Approaches to Teaching Homer's *Odyssey*

Approaches to Teaching Homer's *Odyssey*

Edited by

Lillian E. Doherty

The Modern Language Association of America
New York 2026

85 Broad Street, New York, New York 10004
www.mla.org

To order MLA publications, visit www.mla.org/books. For wholesale and international orders, see www.mla.org/bookstore-orders. The EU-based Responsible Person for MLA products is the Mare Nostrum Group, which can be reached at gpsr@mare-nostrum.co.uk or the Mare Nostrum Group BV, Mauritskade 21D, 1091 GC Amsterdam, Netherlands. For a copy of the MLA's risk assessment document, write to scholcomm@mla.org.

Approaches to Teaching World Literature 182
ISSN 1059-1133

Library of Congress Cataloging-in-Publication Data

Names: Doherty, Lillian Eileen, 1952- editor
Title: Approaches to teaching Homer's Odyssey / edited by Lillian E. Doherty.
Description: New York : The Modern Language Association of America, 2026. |
Series: Approaches to teaching world literature, 1059-1133 ; 182 |
Includes bibliographical references.
Identifiers: LCCN 2025041913 (print) | LCCN 2025041914 (ebook) |
ISBN 9781603297097 hardcover | ISBN 9781603297103 paperback |
ISBN 9781603297110 epub
Subjects: LCSH: Homer. Odyssey | Homer—Study and teaching | BISAC: LANGUAGE ARTS & DISCIPLINES / Study & Teaching | LITERARY CRITICISM / Fairy Tales, Folk Tales, Legends & Mythology | LCGFT: Literary criticism | Essays
Classification: LCC PA4167 .A67 2026 (print) | LCC PA4167 (ebook)
LC record available at https://lccn.loc.gov/2025041913
LC ebook record available at https://lccn.loc.gov/2025041914

CONTENTS

ACKNOWLEDGMENTS

I am extremely grateful to the contributors and to the acquisitions editor, James Hatch, who persevered and had patience with me during the prolonged work on this volume. Many others helped along the way, and I hope to be pardoned for not naming them all. I learned a good deal from the earlier volume in this series titled *Approaches to Teaching Homer's* Iliad *and* Odyssey, edited by Kostas Myrsiades. I want to thank in particular the members of the MLA who completed the survey on their teaching of the *Odyssey*, the external readers and the Publications Committee of the MLA, Eric Lindquist of McKeldin Library at the University of Maryland for help locating books and articles, Lilia Ellis for bibliographic material on trauma theory, my colleague Katherine Wasdin for bibliographic material on race in antiquity, and my student Tolomeo Mújica-Martorell for reading the entire *Odyssey* (and *Iliad*) with me during the pandemic.

PREFACE

The *Odyssey* is one of the oldest surviving works of European literature,[1] yet it still compels interest for its wonderful story and complex characters. It is often assigned in middle and high schools, colleges, and universities. Earlier generations—including the ancient Greeks themselves—have found aspects of the work to criticize, yet recent social and cultural developments in the United States have rendered certain of its aspects especially problematic. In particular, the double standard of sexual conduct implicit in the work and the cultural chauvinism of the hero, Odysseus, increasingly elicit criticism even from those who, like myself, love the poem and strive to engage students' interest in it. The challenge is to balance this criticism with appreciation of a uniquely durable and multifaceted work—a work as "many-minded" πολύμητις as its hero.

A volume in this series on both the *Iliad* and the *Odyssey*, edited by Kostas Myrsiades, appeared in 1987; it remains valuable in many ways, but an update is called for given the evolution of scholarship and the concerns related to sociocultural changes mentioned above. This volume thus focuses on the *Odyssey* alone, although sometimes it elicits comparison to the *Iliad*.

Like many works of ancient Greek literature, the *Odyssey* has carried, and still carries, considerable cultural prestige. While its influence in some eras has been eclipsed by that of the *Iliad*, it has inspired admiration and emulation from antiquity to the present. Its hero, famous for his cleverness, has also inspired suspicion and condemnation for his deceptions: to cite just a few examples, the character of Odysseus, called Ulysses by the Romans, plays nefarious roles in a number of Athenian tragedies (such as Sophocles's *Philoctetes*) and in Vergil's *Aeneid* and is consigned by Dante to one of the lowest circles of Hell in the *Inferno*.[2] A recent, justly acclaimed translation, by Emily Wilson, renders Odysseus's characteristic epithet, *polytropos*, as "complicated" (Odyssey [Norton Critical Edition] 1.1), capturing the ambiguity of his portrayal and of the personality with which the poem endows him. This very complexity, which includes the moral ambiguity attached to his deeds, makes him an ideal subject of study and discussion in the contemporary classroom. The figure of his wife, Penelope, is drawn with even greater ambiguity, since her motives and even her understanding of events are kept obscure (for example, when does she recognize Odysseus?). The concept of identity may be a modern one, but the characters of the *Odyssey* in their permutations—a king disguised as a beggar, a woman unsure whether she is a widow or a wife—raise questions about identity that should resonate with students. In addition to its characters, the themes of wandering and homecoming, parent-child relationships, and "the ethics of revenge" (Loney) make the *Odyssey* a compelling object of study. The poem has been studied by veterans, refugees, and incarcerated people as well as high school and college students and has something to say to each of these groups.

For those who know Greek, the Greek text of quotations from Homer is included in this volume, along with English translations. Many of those who teach the *Odyssey* in English have no background in the language and literature of ancient Greece; a volume like this, while not itself a full introduction to Homer, aims to support teachers at all levels by providing basic information about the origins of the epic and the merits of translations in common use. The section “The Instructor’s Library” also surveys contemporary interpretive approaches and influential works of criticism. The heterogeneous nature of the essays—some more explicitly and practically pedagogical than others—is a result of the effort to make this an inclusive volume for instructors wanting to jump-start a course on the *Odyssey*. Readers are invited to focus on those essays that meet their needs and whet their interest. Some essays could even be assigned to students. I have let the contributors speak for themselves and have not tried to harmonize their views, which on some points differ substantially.

NOTES

1. Both “European” and “literature” are problematic descriptions of the *Odyssey*, as is addressed in this volume, but the work is still widely understood in these terms in most Western scholarship.

2. On Dante’s Ulisse, see the essay by Van Peteghem in this volume.

Introduction

Lillian E. Doherty

Origins in an Oral Tradition

Scholars are now agreed that the *Odyssey*, like the *Iliad*, was the product of a long oral tradition, probably stretching back centuries. Beyond this generally accepted conclusion, which is based on the nature of the dialect and the style of composition, everything else about the origin of the poem is uncertain: the date and place of composition, the identity of the author or authors, the nature of the intended audience, and the way in which the poem was originally written down. The so-called Homeric question, which encompasses all of the above, has become famous; in its particulars, it will probably never be answered,[1] but the consensus that the poems emerged from an oral tradition is based on features of the text itself as well as on ways in which it parallels other living oral traditions.

One of the most distinctive features of Homeric poetry is its pervasive use of epithets for the gods and heroes: cloud-gatherer Zeus, bright-eyed Athena, swift-footed Achilles, Odysseus of many wiles, and so on. Even objects and natural phenomena have their epithets; the most famous is probably rosy-fingered Dawn.[2] These epithets fit into specific portions of the dactylic hexameter line, which is the basic metrical unit of the epic. But the principle goes far beyond the epithets: a majority of the lines are made up of adaptable word-units of specific metrical value that fit one or more segments of the hexameter. These units are often called *formulas*, but that term is misleading because it suggests a kind of automatism in the composition that is very far from the reality. In fact, a poet in an oral tradition like the one from which the *Odyssey* emerged used metrical units as *words*, fitting them into new patterns, as any poet would do. The difference is that the oral poet composed in performance, not reciting a memorized text but actively composing new lines on each occasion. The formulas made this possible by providing units that could quickly be arranged into regular metrical lines.

The key to understanding this feature of the Homeric epics was provided by Milman Parry, an American classicist[3] who studied in Paris in the 1920s and who was building on the work of his teacher Antoine Meillet. Convinced by his own analysis of the text of Homer that the epic was the product of an oral performance tradition, Parry tested his hypothesis by visiting and recording oral poets in Bosnia, which was then part of Yugoslavia. By comparing different recordings of the "same" epic poem performed on different occasions, Parry was able to prove that the poets were actively recomposing as they sang, using traditional but flexible metrical units. Parry died young, but his work was continued by his student Albert Lord, whose 1960 book *The Singer of Tales* became the classic statement of their theory.

There followed a long period in which the theory was debated and refined by scholars inside and outside the field of classics. Some rejected it because it seemed to make Homer into an automaton, slotting prefabricated "formulas" into predictable patterns. It took a wider perspective, provided in part by anthropologists such as Ruth Finnegan,[4] whose early work was in Africa, to demonstrate that the Homeric epics were the product of one among many oral traditions throughout the world. More sophisticated models of oral composition grew out of comparative studies such as those of Lord's student Gregory Nagy, or those of John Miles Foley, who extended Parry's and Lord's research in Serbia and showed that Old English poetry used some of the same techniques.[5]

Parallel to the use of small metrical units on the level of the line, larger units—called "themes" by Lord, or, more often, "type scenes"—can be seen as the building blocks of the narrative. These include recurring events such as assemblies, the entertainment of a guest, the arming of a warrior, or the arrival of a ship at a destination. "Ring composition" is another technique used by the oral poet to frame scenes and (especially) speeches. A notable example is Odysseus's conversation with the shade of his mother in the *Odyssey*, book 11, lines 171–203:[6] he asks her a series of questions, which she answers in reverse order.

In an effort to understand how a performing poet could construct and retain a work as long as the *Iliad* or *Odyssey*, several scholars have identified larger narrative components made up of sequences of scenes. The details of their hypotheses have not met with general agreement, but it seems likely that some such technique was used to assemble the wider epic frame. Examples include, for the *Iliad*, Cedric Whitman's *Homer and the Heroic Tradition* as well as Bruce Louden's *The* Odyssey*: Structure, Narration, and Meaning* and Egbert Bakker's *The Meaning of Meat and the Structure of the* Odyssey.

Textualization

Although the Parry-Lord hypothesis is now the consensus view, there are still significant disagreements over the date of composition and the method by which the Homeric epics were recorded in writing. Most of the bards studied by Parry could not read or write, and scholars trained in a thoroughly textual tradition had trouble with the idea that works as long and complex as the *Iliad* and *Odyssey* could be composed without the aid of writing. Some, like the eminent British classicist Martin L. West, have continued to argue for a literate Homer (*Making*). The poems could not be written down until the Greeks had adapted the alphabet from the Phoenicians; this seems to have happened no later than the mid–eighth century BCE, to judge by the appearance of the first alphabetic inscriptions in Greek during this period, although much earlier dates have been proposed (see, e.g., Waal; Clay et al.). It is often confidently asserted that the epics were composed in the eighth century BCE. Lord, who believed that literacy inevitably put an end to oral traditions, hypothesized that their earliest written form was a dictated text—that is, one produced by a scribe working with an illiterate bard. This view is still shared by a number of scholars, such as Minna Skafte Jensen, who has argued for it at length. A minority view elaborated by Barry B. Powell even holds that the Greek alphabet was adapted from the Phoenicians specifically to record the Homeric poems (*Homer and the Origin*).

But in the context of a true oral performance tradition, there would have been no need—or use—for a written text.[7] As Gregory Nagy has shown, the word "write" (*graphein*) was not used in reference to Homer until the middle of the second century BCE; before this, his activity is described as "making" or "composing" (*poiein*; *Homer* 31–32). Nagy has developed an influential model for the process by which the Homeric epics, still conceived as oral poems, became progressively fixed over many centuries before being written down. Two major stages in the "crystallization" of the epics, according to Nagy, took place in the context of religious festivals: the Panionia, a joint celebration of twelve Greek cities where the Ionic dialect was spoken,[8] and the Panathenaia, an annual festival of the Athenians, first celebrated in the sixth century BCE (21–22).

Even after the poems were recorded in writing, oral performance remained an important feature of their transmission. The ancient evidence, including quotations of Homer by authors of widely varying dates, suggests that the poem's wording remained fluid until quite late. Nagy's model, which is widely accepted by American classicists, has inspired the creation of the Homer Multitext project, led by Casey Dué and Mary Ebbott (homermultitext.org). This project, made possible by digital technology, provides multiple open-source editions of manuscripts of the epics, intended to facilitate their comparison. Readers interested in the details of Nagy's theory, which he elaborated in a series of volumes, may find a concise account of it in his contribution to *The Cambridge Guide to Homer* ("From").

An interesting alternative to this view is that of Zlatan Čolaković, a Croatian scholar who argued on the basis of the Bosnian corpus that Homer was a "post-traditional" poet, trained in the oral-compositional techniques but blending themes and genres that were traditionally kept separate and embellishing his compositions to untraditional lengths. Čolaković believed that like the "post-traditional" Bosnian poet Avďo Međejović, who produced an epic as long as the *Odyssey*, Homer must have dictated the two epics, later performances of which were produced by memorization.

Older Influences

Further in the background, three strands have been thought to contribute to the Greek oral tradition. These are customarily referred to as the Indo-European, the Near Eastern (or Eastern Mediterranean), and the international folktale. Greek belongs to the Indo-European family of languages, made up of subfamilies such as Indo-Iranian, Balto-Slavic, Germanic, Italic, and Celtic, all derived from a parent language reconstructed by linguists and referred to as Proto-Indo-European.[9] It is assumed that along with the linguistic features that first revealed these relationships—such as parallels between forms of the verb "to be"—some kind of narrative tradition was passed on to the descendant cultures. The picture is complicated, especially for Greece, by the fact that speakers of Indo-European languages in the Eastern Mediterranean linguistic family (such as Hittite and Mycenaean Greek) lived in close proximity to speakers of languages from the Afro-Asiatic family (such as Akkadian and Egyptian), so that the linguistic and narrative traditions became intermeshed. We know this because of the many surviving ancient documents from the Near East and Egypt, which are much older than the earliest examples of Greek writing and which include literary versions of stories with points of connection to the Greek tradition. In fact, the influence of non-Indo-European myth and religion seems stronger in the Greek tradition, and especially in the *Odyssey*, than the Indo-European influence. Some plausible connections to Homer from the Indo-European inheritance are the quasi-divine figures of Helen and her twin brothers, the motif of an archery contest for a bride,[10] and the curious role of the Phaeacians as "ferrymen" (E. Cook, "Ferrymen"; Edmunds; Frame, *Myth*).[11] Both the important Homeric value of *kleos* ("fame" or "glory") and even a Homeric formula for it, *kleos aphthiton* ("imperishable fame"), have parallels in the Sanskrit epics.[12] Yet the myth of a sea voyage ending in the loss or renunciation of immortality is shared by the *Odyssey* and the *Epic of Gilgamesh*, which survives in multiple (if fragmentary) versions in the Afro-Asiatic languages Akkadian and Babylonian. An example of probable blending of Near Eastern and Indo-European traditions is the belief in a happy afterlife for a lucky few in "Elysium": the word has Indo-European roots, but the idea of two contrasting fates for the dead—an Elysian extension of life on earth versus a shadowy existence, or worse, in a nether world—also reflects Egyptian and Akkadian beliefs (Puhvel; E. Cook, "Ferrymen").[13]

Some central plot elements in the *Odyssey*—the Cyclops episode and the reunion of Odysseus and Penelope—may be traced to the tradition of the international folktale, where "Ogre Blinded" and "Homecoming Husband" are well-attested tale types. Because of the difference in genre between the *Odyssey* and most other surviving versions of these tales, classical scholars have tended to be unaware of the thematic parallels or to assume they are due to the influence of the Homeric poem. An important exception is William Hansen, whose compilation of Greek and Roman stories with international origins, *Ariadne's Thread*, is a valuable resource (see also Hansen, "Homer"; Page). All these linguistic and cultural strands—Indo-European, Near Eastern, and international—have been skillfully blended in the Homeric *Odyssey*, whose shapers were likely unaware of their disparate sources.

The Epic Cycle

A further complication in our understanding of the Homeric tradition is the relationship between the *Odyssey*, the *Iliad*, and the lost epics collectively known as the epic cycle. The stories of the two surviving epics are closely connected: Odysseus is a major character in the *Iliad*, and in books 11 and 24 of the *Odyssey*, his achievement is explicitly compared with that of Achilles, the central figure of the *Iliad*.[14] Because the events it narrates follow those of the *Iliad*, the *Odyssey* has often been thought of as a sequel. On linguistic grounds, Richard Janko (*Homer* and "πρῶτόν τε καὶ ὕστατον") has argued that in fact it was composed later, though not much later. If the two evolved simultaneously within the oral tradition, as Nagy has argued in "From Song to Text," bards must have made a deliberate effort to differentiate them, because neither includes more than a passing reference to events fully narrated in the other. There is a clear rivalry between their heroes, who are very different characters, each representing different forms of heroic achievement. This is especially explicit in book 11 of the *Odyssey* (lines 488–91), where Odysseus meets the shade of Achilles, and Achilles himself is portrayed as putting the highest value on survival, which, unlike Odysseus, Achilles has not achieved.

At the same time, both epics represent selections of events from a longer series of tales connected with the Trojan War, starting with the wedding of Achilles's parents and the conception of Helen and extending beyond the end of the *Odyssey*. Although these events were the basis for a series of shorter epic texts that were known to Aristotle in the fourth century BCE and summarized later by Proclus, whose prose outlines are our best evidence for them,[15] they must reflect a wider oral tradition that preceded the formation of the Homeric poems. The shorter cyclic epics, which included the *Cypria*, *Aethiopis*, *Ilias mikra* (*Little Iliad*), *Iliou persis* (*Sack of Troy*), *Nostoi* (*Returns*), and *Telegony*, did not repeat the events of the *Iliad* or *Odyssey*—which in turn avoid repeating each other—but filled in the events before, between, and after the two longer epics. In his *Poetics* Aristotle famously compared these shorter texts with the longer epics and found them wanting because they were episodic, lacking the type of plot structure he preferred (1459a-b). Classical scholars have tended to accept his judgment, which they could not otherwise evaluate because the cyclic epics are lost.

In the twentieth century one group of scholars began to take the cyclic epics more seriously. Their approach is called Neoanalysis because it revises the otherwise discredited methods of the Analysts, scholars who in the nineteenth century had pointed to minor inconsistencies in the structures of the Homeric poems and argued that they were assembled out of shorter discrete poems, also known as "lays."[16] The Neoanalysts accepted the coherence of the Homeric epics but argued that some of the lost cyclic epics may have preceded them; in particular, a case was made that the *Aethiopis* influenced the structure of the *Iliad*.[17] More recently, interest in the cyclic epics has been revived as part of a focus on "traditional referentiality," a parallel in oral tradition to what literary scholars call "intertextuality." As currently understood, the oral tradition must have included versions of the narratives that later coalesced into the cyclic epics: just as the *Odyssey* assumes knowledge of the events of the *Iliad*, both

Homeric epics assume that their audiences will be familiar with the mythic background of the Trojan War.

Audiences

This brings us to the question of who made up those audiences. Our uncertainty about the composition of the epics is matched by uncertainty about their original audiences and about the venues and social contexts in which the oral epic was performed. This question in turn is embedded in the vexed issue of the relationship between "Homer" and history. Since the beginnings of modern archaeology, attempts have been made to situate the epics in historical contexts; these attempts have their own ideologically inflected history, well summarized by Susan Sherratt. The question is further complicated by the composite nature of the material culture described in the epics. Several specific types of objects described there have been found by archaeologists; these include not only the boar's tusk helmet worn by Odysseus in book 10 of the *Iliad*, which is Mycenaean, but also iron tools and cremation burials, which belong to later periods. Equally controversial is the effort to describe "Homeric society"—that is, to identify a constellation of social and cultural institutions and attitudes that could situate the poems in a particular historical period. *The World of Odysseus*, by Moses Finley, now dated, was a pioneering work in this area.[18] His view that the social world described by Homer corresponds to the eleventh to tenth centuries BCE has been challenged, notably by J. P. Crielaard ("Homer" and "Homeric Communities"), who has argued in detail for a setting in the early Archaic age (eighth to seventh centuries BCE), and by James Whitley ("Homer's Entangled Objects" and "Homer"), who rejects any notion of an identifiable Homeric society.[19] Yet if the values and practices do not correspond to those of any specific era, they have not proved a barrier to the poem's popularity, in antiquity or later. This volume does not delve into the exact historical location of the epics but focuses on their internal coherence—and, at times, their contradictions.

The *Odyssey* describes two different bards, Phemius in the palace of Odysseus and Demodocus in the palace of Alcinous. They perform relatively brief episodes of heroic material connected with the Trojan War: the use of the wooden horse to take the city, the homeward returns of the Greeks after the war, a quarrel between Achilles and Odysseus.[20] The audiences for their performances are aristocratic and predominantly male; the exception, in each case, is the lady of the house: Penelope in Ithaca and Arete in Scheria. The principal characters of the epic are also aristocratic, as is the implicit ideology: thus the poem defends the right of Odysseus to rule and to restore the honor of his house by killing the suitors who court Penelope in his absence. But there is also, in the *Odyssey* specifically as opposed to the *Iliad*, a significant focus on the experiences of lower-class characters, including those of the hero himself when disguised as a beggar. Peter Rose has argued that the mistreatment of Odysseus in his disguise suggests an effort by the poet to appeal to lower-class members of the external audience, who are thus induced to cheer the hero's vengeance and restoration to the throne ("Class Ambivalence"). I have myself argued on the basis of the portrayals of Penelope and Arete that the poet is making a similar effort to appeal to aristocratic women in his audience (*Siren Songs*).

Yet the occasions for bardic performance in the poem may not reflect the actual, or only, performance context for the Homeric poems, or indeed for other poems in the oral tradition. The length of the epics, which would have taken days to perform, as well as the evidence of the so-called Homeric Hymns, have suggested the context of a religious festival as one possibility. The hymns are narrative poems, some quite long, in Homeric dialect and meter, which praise individual gods, including Demeter, Apollo, Aphrodite, and Hermes.[21] The *Hymn to Apollo* explicitly situates its anonymous author at a festival for the god on the island of Delos. This author describes himself as "a blind man who lives in rocky Chios" τυφλὸς ἀνήρ, οἰκεῖ δὲ Χίῳ ἔνι παιπαλοέσσῃ (my trans.; line 172), one of the sources for the tradition that Homer fit that description. Thucydides's *History* refers to the same hymn as a *prooimion*, or "prelude" (3.104); this has led to the hypothesis that the hymns were performed as preludes to performances of the epics. Like so many Homeric questions, this one about performance contexts cannot be definitively answered. Our understanding of the original or intended audience must be inferred from the poems themselves. As Ruth Scodel has argued, the "socially inclusive rhetoric" of the epics is designed to appeal to a wide audience, whose members may occupy different places in a stratified social hierarchy (177).

Religion

The Homeric vision of the gods—both the powerful Olympian gods and the lesser divinities such as Circe, Calypso, and Ino—was hugely influential in later Greek (and Roman) culture. The historian Herodotus even claimed that Homer and Hesiod—who, next to Homer, is identified as the author of the oldest Greek poems, the *Theogony* and *Works and Days*—gave the gods their authoritative epithets and identified their spheres of influence (2.53). These figures should be understood not as personified abstractions but as real gods who can intervene directly and decisively in the lives of the characters. They are neither omniscient nor omnipotent, but they are immortal, which gives them a very different perspective and, in some cases, different values from the human characters. In book 4 of the *Iliad*, this difference is dramatized when Zeus and Hera make peace between themselves by restarting the war, while the humans expect them to see to it that the outcome of the duel between Menelaus and Paris is respected. Although the gods are often at odds with each other, they ultimately value "getting along"—since they have to live together forever—over their commitments to their human protégés. Thus Athena explains to Odysseus that she could not help him overtly until he reached Ithaca, because she did not want to fight with her uncle Poseidon (13.341–43), and it is the absence of Poseidon (1.22–27) that allows her to raise the issue with the other gods in the first place.

Although the gods in Greek myth are to be understood as real gods, there is an important difference between the ways in which they were portrayed in myth and in cult—that is, in acts of worship. In myth, they are thoroughly anthropomorphized, with strong personalities, likes, and dislikes. They may behave in ways that humans consider immoral, as when Ares and Aphrodite are caught in the act of adultery (*Odyssey* 8.266–366). In cult, the emphasis is on their positive intervention in human affairs: their gifts, for example, of grain, wine, and healthy children and their power to save those in danger, such as men at war or at sea and women in childbirth. There was, however, an overlap between these two views of the gods: they were thought capable of withholding their gifts if displeased or not sufficiently placated with offerings. At the same time, the poets had considerable freedom to imagine their interactions with one another and with humans, to the point of reporting their conversations and their thoughts. These insights could be attributed to the inspiration of the Muse, herself a goddess.[22] There was no systematic theology in Archaic and Classical Greece, no "articles of faith" to which people had to adhere. Nor was there a canon of scripture equivalent to the Bible or the Vedas; even the Homeric and Hesiodic poems, authoritative as they were, were never seen as sacred texts. Some philosophers criticized the traditional beliefs, but if they offered alternatives, these were never accepted by the majority. The essential thing was to perform the traditional sacrifices and celebrate the festivals, keeping the gods happy so they would do their part in preserving the community.

The Homeric gods also differ from the gods as they were actually worshipped in that they are Panhellenic—that is, common to all the Greeks. Each region, *polis* ("city-state"), or village had its patron deities, with localized epithets and local rituals. Even the Olympians had localized forms, such as Zeus of Mount Lykaion, Athena of Alea, or Artemis of Ephesus.[23] In the epics, by contrast, each of the Olympians is a distinct individual whom Greeks of different regions could recognize. In relation to one another they constitute a kind of "super" aristocracy, comparable to human elites in their power and privilege—except that they enjoy the ultimate privilege of immortality. Like ancient Greek aristocrats, they base their status on family ties, and there is a pecking order among them, with a few at the very top; even some of the Olympians (Zeus, of course, but also Hera, Apollo, Demeter, Athena, Artemis, and Aphrodite) outrank others (Hermes, Hephaestus, Ares). At the base of the hierarchy are the numerous minor divinities, such as nymphs and satyrs, whose immortality may be qualified: in the *Hymn to Aphrodite*, the nymphs associated with trees, for example, are said to live only as long as their trees (lines 264–72). Some mythic monsters can be killed, but others, like Scylla, are immortal, as Circe warns Odysseus when he proposes to fight her (*Odyssey* 12.118). Mortal heroes were also honored with cults in the Archaic and Classical periods, but these cults do not figure overtly in the epics.[24]

Much has been written about the difference between the attitudes of the gods in the *Iliad* and in the *Odyssey*;[25] in the opening scene of the latter (1.32–43),

Zeus states that mortals suffer more than necessary because they disregard the warnings of the gods against behaving badly. In the *Odyssey* as compared to the *Iliad*, the gods are more distant, and fewer of the Olympians play major roles; the most important are Athena, the patron and helper of Odysseus, and Poseidon, whose son Odysseus has blinded and who in revenge seeks to delay the hero's return home. Calypso and Circe, though lesser divinities, are true, immortal goddesses.[26] (Circe, though versed in magic, is not a "witch" in our understanding of that word, which is sometimes applied to her.) Like Poseidon, they create significant diversions for Odysseus. Calypso even offers to make him immortal if he will stay with her as her husband; his choice to leave her for his mortal wife and kingdom is decisive for the plot of the epic and ensures his lasting fame (*kleos*).

Already in antiquity there were those who assigned allegorical significance to the gods, sometimes with the explicit aim of defending Homer against accusations of blasphemy for portraying them as committing immoral acts (Lamberton). This allegorical approach has been largely rejected in recent times, but it played an important part in the reception of Homer for many centuries and is considered in the next section.

Reception History

Since antiquity, the *Odyssey* has sparked creative responses from writers and artists in a multitude of genres and media. In recent scholarship the term "reception" has largely replaced earlier references to "the classical tradition," given that scholars now seek to focus on the creative reuse of ancient literature, art, and culture rather than on their influence in later ages. This form of reception began in antiquity, as the dramatists, for example, recast and reimagined the plots and characters of the entire epic tradition, not just the Homeric poems (Kim).[27] Julie Van Peteghem's, Sheila Murnaghan's, and Brett Rogers's essays in this volume deal with specific instances of reception of the *Odyssey*. This section gives a brief overview of the bigger picture.[28]

As the oldest surviving texts in the Greek tradition, the Homeric epics have been widely read and seen as authoritative in later eras: in the Greco-Roman world, the Byzantine and early modern European worlds, the Enlightenment and subsequent (including colonized) European spheres, and even sporadically outside those spheres. It has often been assumed by scholars and teachers that this authority is salutary, and the poems have been praised not only for their content and composition but also for inspiring some of the world's great literature. Yet from early times there have been contrasting approaches in the reception of Homer, with some works implicitly celebrating its characters and themes, while others disparaged them. In recent times as well, oppositional voices have contested the value of the epics—not their literary value but their role as exemplars that sustain colonialist ideology and provide models of heroism and masculinity that have been characterized as "toxic."[29] Others, in turn, have argued that the epics do not endorse without qualification the forms of heroism they portray. The *Odyssey* in particular, though it defends Odysseus by blaming his crew for their own deaths (1.5–10), can be seen as giving voice to characters critical of him.[30] This critical stance has been prominent in some ancient as well as modern works of reception.

In Greco-Roman antiquity, in the words of Lawrence Kim, "Homer is monumental, canonical, and ubiquitous; referred to simply as 'the poet'" (417). As Kim notes, in the sixth and fifth centuries BCE, works other than the *Iliad* and *Odyssey* were attributed to Homer, so when his authority is invoked it is not necessarily traceable to the poems we have (418). Likewise, from the Archaic to the Hellenistic age and even in Rome, the epics, and especially the *Iliad*, were used as school texts, so that educated persons knew them well and cited them as culturally authoritative (Most 171–82; Cribiore 194–97). Yet precisely because of Homer's outsize influence, philosophers such as Heraclitus of Ephesus (ca. fifth century BCE) and poets such as Pindar (mid–fifth century BCE) singled him out for critique (Kim 420). The later criticisms of Plato (fourth century BCE) are especially well known, culminating in the proposal to expel Homer from the ideal state for his pernicious portrayals of the gods and heroes (*Republic* 376e–392a, 605c–608b).

In fact, even when Homer is not himself a target, the figure of Odysseus is often condemned for immoral behavior. In the surviving tragedies, only Sophocles's *Ajax* portrays him with any sympathy, whereas in the same author's *Philoctetes*, Odysseus is conniving and unscrupulous. Wherever the hero appears or is spoken of in Euripides (e.g., *Trojan Women*, *Iphigenia in Aulis*), the same unscrupulous opportunism is attributed to him. In these works he is implicitly compared to the Sophists, a new group of specialists who were teaching rhetoric in Athens at the time and who were held responsible, rightly or wrongly, for the corruption of political discourse. Yet the frequent appearances of Odysseus in tragedy are testimony to the potential of the character for creative reuse, a potential that has been thoroughly explored in later works of reception.

While Plato condemned the ethical implications of the epics, his student Aristotle praised their formal and aesthetic properties in his *Poetics* (1451a, 1459a-b). These properties are the basis of his influential preference for the *Iliad* and *Odyssey*, which by his time must have been known in something like their canonical forms, over the other cyclic epics.[31] In the cultural centers of the Hellenistic period (323 to 31 BCE), and especially in Alexandria under the rule of Alexander the Great's successors the Ptolemies, the epics were the focus of sustained scholarly study and creative emulation—for instance, in the *Argonautica* of Apollonius of Rhodes, a Hellenistic epic on the quest for the Golden Fleece. This was the era of the commentaries that found their way into the margins of later manuscripts as scholia (marginal notes). Thus the Greek-speaking heirs of Alexander deployed Greek culture as a unifying ideological force throughout the lands they conquered, and the Homeric epics remained central to that culture.

A philosophical school that approved of Homer on the whole, and of Odysseus in particular, was that of the Stoics. This Greek school was founded about 300 BCE by Zeno of Elea, whose writings in defense of Homer survive only in fragments; his arguments were elaborated by followers in both Greece and Rome, including Plutarch, who in turn influenced the scholars of the Renaissance (Stanford, *Ulysses Theme* 121, 265n6). The Neoplatonists used allegorical interpretation to defend the morality of Homer's gods and understood Odysseus as a figure for the soul in its journey through "the realm of matter" (Lamberton 127).[32] The Christian church fathers adopted a similar allegorical approach as a way of preserving what they saw as positive in the cultural legacy of polytheistic Greece and Rome.

Another strand in the ancient Greek and Roman reception of the *Odyssey* involved the plot elements of the journey and the reunion of lovers. These formed the basis for the genre of the (ancient) novel, an extended fictional narrative in prose.[33] Each of the five surviving Greek novels from antiquity, dated to the first through fourth centuries CE, describes the adventures and trials—many of them at sea—of a young couple who remain faithful to each other despite the attacks and attentions of others and are ultimately reunited. The two surviving ancient Roman novels, Apuleius's *Metamorphoses* (also known as *The Golden Ass*) and Petronius's *Satyricon*, while not focused on heterosexual couples, also involve long journeys and fantastic adventures; the *Satyricon* in particular has been seen as an ironic riff on the *Odyssey* (Mordine).

Perhaps the most influential work of Homeric reception in antiquity is Vergil's *Aeneid* (late first century BCE). In the account of the fall of Troy by the work's protagonist, Aeneas, in book 2, Odysseus ("Ulysses" to the Romans) is the villain who devises the Trojan horse, taking by deceit the city that could not be taken by force of arms. In Vergil's account the Trojans are the ancestors of the Romans, whose self-image as direct and honest makes them foils for the devious Greeks. Given the prominent place the *Aeneid* quickly assumed in the Roman canon, this portrayal had a decisive effect on attitudes toward Odysseus in Roman and medieval European literature, despite more positive portrayals in works such as Horace's *Epistle* 1.2 and Ovid's *Tristia* (Stanford, *Ulysses Theme* 142–43) that focused on the "much-enduring" Odysseus.[34]

While Homer continued to be read in the eastern Mediterranean in subsequent centuries,[35] knowledge of Ancient Greek was extremely rare in western Europe during the Middle Ages. Thus Dante Alighieri's famous portrayal of "Ulisse," the Italian for Ulysses, in canto 26 of the *Inferno* (discussed by Van Peteghem in this volume) was based on Vergil and other late antique sources rather than any direct knowledge of the Greek text. In addition to the *Aeneid*, prose versions of the Troy story attributed to authors known as Dictys Cretensis and Dares Phrygius were widely read (in Latin, though evidently from Greek origins; Desmond 439–40) and promulgated views not only of Odysseus but also of Homer as unscrupulous and deceitful (Stanford, *Ulysses Theme* 146–58). The medieval French *Roman de Troie* (*The Romance of Troy*), by Benoît de

Sainte-Maure, strongly influenced by the accounts of Dictys and Dares, perpetuated these portrayals and in turn influenced later medieval and early modern vernacular works. Some medieval monarchs of Europe, encouraged by these works to identify with the Trojans, even claimed descent from them (Stanford, *Ulysses Theme* 288).

Not until the late fifteenth century was knowledge of Greek revived in western Europe, as part of the rediscovery and emulation of ancient literature and art often referred to as the Renaissance. Exiles from Constantinople after its fall to the Ottomans brought manuscripts and expert knowledge to Italy. Consequently, the reception of Homer entered a decisive phase with the appearance of the epics and related scholia in print, roughly between 1470 and 1535 (Wolfe 491–92).[36] These publications coincided with an increased interest in the study of the Greek language; as Jessica Wolfe notes, "many early printed texts of Homer's poems were designed with elementary students of Greek in mind" (492). Translations into Latin, and then into the vernaculars of Europe, followed, including, notably, that of George Chapman,[37] which appeared in stages between 1598 and 1624 and later inspired John Keats's famous poem. As Stanford notes in *The Ulysses Theme*, his classic overview of the reception of the *Odyssey*, the increasing importance of the liberal arts in the education of upper-class men in early modern Europe led to wider acquaintance with Homer and the proliferation of works of reception (298).

Stanford himself wisely avoids cataloging these many works, which a volume like the present one can scarcely include. He traces two strands in the early modern reception of the figure of Ulysses (*Ulysses Theme* 162–210): the Iliadic "man of policy," as portrayed, for example, in Shakespeare's *Troilus and Cressida*, and the Odyssean "wanderer," evoked by Pedro Calderon de la Barca in *El mayor encanto amor* (*Love the Greatest Enchantment*). Stanford then sees these strands as "re-integrated" in the *Ulysses* of James Joyce and the *Odyssey* of Nikos Kazantzakis (211–40). In the twenty-first century, other classicists have taken up where Stanford left off: see, in particular, *Homer in the Twentieth Century*, by Barbara Graziosi and Emily Greenwood, and *The Return of Ulysses*, by Edith Hall.[38]

Somewhat paradoxically, the so-called culture wars of the late twentieth and early twenty-first centuries have coincided with a proliferation of works in new and old media that recycle elements of classical myth and literature, including the Homeric epics. Indeed, the field of reception studies has become increasingly important to the academic discipline of classics itself; enrollment in Ancient Greek and Latin has declined, but works of reception continue to multiply, and student interest in these works remains high. While the present volume is written by, and addressed primarily to, North American teachers of literature, it is meant to be used in a wide variety of courses that I hope will include works of reception from many countries and eras. To provide just one example, Justine McConnell has noted that "postcolonial and anticolonial *Odysseys*" (6) are especially prominent in the literature of the African diaspora, demonstrating that "the Homeric epics do not belong inherently to Europe, that they can be as African, Caribbean, and American, as they are European, as 'black' as they are 'white'" (9). A recent volume entitled *Homer's Daughters*, by Fiona Cox and Elena Theodorakopoulos, examines some of the many recent works of Homeric reception by women and includes an epilogue by Emily Wilson titled "Translating Homer as a Woman." For more specific examples of approaches to the *Odyssey* using works of reception, see the essays in this volume by Van Peteghem, Murnaghan, and Rogers.

The above overview has not yet mentioned the reception of Homer in music and the visual arts. These have been equally fruitful areas for the exploration of Odyssean themes and characters, from the composer Claudio Monteverdi's *Il ritorno d'Ulisse in patria* (*The Return of Ulysses to His Homeland*) to the singer-songwriter Suzanne Vega's *Calypso* and from Attic vases to the artist Romare Bearden's series *A Black Odyssey*.[39] In electronic media as well—from film and television to podcasts and computer games—the Homeric epic continues to be recast and renewed (Winkler, "Homer and Homerica"; Jenkins; and Rogers in this volume). Many students will create works of reception of their own, seizing on what they find meaningful in the poem and transforming it to speak to their contemporaries.

Contents of This Volume

This volume, like others in the MLA Approaches to Teaching World Literature series, is divided into two parts: part 1, "Materials," is an overview and assessment of supporting resources, with sections titled "Classroom Texts" (including translations) and "The Instructor's Library," and part 2, "Approaches," is a collection of essays, organized in sections, describing different approaches to teaching the *Odyssey*. Some of the essays are more specific than others about classroom exercises and assignments, but all are informed by the authors' experiences of teaching the epic and identify issues that should intrigue and engage students. Their diverse approaches to teaching are at times matched by a diversity of interpretations, which I have not attempted to reconcile.

The opening section, titled "The *Odyssey* and the Greek Epic Tradition," offers suggestions for introducing the background on oral composition and the coexistence of different versions of certain foundational myths in the Greek oral tradition. Casey Dué calls her students' attention to the existence of textual variants and of differing opinions, even in antiquity, on where the epic should end. Laura Slatkin's essay also focuses on the interplay of epic traditions but emphasizes the ways in which the *Odyssey* "mediates" among them without effacing those it avoids. The essay by Marya Fisher advocates for the inclusion of ancient material culture in literature courses that include the *Odyssey*. In demonstrating how the study of visual art and archaeology can complement the study of the Homeric text, Fisher identifies "pedagogical pitfalls" in the use of these materials and offers specific strategies to help instructors avoid them.

In the second section, "Literary and Theoretical Approaches," some essays can be readily identified with specific existing bodies of scholarship, while others are inspired by forms of close reading. Rachel Lesser's essay, "Gender in the *Odyssey*," takes a resolutely feminist approach to the gender ideology implicit in the epic; Kirsten Lodge's "Polyphemus and Postcolonialism" uses postcolonial theory to read the Cyclops episode against the grain, seeing Odysseus as a potential colonizer who assumes the Cyclopes are "uncivilized" and attempts to impose his own cultural values on them. Jennifer Ballengee, inspired by Kwame Anthony Appiah's critique of Western civilization, seeks to destabilize that construct for her students by tracing its history and connecting the *Odyssey* with the contemporary issues of migration and globalization. Maria Fahey uses an ostensibly more traditional approach to the similes in the epic, yet she, too, encourages students to be aware of ways in which these can be "productively disorienting" by insisting on the likeness of unlike things. In different ways, Bruce King, Laura Slatkin, and I (in my contribution to this section) show how the *Odyssey* can be read in relation to the *Iliad*. Teachers can use comparative readings of the two epics to demonstrate, in King's reading, the historically contingent nature of kinship structures or, in mine, the complementarity of two kinds of heroism: that of the warrior facing his mortality and that of the survivor. My essay also tackles the issue of balancing critique with appreciation in presenting the epic and its hero to twenty-first-century students.

In recent decades, as reception studies have become a vital component of classical scholarship, classicists have produced comparative studies of many postclassical works and have used them in courses, both for their intrinsic value and for the light they can throw on the *Odyssey* itself. One of the earliest works to use the myth of Odysseus as a touchstone, Dante's *Inferno*, is the focus of Julie Van Peteghem's essay, "Dante's Canto of Ulysses." In courses ranging from introductory surveys to graduate courses in Italian, Van Peteghem uses the passage in canto 26 describing Ulysses's punishment as an introduction to medieval literature and to reception studies. Modern lyric poetry in English provides an entry into the epic for Sheila Murnaghan's students. Rather than treat the poems of H.D., Katha Pollitt, and Joseph Brodsky in a separate unit, Murnaghan reads them alongside a translation of the *Odyssey*, encouraging students to see the act of reception "as (in many cases) a selective, pointed, and personally inflected enterprise." This section of the volume closes with an essay describing the use of modern media to stimulate reflection on the importance of genre and cultural context in the interpretation of a work. Brett Rogers's "2001 Space Odysseys" describes his use of popular culture—including television, comics, and games—for a range of pedagogical purposes. His essay gives specific examples of works he has used in different kinds of courses to achieve different learning goals.

The essays in the final section of the volume, "Classroom Contexts," contain ideas designed for specific circumstances that would also work well in other settings. Patricia Vreeland outlines her strategies for teaching the *Odyssey* to ninth-grade students, Henry Alley describes how to combine discussion of the epic's characters with the process of planning and writing an essay, and Jamie Brummer addresses the value of the epic for teaching about the construction of masculinity at an all-boys' high school. The volume concludes with an essay by Michael Morgan and Olga Faccani on their work reading the *Odyssey* with incarcerated youth as a basis for a theater program exploring Odysseus's journey as retold in the young men's own voices.

The order in which one reads the essays will be determined by the interests and needs of the individual instructor. The titles are descriptive for the most part and can guide the reader to the most relevant essays. Those in "Classroom Contexts" offer the most focused pedagogical advice, but many others suggest specific types of assignments. A good starting place might be Rogers's essay on teaching the *Odyssey* with pop culture, since it recommends the approach of backward design, in which learning goals are identified first and course design follows. If the instructor's need is for ideas about teaching the origins of the epic and its relationship to other genres, the first two essays are especially appropriate for that. While teachers at all levels can profit from the advice in any given essay, strategies for teaching at the high school level are featured especially in Brummer and in Vreeland. The essays by Lodge, King, Lesser, and Van Peteghem focus on approaches used in college-level world literature or great books courses, although these approaches, as well as Ballengee's and my own, would be appropriate for courses in classical mythology as well. Concrete suggestions for classroom activities are especially prominent in the essays by Alley, Dué, Van Peteghem, and Vreeland, while broader pedagogical strategies (which are nonetheless applied specifically to Homer) are discussed in the essays by Ballengee, Fisher, King, and Murnaghan. The essays by King and Lesser, in particular, focus on the ways in which the *Odyssey* can be seen to affirm specific cultural norms, while those by Brummer and Lodge (and others) identify ways in which the epic calls these norms into question.

It is my hope that teachers in many settings will find these essays helpful and indeed inspiring, just as I have been inspired in the process of collecting and editing them.

NOTES

1. For those interested in the related—and likewise unresolved—question of whether there was a "real" Trojan War, see Saïd 75–78; Cline.

2. Modern translations may omit many of the epithets or translate them differently from one place to another, assuming that a modern audience would find the repetitions boring. One translator who renders the epithets identically every time is Richmond Lattimore (in both his *Iliad* and *Odyssey*).

3. For a life of Parry, see Kanigel.

4. See especially Finnegan and, more recently, the first four chapters of Jensen.

5. Foley was an American professor of classics and comparative literature who founded the journal *Oral Tradition*. See his *Immanent Art*.

6. Line references to the *Odyssey* (and *Iliad*) in this volume are to the Greek text unless otherwise noted. The number of lines in different translations may vary dramatically. Three translations with the same number of lines as the original are those of Lattimore (Iliad; Odyssey [1967]), Mendelsohn (Odyssey), and Emily Wilson, though Wilson's line numbers do not correspond as closely to the Greek text.

7. This is the crux of Jensen's view, based on an overview of fieldwork studies of modern oral traditions in India, Africa, and the Near East.

8. The theory of a Panionian setting for the initial shaping of the epics was first proposed by Douglas Frame (*Hippota Nestor* 551–620).

9. For an overview of the reconstruction of the Indo-European language family, see "Indo-European Languages."

10. Jamison describes a series of detailed parallels between the Indic *svayamvara* (a contest in which a bride chooses her own husband) and the contest for the hand of Penelope in the *Odyssey*. See also E. West.

11. A more controversial attempt to derive substantial elements of the *Odyssey* from Indo-European tradition is intricately argued in Frame, *Hippota Nestor*.

12. The parallel was first noted by the German scholar Adalbert Kuhn (467). More recent discussions include Nagy, *Comparative Studies*, and M. West, *Indo-European Poetry* 406–10.

13. Griffith argues for an Egyptian origin of Elysium.

14. There are also parallels between the narrative structures of the two epics; see Doherty in this volume.

15. Most of Proclus's summaries have come down to us in the scholia (marginal notes) to the manuscript of the *Iliad* known as the "Venetus A." Some ancient authors sketch out an even wider "cycle" that includes mythic material from the creation of the world to the end of the heroic age. For the fragments and summaries, with English translation, see M. West, *Greek Epic Fragments*; the most complete edition is Bernabé. Episodes from several of the cyclic epics (combined with details of versions found in other ancient works) are described in Apollodorus's *Library*, Epitome 3.1–35, 5.1–25, 6.1–15, and 7.34–40. For a one-volume translation of Apollodorus with explanatory notes, see Apollodorus, *Library of Greek Mythology*.

16. The Analysts were opposed by the Unitarians, who argued for the essential unity of the epics. The debate between Analysts and Unitarians has been superseded by awareness of the oral tradition and the ongoing debate over the degree to which writing was involved in the composition of the epics.

17. The leading proponents of Neoanalysis or related approaches are Ioannes Kakridis, Wolfgang Schadewaldt, Wolfgang Kullmann, and Georg Danek. A comprehensive set of essays by contemporary scholars who take differing views on the relationship between the Homeric and cyclic epics may be found in Fantuzzi and Tsagalis. See in particular the essay of Jonathan Burgess in the same volume ("Coming"), whose work on the epic cycle has put the issues in a new and clearer light.

18. The book was reprinted as recently as 2002, with an introduction by Bernard Knox.

19. For a clear overview of the issues, see Raaflaub. See Fisher in this volume on the use of visual art as evidence in the debate.

20. An exception is Demodocus's tale of Aphrodite, Ares, and Hephaestus in book 8 of the *Odyssey*, which features divine characters.

21. Many modern translations of the hymns are available. Some of the most widely used translations are by Apostolos Athanassakis and Diane Rayor; there is a version

with Greek on facing pages in the Loeb Classical Library edition by Martin L. West (*Homeric Hymns*).

22. Although Hesiod describes the Muses as plural, the epic narrator invokes a single Muse.

23. For more examples, see Burkert 119–20.

24. For example, there was a cult of Menelaus and Helen at Sparta; but although in the *Odyssey* these figures are said to be destined for a happy afterlife in the Elysian Fields (4.561–70), their cult is not mentioned. See Burkert 203–08 on the relationship between heroes and gods. Nagy argues for an implicit ritual antagonism between specific heroes and gods (*Best*).

25. A recent contribution to this discussion is Graziosi and Haubold, *Homer* 75–80, which argues that the *Odyssey* is set in an era when "the separation between gods and mortals is further advanced than in the *Iliad*" (77).

26. The word "nymph" (*numphē*), sometimes used in reference to Calypso and Circe in the epic and in translations, may also be used of a human bride or marriageable woman but is the conventional term for a category of lesser goddesses, usually associated with springs, trees, or the sea.

27. For detailed treatment of the ancient reception of the epic cycle, see Fantuzzi and Tsagalis.

28. For more detailed treatment of the reception history, see Hall; Pache 411–561 (the section "Homer in the World"). Dated, but still indispensable, is Stanford, *Ulysses Theme*; see also Graziosi and Greenwood.

29. See Venkatraman; Cox Gurdon. See also the essays by Lesser and Lodge in this volume.

30. Notably even the Cyclops (9.452–55). See the essay by Lodge in this volume.

31. For Aristotle's critique of the cyclic epics, see his *Poetics* 1459a-b and the section on the epic cycle in this introduction.

32. For more detailed discussion of the ancient philosophers' reception of Homer, see Lamberton; Kim. On the late Platonist Porphyry, see Lamberton 127.

33. For an introduction to the ancient novel and a collection of translations, see Reardon.

34. In *De finibus*, Cicero also praised Odysseus for seeking knowledge. See Van Peteghem in this volume.

35. See Mavroudi on the reception of Homer in Byzantine literature.

36. For detailed accounts of the Renaissance reception of Homer, see Wolfe; Grafton.

37. See "Classroom Texts" in part 1 of this volume for a discussion of translations into English, including Chapman's.

38. For a review of these and related works, see Burgess, "Recent Reception."

39. This series of collages and paintings formed the basis of an exhibition that toured from 2015 to 2017 and is archived online by the Smithsonian ("Romare Bearden"). See O'Meally for a presentation in book form with commentary.

Part One

MATERIALS

Classroom Texts

Greek and Dual Language Editions

The Greek editions of the *Odyssey* most frequently used by scholars are those of Thomas W. Allen and D. B. Monro in the Oxford Classical Texts series (*Odysseae Libros I–XII*, *Odysseae Libros XIII–XXIV*); Helmut van Thiel; and Karl Friedrich Ameis, Karl Hentze, and Paul Cauer. While the Oxford Classical Texts edition is still used in classrooms, it includes no commentary; most teachers of Greek therefore prefer the edition of W. B. Stanford, which includes a useful, if somewhat dated, commentary and a good basic introduction to the Homeric dialect. The text on the *Perseus Digital Library* website is especially appealing to students because it is open-source and hyperlinked to a translation and to various study aids; this edition uses the version of W. Walter Merry, James Riddell, and D. B. Monro (Merry et al.). *The Chicago Homer* is another open-source database with searchable Greek and English texts of the *Iliad*, *Odyssey*, and Homeric Hymns (Kahane and Mueller). There are also open-source editions of books 6–8 and 9–12 (and a beta version of books 17–20), edited by Geoffrey Steadman, with running vocabulary and notes, which may be printed on demand (*Homer's* Odyssey *6–8*, *Homer's* Odyssey *9–12*, *Homer's* Odyssey *17–20*). The notes contain some errors, but the running vocabulary is very useful to students. Two other options for those beginning to read Homer are *An* Odyssey *Reader*, edited by P. A. Draper, with selections in Greek from books 1–12, and *The Triumph of Odysseus* from the Joint Association of Classical Teachers, which contains the full text of books 21 and 22; both also contain running vocabulary and notes. A caveat, however: it can be difficult for students beginning with one of these texts to wean themselves from the vocabulary lists. Instructors will need to help students build their own working vocabularies of the most commonly used words. William B. Owen and Edgar J. Goodspeed's *Homeric Vocabularies* lists commonly used words by frequency and is a good starting point for vocabulary building.

For advanced students, the "Cambridge green and yellows" editions (in the Cambridge University Press Greek and Latin Classics series) are ideal; though not yet available for all the books, they include books 6–8, 9, 13–14, 17–18, and 19–20 at the time of this writing (Garvie; Bakker, *Homer*; Bowie; D. Steiner; Rutherford). Volumes for books 11 and 16 are in preparation.[1]

I have begun by listing the Greek editions without translations since many instructors prefer those, but there is also an edition of book 1 with an English translation on facing pages by Simon Pulleyn. Still in print, and available in many libraries, is the old edition of the entire poem with facing translation in the Loeb Classical Library; although the original translation by A. T. Murray has been updated in reprintings by George Dimock, the vocabulary and syntax are still quite old-fashioned. This edition is chiefly useful for those who know some Greek and want to check the original text of specific lines. Richmond Lattimore's and

Daniel Mendelsohn's translations follow the Greek text line by line and may also be used to locate specific passages. The *HathiTrust* digital library has a complete online text in Greek with the old-fashioned but readable translation by George Herbert Palmer.

Several textbooks aim to teach Ancient Greek with the express purpose of enabling students to read Homer. The most user-friendly of these is *A Reading Course in Homeric Greek* in its third revised edition (Schoder and Horrigan), which seeks to prepare students to read the *Odyssey* in particular. (Clyde Pharr's *Homeric Greek* leads into book 1 of the *Iliad*.) Composed by two Jesuit educators, Schoder and Horrigan's *Reading Course* also includes excerpts from the New Testament and the Septuagint (the Ancient Greek translation of the Hebrew Bible); the grammatical explanations and explanatory essays have been updated in the most recent edition. Frank Beetham's *Beginning Greek with Homer* also prepares students to read the *Odyssey* (book 5 in particular) but is much denser and heavily front-loaded with grammar; it may be more suitable for students who have already studied Latin and will be able to grasp the structure of an inflected language.

Commentaries and Study Aids

Commentaries on the text of Homer have existed since antiquity and modern versions exist in many languages.[2] Most commentaries are intended for those reading the epics in Greek; the most current, a thoroughly revised edition of the old "Ameis-Hentze-Cauer" edition (Ameis et al.; a German commentary published from 1868 to 1913), is the Basel Commentary, which deals with the *Iliad* only and is still in the process of publication (Bierl and Latacz). The publisher's website states that "the commentary primarily aims at students and academic teachers (at schools and universities), not only of Classics but also of cultural and literary studies as well as of humanities in general" ("*Homer's* Iliad"). As of this writing, eleven out of a projected twenty-five volumes have appeared in English translation; the first, *Prolegomena*, includes information relevant to the *Odyssey* on the dialect, meter, and background of Homer. The commentaries on the full text of the *Odyssey* are older; in English, the most recent is the rather specialized narratological commentary by Irene de Jong (*Narratological Commentary*), discussed below in "The Instructor's Library." The most affordable and best adapted to the needs of students of Greek is that included in the edition by Stanford mentioned above. There is also a commentary in three volumes (without the Greek text), each covering eight books of the *Odyssey* and written by different scholars; the general editor is Alfred Heubeck.[3] This commentary addresses variant readings and issues of Homeric morphology and syntax, and includes information from the ancient scholia as well as references to modern works of scholarship (many of them in German). The approach is conservative, emphasizing clarification of linguistic, geographic, mythological, and cultural issues as understood in the late twentieth century.

For those without Greek, there are useful line-by-line commentaries to the translation of Lattimore by Peter Jones and to that of Robert Fitzgerald by Ralph Hexter. A new one-volume *Oxford Critical Guide to the* Odyssey, designed to be useful to those who do not read Greek, is in preparation as of this writing, edited by Joel Christensen.

There are two Greek-to-English lexicons of the Homeric dialect: that of Richard John Cunliffe and that of Georg Autenrieth, translated from the German text of 1873. They are very similar, but Cunliffe is superior in providing the gender of nouns. Both are still in print as of this writing, and the Autenrieth edition is available in searchable format as part of the *Perseus Digital Library*. This digital collection, hosted by Tufts University, is an invaluable online resource for the study of Greek and Latin texts.

Concordances—works that itemize all occurrences of specific words in a text—have been made more or less obsolete in the digital era with the advent of searchable texts. The most accessible (open-source) searchable texts of the *Odyssey* are those in the *Perseus Digital Library* and the *Chicago Homer*, mentioned above. The *Thesaurus Linguae Graecae* (stephanus.tlg.uci.edu/index.php), a searchable database of the entire surviving corpus of Greek literature, requires a personal or institutional subscription, but the abridged *Thesaurus Linguae Graecae* of certain canonical authors, including Homer, is available for free browsing and searching (stephanus.tlg.uci.edu/abridged.php). For those who prefer a print concordance, there is one for the *Odyssey* by Henry Dunbar, revised by Benedetto Marzullo. A newer one by Joseph Tebben, published in print but based on a computer search of the van Thiel edition, includes words omitted from the Dunbar-Marzullo concordance but has other drawbacks (Hainsworth).

Translations

Translations of the *Odyssey* are legion. This is both a problem and an opportunity for teachers who have the option to select an edition for their course. A good class exercise, if there is time—ideally, when students begin reading the text—is to give students several translations of the proem (the first ten lines) to compare.[4] At least one of these should be an older translation, such as that of George Chapman or Alexander Pope, to make the point that contemporary language lacks the formal poetic diction that once existed in English; the Homeric dialect is similarly formal and this makes it very difficult to convey the style of the original in contemporary English.[5] In fact, the Homeric dialect is artificial, a composite developed over time expressly for the performance of oral epic. It contains forms from several dialects of Greek and can include multiple forms of a single word or case that fit different places in the hexameter line. The epithets that dot the text are another feature of this formality, and many translators drop at least some of them or vary their renderings of a single epithet: Stanley Lombardo's Athena, for example, has eyes that are "owl-grey" (1.49), "seagrey" (1.192), "grey as saltwater" (1.331), "flash[ing]" (2.424), or "glinting" (3.14)—all renditions of γλαυκῶπις (*glaukōpis*), whose meaning is disputed. The only translators to my knowledge who render the epithets identically each time are Lattimore and Mendelsohn.

Despite this formality of diction, the syntax is straightforward: for the most part, the sentence structure is paratactic—that is, composed of simple clauses strung together rather than complex sentences with subordinate clauses. This structure was well suited to the original performance context, in which the poet was composing as he sang and the audience was listening rather than reading; Egbert Bakker has shown in detail how the syntax corresponds to that of ordinary speech (*Poetry*). As a result, the narrative tends to flow rapidly, even in the character speeches, which often include narratives of their own: Homer's characters are storytellers themselves.

To these characteristics—rapidity and "plainness and directness" of expression—Matthew Arnold adds "sustained nobility of tone," but a more contemporary description might be "dignity."[6] This is especially challenging for a contemporary translator to convey since the prevailing tone in much modern narrative, and even much poetry, is ironic. "Chapman's Homer," famously praised by John Keats, captures this dignity but is unreadable for contemporary undergraduate students and adds many of Chapman's own flourishes to the text. Pope's version is also a striking poem in its own right but too grandiloquent for Homer's tone and equally inaccessible for many of today's students; like Chapman's, it interrupts the forward momentum of the original with its rhyming couplets. (Homer does not use end rhyme.)

Another reason to give students a few passages of these older translations is that they convey the effect of regular poetic meter, which is true to the original. Emily Wilson is the most recent translator as of this writing to attempt a truly metrical version of the text in English (Odyssey [2018]); using iambic pentameter, she captures the directness and forward momentum of the original. In some places her translation is more explicit than most, such as in calling the enslaved characters "slaves" rather than "attendants" or "maids." It is also somewhat tendentious in certain details; the translator has made clear her own criticisms of the poem's implicit ideology, and this critical stance is sometimes evident in the wording (W. Mason). For example, her translation reads, "All the other Greeks / who had survived the brutal sack of Troy" (1.11–12) where the Greek original simply states, "All those who had escaped sheer destruction" ὅσοι φύγον αἰπὺν ὄλεθρον (1.11); where in the Greek Helen describes herself as "shameless"—literally, "dog-faced" κυνώπιδος (4.145)—Wilson translates the same line as "They made my face the cause that hounded them" (4.148). Despite this caveat, Wilson's translation is a good choice for those seeking a contemporary poetic version.

The translation by Daniel Mendelsohn, brand new as of this writing, includes a detailed note on the translation (Odyssey 57–80) that critiques Wilson's for its brevity: Wilson's decision to maintain the same number of lines as in the Greek while using the shorter iambic pentameter meant that she had to omit much of the detail of the original. Mendelsohn's own translation is also poetic but not as metrically regular as Wilson's; his lines are largely dactylic, but of varying lengths, so that the overall effect is somewhat more prosaic. Inevitably, readers will disagree about their preferences, and teachers who have a choice of translations should choose the one about which they can be most enthusiastic.

Of the other poetic translations available, the most effective *as poetry*, in my view, are those of Robert Fitzgerald, Allen Mandelbaum, and Stanley Lombardo. Like Wilson's, these deliberately vary the formulaic epithets and take some liberties with imagery. Fitzgerald and Mandelbaum adopt a loose form of iambic pentameter, while Lombardo uses free verse and is more colloquial, which makes his version more accessible to students; his translation also has a real poetic sense and conveys some of the alliteration and assonance of the original. Mandelbaum makes the greatest efforts to convey these sound effects and even uses rhyme with some frequency in his translation. This gives his version an artful quality that I find at odds with Homer's original text: Homeric style does not call attention to itself.

Many other modern translations are printed as nonmetrical poetry but are otherwise close to prose. Lattimore, who describes his meter as "a free six-beat line" (Iliad 55), preserves the length and heft of the hexameter, but his version is much less flowing compared with those of Fitzgerald and Wilson, and even with the free verse of Lombardo. This is especially evident when reading the epic aloud, which is sometimes done by classics departments and clubs when staging a "Homerathon."[7] Robert Fagles, the author of another popular translation, has stated in an interview that the epics were "meant to be heard, not read" and that while working on his own version he started every day by reading the relevant lines aloud in Greek. Yet he also admitted, "My English is hardly ever forthright and direct; it's more understated, lacking in forward drive" (Storace 157). For oral reading I find his translation more suitable than Lattimore's, but less so than Wilson's or Lombardo's.

Other free-verse translations that read more like prose include those of Albert Cook, Barry Powell (*Homer: The* Odyssey), and Peter Green. Cook's has been praised for its closeness to the literal sense of the original; it was used as the basis for a Norton Critical Edition, now in its second edition and still in print alongside the new Norton Critical Edition by Wilson. These editions include background essays by scholars (different selections in each edition) as well as excerpts from ancient commentators. The paperback editions of the other translations discussed so far also have excellent introductions, especially Bernard Knox's introduction to Fagles's translation; Sheila Murnaghan's introduction to Lombardo's translation (Murnaghan, Introduction); Wilson's introduction to her own translation (Odyssey [2018] ix–xxxix), expanded in the Norton Critical Edition (Odyssey [2020] ix–lx); and Mendelsohn's introduction to his translation (12–56). These provide all the information a student needs to begin to make sense of the text.

A little should be said of the prose versions, since some teachers find that students have difficulty with even the more successful verse translations. The most commonly used of those in prose is that of E. V. Rieu in the Penguin Classics edition. Since its initial publication in 1947, its diction has been updated by Rieu's son D. C. H. Rieu and Peter Jones; the new version reads fluently. Unfortunately, like those of Walter Shewring and Martin Hammond, it has no real style, and the prose translations with style—those of Samuel Butler, W. H. D. Rouse, and T. E. Lawrence—contain enough archaic language and syntax to deter a student, though all are still in print.[8] Butler and Rouse are especially lively and make the epic read like a novel.

Many dramatic adaptations of the *Odyssey* have been produced, including those of Derek Walcott, Mary Zimmerman, and Simon Armitage (*Homer's* Odyssey). These could serve as introductions to the epic as well as to the field of classical reception studies since all are interpretations and reshapings as well as dramatizations. Some students may already be familiar with the novels that offer different perspectives (often those of the female characters) on the story, such as Madeline Miller's *Circe*. One of the earliest and best of these is Margaret Atwood's *Penelopiad*.

Several of the respondents to the MLA preliminary survey on teaching the *Odyssey*, when asked about textbooks they used, mentioned graphic novels and even children's versions (such as that by Geraldine McCaughrean) as "gateway books" that facilitate entry to the text. These editions are especially recommended for students with limited reading skills. Two of the graphic novels follow the plot rather closely: the version by Roy Thomas and Greg Tocchini portrays all the female characters, including Penelope, in skimpy costumes, while the version by Gareth Hinds intended for high school and adult readers is more realistically illustrated; both include the sex and violence of the original. Those by Russell Punter and by Diego Agrimbau, however, portray the Cyclops with a different skin tone than that of the Greek characters, an invidious choice given the criticisms of Sarah Derbew ("Definitions") and Jackie Murray (see "The Instructor's Library" below). Though not a comprehensive listing, these versions may provide a starting point for those interested in this approach to the text.

Audio and Video Resources

When I teach the *Odyssey* in translation, I always read the proem aloud in Greek to students to make the point that it was not originally composed in English. An instructor who does not know Greek might play the recording of the proem by Ioannis Stratakis in a "reconstructed Ancient Greek" ("Homer"). There are also unabridged audio versions of the Fagles translation read by the actor Ian McKellen, of Lombardo's and Mendelsohn's read by the respective translators, and of Wilson's read by Claire Danes. Wilson herself has made videos on *YouTube* in which she reads—with relish and drama (and props)—excerpts of her version ("Emily Wilson's *Odyssey* Translation"). Other audio versions (including Armitage's dramatization) are available on audiobook sellers' websites (see, e.g., Armitage, Odyssey). The *Internet Archive* has excerpts (originally on Caedmon Records) read by the British actor Anthony Quayle.

The 1997 miniseries featuring Armand Assante as Odysseus, available on *Freevee* (formerly *IMDb TV*), is visually striking and sure to grab students' attention; the challenge, then, will be to persuade them to read the text as well. To address this issue instructors can devise a comparison assignment since the miniseries, like any dramatization, is one interpretation of the original (and very different in detail).[9] Films that can be approached as receptions of the *Odyssey*, such as Martin Ritt's *Sounder* or Joel Coen and Ethan Coen's *O Brother, Where Art Thou?*, can also be the basis for such comparisons.

There are a number of short videos on *YouTube* that purport to summarize the plot of the epic; those I have previewed are all incorrect in one or more details, and most begin the story with Odysseus rather than Telemachus. But for some students an introduction like this may be useful—as long as they do not substitute it for actually reading the work. A valuable video introduction to the text is the one on *Annenberg Learner*, which does not summarize the plot but features a diverse set of commentators, including the comic book author Roy Thomas and the playwright Mary Zimmerman in addition to several classics professors ("Invitation"). A shorter and more provocative video commentary by John Green might be good for sparking class discussion.

Many other online resources are available to help fill in the mythic and geographic background to the epic, but students should beware of amateur sites lacking factual details and authoritative authorship. One of the most dependable and exhaustive sites on Greek (and Roman) mythology, including the names and identities of the gods, is the *Theoi Project*, edited by Aaron J. Atsma (www.theoi.com), which in addition to plot summaries of the myths includes visual art from antiquity and translated excerpts from many ancient texts. General introductions to mythology—in any medium—are less helpful, especially if they take a doctrinaire approach to interpretation, insisting, for example, on Joseph Campbell's version of "the hero's journey" (*Hero*) or on the view of myth as a primitive explanation of natural phenomena.

Maps of the Mediterranean in antiquity are readily available online. But the geography of the *Odyssey*, including even the identity of Ithaca, is contested, despite the existence of a Greek island with that name. Although many attempts have been made to "place" Odysseus's other landfalls in the Mediterranean, they are probably as imaginary as their inhabitants. All that students need to know are the relative locations of Troy and mainland Greece, as well as those of Crete, Pylos, and Sparta; whichever island Ithaca is, it must be one of the Ionian islands, located off the western coast of Greece.

The Instructor's Library

The literature on Homer is vast and can be daunting even to the specialist. This section offers an overview of the most salient approaches and recommends some specific studies that may be useful to instructors. Some of these studies deal with the *Iliad* as well as the *Odyssey*.

Of the general works on Homer, the most comprehensive are the *Homer Encyclopedia* in three volumes, edited by Margalit Finkelberg, and the recent *Cambridge Guide to Homer*, an outstanding work of collaborative scholarship, edited by Corinne Ondine Pache. The single-volume *Cambridge Companion to Homer*, edited by Robert Fowler, is compact enough to be used as a textbook in an advanced course yet thorough in its coverage. The 1997 *New Companion to Homer*, edited by Ian Morris and Barry B. Powell, designed as an update to the 1962 *Companion to Homer*, edited by Alan Wace and Frank Stubbings, is itself already somewhat dated (Janko, Review).

There are many collections of essays on the *Odyssey* or on both Homeric epics, including a special issue of *College Literature* titled *Reading Homer in the Twenty-First Century*, edited by Kostas Myrsiades. Two collections, both entitled *Approaches to Homer*, one by Carl Rubino and Claudia Shelmerdine and the other by Robert J. Rabel, include valuable essays on both the *Iliad* and the *Odyssey*. Collections of previously published articles on the *Odyssey* in particular include *Essays on the* Odyssey, edited by Charles H. Taylor; *Reading the* Odyssey, edited by Seth Schein; and the volume *Homer's* Odyssey in the series Oxford Readings in Classical Studies, which I edited (Doherty, *Homer's* Odyssey). Harold Bloom's volume *Homer's The* Odyssey is primarily composed of excerpts from an earlier generation of scholars, interesting for what they reveal about the history of Homeric criticism.

An engaging work written in a lively style that may be of special interest to teachers is *A Companion to Homer's* Odyssey, by James Morrison. In addition to individual chapters on each book of the epic, it includes introductory essays, sidebars on the Greek language, a list of characters with a pronunciation guide, and suggestions for classroom activities. A work in preparation at the time of this writing, the *Oxford Critical Guide to the* Odyssey, edited by Joel Christensen, will also devote chapters to the individual books of the epic; this guide is intended for a more advanced audience than Morrison's *Companion*.

This volume's introduction discusses works on the poetics of the oral tradition; prominent scholars who work on this topic include, among others, Egbert Bakker (*Poetry*), Jonathan Burgess ("Coming Adrift," *Tradition*), Barbara Graziosi and Johannes Haubold, Gregory Nagy, and Christos Tsagalis. A collection of essays with this focus is *Written Voices, Spoken Signs*, edited by Bakker and Ahuvia Kahane. Casey Dué's and Laura Slatkin's essays in the present volume use a similar approach.

For classical scholars, the approach of close reading remains basic, and informs most of the college literature courses they teach as well as much of their published scholarship. An especially sensitive close reader is Sheila Murnaghan, whose *Disguise and Recognition in the* Odyssey probes the implications of Odysseus's disguise and the sequence of his recognitions by his son, wife, and father.

Jasper Griffin also offers a nuanced and perceptive, if more conventional, reading of the epic, with particular attention to its style, in *Homer: The* Odyssey.

Narratology is interested in the relationships among narrators, focalizers (those whose perspectives inform the telling), and audiences, or narratees. As extended narratives with many speakers and passages of dialogue, the epics lend themselves to this approach. Narratology has been embraced by Homerists, despite its origins in the analysis of folklore and modern fiction (e.g., Vladimir Propp's work on the Russian folktale and Gérard Genette's study of Proust), for the light it has shed on the narrative structure of the epics. Foundational work in this area has been done by Irene de Jong; her *Narratological Commentary on the* Odyssey builds on her earlier groundbreaking study, *Narrators and Focalizers: The Presentation of the Story in the* Iliad. The focus on audiences is stronger in reader-response, or audience-oriented, criticism, which explores the ways in which the poems may have been understood by early listening audiences or by later literate ones. An important work in this vein is *Listening to Homer*, by Ruth Scodel.

In their efforts to reanimate the bards of epic tradition, Homerists have also borrowed the approaches of linguistic theory and performance studies. Some of this work focuses on the *Iliad*, such as Richard Martin's *The Language of Heroes*, but much of it is also applicable to the *Odyssey*. Knowledge of Ancient Greek is necessary to understand works such as Bakker's *Poetry in Speech*, which demonstrates how the class of words called "particles" helps to establish and maintain the bard's connection with his audience. But some studies, such as *Homer in Performance*, edited by Jonathan Ready and Christos Tsagalis, are more accessible to those without Greek.[10] The goal of this approach is to reconstruct the original context of performance to the extent possible, with emphasis on the activity of the performer. Comparative material from other epic traditions and related oral genres helps illuminate the range of possibilities. The interesting result is a more nuanced understanding of the so-called Homeric question,[11] as evidence emerges that even within a particular time and place, performers may have different preferences for innovation or preservation of episodes and lines. It has also emerged that whereas epic is usually seen as a masculine genre, women in other traditions may perform it, or may perform related stories in different poetic genres (see, e.g., Vidan; Narayana Rao). As discussed by Olga Levaniouk, a surviving fragment of a poem by Sappho about the wedding of Andromache and Hector is evidence that similar practices may have existed in Greece ("Did").

In the 1970s and 1980s, the approaches of structuralism and deconstruction produced some valuable interpretations of Homer (and of Hesiod). These approaches, originating in anthropology (especially in the work of Claude Lévi-Strauss), focused on the ideologies implicit in myth and ritual, which they detected in persistent oppositions such as endogamy versus exogamy or eating raw versus cooked food. Pierre Vidal-Naquet's essay "Land and Sacrifice in the *Odyssey*" contrasts the social structures and practices of the "real world" as portrayed in Ithaca, Pylos, and Sparta with the fantastic world of Odysseus's wanderings and the "utopia" of Scheria, an island Odysseus arrives at in his journey. *Cunning Intelligence in Greek Culture and Society*, by Marcel Detienne and Jean-Pierre Vernant, is a wide-ranging study of the cultural value of *mētis*, the cunning that is Odysseus's most prominent trait. "The Economic Man," by James Redfield, applies a modified form of structuralist analysis to the adventures of Odysseus.[12] Deconstructive criticism, as introduced by Jacques Derrida and Jacques Lacan, emphasized the instability inherent in the systems of oppositions discerned by structuralists—an instability that extended to the meanings of words and literary works. Virtuosic studies of the *Odyssey* in this vein are John Peradotto's *Man in the Middle Voice* and Pietro Pucci's *Odysseus Polutropos*.

Attention to gender roles as reflected in the epic, and the ways in which these roles constrain the female characters, has informed a significant number of studies of the *Odyssey* since the 1980s. A central insight is the awareness that there exists in each society and in each era a "sex-gender system,"[13] in which gender roles are culturally assigned; though originating in the social sciences, this insight has been fruitfully applied to literature and the arts. Feminist criticism takes many forms since attention to gender can be combined with many other approaches. For example, Nancy Felson's *Regarding Penelope: From Character to Poetics* combines narratological and audience-oriented approaches to examine the "possible plots" in which Penelope finds herself cast and in which she can be seen as playing active, if circumscribed, roles. Feminist scholars have found themselves on both sides of the debate about when Penelope recognizes Odysseus; Murnaghan in "Penelope's *Agnoia*" emphasizes that Penelope's ignorance is imposed by her husband and reflects a "generalized suspicion of women" that informs the epic (108); John Winkler, while acknowledging these constraints, argues for her strong suspicion of the "beggar's" identity and her active participation in the epic's denouement (129–61). In the present volume, the essay by Rachel Lesser takes a feminist approach. The recent translation by Emily Wilson, with its extensive introduction, is also informed by a feminist perspective.

More recently, postcolonial insights have been applied to the *Odyssey*, and specifically to its treatment of the cultures Odysseus encounters in his wanderings. Kirsten Lodge in this volume takes this approach to the analysis of the Cyclops episode. Justine McConnell, in *Black Odysseys*, combines a postcolonial analysis of the ancient epic with a study of its reception in the African diaspora. Like feminist studies, postcolonial approaches tend to be critical of the epic and of its hero, which are seen as assuming the superiority of their own cultural norms. These approaches share an awareness of ideologies implicit in the work, which have continued to inform Western culture and traditional readings of Homer. The dilemma this can create for teachers who wish to convey enthusiasm for the work is discussed below and in my essay in this volume.

A related approach with radical implications for the interpretation of classical literature as a whole is that of critical race theory, developed outside the field of classics but used within it by scholars such as Jackie Murray and Sarah Derbew

("Definitions") to uncover what they call the "racecraft" of works like the *Odyssey*. This approach is in fact a kind of deconstruction, in that it not only critiques but also excavates in detail the normative behavior patterns that "construct" hierarchical social groups in literature as in society. The word *race* is used in these studies independently of the focus on skin color central to its modern usage: in Derbew's definition, race is "an outward-facing category that allows people to categorize and essentialize others," thereby depriving them of humanity ("Definitions" 25).[14] Murray (esp. 145–51) uses this approach to argue that the *Odyssey*, told from the perspective of the dominant group (male heroes), racializes the group of herders, including not only Eumaeus and Melanthius but also the Cyclopes, through the processes of "monstrification and double standards in social interactions"—the latter including "centering" of the dominant group's perspective, "ritual deference" expected by one group from another, and asymmetry in sexual and kinship relations (144–45). While focusing on the specifics of ancient literature and culture, these scholars simultaneously grapple with the persistence of racism in the contemporary world and with the racist legacy of classical scholarship. In that way, critical race studies are like feminist and postcolonial approaches to the study of ancient texts: inspired by contemporary progressive movements, they are informed by the scholars' own positionality and by their desire to reach students who live in a world where race and gender are subject to active reevaluation.

The relatively few older studies of class distinctions in the *Odyssey*, which do not mention race, are divided between a deconstructive approach similar to Murray's and a more positive evaluation of the epic's portrayal of the lower classes. The fact that Odysseus himself is disguised as a beggar for much of the poem and is mistreated by the suitors is seen by Peter Rose as evidence that the poet, in his description of "the compulsion of hunger and the concomitant humiliations of the hungry wanderer," is channeling a "barely suppressed rage" at those humiliations ("Class Ambivalence" 142).[15] William G. Thalmann, by contrast, argues in detail that the epic makes a "self-conscious presentation of a justly hierarchical society" (*Swineherd* 20), in particular by its portrayal of "good slaves" as allied with Odysseus and "bad slaves" as allied with his opponents, the suitors. Both Rose and Thalmann see the epic as participating in the social and political struggles of the late eighth century BCE, when most scholars assume the *Odyssey* was composed.

A recent theoretical approach to the interpretation of Homer is that of the new materialisms—plural because there are several strands to this concept. As explained and deployed by, for example, Lilah Grace Canevaro, it involves taking seriously the materiality of objects with which the characters interact and that become "manifestations of [characters'] agency" (17). For Canevaro, this is especially important in the case of female characters such as Helen and Penelope, who use their weaving as a form of communication with one another as well as with male characters. By contrast with the "merging of object and person" (24) that can occur in the case of men and their weapons, Canevaro observes that female characters use objects as proxies or surrogates in their attempts to exercise what agency they can, given the constraints of their social position (cf. Purves).

Another recent approach, that of trauma theory, is central to Joel Christensen's *The Many-Minded Man*. Building on the work of psychologists and classical scholars who have read Greek epic and tragedy with combat veterans, Christensen argues that on Calypso's island Odysseus finds himself isolated and depressed, in a condition of "learned helplessness" (8). He must reconstruct his identity by means of both action (e.g., building the raft) and narration (e.g., telling his story to the Phaeacians). In this view, the *Odyssey* has a therapeutic dimension, based on "the relationship between the narrative self and the *self as agent*" (7).

That members of communities that may have experienced trauma, such as veterans and incarcerated people, can themselves connect with ancient works such as the *Odyssey* and find their experiences validated in them has been shown by projects such as *Ancient Greeks / Modern Lives*, led by Peter Meineck (ancientgreeksmodernlives-blog.tumblr.com); *Theater of War*, led by Brian Doerries (theaterofwar.com); the *Medea Project* of Rhodessa Jones (themedeaproject.weebly.com); and the prison education efforts of members of the Classics and Social Justice affiliated group of the Society for Classical Studies (classicsandsocialjustice.com). An early participant in this movement is the psychiatrist Jonathan Shay, who used the *Iliad* and *Odyssey* in his work with combat veterans of the Vietnam War and more recent wars. While Shay found the *Iliad* valuable as a text with which the veterans could engage and that could be used to help them heal from what he called the "moral injury" of battle (*Achilles*), he read the *Odyssey* as "a detailed allegory of many a real veteran's homecoming" (*Odysseus* xv) in which, for example, the episode of the Lotus-Eaters represents the lure of drugs as a "flight from pain" (35–41), while that of the Cyclops represents "the flight from boredom" (42–46). To Shay, "Odysseus stands for the veterans, but as a deeply flawed military leader himself, he also stands for the destroyers of trust" (xv), the officers whose incompetence and careerism led to increased casualties (166–67). While most encounters with the epics today still take place in the classroom, Shay's reading puts them back into the context of actual war and its aftermath, which many members of ancient audiences would have experienced. A recent volume edited by Emilio Capettini and Nancy Sorkin Rabinowitz explores the related ways in which ancient texts, including the Homeric epics, are used to engage with people in prisons and provides pedagogical guidance for these efforts. For an example of such a project, see the essay by Michael Morgan and Olga Faccani in this volume.

A final approach that may be combined with any of the foregoing is that of reception studies, which replaces the older study of "the classical tradition." Reception studies puts the emphasis on the ways in which later artists and writers have received, questioned, and reimagined classical works. A fuller account of this approach is given in the introduction to this volume.

My own experience of teaching the *Odyssey* in both Greek and English over the course of forty years has led me to seek a balance between the approaches I have described as critical, in the negative sense, and more positive perspectives on the poem. While my own research has made me wary of the ways in which the text draws the audience (and especially the female audience) into tacit agreement with its implicit ideology (Doherty, *Siren Songs*), I continue to value the work for its many attractive qualities: its compelling story, vivid characters, clever plotting, and reflection on its own status as poetry. Perhaps above all, I value its emphasis on the possibility of survival against the odds—its comic rejoinder to the *Iliad*'s tragic vision. It is the balance between critical and appreciative approaches that in my view will continue to persuade students that the *Odyssey* and other ancient works of literature are worth their time and attention.

NOTES

1. Discussed in emails with Cambridge University Press of 16 June 2025.

2. For an overview of the history of Homeric commentaries, with an emphasis on the *Iliad*, see Latacz.

3. As the preface to the first volume explains, this is a revised version of a commentary originally published by Mondadori in Italy.

4. Especially in a comparative or survey course, it can also be instructive to compare the proem of the *Odyssey* with those of the *Iliad* and *Aeneid*.

5. Recommended discussions of the challenges of translating Homer may be found in Arnold; the note on the translation by D. S. Carne-Ross (lxi–lxx) in his introduction to Fitzgerald's translation; Mendelsohn's note on the translation in his introduction to his own translation (Odyssey 57–80); and W. Mason.

6. Arnold also characterizes Homer's thought as "plain and direct" (9). In the *Odyssey* especially, this is open to doubt, as many of the essays in this volume attest.

7. The continuous oral reading of one of the Homeric epics, shared among a group of students and faculty members (ideally from several departments), has become a popular way of celebrating Greek literature and making others aware of it.

8. Recent hardcover editions of Butler and Lawrence, available through online booksellers, are photocopies of older editions. The full text of Butler is available on *Project Gutenberg*.

9. The 1954 *Ulysses* starring Kirk Douglas is dated and introduces inaccuracies; it conflates Circe with Calypso (and implicitly with Penelope) and includes the further misleading premise that Odysseus has lost his memory when he arrives in Phaeacia.

10. The volume combines textual study of the epics with what is known about their performance in antiquity and with comparative material from other traditions. On the epics as scripts for solo performance, see Kretler.

11. For more on the Homeric question, see the first section of the introduction to this volume.

12. Redfield's more influential work on Homer, also inflected by anthropological thought, is *Nature and Culture in the* Iliad.

13. The term originated with the cultural anthropologist Gayle Rubin (159).

14. The concept of race, as used by these scholars, is not interchangeable with social class; for the difference, see J. Murray 144–45.

15. See also Rose, *Sons* 42–140; Farron.

Part Two

APPROACHES

THE *ODYSSEY* AND THE GREEK EPIC TRADITION

The Ends of the *Odyssey*

Casey Dué

Where does the *Odyssey* end? For a typical student, the answer is easy. It ends at book 24, line 548, or on the last page of whatever edition or translation their teacher has assigned to them, or with the oaths brokered by Athena at the end of the poem, in the guise of Mentor. But if you ask a student where the *Odyssey* *should* end, you might get a different answer. Ancient scholarship on the poem tells us that the great Alexandrian critics of the Hellenistic era, Aristophanes of Byzantium and Aristarchus of Samothrace, wanted verse 296 of book 23 to be the "end" (*peras* or *telos*):[1] "When she had conducted them to their room she went back, and they then came gladly [*aspasioi*] to the rites of their own old bed" ἐς θάλαμον δ᾽ ἀγαγοῦσα πάλιν κίεν. οἱ μὲν ἔπειτα / ἀσπάσιοι λέκτροιο παλαιοῦ θεσμὸν ἵκοντο.[2] And this moment in the poem, in which Penelope and Odysseus reunite at last in their marital bed, is indeed the one many students would choose to end on as well. (I know because I always ask them.)

For most works of literature, the question of where to end is nonsensical. We must interpret each work as the author composed it. But the *Odyssey* is not like most works. Modern scholarship, beginning with the pathfinding research and fieldwork of Milman Parry and Albert Lord,[3] has demonstrated that the *Odyssey* was composed within a dynamic and multiform oral tradition that was centuries, possibly millennia, in the making. Although it was composed by poets working within a highly traditional medium—who were using a highly traditional language to weave tales made up of highly traditional characters, plots, and themes—before the Archaic era, no single performance of the poem was canonical. In the earliest stages of the history of this poem, performers told the story anew each time. Each performance of the song was a new composition with a variety of traditional possibilities for how to tell the story and bring it to a conclusion that depended on the occasion, time allowed, and interaction with the audience. In my courses, including those aimed at a general audience of students who may never have encountered Greek literature before, I challenge the students to approach the *Odyssey* as an orally composed and performed poem—that is, as dynamic rather than fixed and static. The implications of its oral composition for our understanding of the poetics of the *Odyssey* are manifold. How was such a poem received by ancient audiences, and how, in turn, do we interpret it?

Not only is the *Odyssey* about a "complicated" man, to cite Emily Wilson's justly admired translation of Odysseus's Greek epithet in the first line of the poem, *polutropos*, but the *Odyssey* itself is complicated, not least because it is "multiform," to use Lord's term.[4] I therefore focus in this essay on the text's beginning and even more on its ending. How does where the poet begins and ends the poem affect the audience's understanding of it as a whole? If an audience knows the story already, does it matter where the poet begins? I then explore the concept of τέλος (*telos*), or "ending," for an oral poem. After considering the ending that Aristophanes and Aristarchus preferred, I then, as I do with my students, look at how the *Odyssey* we know actually ends, in order to show how that later ending—that is, the last book of the *Odyssey*—articulates the central themes of the *Odyssey* as we now know it. Ultimately, quite a lot is lost if book 24 is omitted.

But my essay cannot end even there, nor can any discussion of the *Odyssey* with students, because the story of Odysseus does not end there. In book 11 of the *Odyssey*, Odysseus consults the prophet Tiresias in the underworld, who tells him that he still has much wandering to do even after he returns home to Ithaca. How are we to understand Tiresias's prophecy in terms of the poem's overarching theme of "homecoming" (*nostos*)? What's more, many variations on what happens in the story of Odysseus, Penelope, and Telemachus after Odysseus returns home survive from antiquity, some of which indicate that Penelope has not been faithful. (I have included some ancient testimony in an appendix to this essay, which can be used as a handout for students, together with some questions for discussion.) If we know that alternative *Odysseys* were at least potentially out there, how does the experience of the *Odyssey* in performance change for ancient audiences, and for us? By giving students a glimpse of these possibilities, we help them to see that interpretation of an oral poem must be approached differently than that of modern works of literature composed in writing.

Because we now understand that the *Odyssey* was composed within an oral traditional system that evolved over many centuries, we can assert with confidence that in the earlier stages of the history of this poem the performers had choices about where to begin and end each performance, and countless other choices in between. The *Odyssey* gives us a glimpse of this flexibility in its opening invocation in book 1: the poet asks the Muse to tell the story of Odysseus's wandering, starting from whatever point she chooses. In book 8 of the *Odyssey*, the Muse inspires the singer Demodocus "to pick up a story thread and sing about a matter whose glory in song had reached wide heaven" ἀειδέμεναι κλέα ἀνδρῶν, / οἴμης τῆς τότ' ἄρα κλέος οὐρανὸν εὐρὺν ἵκανε (73–74). In other words, Demodocus, inspired by the Muse, dips into the epic tradition and pulls out from among the many tales he could tell the story of a quarrel between Agamemnon and Odysseus. Where a singer starts and stops in such a tradition is significant, not least because there was more than one place to do so. The beginning and ending focus and give an arc to the action and draw out crucial themes; they provide an essential structure within a wide-ranging poetic tradition that is fluid and dynamic. The *Odyssey* opens with nine verses that preview much of its plot. Similarly, the *Iliad* in its opening verses gives an overview of the action that sets its plot in motion. Indeed, the theme of each work is distilled into its very first word, "man" (*andra*) for the *Odyssey* and "wrath" (*mēnin*) for the *Iliad*. Yet neither poem previews how precisely it will end. In this way the option of where to end is kept open for the poet.

Even much later, several centuries after the *Odyssey* had become an essentially fixed poem with defined parameters for the Greeks, ancient scholars knew about more than one ending and, in fact, argued about what the ending should be. Their scholarship, which took the form of commentaries on the *Iliad* and *Odyssey* in antiquity, was later selectively copied in the margins of medieval manuscripts of these poems, and these excerpted comments are known collectively as scholia. One such scholion, on book 23, line 296,[5] has to do with this very question of the end of the *Odyssey*, and it has itself survived in two forms—that is to say, the comment is transmitted differently in different manuscripts. Here are both versions:

Version 1

Ἀριστοφάνης δὲ καὶ Ἀρίσταρχος πέρας τῆς Ὀδυσσείας τοῦτο ποιοῦνται.

"Aristophanes and Aristarchus make this the *peras* ['limit'] of the *Odyssey*."

Version 2

τοῦτο τέλος τῆς Ὀδυσσείας φησὶν Ἀρίσταρχος καὶ Ἀριστοφάνης.

"Aristarchus and Aristophanes say that this is the *telos* ['goal,' 'completion,' 'end'] of the *Odyssey*."

As I noted at the outset of this essay, Aristarchus and Aristophanes were two of the premier editors of the Homeric epics in antiquity. Both were heads of the library of Alexandria, and together with their predecessor Zenodotus they are referred to throughout the surviving scholia as the authorities for textual disputes and various questions of reading and interpretation. Arguably one of the most significant preserved multiforms of all is the one previously mentioned on book 23, line 296, if we are understanding the comment correctly. Throughout the scholia various kinds of editions are cited as evidence for the readings attested in the debates of ancient scholars. Could it be, as these two comments suggest, that there were versions of the *Odyssey* that ended at book 23, line 296? Certainly there would be nothing to stop a performer from closing his performance there. Were there actual editions of the *Odyssey* in the library of Alexandria that ended this way? If so, they have left no trace (beyond the quoted scholia) in the textual transmission of the poem.

Many have resisted the notion that an edition of the *Odyssey* ending at book 23, line 296, could have existed, and the extensive argumentation on this question in modern scholarship is intricately intertwined with broader, long-standing debates about both the nature of Homeric poetry and the work of the Alexandrian editors. The Analysts of the nineteenth century, for example, were quite willing to view the remainder of the *Odyssey* as inferior and tacked on, while the Unitarians in the twentieth century vehemently defended the complete poem as we know it.[6] Modern scholars (going as far back as the twelfth-century-CE Eustathius) have tried to find alternative explanations for the word *telos*—for example, by viewing it through a more literary, Aristotelian lens and not as a literal "end." It is difficult to do the same, however, for *peras* (and we should note that Aristotle himself discusses the slaughter of the suitors in book 22 as being the *telos* of the *Odyssey* in his *Poetics* [1455b17–24]).

I don't intend to offer a solution in this essay. Rather, I wish to show how it is possible to encourage students to consider multiple possibilities and to appreciate the *Odyssey* as a multiform entity. I look first to the ending that many ancient critics of Homeric poetry preferred as the ending. After that I look at how contemporary editions of the *Odyssey* actually end and see what we can learn about how the later ending after book 23 affects our understanding of the poem. Yet even while making a case for book 24 of the *Odyssey*, I want to be clear that any of these endings could have and almost certainly did occur in performance, and one is not more valid than the other in that context.

Odysseus is in many ways a suitor at the end of the *Odyssey*. And while I realize not everyone—including my students—would agree with my own view that Penelope knows precisely to whom she is talking when she tells the disguised Odysseus about her dream of the twenty geese that are killed by an eagle who subsequently reveals himself to be her husband (19.509–81; a topic for another essay), I believe that she is in a position to choose whether she wants Odysseus now that he is home, or whether she prefers one of the suitors. (On the gender dynamics at work here, see also Rachel H. Lesser's contribution to this volume.) In book 21, like the rest of the suitors, Odysseus participates in (and wins) the contest of the axes, which has been expressly set up by Penelope as a mechanism for choosing a husband. And in fact, once the other suitors are dead and Odysseus has won, he is presented (with Athena's help) as a bridegroom, and their reunion is portrayed as a wedding.

Immediately after the slaughter of the suitors, those remaining in the house begin to celebrate. This is done ostensibly to deceive the people of Ithaca about the slaughter that has just occurred, but the comparison to a wedding is clear:

> First they washed and put on their *khitons*,[7]
> and the women prepared themselves. The divine singer took up
> the hollow *phorminx*,[8] and he stirred in them the desire
> for sweet song and faultless dance.
> The great house resounded with the feet
> of the men playfully dancing and of the women with their beautiful sashes.
> And so one would say as he heard from outside the house:
> "Surely someone has married the much wooed queen.
> Cruel woman, she didn't hold out to the end in her protection
> of the great house of the husband of her youth, until he came home."
> So someone would say, but they did not know what things had been done.
>
> πρῶτα μὲν οὖν λούσαντο καὶ ἀμφιέσαντο χιτῶνας,
> ὅπλισθεν δὲ γυναῖκες· ὁ δ᾽ εἵλετο θεῖος ἀοιδὸς
> φόρμιγγα γλαφυρήν, ἐν δέ σφισιν ἵμερον ὦρσε
> μολπῆς τε γλυκερῆς καὶ ἀμύμονος ὀρχηθμοῖο.
> τοῖσιν δὲ μέγα δῶμα περιστεναχίζετο ποσσὶν
> ἀνδρῶν παιζόντων καλλιζώνων τε γυναικῶν.
> ὧδε δέ τις εἴπεσκε δόμων ἔκτοσθεν ἀκούων
> 'ἦ μάλα δή τις ἔγημε πολυμνήστην βασίλειαν
> σχετλίη, οὐδ᾽ ἔτλη πόσιος οὗ κουριδίοιο
> εἴρυσθαι μέγα δῶμα διαμπερές, ἧος ἵκοιτο.'
> ὣς ἄρα τις εἴπεσκε, τὰ δ᾽ οὐ ἴσαν ὡς ἐτέτυκτο. (23.142–52)

The townspeople don't know what has been happening, but they are correct that Penelope is getting married at last. She is remarrying Odysseus after his long absence. Odysseus then becomes a bridegroom as the passage continues:

> Meanwhile great-hearted Odysseus in his own home
> the housekeeper Eurynome washed and anointed with olive oil,
> and around him she put a beautiful cloak and a *khiton*.
> Athena in turn poured much beauty down over his head,
> such that he was taller and broader to look upon. And down from his head
> she sent dark hair, like a hyacinth blossom.
> As when a man pours gold around silver,
> a craftsman, whom Hephaestus and Pallas Athena have taught
> every kind of skill, and he accomplishes lovely works,

so did she pour grace around his head and shoulders.
He went from the bath looking like the immortals in form,
and he sat back down again on the seat from which he had risen,
opposite his wife, and he addressed her with words.

αὐτὰρ Ὀδυσσῆα μεγλήτορα ᾧ ἐνὶ οἴκῳ
Εὐρυνόμη ταμίη λοῦσεν καὶ χρῖσεν ἐλαίῳ,
ἀμφὶ δέ μιν φᾶρος καλὸν βάλεν ἠδὲ χιτῶνα·
αὐτὰρ κὰκ κεφαλῆς χεῦεν πολὺ κάλλος Ἀθήνη
μείζονά τ᾽ ἐσιδέειν καὶ πάσσονα· κὰδ δὲ κάρητος
οὔλας ἧκε κόμας, ὑακινθίνῳ ἄνθει ὁμοίας.
ὡς δ᾽ ὅτε τις χρυσὸν περιχεύεται ἀργύρῳ ἀνὴρ
ἴδρις, ὃν Ἥφαιστος δέδαεν καὶ Παλλὰς Ἀθήνη
τέχνην παντοίην, χαρίεντα δὲ ἔργα τελείει,
ὣς μὲν τῷ περίχευε χάριν κεφαλῇ τε καὶ ὤμοις.
ἐκ δ᾽ ἀσαμίνθου βῆ δέμας ἀθανάτοισιν ὁμοῖος·
ἂψ δ᾽ αὖτις κατ᾽ ἄρ ἕζετ᾽ ἐπὶ θρόνου ἔνθεν ἀνέστη,
ἀντίον ἧς ἀλόχου, καί μιν πρὸς μῦθον ἔειπε. (23.153–65)

This kind of imagery finds a counterpart in the poetry of Sappho, where, for example, Hector and Andromache are compared to the gods on their wedding day (fragment 44)[9] and lovers are described with botanical images, including hyacinths. Here Odysseus is made to look like the young bridegroom that he once was on his original wedding night to Penelope. Like the couple of Sappho 31, they sit opposite one another, with Odysseus in the position of the godlike groom.

What immediately follows this passage is not a joyful and long-awaited reunion, however, but one of the most famous tricks of the *Odyssey*. Odysseus offers to sleep alone, and Penelope outmaneuvers him by offering to bring him his bed outside their bedroom, something only the real Odysseus would know to be impossible. His angry reply is the final proof that Penelope needs to confirm that he is in fact her husband. Their essential like-mindedness is then confirmed by a simile that depicts Penelope's relief in distinctly Odyssean terms:[10]

As when land appears welcome (*aspasios*) to men who are swimming,
men whose well-built ship Poseidon has smashed on the sea,
oppressed by the wind and a massive wave,
but a few have escaped from the grey sea towards land,
swimming, but a great deal of brine is encrusted on their skin,
and eagerly (*aspasioi*) they step upon the land, after escaping evil,
so was her husband welcome to her as she looked upon him,
nor did she release her white arms from his neck.

ὡς δ᾽ ὅτ᾽ ἂν ἀσπάσιος γῆ νηχομένοισι φανήῃ,
ὧν τε Ποσειδάων εὐεργέα νῆ᾽ ἐνὶ πόντῳ

ῥαίσῃ, ἐπειγομένην ἀνέμῳ καὶ κύματι πηγῷ·
παῦροι δ᾽ ἐξέφυγον πολιῆς ἁλὸς ἤπειρόνδε
νηχόμενοι, πολλὴ δὲ περὶ χροῒ τέτροφεν ἅλμη,
ἀσπάσιοι δ᾽ ἐπέβαν γαίης, κακότητα φυγόντες·
ὣς ἄρα τῇ ἀσπαστὸς ἔην πόσις εἰσοροώσῃ,
δειρῆς δ᾽ οὔπω πάμπαν ἀφίετο πήχεε λευκώ. (23.233–40)

Odysseus is of course the shipwrecked sailor who has managed to reach the shore, but in the simile Odysseus is the land and Penelope is the sailor. Both are *aspasioi*: Odysseus is as welcome to Penelope as the land is to the shipwrecked sailors of the simile, but so, too, are the sailors *aspasioi* (in this sense, "eager") to reach the land.

It is at this point that their remarriage can truly take place. And it is at this point that Odysseus can stop testing Penelope with lying tales and tell her the truth of what lies ahead—the additional trials and journeys foretold by the prophet Tiresias in book 11. Athena prolongs the night so that dawn does not interfere too soon. Meanwhile Eurynome and Eurycleia prepare the marriage bed, and Eurynome leads them to it by torchlight, much as in an actual marriage procession:

So they spoke such things to one another.
Meanwhile Eurynome and the nurse prepared the marriage bed
of soft coverings by the light of shining torches.
Then when they had hastily covered the intricately made bed,
the old woman went home to sleep,
and Eurynome led the way for them as their bedroom attendant
as they went to bed, holding a torch in her hands.
Upon leading them to the bedroom she went back. They then
came eagerly (*aspasioi*) to the rites of their own old bed.[11]

ὣς οἱ μὲν τοιαῦτα πρὸς ἀλλήλους ἀγόρευον·
τόφρα δ᾽ ἄρ᾽ Εὐρυνόμη τε ἰδὲ τροφὸς ἔντυον εὐνὴν
ἐσθῆτος μαλακῆς, δαΐδων ὕπο λαμπομενάων.
αὐτὰρ ἐπεὶ στόρεσαν πυκινὸν λέχος ἐγκονέουσαι,
γρηῢς μὲν κείουσα πάλιν οἶκόνδε βεβήκει,
τοῖσιν δ᾽ Εὐρυνόμη θαλαμηπόλος ἡγεμόνευεν
ἐρχομένοισι λέχοσδε, δάος μετὰ χερσὶν ἔχουσα·
ἐς θάλαμον δ᾽ ἀγαγοῦσα πάλιν κίεν. οἱ μὲν ἔπειτα
ἀσπάσιοι λέκτροιο παλαιοῦ θεσμὸν ἵκοντο. (23.288–96)

There are no more contests, no more tests, and no more lies; Odysseus has defeated all other suitors, proven his identity, and won Penelope's hand. Their reunion in their marriage bed makes for a satisfying ending.

A passage from book 24 of the *Odyssey*—and I am aware of the perversity of using book 24 in this way—supports a reading of the poem that makes the remarriage with Penelope in book 23 the culminating event. In this passage, the slain suitors have descended to the underworld, where Achilles and Agamemnon are conversing. Agamemnon proclaims Achilles to be "blessed" (*olbios*) for having died at Troy (24.36), and as a result of his magnificent death and funeral, he will have *kleos*, or eternal glory in song (24.93–94). When Agamemnon learns from the suitors of the events that led to their deaths, he likewise proclaims Odysseus *olbios*:

> Blessed son of Laertes, much devising Odysseus,
> truly you have acquired a wife of great merit.
> How good was the intelligence of faultless Penelope,
> daughter of Icarius. How well she remained mindful of Odysseus,
> the husband of her youth. The glory of her excellence
> will never die, and the immortal gods will create a song for mortals
> in praise of prudent Penelope.
>
> ὄλβιε Λαέρταο πάϊ, πολυμήχαν᾽ Ὀδυσσεῦ,
> ἦ ἄρα σὺν μεγάλῃ ἀρετῇ ἐκτήσω ἄκοιτιν·
> ὡς ἀγαθαὶ φρένες ἦσαν ἀμύμονι Πηνελοπείῃ,
> κούρῃ Ἰκαρίου· ὡς εὖ μέμνητ᾽ Ὀδυσῆος,
> ἀνδρὸς κουριδίου. τῷ οἱ κλέος οὔποτ᾽ ὀλεῖται
> ἧς ἀρετῆς, τεύξουσι δ᾽ ἐπιχθονίοισιν ἀοιδὴν
> ἀθάνατοι χαρίεσσαν ἐχέφρονι Πηνελοπείῃ. (24.192–98)

This passage, which of course would not be included if the poem were to end at book 23, line 296, suggests that remarriage with Penelope is the goal of the *Odyssey*, and the key to Odysseus's glory in song, his *kleos*.

Surely there were performances of the *Odyssey* in antiquity that prioritized remarriage with Penelope as the poem's driving goal. But our *Odyssey*—that is, the one we know today—has another overarching theme, which is the transfer of *kleos* from father to son. Our *Odyssey* begins with four books about Odysseus's son Telemachus, who initially barely knows who his father is—"My mother tells me that I am his, but I myself / don't know—for no one really knows his own sire" μήτηρ μέν τ᾽ ἐμέ φησι τοῦ ἔμμεναι, αὐτὰρ ἐγώ γε / οὐκ οἶδ᾽· οὐ γάρ πώ τις ἑὸν γόνον αὐτὸς ἀνέγνω (1.215–16)—but by book 4 Telemachus weeps upon hearing stories about him (113–16). Odysseus does not retake his house from the suitors solo, but as part of an ambush pair with Telemachus.[12] Telemachus is the only one that Odysseus does not test with disguises and lying tales; he tells him straight out who he is (16.187–89).

If the poem were to end at book 23, line 296, readers would not get the other side of this equation, which is the connection between Odysseus and his own father, Laertes. The final reconnection of our *Odyssey* comes not with Penelope but with Laertes, suggesting that this connection between father and son is in fact the *telos* of the *Odyssey*. As with Penelope, the reconnection between Laertes and Odysseus requires testing and proof. Odysseus must show his scar, and reveal his knowledge of the intricacies of Laertes's orchard. But once those proofs are given, Laertes unreservedly embraces him and nearly faints with joy.

One of the very last exchanges of the poem highlights the reestablished link between Laertes, Odysseus, and Telemachus and the continuity across generations:

> Quickly [Odysseus] addressed his dear son Telemachus:
> "Telemachus, now you yourself will know, having come to the place
> where the best of the fighting men are distinguished,
> not to bring shame in any way upon the line of your forefathers, who indeed before this
> excelled in battle might and manliness throughout the whole world."
> Prudent Telemachus then in turn addressed him in answer:
> "You will see me if you wish, dear father, in my heart (*thumos*)
> not in any way shaming your family line, as you say."
> So he spoke, and Laertes rejoiced and spoke words:
> "What a day this is for me, dear gods! Truly I rejoice in it.
> My son and my grandson are vying with one another in excellence."

> αἶψα δὲ Τηλέμαχον προσεφώνεεν ὃν φίλον υἱόν·
> 'Τηλέμαχ', ἤδη μὲν τόδε γ' εἴσεαι αὐτὸς ἐπελθών,
> ἀνδρῶν μαρναμένων ἵνα τε κρίνονται ἄριστοι,
> μή τι καταισχύνειν πατέρων γένος, οἳ τὸ πάρος περ
> ἀλκῇ τ' ἠνορέῃ τε κεκάσμεθα πᾶσαν ἐπ' αἶαν.'
> τὸν δ' αὖ Τηλέμαχος πεπνυμένος ἀντίον ηὔδα·
> 'ὄψεαι, αἴ κ' ἐθέλησθα, πάτερ φίλε, τῷδ' ἐπὶ θυμῷ
> οὔ τι καταισχύνοντα τεὸν γένος, ὡς ἀγορεύεις.'
> ὣς φάτο, Λαέρτης δ' ἐχάρη καὶ μῦθον ἔειπε·
> 'τίς νύ μοι ἡμέρη ἥδε, θεοὶ φίλοι; ἦ μάλα χαίρω·
> υἱός θ' υἱωνός τ' ἀρετῆς πέρι δῆριν ἔχουσι.' (24.505–15)

In book 1 of the *Odyssey*, Athena (disguised as Mentes) tells Telemachus to follow the example of Orestes by taking action on behalf of his father, so that he, too, will be spoken well of by future generations (1.298–302). Telemachus replies (with the same speech introduction that we find here in book 24, line 510) that Athena in her disguise as Mentes has spoken to him as a father would to his son. By book 24, we know that Telemachus has indeed lived up to the expectations set by his father, as Odysseus has lived up to those of Laertes.

Our *Odyssey* is not the story of Odysseus and Penelope, though their story is a big part of it. Penelope herself gets *kleos* because of her critical role; Agamemnon says that her song of glory will be composed by the gods themselves, and that song is presumably the *Odyssey*. But the *Odyssey* is more complicated than that. It is a "journey of a soul," to quote my own teacher and mentor Gregory Nagy, for both Odysseus and Telemachus, one that ties together the concept of homecoming (*nostos*) with regaining one's consciousness and identity, resulting in a song of *kleos* that will never die (Nagy, *Ancient Greek Hero* 482, 10§32). All these ideas come together in the image of Odysseus and Laertes and Telemachus becoming a fighting team in book 24 before Athena puts a stop to the hostilities. *Kleos* is inherited from one's father and ancestors and lives on in one's son—if he proves himself worthy of it. This is an important theme in the *Iliad* as well, which ends as it does with the lamentation of a father for his son and a son for his father.

A poet in a traditional song culture like that of the ancient Greeks could compose poetry in performance using techniques, plots, characters, and an ever-evolving corpus of formulaic language that he had inherited from many previous generations of singers. The material and techniques were traditional, but each performance was a new composition—a recomposition, in and for performance. This dynamic necessarily affects how ancient epic poetry is understood and appreciated. To make an even more modern analogy than Parry and Lord's South Slavic one, for an audience that knows Anakin Skywalker will become Darth Vader, *Star Wars* is no less full of drama and tension as he proceeds down that path. Many a *Star Wars* fan has been content to watch that story replay itself again and again upon subsequent viewings.[13] But for the audience of the Homeric epics there was an additional layer of tension. Certainly Odysseus was always going to make it home from Troy, but the song that narrated that return was always being composed anew. Not only might different singers arrange the song differently, and not only might there be variations on what episodes were included in any given performance; there was always the lurking possibility, however unlikely, that the current performance would turn out differently. As I noted at the outset of this essay, it seems that in not all versions of the *Odyssey* was Penelope faithful to Odysseus, and there were many variations in antiquity on what came next. An *Odyssey* that did not end with what we know as book 24 could have gone in any number of directions, to judge by ancient testimony.

An *Odyssey* that ended at what we know as book 23, line 296, is thematically different from one that ends at book 24, line 548. One emphasizes the loving reunion of two long-separated and long-suffering and exceptionally like-minded spouses, while the other emphasizes the transfer of *kleos* from father to son and the restoration of a king to his kingdom. But what about an *Odyssey* that is decidedly different from the one we know, one in which Penelope has not been faithful? Both Pausanias and Apollodorus (two later sources) refer to such a version, and both link this version to the local lore of Mantineia, in Greece, which claimed that she died (and presumably was buried) there (see the appendix). I personally find it unlikely that such a version was ever considered canonical or "in accordance with destiny" κατὰ μοῖραν (*Odyssey* 8.496), much as Achilles in the

Iliad was never going to choose to leave Troy and live a long, unremembered life. There were limits to the multiformity of the epic tradition. But that does not mean that poets could not play off a known local mythological alternative when composing their tale. Throughout our *Odyssey* it is hinted that Penelope could turn out to be like Clytemnestra, the wife of Agamemnon, who together with her lover Aegisthus killed him upon his return from the Trojan War. As we have seen, the fact that Penelope does not is the key to Odysseus's success.

And what are we to make of a narrative like the *Telegony*, which does not end with Odysseus and Penelope happily reunited, and in which not only is Odysseus killed by his son and Circe's, Telegonus, but Penelope ends up marrying that son? It is difficult to reconstruct the poetics of that lost epic from the few surviving references, but clearly the themes of that poem were very different from those of our *Odyssey*. The *Odyssey* we know, with its predictions of Odysseus's future wanderings, does not categorically preclude such an ending, at least for Penelope—Tiresias tells Odysseus that his death will come "from the sea" (11.134), and Telegonus is not mentioned—but it certainly does not reference it. If it had, we would understand the poem very differently. Where the story ends matters.[14]

When we understand the *Iliad* and *Odyssey* to have been composed this way, we cannot stake rigid claims upon any one version of the text, as if the poem were fixed and unchanging. Attested variations are, at least potentially, authentically generated performance multiforms and have something to teach us about the compositional process and the poetics of the system in which they were generated. Not all variations on the *Odyssey* could have been known to all singers and all audience members at all times and in all places, yet each has the potential to reveal something about the poetics of the tradition in the time and place in which that multiform is attested. Even much later sources that point to other ways of telling the tale can inform the reading of the *Odyssey* that has come down to us. For this reason, I share with my students some of the alternatives that have survived in later sources using the handout that I have appended here. Many are now familiar with some of them, thanks to the popularity of Madeline Miller's novel *Circe*, which includes within the confines of its narrative material from the (now lost) poems of the epic cycle, as they have been summarized by the ancient scholar Proclus.[15]

Our *Odyssey* is not the only *Odyssey* that ever existed. But the *Odyssey* we have, which was shaped within the Panhellenic performance context of the Panathenaic festival in Athens, did win out, so to speak, over all other versions (Dué; Nagy, "From Song"). As I have noted, the evidence for other *Odysseys* generally comes from later sources. We only catch glimpses of them in the ancient scholarship on the poem that has survived in our medieval manuscripts. But the existence of alternatives—not to mention other points of starting and stopping—is very much in keeping with what we know about oral poetry. The contemplation of alternative endings is itself a kind of fidelity to the *Odyssey*.

NOTES

For the arguments made in this essay, I am indebted to my work with Gregory Nagy when I was his student, including my work as a teaching fellow for his course on the ancient Greek hero. The content of that course has since been published in Nagy, *Ancient Greek Hero*.

1. In what follows I discuss two different versions of this note that survive in medieval manuscripts.
2. This translation has been adapted slightly from that of Samuel Butler. Other translations are my own unless otherwise noted.
3. For more on the work of Parry and Lord, see the introduction to this volume.
4. On the term "multiform," see Lord 100–01.
5. The commentaries on the *Odyssey* in Heubeck et al. 3: 342–45 and Stanford, *Homer* 2: 404–06 discuss the controversial scholion on book 23, line 296, in detail, with additional bibliography cited ad loc.
6. For more on the Analysts and the Unitarians, see the introduction to this volume.
7. A *khiton* is an ancient Greek garment that is much like a tunic, but fastened at the shoulder and belted at the waist.
8. A *phorminx* is an ancient stringed musical instrument, similar to a lyre.
9. The fragment numbers of Sappho are based on the Greek text of Lobel and Page. Good translations are those of Carson; Rayor and Lardinois.
10. On this simile, see also H. Foley, "'Reverse Similes.'"
11. For the last verse I have adapted the translation of Samuel Butler.
12. For more on Odysseus and Telemachus as an ambushing team, see Edwards; Dué and Ebbott.
13. *Star Wars* has been recomposed as an epic poem by Jack Mitchell.
14. For more on the future adventures of characters in Greek epic, see Simms.
15. On Proclus, see Marks, "Epic Traditions," and the introduction to this volume.

APPENDIX: AFTER THE *ODYSSEY*

We think of the *Odyssey* as the definitive story of Odysseus, Penelope, and Telemachus, but it was not; many other versions, especially of the end of the story, existed in antiquity. Below are several ancient accounts of the way the story ends, beginning with the *Odyssey* itself. Proclus was an ancient scholar whose surviving summary of the now lost epics of the so-called epic cycle gives us a great deal of information about narratives those epics contained. Pausanias published a book of travel writing in the second century CE. Apollodorus is the author of a compendium of mythology usually dated to the first or second century CE.

Ending A

"You want to know," said Tiresias, "about your return home, but a god will make this hard for you. I do not think that you will escape the eye of Poseidon, who still nurses his bitter grudge against you for having blinded his son. Still, after much suffering you may get home if you can restrain yourself and your companions when your ship reaches the Thrinacian island, where you will find the sheep and cattle belonging to the sun, who sees and gives ear to everything. If you leave these flocks unharmed and think of nothing but of getting home, you may yet after much hardship reach Ithaca; but if you harm them, then I forewarn you of the destruction both of your ship and of your men. Even though you may yourself escape, you will return in bad plight after losing all your men, in another man's ship, and you will find trouble in your house, which will be overrun by high-handed people, who are devouring your substance under the pretext of paying court and making presents to your wife.

"When you get home you will take your revenge on these suitors; and after you have killed them by force or fraud in your own house, you must take a well-made oar and carry it on and on, till you come to a country where the people have never heard of the sea and do not even mix salt with their food, nor do they know anything about ships, and oars that are as the wings of a ship. I will give you this certain sign which cannot escape your notice. A wayfarer will meet you and will say it must be a winnowing shovel that you have got upon your shoulder; then you must fix the oar in the ground and sacrifice a ram, a bull, and a boar to Poseidon. Then go home and offer hecatombs to the gods in heaven one after the other. As for yourself, death shall come to you from the sea, and your life shall ebb away very gently when you are full of years and peace of mind, and your people shall be prosperous. All that I have said will come true."*

Ending B

After the *Nostoi* comes the *Odyssey* of Homer, and then the *Telegony* in two books by Eugammon of Cyrene, which contain the following matters. The suitors of Penelope are buried by their kinsmen, and Odysseus, after sacrificing to the Nymphs, sails to Elis to inspect his herds. He is entertained there by Polyxenus and receives a mixing bowl as a gift; the story of Trophonius and Agamedes and Augeas then follows. He next sails back to Ithaca and performs the sacrifices ordered by Teiresias, and then goes to Thesprotis where he marries Callidice, queen of the Thesprotians. A war then breaks out between the Thesprotians, led by Odysseus, and the Brygi. Ares routs the army of Odysseus and Athena engages with Ares, until Apollo separates them. After the death of Callidice Polypoetes, the son of Odysseus, succeeds to the kingdom, while Odysseus himself returns to Ithaca. In the meantime Telegonus, while traveling in search of his father, lands on Ithaca and ravages the island: Odysseus comes out to defend his country, but is killed by his son unwittingly. Telegonus, on learning his mistake, transports his father's body with Penelope and Telemachus to his mother's island, where Circe makes them immortal, and Telegonus marries Penelope, and Telemachus marries Circe.†

Ending C

In addition to the roads mentioned there are two others, leading to Orchomenus. On one is what is called the stadium of Ladas, where Ladas practised his running, and by it a sanctuary of Artemis, and on the right of the road is a high mound of earth. It is said to be the grave of Penelope, but the account of her in the poem called *Thesprotis* is not in agreement with this saying. For in it the poet says that when Odysseus returned from Troy he had a son Ptoliporthes by Penelope. But the Mantinean story about Penelope says that Odysseus convicted her of bringing lovers to his home, and being cast out by him she went away at first to Lacedaemon, but afterwards she removed from Sparta to Mantinea, where she died.‡

Ending D

And after sacrificing to Hades, and Persephone, and Tiresias, he journeyed on foot through Epirus, and came to the Thesprotians, and having offered sacrifice according to the directions of the soothsayer Tiresias, he propitiated Poseidon. But Callidice, who was then queen of the Thesprotians, urged him to stay and offered him the kingdom; and she had by him a son Polypoetes. And having married Callidice, he reigned over the Thesprotians, and defeated in battle the neighboring peoples who attacked him. But when Callidice died he handed over the kingdom to his son and repaired to Ithaca, and there he found Ptoliporthes, whom Penelope had borne to him.

When Telegonus learned from Circe that he was a son of Odysseus, he sailed in search of him. And having come to the island of Ithaca, he drove away some of the cattle, and when Odysseus defended them, Telegonus wounded him with the spear he had in his hands, which was barbed with the spine of a sting-ray, and Odysseus died of the wound. But when Telegonus recognized him, he bitterly lamented, and conveyed the corpse and Penelope to Circe, and there he married Penelope. And Circe sent them both away to the Islands of the Blest.

But some say that Penelope was seduced by Antinous and sent away by Odysseus to her father Icarius, and that when she came to Mantinea in Arcadia she bore Pan to Hermes. However others say that she met her end at the hands of Odysseus himself on account of Amphinomus, for they allege that she was seduced by him.

And there are some who say that Odysseus, being accused by the kinsfolk of the slain, submitted the case to the judgment of Neoptolemus, king of the islands off Epirus; that Neoptolemus, thinking to get possession of Cephallenia if once Odysseus were put out of the way, condemned him to exile; and that Odysseus went to Aetolia, to Thoas, son of Andraemon, married the daughter of Thoas, and leaving a son Leontophonus, whom he had by her, died in old age.**

Questions for Discussion

Does this knowledge of alternative versions of the *Odyssey* story and its ending affect your reading of the poem? What added significance do books 13–24 take on in light of existing versions in which Penelope's fidelity is not assured?

Our *Odyssey* alludes to some of the events related in the epic cycle, Pausanias, and Apollodorus, even though they don't take place within the poem itself. Which of these events are consistent with the narrative of the *Odyssey*, and which seem inconsistent with or even contradicted by our *Odyssey*?

What do these multiple versions tell us about the song culture in which the *Odyssey* was composed? What are some of the reasons for the existence of multiple versions of the Odysseus tale?

* Translation adapted from that of Samuel Butler (11.100–37).

† Proclus's summary of the epic cycle. Translation adapted from that of H. G. Evelyn-White (531).

‡ Translation adapted from that of W. H. S Jones (Pausanias 3: 8.12.5–6).

** Translated by James G. Frazer (Apollodorus, *Library* [Frazer], Epitome 7.34–40).

The *Odyssey* and Epic Traditions

Laura M. Slatkin

The *Odyssey*, like its central figure, is a many-sided creation, and can be approached in a multitude of ways. Although it is often taught as a self-enclosed, stand-alone work (as a character study, a family romance, or the original bildungsroman template, among other readings), the poem itself invites its audience to approach it through its relation to other treatments of its subject: to alternative narratives about Odysseus and his exploits that appear elsewhere in early oral traditional poetry and that variously inform our *Odyssey* throughout. Odysseus has a significant presence in the *Iliad* as well as in the Archaic period poems known as the epic cycle, and he makes an appearance, directly or indirectly, in Hesiod's *Theogony* and the Hesiodic *Catalogue of Women*.

Recognizing the ways in which the *Odyssey* interacts with alternative traditions about Odysseus and his homecoming allows us to register the poem's specific contours. By tracking its involvement in, differentiation from, and occasional subsuming of those related but divergent narrative pathways, we can see that the *Odyssey*'s response to these alternatives is central to its distinctive poetics. One way of approaching what is most Odyssean about the poem, we might say, is to read it with and against the background its early audiences would have known.

As Casey Dué helpfully asks in the first essay in this volume, "If we know that alternative *Odysseys* were at least potentially out there, how does the experience of the *Odyssey* in performance change for ancient audiences, and for us?" This is a question worth raising with students at the beginning of any study of the *Odyssey*. Offering students brief passages from other early poems in which Odysseus is featured—particularly from the *Iliad* and from summaries of the epic cycle—attunes our collective ears to the emerging power and carefully shaped logic of this specific narrative. I have found that while some students may be acquainted with the *Odyssey*, many are being introduced to it for the first time, though a few elements of its plot may be familiar to them; this is the case in university courses as well as in alternative programs such as those in correctional facilities, as my teaching experience in the past decade has shown me. Rather than plunge students unaccustomed to the dynamics of oral poetry into a potentially overwhelming array of texts and traditions, my hope is to facilitate an orientation toward reading and hearing that the poem itself manifests and encourages: an alertness to narrative as mediated and shaped, and to story as emergent rather than fixed or predetermined. What follows here are reflections on the *Odyssey* under the sign of this orientation: its preoccupation with mediation and narrative alternatives—that is, its foregrounding of narrative pathways variously chosen, averted, and shadowed forth.

One of the governing conditions of the *Odyssey*'s interaction with that background repertoire is its representation of itself as the story of aftermath: it has to reckon continuously with its relation to the story the *Iliad* tells—to the stamp that the Iliadic narrative has put on characters and plot trajectories. The *Odyssey*, in this sense, is always already in the position of mediating. It overtly acknowledges Iliadic "antecedents" while adjusting them to its own horizons and navigating the expectations that an audience familiar with the shape of the *Iliad*—that epic of no return—would bring to this "homecoming" (*nostos*) poem.

Students are often intrigued and surprised to think of the poem's eponymous hero as a figure who is being reclaimed, not simply celebrated. Audiences familiar with the *Iliad*, however, come to the *Odyssey* with distinctly low expectations of Odysseus, who conspicuously does not represent the warrior-hero ethos—defined by full-frontal courage, loyalty, and capacity for self-sacrifice—that earns the "glory" (*kleos*) the *Iliad* confers. Although Odysseus figures prominently at several key points, he is undistinguished on the *Iliad*'s battlefield. In contrast, for example, to Achilles or Diomedes or Ajax (among others), Odysseus never appears in the kind of single combat that highlights the prowess and courage of an esteemed warrior. Principally appearing on the scene to urge others to fight (e.g., *Iliad* 2.278–332, 19.216–37), he takes on that role most notably as the smooth-talking mouthpiece of Agamemnon, conveying to the affronted Achilles the king's bid to lure him back to the fight with the promise of material wealth (9.225–306).

On the field of battle, when appealed to for assistance in rescuing the beleaguered Nestor, for example, Odysseus ignores the request and makes a rapid exit from the site of conflict (*Iliad* 8.90–98), heading instead back to his ships. And where are they? While the ships of Achilles and Ajax are stationed at the vulnerable edges of the fleet, Odysseus has positioned his in the more protected middle. His most elaborate confrontation with the Trojans, moreover, is not a face-to-face duel in broad daylight, like that of Achilles and Hector, but a spying mission undertaken under cover of night. Odysseus and Diomedes come upon the luckless Trojan Dolon as he is attempting to reconnoiter among the Achaeans; after duplicitously promising him safety in exchange for information about the Trojan defenses, they promptly cut off his head as he begs for mercy and proceed to slaughter the nearby newly arrived Trojan allies as they sleep (*Iliad* 10.333–497). The wiliness and circumspection that are his hallmarks are denoted by such epithets as *polymētis* ("of many stratagems" or "very crafty") and *polymēchanos* ("of many devices"), which belong exclusively to Odysseus in both the *Iliad* and the *Odyssey*.

These qualities of Odysseus, foregrounded in the *Iliad*, align with the ways he is represented in the epic cycle, according to the summaries of their contents: the *Cypria*, which gave an account of the origins of, and preparation for, the Trojan War, recounted that when the Achaean leaders were trying to recruit warriors for the expedition, Odysseus pretended to be insane in order to avoid having to join them, until his ruse was exposed (Apollodorus, Epitome 3.6–7). And according to the cyclic poem known as the *Little Iliad* (*Ilias mikra*), which narrates the final stages of the war, Odysseus was responsible for several schemes involving subterfuge, and he assumed a decisive role in the conquest of Troy, which was ultimately accomplished not in open combat on the battlefield but through his notorious deceptive stratagem of the wooden horse. The *Little Iliad* also narrated Odysseus's dubious victory over Ajax in the contest over the armor of Achilles, brought about by the maneuvering of his ally Athena (West, *Greek Epic Fragments* 118–41); this and other episodes from the epic cycle poems, such as Odysseus's arranging for the death of the infant Astyanax (142–53), provided rich material for fifth-century Athenian tragedy, including Sophocles's *Ajax* and *Philoctetes* and his lost *Odysseus Acanthoplex* as well as Euripides's *Trojan Women* and *Hecuba*.

Given the reputation that precedes him into the *Odyssey*, then, how does the song forming itself around Odysseus face the challenge of recuperating him, of making him someone with whom its audience sympathizes, and whose goal of returning home it endorses? From the outset, it represents his homecoming not as a merely private matter but as the divinely authorized rescue of a household and community under siege: as the goal articulated and sponsored by Zeus and Athena that not only allows for, but in fact proposes, taking revenge on Penelope's suitors as a matter of restoring social order. The *Odyssey* responds to alternative traditions about Odysseus not by effacing them but by acknowledging and recoding them. In a move of stunning virtuosity, it takes Odysseus's distinguishing characteristics (unsavory, at best, from the perspective of the *Iliad* and epic cycle)—namely, his cunning, his instinct for self-protection, his smooth-talking fluency, his elusiveness—and makes them precisely the qualities he needs to achieve his divinely approved return.

The opening book of the poem, launched by a council of the gods, orients the audience to the *Odyssey*'s narratological mode—to its poetics of mediation—through which it points to alternative directions the storyline might follow: neither expunging nor embracing them, it addresses and reintegrates their potential to reconfigure its trajectory. The poem begins by signaling the problem of how to tell the story of Odysseus. From the perspective of the *Odyssey*'s external audience, the plan for moving Odysseus homeward, attributed to divine intervention, is arrived at indirectly. His return would seem to be a byproduct of the gods' reflections on Agamemnon's catastrophic homecoming, on which Zeus's attention is focused: "He thought in his heart of handsome Aegisthus / Whom Agamemnon's famous son, Orestes, killed" μνήσατο γὰρ κατὰ θυμὸν ἀμύμονος Αἰγίσθοιο, / τόν ῥ' Ἀγαμεμνονίδης τηλεκλυτὸς ἔκταν' Ὀρέστης (1.29–30).

At the start, then, it appears as though the poem opens the possibility of following an Oresteian route, suggested by Zeus's train of thought about the slaughter of the returning king and his son's revenge on his mother's murderous suitor—the very direction pursued by the epic cycle's *Homecomings* (*Nostoi*) of the Achaeans from Troy. In response to Zeus, however, Athena, while approving the example of the suitor's death at the hands of his victim's son, introduces a different narrative path, by which Odysseus will be rescued and brought safely back to Ithaca (1.44–62) while his son travels in search of him (1.80–95).

How is the story of Odysseus's journey to be narrated? How will his *nostos* be sung? This is presented as a question for the *Odyssey*'s internal audience as well—in the first place, for those in Odysseus's household. Book 1 takes us from the gods' conversation on Olympus to Athena's arrival on Ithaca, where the bard Phemius entertains Penelope's suitors at their feast: "The famous bard was singing to them, and in silence / they sat listening: he sang of the Achaeans' wretched homecoming from Troy, / which Pallas Athena inflicted upon them" τοῖσι δ' ἀοιδὸς ἄειδε περικλυτός, οἱ δὲ σιωπῇ / ἥατ' ἀκούοντες· ὁ δ' Ἀχαιῶν νόστον ἄειδε / λυγρόν, ὃν ἐκ Τροίης ἐπετείλατο Παλλὰς Ἀθήνη (1.325–27).[1] In the middle of his performance, Penelope interrupts the singer and requests a different song. The one he is in the midst of is too sad because, from the Ithacan point of view, there can be no singing about homecoming that includes Odysseus:

> Then, weeping, she addressed the divine singer:
> "Phemius, since you know many other things that enchant people,
> deeds of gods and heroes, such as bards make famous,
> sing of those, as you sit next to the suitors, and let them silently
> drink their wine; but cease from this sorrowful song
> which always breaks the heart in my breast,
> since it above all brings me unforgettable grief.
> For I long for the husband I remember,
> whose fame was widespread through Hellas and middle Argos."
>
> δακρύσασα δ' ἔπειτα προσηύδα θεῖον ἀοιδόν·
> 'Φήμιε, πολλὰ γὰρ ἄλλα βροτῶν θελκτήρια οἶδας,
> ἔργ' ἀνδρῶν τε θεῶν τε, τά τε κλείουσιν ἀοιδοί·
> τῶν ἕν γέ σφιν ἄειδε παρήμενος, οἱ δὲ σιωπῇ
> οἶνον πινόντων· ταύτης δ' ἀποπαύε' ἀοιδῆς
> λυγρῆς, ἥ τέ μοι αἰεὶ ἐνὶ στήθεσσι φίλον κῆρ
> τείρει, ἐπεί με μάλιστα καθίκετο πένθος ἄλαστον.
> τοίην γὰρ κεφαλὴν ποθέω μεμνημένη αἰεί,
> ἀνδρός, τοῦ κλέος εὐρὺ καθ' Ἑλλάδα καὶ μέσον Ἄργος.' (1.336–44)

Telemachus, in reply, insists that Phemius should continue nevertheless, because the latest song in the bard's repertoire is the one everyone wants to hear:

> Mother, why do you resent that the faithful bard
> gives pleasure as his mind moves him to? Singers are not to be held
> responsible;
> rather it is Zeus who is responsible
> and visits whatever he wishes on men who toil, on each one of them.
> That man deserves no blame for singing the Danaans' doomed return,
> since people always especially praise
> the song that is the latest to reach the audience.

Let your heart and spirit bear to listen;
for Odysseus is not the only man who lost his day of homecoming
from Troy; many other men perished as well.

μῆτερ ἐμή, τί τ' ἄρα φθονέεις ἐρίηρον ἀοιδὸν
τέρπειν ὅππῃ οἱ νόος ὄρνυται; οὔ νύ τ' ἀοιδοὶ
αἴτιοι, ἀλλά ποθι Ζεὺς αἴτιος, ὅς τε δίδωσιν
ἀνδράσιν ἀλφηστῇσιν, ὅπως ἐθέλῃσιν, ἑκάστῳ.
τούτῳ δ' οὐ νέμεσις Δαναῶν κακὸν οἶτον ἀείδειν·
τὴν γὰρ ἀοιδὴν μᾶλλον ἐπικλείουσ' ἄνθρωποι,
ἥ τις ἀκουόντεσσι νεωτάτη ἀμφιπέληται.
σοὶ δ' ἐπιτολμάτω κραδίη καὶ θυμὸς ἀκούειν·
οὐ γὰρ Ὀδυσσεὺς οἶος ἀπώλεσε νόστιμον ἦμαρ
ἐν Τροίῃ, πολλοὶ δὲ καὶ ἄλλοι φῶτες ὄλοντο. (1.346–55)

How to tell the story of Odysseus? The *Odyssey* here calls attention to its own development as it takes shape in performance, in the context of its interaction with other songs and other treatments of its subject. The generative investigations into the formation of Homeric epic offered by Albert Lord's pioneering study, *The Singer of Tales*, make clear that such narrative adaptability is fundamental to the compositional process of oral traditional song. Lord writes, "In a traditional poem . . . there is a pull in two directions: one is toward the song being sung and the other is toward previous uses of the same theme" (228). The *Odyssey* here, as throughout, reflects and highlights that "pull," acknowledging the impact of the dynamic between audience and performer in the process.[2] We see this at work in several dimensions: "The famous bard was singing to them, and in silence / they sat listening: he sang of the Achaeans' wretched homecoming from Troy, / which Pallas Athena inflicted upon them" τοῖσι δ' ἀοιδὸς ἄειδε περικλυτός, οἱ δὲ σιωπῇ / ἥατ' ἀκούοντες· ὁ δ' Ἀχαιῶν νόστον ἄειδε / λυγρόν, ὃν ἐκ Τροίης ἐπετείλατο Παλλὰς Ἀθήνη (1.325–27). What we know of two of the epic cycle poems in particular, the *Sack of Troy* (*Iliou persis*) and the *Homecomings* (*Nostoi*), makes us aware that their narratives featured Athena's fury at the victorious Greek warriors, inflicted upon them on their homeward journeys; the summary of the cycle's *Sack of Troy* indicates that the goddess is outraged by their sacrilegious brutality at the fall of Troy and "begins to plan [their] destruction."[3] In our *Odyssey*, however, Athena is Odysseus's champion, as her intervention on his behalf in the council of the gods makes evident, and as the rest of the poem will elaborate. Here we have an example of the *Odyssey*'s characteristic move of mediation: it signals its awareness of the tradition of Athena's anger at the Greeks,[4] making explicit reference to it but ascribing it to a different *nostos* song—the song sung by Phemius and interrupted by Penelope—again, neither expunging nor embracing it for its own story but redirecting it. Athena's anger is fully present in the *Odyssey* but turned against Penelope's *suitors*; the implacable Poseidon becomes Athena's replacement as a spoiler of homecoming.

As the exchange above marks the responsiveness between audience and singer, the poem at the same time draws attention, here and elsewhere, to the disparity between the perspective of its external audience—who know from book 1 about Athena's plan for Odysseus—and that of the listeners within the poem. As much as Telemachus speaks in favor of the most recent song in the bard's repertoire, neither he nor Phemius, nor the Ithacan audience, perceives that the very latest song is the one that is forming around them—the song of which they are the subject.

The uncertainty expressed by Telemachus about where or whether Odysseus can fit into a song of return underscores the poem's negotiation of possible trajectories, a mediation reflected most explicitly and fully in the development of Telemachus's own role. Although the *Odyssey* firmly establishes the Ithacan royal lineage as carried by the single son of a single son, from Laertes to Odysseus to Telemachus, Hesiod's *Theogony* (1011–18) transmits a parallel tradition in which several sons were born to Odysseus, two by Calypso and three by Circe. The adventures of one of his sons by Circe, Telegonus, were featured in the epic cycle's final poem, the *Telegony*, which narrated an episode in which Odysseus left Ithaca after his homecoming there from Troy, journeyed to Thesprotia and begot yet another son, this time with the Thesprotian queen, whom he married; later Odysseus returned to Ithaca.[5] According to the summary we have of the poem, the *Telegony* both raised the issue of succession to the throne[6] and dramatized the calamitous consequences of a son not knowing his father: Telegonus arrives on Ithaca and, unable to recognize Odysseus, unwittingly kills him in battle and thereupon marries Penelope.

As with its allusion to Athena's anger, the *Odyssey* acknowledges the tradition elaborated in the epic cycle but redirects it toward its narrative *telos*, in which the family of the "like-minded" husband and wife,[7] along with their loyal son, will be reunited, and their household definitively restored. Although other female figures he encounters (human and divine) desire him as a husband (most explicitly, Calypso and Nausicaa), the Odysseus of our *Odyssey* will have no other marriages or additional progeny. The possibility of a murderous filial confrontation is transformed into a potential contest on the level of narrative structure: in the absence of the hero, will his son—on whom the first four books of the poem are focused—usurp not the kingdom but the plot?

In defining its own direction in relation to the prospect that it might become the son's story rather than the father's, the *Odyssey* highlights the challenge of both honoring the song of battlefield glory and extricating itself from it: rather than killing his father (like Telegonus), Telemachus, expressing vicarious nostalgia for the *Iliad*'s story, wishes his father had died a hero's death at Troy (1.236–40). The *Odyssey* models its negotiation of alternative roles for Telemachus, as Athena reinforces the apparent open-endedness and uncertainty of his (literal and figurative) path; initially she asserts, "your father hasn't died" (1.196–205), but then she advises him how to proceed, "if you find that your father has died . . ." (1.289–96). Directing him to discover either the *kleos* or the *nostos* of his father, the goddess invokes by name two genres of song, leaving unspecified which one the story of Odysseus and Telemachus might become.

What direction will the poem take once Telemachus sets out on his journey, given that, as Athena's "if/thens" suggest, there is no fixed path for how the parallel arcs of father and son will converge? Here two options come to the fore, the first recalling the epic cycle's *Nostoi*: the paradigm introduced at the outset of the poem, and returned to continually, is that of the son as avenger, with the story of Orestes as the prototype, earning *kleos* for himself. The gods have this possibility in view (1.40–41, 298–302), and Nestor reiterates it in conversation with Telemachus himself (3.306–17). The other option returns to, and reconfigures, the plot of the *Telegony*: Athena proposes that Telemachus may come into his own as his late father's heir, arranging his father's funeral rites, marrying Penelope *off*, and taking over the kingdom (1.289–97).

These narratives, in which the hero's son either murders or marries his father's wife—either exacting vengeance for his father or becoming the usurper of his household—are adverted to in the *Odyssey* and transformed, perhaps most suggestively in the latter case, in book 21, when Telemachus all but strings the bow to become the winner in the contest for Penelope's hand (21.101–29). The poem takes note of such possible outcomes for its trajectory and assimilates them, developing instead its story of marital fidelity and family solidarity—always subtly shadowed by what might have been.

Telemachus exacts retribution not for but *with* his father, becoming his co-avenger against the suitors. The final episode of the poem treats the son's allegiance with his father as his comrade-in-arms as the endpoint of the route it has threaded for him; he fights neither over his father nor against him but alongside him in their pitched battle against the suitors' relatives—thereby evoking the *Iliad* and moving beyond it. As the son's potential challenge to his father is precluded—rendered instead as a cooperative competition between them (24.505–12)—the last word on the displacement of the Telegonus possibility is given to Laertes, who rejoices at their collaborative rivalry: "So he spoke, and Laertes was joyful, and said: / 'What a day is this for me, dear gods? I am overjoyed. / My son and my son's son are vying with each other over their valor'" ὣς φάτο, Λαέρτης δ' ἐχάρη καὶ μῦθον ἔειπε· / 'τίς νύ μοι ἡμέρη ἥδε, θεοὶ φίλοι; ἦ μάλα χαίρω· / υἱός θ' υἱωνός τ' ἀρετῆς πέρι δῆριν ἔχουσι' (24.513–15). Here it may be useful to distinguish between the *Odyssey*'s acknowledgment and reintegration of alternative storylines as narratological exploration and the *Iliad*'s repeated expression of counterpressures on its plot, especially in the form of contrafactual statements, in which the logic of the plot is said to have been *almost* derailed (or was feared to be), as in book 17, line 321, "and the Argives, even beyond Zeus's destiny [*huper Dios aisan*], might have won glory" Ἀργεῖοι δέ κε κῦδος ἕλον καὶ ὑπὲρ Διὸς αἶσαν, or book 2, lines 155–56, "Then for the Argives a homecoming beyond destiny [*huper mora*] might have been accomplished, / had not Hera spoken a word to Athena" ἔνθα κεν Ἀργείοισιν ὑπέρμορα νόστος ἐτύχθη / εἰ μὴ Ἀθηναίην Ἥρη πρὸς μῦθον ἔειπεν.

The *Iliad*'s action might have taken a turn "beyond destiny" (*huper aisan* or *huper moron/mora*): this may be understood, as Gregory Nagy has shown, to mean a turn that would contravene narrative tradition (*Best* 40, 40n2). The *Odyssey*, by contrast, does not represent its own storyline as bound to "destiny"—although it certainly registers futurities, especially in the enigmatic prophecy delivered by Teiresias, repeated by Odysseus to Penelope, and assented to by Penelope: Odysseus will make one further journey after his homecoming, but in contrast to the course of his travels in the *Telegony*, he will ultimately return to Ithaca, to remain in his household for good (*Odyssey* 11.119–37, 23.247–87). Unlike the *Iliad*, the *Odyssey*'s route to its goal is not said to be tied to fulfilling the "will of Zeus" (*Dios boulē*; *Iliad* 1.5): the *Odyssey* is always the poem of "both/and," such that Odysseus's homecoming is made to seem at once divinely guaranteed and, intermittently, fortuitous and contingent.

The *Odyssey*'s signposting of its alternative plot possibilities, in this sense, does not undermine its own structure, but is in fact itself a sign of its capacity to assimilate other options and variants, and is integral to its mode of taking storytelling itself to be a central subject. Raising interpretation to the level of theme, the poem shows the characters themselves participating in the process, as narrators and as interpreters of the place to which the narrative has brought them—and reminding the audience that it could have been otherwise.

We may think, for example, of Amphimedon's account in book 24 of how he and his fellow suitors have landed in the underworld and his interpretation of their slaughter—which, from the standpoint of Zeus's opening statement invoking the Aegisthus narrative, is the *telos* of the poem. Amphimedon's interpretation is that Odysseus and Penelope conspired together in setting up the contest of the bow (24.167–69). Here the poem of "both/and" at the same time alerts us to the conditioned, limited perspective of the narrator of his own story, validates his intuition of Penelope's sympathy for the outcome of the contest, and allows for the ambiguity in Penelope's recognition of Odysseus—could she (as a number of scholars have proposed) have seen through the beggar's disguise from the start and known him for who he truly was?

Most striking is Penelope's retrospective interpretation of events, and it is fitting to conclude these reflections on the poem with her, insofar as Odysseus's restoration in his household depends at least as much on the role she plays in it as it does on the actions and intentions of Telemachus and Odysseus. It is given to Penelope in book 23 to explain the unanticipated suspense by which the *Odyssey* postpones her acceptance of her husband's identity—and to articulate the link between its deferral and the alternative possibility that this epic knows and rejects. Here, at their reunion—at the poem's provisional *telos* (at least from the point of view of its audience, if not from the point of view of Zeus, who never mentions Penelope)—the *Odyssey* circles back to the *Iliad*, to assert once again its connection with that ostensibly prior narrative, from its formation to its consequences, and to mark its dissimilarity from the "prior" story—even as it marks its legacy from it as well.

And yet Penelope's account, as the explanation of why she resisted embracing her husband, gives not a unitary reading of the potential precedent for her story but a compound interpretation:[8]

> But do not be angry with me now, or resentful,
> because I did not at first, when I saw you, welcome you as I do now.
> For the heart in my breast always shuddered
> at the thought that some mortal man might arrive and deceive me
> with words, since many men contrive for evil gain.
> And neither would Argive Helen, the offspring of Zeus,
> have made love with a man from another country,
> if she had known that the warlike sons of the Achaians
> would bring her back home again to the dear land of her fathers.
> But surely a god prompted her to do the shameful deed;
> and never before had she taken into her heart this
> wretched folly, from which came grief for us as well.

> αὐτὰρ μὴ νῦν μοι τόδε χώεο μηδὲ νεμέσσα,
> οὕνεκά σ' οὐ τὸ πρῶτον, ἐπεὶ ἴδον, ὧδ' ἀγάπησα.
> αἰεὶ γάρ μοι θυμὸς ἐνὶ στήθεσσι φίλοισιν
> ἐρρίγει μή τίς με βροτῶν ἀπάφοιτ' ἐπέεσσιν
> ἐλθών· πολλοὶ γὰρ κακὰ κέρδεα βουλεύουσιν.
> οὐδέ κεν Ἀργείη Ἑλένη, Διὸς ἐκγεγαυῖα,
> ἀνδρὶ παρ' ἀλλοδαπῷ ἐμίγη φιλότητι καὶ εὐνῇ,
> εἰ ᾔδη ὅ μιν αὖτις ἀρήϊοι υἷες Ἀχαιῶν
> ἀξέμεναι οἶκόνδε φίλην ἐς πατρίδ' ἔμελλον.
> τὴν δ' ἤτοι ῥέξαι θεὸς ὤρορεν ἔργον ἀεικές·
> τὴν δ' ἄτην οὐ πρόσθεν ἑῷ ἐγκάτθετο θυμῷ
> λυγρήν, ἐξ ἧς πρῶτα καὶ ἡμέας ἵκετο πένθος. (23.213–24)

On one reading, Penelope's account suggests, Helen was deceived by someone out for evil gain (*kaka kerdea*); on another reading, which would make for a different story, Helen willingly decided to go to bed with a man from elsewhere because she didn't foresee that the Achaeans would go to war and bring her back home; on still another reading—which would make for still a different story—a god prompted Helen to act because on her own, she herself would never have embraced "wretched folly" (*atē*). Penelope here, one might say, channels the inscrutability of Helen (even to Helen herself) in the *Iliad* but renders it as a latent ambiguity or a conceivable variant, narrowly escaped, in her own story.

With this in mind, we might say that the long-awaited finality of homecoming culminates in the explicit recognition of a range of narrative opportunities that the *Odyssey* signals, not as a narrative obstacle or a counterfactual but as its mode of proceeding *per se*. In highlighting those opportunities and subsuming them, the poem of many ways defines its distinctive course.

NOTES

My thanks to Sara Bershtel, Jonathan Burgess, Rachel Eisendrath, Amy Johnson, Bruce King, Richard Martin, Gregory Nagy, and above all to Maureen McLane, for illuminating, ongoing conversations on Homeric poetry, and to my students in the University of Chicago's Committee on Social Thought for all they've taught me about the *Odyssey*. This essay is offered in memory of Gloria Ferrari and Corinne Pache.

1. Unless otherwise indicated, all translations are my own.

2. For further discussion of Lord's insights, see Slatkin, "Composition."

3. Excerpted from Proclus's summary of the *Sack of Troy* (*Iliou persis*): "They kill many, and the city is taken by force. Neoptolemos kills Priam, who has taken refuge at the altar of Zeus Herkeios. . . . Ajax son of Oïleus takes Kassandra by force, dragging her away from the wooden statue of Athena. . . . Then the Achaeans put the city to the torch. They slaughter Polyxena on the tomb of Achilles. Odysseus kills Astyanax, and Neoptolemos takes Andromache as his prize. The rest of the spoils are distributed. . . . Then the Greeks sail off [from Troy], and Athena begins to plan destruction for them at sea" (Nagy, "Proclus' Summary").

4. For a suggestive, alternative reading of Athena's anger and its effects in the *Odyssey*, see Clay.

5. The *Telegony* also made reference to an additional son, Ptoliporthes, a child of Odysseus and Penelope and therefore a brother to Telemachus.

6. According to the summary, the Thesprotian queen's son, rather than her husband Odysseus, followed her to the throne.

7. The *Odyssey*'s term for such affinity is *homophrosunē* ("like-mindedness"; 6.181, 15.198).

8. I am grateful to Emma Eigen and Chenxi Zhang for their valuable insights into Penelope as interpreter and explicator of her own story.

The Material Culture of Epic: Teaching the *Odyssey* with Greek Art, Architecture, and Archaeology

Marya Fisher

To teach Homer's epics without considering material culture is to put oneself at a great pedagogical disadvantage. This is especially true for educators teaching students in undergraduate survey classes or high school classrooms, who may never have encountered the texts in a meaningful way before. While the verse itself richly illustrates the battles fought, the lives lived, and the objects exchanged, encountering images of archaeological sites and objects can allow students to access the world described in the text and to consider the epics in their original contexts.

Yet the complications of understanding and teaching material culture in responsible ways may make educators with a background in philology avoid engaging with it altogether in the classroom. Rather than introduce the complications inherent in looking at objects, educators will often focus exclusively on the texts themselves. Whether we intend to or not, however, we are introducing images into our classrooms when we use printed editions of the epics: most editions used in classrooms, be they in the original Greek or in translation, have cover art derived from works of ancient art. The first volume of W. B. Stanford's *Odyssey* (books 1–12), a Greek edition and commentary I use in my own teaching practice, displays—in its current edition—a detail of a Boeotian black-figure skyphos currently in the Ashmolean Museum (G249), which belongs to a class of vases known as Cabirion ware (see Boeotian black-figure skyphos). Likewise, the Penguin Classics edition of Robert Fagles's translation of the *Odyssey*, commonly used in classrooms, has as its cover image the interior of an Attic black-figure Little Master cup, depicting Herakles fighting Triton, encircled by a ring of dancing women (Tarquinia, Museo Nazionale Tarquinese RC 4194; see Black-figure Little Master cup). Both of these are evocative, ancient Greek images, but neither can be used as a straightforward illustration of the texts it decorates: the former is an example of a particular type of iconography found only in association with a single cult site in Thebes, characterized by its grotesque depiction of myth, which may or may not actually be an illustration of ritual or dramatic activities;[1] the latter is an Attic depiction of a story that does not appear at all in the epic, that of Herakles and Triton.[2] Both of these images, while Greek, were painted hundreds of years after the period in which the epic was set in writing, and are reflective of the very different specific contexts in which they were originally created and received.[3] These are just two examples of a widespread practice of illustrating the epics with ancient art that is either unconnected or connected in a complex way with the texts themselves. If you look at your bookshelves, you'll immediately see this phenomenon at work: on recent editions of Homer, there are images from a variety of ancient cultures, from Minoan Crete to Classical Athens to Roman Campania.[4] These illustrations mean that whether or not an educator intends to have images in their classroom, there are images in the classroom. Students will associate these images with the texts, and in doing so, will draw their own connections between them. As educators, it is important that we contextualize these images for students.

It is easy, however, to assert that material culture should be taught, and far less so to teach it in a responsible way. When teaching material culture to students, I always begin by asking them to describe the object in concrete terms rather than immediately try to identify the scene, which tends to be the natural response. This allows students to consider the object as a whole, and really look at it, before beginning to guess at its meaning. Depending on the age and disposition of the students, it may be useful to invite them to draw what they see during this process of description, as it may help them identify details that they would ordinarily have missed.[5] In these descriptions, I ask my students to consider the following qualities.

Materiality. What an object is made of is fundamental to the study of material culture; it can indicate how and why it was created, as well as how it was used in antiquity. Whether a material was local to the object's production or needed to be imported could have a major impact on its value. Understanding the material—along with scale—can indicate how portable the object was, and whether it was meant to be moved. Examining and understanding material is essential to understanding an object, its original context, and use.

Scale. In material culture, size matters. It impacts our understanding of an object's production, value, and use. Noting the scale of an object is especially important for your students when teaching from images rather than the objects themselves (as in a museum setting), which can make all objects appear to be the same size, even when they vary greatly.

Style. Unlike material and scale, style can seem more daunting to describe. In my teaching, I have students understand style as the answer to the question of how the subject is articulated. To get at the style of an object, it can be useful to think through questions of whether the subject is drawn from life or whether it has been abstracted in some way: If the form has been abstracted, how has it been done? Does the abstracting draw attention to particular aspects of the form? (For example, in a depiction of the human form, are parts of the anatomy, such as the eyes, highlighted?) In discussing style with students, it is useful to divorce the idea of style from that of skill. Classical Greek sculpture does not necessarily look more naturalistic than Archaic because the artists were more skilled than those working in the Archaic period. Rather, style is better conveyed to students as a way of communicating what is important to people in a given time period. An apt example, and one I use often with my own students, is that of changing trends around *Instagram* filters and formats, which shows the way the images we prefer change as styles change, even in a very short period of time.

Only after students have thoroughly described the object do I invite them to comment on its subject matter.

Iconography. If style describes how a subject is shown, iconography describes what is represented. I ask my students to thoroughly consider the formal aspects of a piece of material culture before embarking on identifying its subject because it forces close looking (a practice akin to close reading), which might otherwise be eschewed in favor of guessing. Close looking leads to better iconographic analysis because it promotes the acknowledgment and discussion both of the object as a whole and of its details.

Once students have thoroughly described and analyzed the artifact at hand, I provide information to help them understand the work of art in its original context. The aspects of context that are especially relevant to a discussion of ancient art are chronology, archaeological context, and original use.

Chronology. For ancient artifacts, it is very rare to have precise dates recorded, barring exceptional situations (for example, the erection of the Parthenon on the Athenian Acropolis). For this reason, dates—especially for the types of objects you encounter in museums, which often lack archaeological context—are often determined by the style of the object. While it is not necessary for students to understand archaeological methods or stylistic dating and relative chronologies to consider ancient material culture, it is useful for them to understand the uncertainty inherent in dating any piece of ancient art, especially when thinking about it in relationship to the epics, which also have complex and uncertain chronologies.

Archaeological context. It is often not possible, for various reasons, to understand the original context of a piece of ancient art, either because the piece had multiple contexts in antiquity or because it has been removed from its archaeological context without documentation. However, where archaeological context does exist, it is essential to our understanding of the work of art and should be noted for students to help them understand the object that they are considering.

Original use. The idea of how and why an object was used is important in discussing ancient material culture. Because ancient art was, for the most part, functional in some way, its function is necessarily tied to its meaning. Knowing, for example, whether a ceramic vase was used to mix wine at a symposium or to serve as a monumental grave marker allows a more nuanced reading of the object itself.

Once my students have described and discussed an object, I invite them to put it into conversation with the text. In doing so, I find the following questions important to consider and discuss:

Is there a direct relationship between the image and the text? If so, how should we understand this relationship?

What is the contextual (chronological and geographical) relationship between the text and the object? Which was created first? Could the text have influenced the creation of the object, or vice versa?

Does looking at the object alongside the text help us better understand the text? Does it help us better understand the object?

To give an example of why these questions are useful, I want to consider the one category of objects—Mycenaean boar's tusk helmets and images of them—that are directly represented in the text of the Homeric epics: "And around [Odysseus's] head, he placed / a leather cap made of skin: on the inside / it was stretched firmly with many straps; on the outside the close-set white tusks / of a white-tusked boar supported it / well and skillfully all around . . ." ἀμφὶ δέ οἱ κυνέην κεφαλῆφιν ἔθηκε / ῥινοῦ ποιητήν· πολέσιν δ' ἔντοσθεν ἱμᾶσιν / ἐντέτατο στερεῶς· ἔκτοσθε δὲ λευκοὶ ὀδόντες / ἀργιόδοντος ὑὸς θαμέες ἔχον ἔνθα καὶ ἔνθα / εὖ καὶ ἐπισταμένως . . . (*Iliad* 10.261–65).[6] When teaching this section of text, images of Mycenaean boar's tusk helmets help students visualize what is being described (see, e.g., Boar's tusk helmet); the images, in effect, help illustrate the text. But the conversation about them does not need to end there. Rather, I invite my students to consider how the writer of the *Iliad*'s verse, who lived six centuries after Mycenaean warriors donned such helmets, would know of such an object. Moreover, why, in a poem replete with bronze helmets of the sort worn by the poet's contemporaries in the eighth and seventh centuries BCE, does this six-hundred-year-old Mycenaean helmet appear at this moment in the text? What is important about the context of the passage, and the genealogy given to the helmet that follows (10.266–70), which traces it back at least two generations to the robber Autolykos? Is, perhaps, the appearance of the boar's tusk helmet meant to evoke the deep past and Odysseus's connection to his trickster forebear? By considering the boar's tusk helmet not just as a simple illustration of the text but also as an object with a context of its own, it is possible to enrich discussions of passages in the classroom and introduce complication and nuance to the students' understanding both of the text itself and of the ancient world more generally.

With all this in mind, in the remainder of this essay, I provide examples that pair the epic and material culture from the following categories: Minoan and Mycenean Greek artifacts (contemporary with the "story" of the epics); Geometric Greek artifacts bearing scenes of heroism (contemporary, perhaps, with the oral tradition and codification of the epics); and later Greek Homeric scenes, which first appear in the Archaic period and continue to this day (contemporary with the reception of the epics). The examples provided are not meant to be prescriptive but to inspire other teachers to integrate objects in their teaching of the *Odyssey*. For each, I have included a formal description of the object discussed in order to provide a model for any educators without a background in art history.[7] It is almost always preferable to teach directly from objects rather than images of objects (as the students can get a better sense of scale, dimensionality, and detail), so it may be useful to substitute apt examples from local collections if there are any in your area.

Material Culture of Minoan and Mycenaean Greece

As illustrated in the example above, one class of material culture often paired with the teaching of the *Odyssey* is that of the Bronze Age civilizations of Minoan and Mycenaean Greece (ca. 3200 to 1050 BCE). The material culture of this period was created contemporaneously with the "events" of the epic, a clear motivation for teaching it alongside the epic.[8] What may be less clear is why the relationship between material culture of this period and the verse is not straightforward. The reason is simply that there are very few direct connections between material culture of this period and what is described in the epics. This is because, as noted above, the Mycenaean and Minoan cultures were centuries removed from the epics; the *Odyssey*, therefore, must be read not as a direct reflection of the Bronze Age but as a poetic reception of the stories and culture of this period. Illustrating the texts of Homer with images from this period—that is to say, having them accompany the text without providing context for their relationship with the *Odyssey*—flattens a complex relationship between the material culture and the poem. This, however, should not dissuade educators from using material culture in the teaching of the *Odyssey*, only caution them against using it without providing this understanding to their students. There are many ways to do this, but I suggest two here: first, the *Odyssey* as the reception of the Bronze Age past and, second, the ways in which the *Odyssey* has been used as an interpretive tool to understand Minoan and Mycenaean remains.

The Odyssey *as reception*: This approach to pairing material culture with the *Odyssey* highlights the ways in which the poem represents and interprets the remains of the Minoan and Mycenaean worlds that would have been known at the time of the poem's composition. One of the most evocative pieces of material culture to put into conversation with the *Odyssey* is the Lion Gate at Mycenae.[9] The Lion Gate is the main entranceway to the citadel of Mycenae, surmounted by the monumental relief sculpture that gives the gate its name. The gate is made from four enormous blocks of local stone: the threshold, two uprights, and a lintel. Above the lintel, there is a triangular slab of limestone, which measures about three meters in height, into which the relief sculpture is carved.[10] The relief itself shows two lions, with their forepaws resting on two altars that support a central column.[11] The lions' heads are lost; they were made separately from the relief and attached. The material of the heads and manes is much debated, but may have been gilded metal or stone (Blackwell 452). At the top of the ramp leading into the fortified citadel of Mycenae, this relief greeted visitors of the Bronze Age stronghold. Interestingly, although the city was destroyed, the gate was visible and known throughout antiquity and therefore could have been an influence on the poet of the *Odyssey*.[12] The date of the gate is somewhat contested, but it most likely belongs to the mid–thirteenth century BCE (452).

There is no passage in the epics that references the Lion Gate at Mycenae, but it may be taught alongside the description of the entrance to Alcinous's palace (*Odyssey* 7.88–93).[13] In this passage, the doors of the Phaeacian palace are described as being flanked by dogs made of gold and silver by Hephaestus, which guard the house. The description of the dogs, "which are immortal and unaging forever" ἀθανάτους ὄντας καὶ ἀγήρως ἤματα πάντα (7.94), has long been debated by scholiasts and scholars alike, and pairing its interpretation with that of the Lion Gate adds an extra layer to discussion, raising the question of whether the poet is describing an entrance similar to the gates at Mycenae. Students can explore the ways in which this should inform our reading of the passage and whether the dogs are meant to be understood as animate or inanimate. This pairing may also help students better understand the function of the Lion Gate, since the Odyssean examples were built "in order to guard the house of great-hearted Alcinous" δῶμα φυλασσέμεναι μεγαλήτορος Ἀλκινόοιο (7.93). If indeed Alcinous's gate is related to the one at Mycenae, the Lion Gate, too, may have been built to serve an apotropaic function, to turn away danger from its walls.[14] In these ways, this pairing allows students to deepen their understanding both of the poem and of the material culture of the Bronze Age.

The Odyssey *as interpretive tool*: Another fruitful way to approach the Minoan and Mycenaean material in conversation with the *Odyssey* is to invite your students to consider the ways in which the poem has itself influenced the interpretation and understanding of Bronze Age material by modern archaeologists. This approach admittedly requires a bit more background about the dawn of archaeology in the nineteenth and twentieth centuries, and the introduction of the famous (and infamous) figure of Heinrich Schliemann, a German businessman, amateur archaeologist, and favorite of students for his illogical approaches to excavation, bombastic claims, and compulsive self-aggrandizement.

Born in 1822 in Germany, Schliemann acquired a large enough fortune through his various businesses to fund exploratory journeys to Ithaca and the Troad. On the basis of his findings from those journeys, Schliemann spent the last two decades of his life excavating sites he believed held the key to the historicity of the Homeric epics, beginning with the hill of Hissarlik, a site in northern Turkey that he believed to be the site of Troy, and subsequently moving on to Mycenae and Tiryns, actively working until his death in 1890.[15] Schliemann was never fully accepted by the academic establishment during his own life and has been the subject of suspicion within the archaeological community since his death. Despite this, it is difficult to overestimate his influence both on the field of archaeology and—especially—on its relationship to the Homeric epics. Schliemann understood all he excavated as a direct reflection of the epics; the ways in which he understood what he found, and the ways in which his views underpin our understanding of the material culture of the Bronze Age, are fruitful topics for classroom discussion.

One object excavated and analyzed by Schliemann that provides an excellent pedagogical opportunity is the so-called Mask of Agamemnon (Athens, National Museum 624; see Mask of Agamemnon).[16] The mask itself is made from a sheet of gold, which was hammered over a wooden form (a process called repoussé) to create the image of a three-dimensional face that measures about twenty-six centimeters in height. Details of the face, including the eyebrows, beard, and mustache, were inscribed with a sharp object. There are two holes just below the ears with which the mask could be secured. Dated to the sixteenth century BCE, the mask is highly stylized and individualized, with the forms of the face represented emphatically by relatively simple shapes and lines: the closed eyes are almond-shaped; the lips and nose are linear; the ears are volutes; the beard, mustache, and eyebrows are expressed by linear patterning. The mask was found by Schliemann in Grave Circle A at Mycenae in 1876, laid over the face of one of the nineteen bodies that were buried in the shaft graves there. It is the most famous of five gold masks of this type found in Grave Circle A, all of which were individualized, presumably to represent the deceased. It was among a rich array of funerary gifts: vast quantities of gold jewelry of all types, ceremonial vases made of precious metals, and weapons, both ceremonial and for military use.[17]

Unlike the previous two examples, there is no direct or indirect relationship between the object itself and the epics: there are no descriptions of golden death masks in the poetry, nor is it possible that this mask could have adorned the corpse of a warrior of the Late Bronze Age, as it predates that period by three centuries. This mask, however, presents another teaching opportunity: to illustrate how the epics have framed the understanding of Bronze Age objects. There is a famous—but almost certainly fabricated—story that Schliemann, upon unearthing the mask, sent a telegram to the king of Greece saying, "I have gazed upon the face of Agamemnon" (Dickinson 302). While Schliemann likely never sent such a telegram, he did believe that the graves that he uncovered were those of Agamemnon and the Mycenaean royal family of the epics.[18] And for generations, the question of the so-called Mask of Agamemnon has continued to be a subject of interest and debate among scholars.

This object may also be useful to teach alongside Menelaus's account of his brother's demise (*Odyssey* 4.512–37), as it can encourage students to consider the following questions: Why did Schliemann associate this particular mask with the figure of Agamemnon, and—in particular—his burial? Is there anything in the text of the *Odyssey*, a text Schliemann knew intimately, that would lead him to this identification? How does the association between Agamemnon and the mask change the way we understand and view the object? Was it Schliemann's association of this mask with the Homeric figure that made it such a subject of scholarly debate? And, more broadly, how does giving something a Homeric name, even when scholars accept that it is not Homeric, impact how that object is understood? Does it affect the questions asked of it and the scholarship done? Would we understand this object differently if it had never been associated with the Homeric hero, and would this be to the benefit or detriment of our understanding of the object and the people who created it? By asking these questions of the object and its Homeric associations, students can broaden their study of the *Odyssey* to begin to see its influence, not only on subsequent literature and art but also on whole academic fields of study.

Heroic Scenes of Geometric Greece

Another class of material culture that may be useful to consider with students in the study of the Homeric epics is that of the Geometric period (ca. 900–700 BCE). The Geometric period is of particular interest to students of Homer because it is the period during which many scholars believe that the poems as we know them began to emerge. The artistic production of this period, therefore, can give students insight into the culture in which the stories and ideas in the epics were likely taking shape.

During the Geometric period, an abundance of figural art was produced in Athens. This art, with its often impressive scale and stylized figures made up of simple geometric shapes, provides a wealth of material to consider with students alongside the Homeric epics. Of special note are the funerary vases of the middle to late eighth century, largely found in the main necropolis of Athens, the Kerameikos.[19] There are examples of these vases in museums and private collections across the globe, any one of which would provide a fitting companion piece in the discussion of the Homeric epics. For the sake of clarity, I will use one example that I have often referenced in my teaching, a monumental funeral vase, or krater, in the Metropolitan Museum of Art (14.130.14; see Terracotta krater).

The krater in the Metropolitan Museum is monumental in scale, measuring over three and a half feet high and over two feet in diameter. Although used as a grave marker, the vase has the form of a krater, a large bowl used to mix wine and water in the context of a symposium.

Geometric pots are notable for their exuberant decoration in black silhouette,[20] and the example in the Metropolitan Museum provides a lovely illustration of this: the entire surface of the vase is covered with linear and figural motifs, with two major zones of figural decoration adorning the body of the krater. At the widest point of the vase, there is a frieze—a continuous decorative band—showing a *prothesis*, a funeral scene in which the body is laid out and visited by mourners, who are shown to either side of the couch rending their hair in a show of grief. Below, there is a military scene featuring a procession of chariots and warriors on foot. Areas between the zones and figures are covered in a variety of geometric designs, including checkerboards, meanders, zigzags, and dots. The decoration is highly stylized, with figures and designs made up of the same simple geometric forms; this style emphasizes clarity of the scene over naturalism. It is clear that the deceased on the couch is signaled as the most important figure in the scene above because it is the largest and central; no figures (except for the horses drawing the chariots) overlap. Interestingly, the military scene uses archaizing images—chariots and hourglass-shaped shields[21]—to signal that this zone references the heroic past. The funerary scene is fitting here as these large-scale vases served as monumental markers for the graves of the elite of eighth-century Athens.[22]

These Geometric vases are ideal for teaching alongside the *Odyssey* because they represent a parallel artistic production that emerged during the same period in which the epics were composed. Although there are no definitively Homeric scenes on these vases, they communicate similar ideas and values to those of the epics about masculinity, honoring the dead, and the heroic past. Useful questions to explore with students when pairing these vases with the epics include the following: What, if any, passages in the *Odyssey* are evoked by the images on these vases? How do the representations of the heroic past and heroism on the vases complement or contradict those found in the epics? Why were these scenes used on funerary markers? What do these scenes tell us about the people whose graves were marked by these vases? Does considering these vases alongside the epics clarify, confuse, or add nuance to the values and ideas represented in the poems? Is it a coincidence that these cultural productions were made in the same period? By putting these vases into conversation with the epics, students can deepen and expand their understanding of eighth-century Greek culture by exploring the ideas and values that were communicated by the cultural productions of this period. Considering these objects in tandem therefore allows students to begin to examine the ways in which the eighth-century Greek audience would have understood and contextualized the epics.

Homeric Scenes of Archaic and Classical Greece

Some of the most evocative images that are used to illustrate scenes from the Homeric epics are those found in the vase painting of Archaic and Classical Greece. These images are compelling because they provide visual representations of the episodes found in the epics, from the death of Sarpedon in book 16, lines 426–683, of the *Iliad* (e.g., Cerveteri, Museo Nazionale Archeologico 145139; see Red-figure calyx krater) to the blinding of the Cyclops in book 9, lines 360–412, of the *Odyssey* (e.g., Eleusis, Archaeological Museum 2630; see Eleusis neck amphora). Indeed, many of these scenes are labeled with the names of the heroes of the *Iliad* and the *Odyssey*, an exciting realization for any student of Classical Greek.[23] Yet the ways in which these scenes mirror those told in the epics, and in which the inscriptions help us identify those scenes, belie the complex relationship between object and text. As was true in all previous examples, by thinking about these objects not as illustrations but as artifacts with their own contexts, it is possible to teach them alongside the epics in a way that acknowledges these complications.

One apt example to teach alongside the *Odyssey* is the Mykonos Vase, an early Archaic monumental pithos, or storage jar, dating to about 675 BCE (see Mykonos Vase). The decoration is completely rendered in relief, with the figures emerging from the body of the vase. Like the Geometric krater considered above, the decoration is rendered in a series of horizontal friezes or registers. On the neck is the image of a monumental horse on wheels with portholes that reveal the faces of warriors; other warriors surround the horse, distinguishable by their helmets, round shields, and spears. Below, the three registers decorating the body of the vase are divided into rectangular metopes, or decorative panels, each of which shows a vignette of a violent interaction between a warrior and women, recognizable by their long, patterned dresses, and children, distinguished by their smaller stature. All of the figures are highly stylized, with large round eyes dominating their faces, and exaggerated gestures, which give clarity to the scenes depicted. The pithos, like the monumental Geometric vase, was used in a funerary context, as it was found holding human bones (Ervin).

Although this vase is unique in its decoration, it is not unique in the questions it asks of students as they consider scenes that appear, at first glance, to be illustrations of Homeric episodes. The primary question that one should always ask of students is whether it is possible to tell whether this is truly a Homeric scene; in other words, is this a representation of the story as it is told by the epic or of an alternate version of the myth? In the case of this vase, it is useful to pair it with Menelaus's account of the Trojan horse in book 4 of the *Odyssey*, lines 271–89. As students are guided through the details of the vase (the faces of the warriors visible through the portholes, the warriors surrounding the vase), it becomes clear that if the artist was working from the story of the Trojan horse that is told in the *Odyssey*, he took great artistic license with the representation: for example, the warriors inside the Homeric horse definitely do not have portholes from which to view the scene below. Thinking through the reasons why these choices were made by the artist (in the case of the portholes, to give clarity to the scene, ensuring the viewer understands that the horse is filled with warriors) can both help explain and further complicate the relationship between text and image and, in so doing, add nuance to the discussion of both the object and the epic.

It is worthwhile, in conclusion, to return to the book covers of the *Odyssey*. Each of the editions mentioned in the introduction to this essay displays images that, when contextualized properly, allow for a classroom discussion that may enrich students' understanding not only of the epic but also of the cultures of Bronze Age, Archaic, and Classical Greece. Take just one example: the Cabirion skyphos—a two-handled drinking vessel—on Stanford's edition of the *Odyssey*. A contextual examination of the vase alongside the text of the epic would allow students to explore the ways in which the stories of the epic were received and interpreted in a cult context—in this case, the mystery cult of the Kabeiroi at Thebes—and to consider the ways in which the image of the hero on this vase subverts the depiction of Odysseus in the epic. By helping your students understand the objects, such as those on book covers, as cultural artifacts with their own contexts before pairing them with sections of text, you can enrich their understanding not only of the *Odyssey* but also of the culture that produced it and of the ways its stories were received and interpreted in the Greek world. This introduction to these practices is not meant to be exhaustive or prescriptive but only to provide models that may help teachers integrate material culture into the classroom in ways that convey the intrinsic value of the objects instead of relegating them to the role of illustrations to the Homeric text.

NOTES

1. For a complete discussion of this class of ceramics, see Heimberg; Daumas. For a positive reading of the vase in the context of the symposium, see Derbew, *Untangling*, especially 40–41.

2. For a discussion of this motif on Athenian pottery, see Ahlberg-Cornell.

3. For debates about the date of composition of the *Odyssey*, see the introduction to this volume.

4. Emily Wilson's 2018 edition uses the drawing of a Minoan wall painting; Fagles, noted above, uses an Attic black-figure vase; E. V. Rieu uses a Roman Campanian relief showing Odysseus at the helm of his ship.

5. Thanks are due here to Sofia Gans, my colleague at the Pierrepont School, who introduced this teaching practice to me.

6. Unless otherwise noted, all translations from the Greek are mine.

7. For other models of this sort of description, see museum websites and exhibition catalogs, including the website for the Metropolitan Museum of Art (metmuseum.org/art/the-collection), the Museum of Fine Arts in Boston (collections.mfa.org/objects), and the British Museum (britishmuseum.org/collection).

8. For a review of the arguments surrounding the historicity and date of the Trojan War, see Saïd 75–78; in the years since Saïd, Cline has defended the historicity of the Trojan War on the basis of both the archaeology of Hissarlik and an analysis of Hittite texts.

9. For an illustration of the Lion Gate, see "Lion Gate." For a comprehensive discussion of the Lion Gate and its interpretation, see Mylonas 173–76.

10. Relief sculpture is bound to its backing surface, as opposed to sculpture in the round, which is free-standing. The precise measurement of the relief is somewhat contested because of the difficulty inherent in measuring it in situ (Blackwell 452n14).

11. For a discussion of the identification of these animals as lions, see Blackwell 472–73.

12. The Lion Gate is briefly commented upon in antiquity by Pausanias, the second-century traveler and geographer, in describing the fortifications of Mycenae (2.16).

13. It has been suggested, in fact, that Homer's description of Alcinous's palace was inspired by the Lion Gate (Blakolmer 50).

14. For a discussion of the myriad interpretations of the Lion Gate, see Mylonas 173–76.

15. For Heinrich Schliemann's extraordinary biography, see Ludwig as well as the autobiographical introductions to Schliemann (*Troy*; *Ilios*).

16. It should be noted here that the authenticity of this mask has been called into question by William M. Calder III and by David Traill. This claim, however, seems unlikely; see Demakopoulou; Arentzen. For a claim that Calder and Traill misidentified the mask that Schliemann associated with Agamemnon, see Dickinson. For educators interested in introducing this debate into the classroom, a useful set of articles accessible to nonspecialists can be found in vol. 52, no. 4, of *Archaeology*; see Harrington et al.

17. For the National Archaeological Museum's description of the object, see "Collection."

18. For a more in-depth discussion of Schliemann's references to Agamemnon with regard to this mask, see Dickinson 301–02.

19. For an overview of Attic Geometric pottery and burial practices, see Coldstream 109–23.

20. This was achieved by applying slip (diluted clay solution) onto the leather-hard surface of the clay before firing. This technique differs from the black figure of the Archaic period in that details are not incised into the silhouette. For a technical and detailed discussion of the production of Attic pottery, see Noble.

21. It is important to note that there is an ongoing debate about the nature of these shields, with some scholars arguing that they do not represent real Geometric shields, but memories of those from the Bronze Age (Webster; Snodgrass), while others contend that it was, indeed, an ordinary shield type in the Geometric period (Boardman). The argument that these shields existed in the Geometric period but were meant to reference the heroic past is compelling (Hurwit).

22. For an in-depth study of the mortuary practices in Geometric Athens, see Whitley, *Style*.

23. One way, in fact, that I often motivate and invigorate beginning Greek students is to have them read the myriad inscriptions on the krater known as the François Vase (Florence, Museo Nazionale Archeologico 4209; see François Vase) and try to identify the scenes.

Appreciating a Problematic Text

Lillian E. Doherty

From the perspective of the twenty-first century, it is easy to see what is "wrong" with the *Odyssey*: it can be seen to endorse systems of gender and class privilege and an ethic of revenge that many (though by no means all) of our contemporaries deplore. Should students then be interested in the *Odyssey* solely as an artifact of a bygone era and an object of critique? Much of my own scholarship has been in a critical vein,[1] but as a teacher of undergraduates and MA students (some of whom are themselves serving as teaching assistants in my undergraduate mythology course), I am eager to highlight as well the aspects of the poem that I admire.

This is not as difficult as it may seem at first, because to a certain extent the poem includes a critique of its hero and even, at times, of its own ideology. It does this in the first place by giving voice to characters who are opposed to Odysseus or who perceive their circumstances as unfair. Thus, for example, Polyphemus complains to his faithful ram that "no-account" οὐτιδανός (9.460)[2] Odysseus has taken unfair advantage by getting him drunk, while the crew complain that their leader has received gifts he is not sharing with them (the bag of winds; 10.34–45). Other complaints go further and address the injustice of the gods: Calypso's protest at their double sexual standard (5.118–29), or the crew's that it is unfair to let them die of hunger in the presence of an enormous herd of cattle (12.340–51). The poet also lets us see the hurt that Odysseus's deception causes his wife and father when they weep in his presence. At that point he immediately reveals himself to Laertes, but he "[keeps] his eyes in their lids dry and steady as horn or iron" ὀφθαλμοὶ δ' ὡς εἰ κέρα ἕστασαν ἠὲ σίδηρος / ἀτρέμας ἐν βλεφάροισι (19.211–12) rather than risk confiding in Penelope. As others have shown,[3] implicit analogies between Odysseus and his most savage opponent, Polyphemus, also raise serious questions about the ethics of his revenge.

These are some of the ways in which the *Odyssey* problematizes its own apparent values. But is that self-critique the only feature of the poem that makes it worth reading in our age? I argue that there are also values in the poem that we would wish to affirm—at least, that I myself am still prepared to affirm. It is easy, from our vantage point in the twenty-first century, to deprecate the exaggerated fidelity that is expected of Penelope and to contrast it with the dalliances of the hero, or to criticize Odysseus for his unscrupulous behavior—indeed, other essays in this volume take these critical approaches, and they are fully justified. Yet I cannot help admiring the ultimate success of the hero, which contrasts (pointedly, in the meeting of the two heroes in book 11) with the tragedy of Achilles in the *Iliad*. Odysseus is a survivor, and survival means compromise. Penelope, too, is a survivor, in very different circumstances, a clever woman who finds the means in her own sphere to resist the demands of her unwelcome suitors. I believe it is possible to admire the survival and the mutual bond of these characters while critiquing the implicit ideology of the poem, including its gender disparities and its ethic of revenge.

Odysseus's distinctive epithets, *polymētis* ("of much cunning") and *polytropos* ("of many turns"), emphasize his cleverness and versatility, which are primarily responsible for getting him out of the dangerous or delicate situations in which he finds himself. In contrast to Achilles, who is eloquent in expressing his own feelings but oblivious to those of others,[4] Odysseus anticipates the perspectives of his interlocutors. True, this enables him to manipulate them by tailoring his appeals to them, but it can also demonstrate his respect for them and sensitivity to their feelings. When Calypso, after receiving Zeus's mandate and telling Odysseus he can return home, tries one last time to dissuade him by comparing her immortal beauty to Penelope's mortal form, he assures her that Penelope is inferior in both appearance and stature (εἶδος ἀκιδνοτέρη μέγεθός τε [5.217]); his renewed plea for release emphasizes his desire for home rather than for his wife (5.219–20). His appeal to Nausicaa is similarly framed to address her concerns as he can deduce them from her age and circumstances: in the first place, her fears for safety when faced with a naked stranger, and in the second, her wishes for a happy marriage. By comparing her to Artemis (a flattering comparison, but one seconded by the Homeric narrator; cf. 6.102–09 and 149–52), he assures her that he means to make no sexual advances, and by wishing her happiness in marriage he addresses the foremost concern of young women of marriageable age in this culture. To be sure, he also awakens her interest in him as a potential suitor, but his emphasis on *homophrosynē*, "like-mindedness," as the key element in a successful marriage (6.180–85) evokes his relationship with Penelope and anticipates his reunion with her.

I think it is wrong to see this side of Odysseus as purely manipulative and self-serving. While on some level he is both those things, he also displays an awareness of—and a concern for—the feelings of others. The shade of his mother, whom he meets in the underworld, says she died of longing for his "gentleness" ἀγανοφροσύνη as well as for his "cleverness" μήδεα (11.203). The epic narrator, who not only endorses but also in some ways emulates his hero, begins the poem by insisting that Odysseus "tried hard to win" ἀρνύμενος (1.5), both his own life and the homecoming of his crew. He is indeed "a complicated man," as Emily

Wilson has called him in her translation (Odyssey 1.1), but part of that complication is a mixture of self-concern and concern for others.

The key demonstration of Odysseus's cleverness, of course, comes in the Cyclops episode, where he faces the greatest challenge to his survival. Without some knowledge of Greek it is difficult to appreciate the full impact of this episode, which features not one but two thematically significant puns. The best-known of these involves the false name Odysseus gives to Polyphemus: *Outis* (Οὖτις), a thinly disguised variation on οὔτις, Ancient Greek for "no one."[5] When Polyphemus cries out to the other Cyclopes that *Outis* is killing him, they reply that in that case they can do nothing to help. But the Greek is cleverer still: in the Cyclopes' reply, framed as a conditional sentence ("If Nobody is hurting you and you are alone . . ."; 9.410), Οὖτις becomes μή τις (*mē tis*), which evokes Odysseus's intelligence, the *mētis* of his chief epithet, *polymētis*. So the Cyclopes are also saying, unwittingly, "If cleverness is hurting you . . ." The postcolonial reading of this episode, epitomized by Kirsten Lodge's essay in this volume, is an important corrective to the unthinking validation of Odysseus's victory over Polyphemus. But the episode also portrays the superiority of intelligence to brute force. As a variant of an international folktale,[6] it also portrays the escape of a clever underdog from an unthinking, murderous enemy. In this perspective, the traditional admiration for Odysseus as a hero of survival seems justified. This is the Odysseus who has been reimagined by African American writers and artists such as Ralph Ellison and Romare Bearden.[7]

The other quality of Odysseus that ensures his survival is endurance: the willingness to suffer what he must in order to reach home. His epithet *polytlas*, "much-enduring," captures this facet of his character, as does his response to Calypso when she warns him of the suffering he faces if he leaves her:

> If some one of the gods strikes me on the wine-colored sea,
> I will endure, with a heart in my chest that withstands grief;
> for I have already suffered much and toiled much
> in the waves and in the war; let this, too, be added to that.
>
> εἰ δ' αὖ τις ῥαίῃσι θεῶν ἐνὶ οἴνοπι πόντῳ,
> τλήσομαι ἐν στήθεσσιν ἔχων ταλαπενθέα θυμόν·
> ἤδη γὰρ μάλα πολλὰ πάθον καὶ πολλὰ μόγησα
> κύμασι καὶ πολέμῳ· μετὰ καὶ τόδε τοῖσι γενέσθω. (5.221–24)

There are several points in the epic where Odysseus's endurance is emphasized. In the Cyclops's cave, he is tempted to kill the sleeping giant outright but realizes he could not move the stone blocking the doorway; "so for that time we waited, groaning, for the bright dawn" ὣς τότε μὲν στενάχοντες ἐμείναμεν Ἠῶ δῖαν (9.306). In the Aeolus episode, when he awakes to find that his men have released the winds and driven them far from home after Ithaca had been in sight, he even considers suicide (at least, this is what he claims to the Phaeacians), but again "endures and remains" ἀλλ' ἔτλην καὶ ἔμεινα (10.53). Much later, tossing and turning on the night before his attack on the suitors, he reminds himself that he endured worse when the Cyclops ate his men: "But you endured, until your *mētis* led you out of the cave, though you expected to die" σὺ δ'ἐτόλμας, ὄφρα σε μῆτις / ἐξάγαγ'ἐξ ἄντροιο ὀϊόμενον θανέεσθαι (20.20–21).

This ability to endure is one of the traits Odysseus shares with Penelope. She is often thought of, especially by contemporary readers and critics (including Lesser in this volume), as accepting of her subordinate status and fearful of risking her reputation as a chaste wife. I myself have argued that she can be seen as epitomizing the intended female audience for the epic, honored like Arete in being addressed by Odysseus but confined by his tale to her supporting role (Doherty, *Siren Songs* 176–77). At the same time, it is important to recognize that she shares the attributes of Odysseus that enable his survival. She, too, is exceptionally clever, as the suitors acknowledge in describing her weaving trick (2.88, 116–22), and she endures as even Odysseus is not called upon to do, in loyalty to her role as mother of a young son and wife of a man whose fate is unknown. While she may seem sheltered, and certainly is so by comparison with the enslaved women who wait on her, she is playing a dangerous game by resisting the norm that would have her remarry.[8] In this perspective, her decision to set the contest of the bow, whether or not she intuits that Odysseus is there to win it, is a kind of defeat, accepted because of the threat to her son's inheritance (19.530–34).[9]

In the cleverness and tenacity they share, there is thus a real "like-mindedness" (*homophrosynē*; ὁμοφροσύνη) between Odysseus and Penelope, of the kind the hero had praised to Nausicaa in wishing her a harmonious relationship with her future husband. It has often been noted that Penelope uses her cleverness even against Odysseus to get him to reveal the secret of their bed (23.177–206). Her courage and persistence in withstanding the suitors are described in a simile comparing her to a lion (4.791), which creates another parallel to Odysseus, who is compared to a lion several times (4.335, 17.126, 6.130, 22.402, 23.48). An extraordinary simile (discussed by several other contributors to this volume), describing the joy of a shipwrecked sailor who comes to land, marks the reunion of husband and wife: it begins from the viewpoint of Odysseus, who has been physically shipwrecked more than once, but it concludes from the perspective of Penelope, who is thus shown to have survived a comparable ordeal (23.231–40).[10]

Thus, despite the sometimes exasperating disparity between their circumstances, which must be recognized, Odysseus and Penelope are portrayed as similar in a number of ways that the poet values and celebrates. When they finally embrace, and Odysseus—who had earlier restrained his tears—weeps with Penelope, the narrator describes her as "the wife who fits his heart" ἄλοχον θυμαρέα (23.232). The courage, tenacity, and wit they share can plausibly be seen as contributing to their mutual fidelity. Odysseus is famously unfaithful with Circe and Calypso, but it is less often noted that these are goddesses, whom it is scarcely feasible for him to refuse. The double standard is firmly in place and Odysseus has the best of it. Yet he rejects Calypso's offer of immortality to return to his mortal existence, which includes his bond with his mortal wife.

That cleverness can be a positive trait of women—not merely used for devious and destructive ends, as in the contrasting cases of Clytemnestra and Helen—is epitomized in the character of Athena. She takes a particular interest in Odysseus, for obvious reasons; as she says explicitly when finally revealing herself to him in Ithaca, he may be "the best of mortals for plans and speeches," but she is "known among all the gods for [her] wit and wiles" σὺ μέν ἐσσι βροτῶν ὄχ'ἄριστος ἁπάντων / βουλῇ καὶ μύθοισιν, ἐγὼ δ' ἐν πᾶσι θεοῖσι / μήτι τε κλέομαι καὶ κέρδεσιν (13.297–99). Yet she also takes an interest in Penelope and occasionally intervenes on her behalf, as when she sends a dream to reassure her that Telemachus will get home safe (4.795–807), or inspires her to appear before the suitors and elicit gifts (18.158–62), a stratagem appreciated by the disguised Odysseus (18.281–83).[11] When the couple are reunited, Athena extends the night for them by preventing Dawn from harnessing her horses (23.242–46). They make use of the time not only for physical intimacy but to share their stories, and even to anticipate the hardships they have yet to endure (23.248–87).

In many, perhaps most, respects the marriage of Odysseus and Penelope is incompatible with contemporary Western ideas of what a marriage should be. Yet the epic narrator's emphasis on their shared traits, which include intelligence and courage, makes theirs in some sense a match of equals. Like the shipwrecked sailor of the simile, they are both survivors who have struggled against different but equally painful hardships to rejoin one another. Despite Odysseus's enjoyment of relationships with Circe and Calypso, he is willing to sacrifice the prospect of immortality for the sake of his return home. This return has many dimensions—the claim on his household and kingdom, the relationships with his son and father—but one of them is his bond with Penelope.

A structural parallel between the plots of the *Iliad* and *Odyssey* suggests to me that the epic poets shared to some extent our discomfort with the violent basis of the heroes' fame. In each poem, the violent climax of the action—Achilles's killing of Hector, Odysseus's killing of the suitors—is followed by a nonviolent meeting that is the true culmination of the plot. In fact, in the case of the *Odyssey*, the meeting is doubled: the hero is reunited first with his wife and then with his father. And each of these meetings requires the hero to demonstrate qualities of mind and feeling rather than physical prowess. To adapt Aristotle's terminology in the *Poetics*,[12] each scene involves a "recognition" (*anagnōrisis*) on the part of the hero but also on that of the audience. In the case of Achilles, the recognition is tragic: he is seen as acknowledging Priam's equality in suffering with his own father and with himself. For Odysseus, by contrast, the recognition is a happy one: he realizes how well his wife "fits his heart" by her loyalty and cleverness. In what seems a deliberate parallel with—and "capping" of—book 24 of the *Iliad*, he is then reunited with his own father, who, like Penelope, has kept his memory alive and grieved for his loss.

Ironically, given his portrayal as unusually perceptive and clever, Odysseus is ultimately less self-aware than Achilles. His survival depends not only on awareness of his surroundings but also on an ability to blunt his own feelings. Whereas Achilles lashes out in immediate bursts of anger, Odysseus must conceal his anger with the suitors (as earlier with the Cyclops) for the sake of ultimate victory over them. The habit of suspicion, which has kept Odysseus alive, is no longer appropriate in the meeting with his father, yet he feels compelled to "test" the old man. When Laertes, like Priam at the death of Hector (*Iliad* 22.408–28), reacts with acute distress to his son's false tale of entertaining Odysseus five years before, Odysseus feels a sharp pain, δριμὺ μένος (24.319), in his nose: a unique expression suggesting the unexpected vehemence of the hero's own reaction to the pain he has caused. In both of his reunions, with Penelope and with Laertes, the emotional bond is rooted in the past and evoked by "signs" σήματα (23.110, 24.329): the marriage bed for Penelope and the scar and the trees of the orchard for Laertes. Yet in each case it is not the physical sign but the story behind it that carries conviction: so Odysseus tells how he built the bed, received the scar, and followed his father around the orchard as a boy.

Although the qualities that enable Odysseus to survive are very different from the tragic insight granted to Achilles, the structure of the plot in each case throws the emphasis on the hero's qualities of mind and feeling rather than his battle prowess. Achilles is able to recognize and express the tragic equality between his father and Priam, and to treat his enemy as a guest. Odysseus is able to renew the bonds he created in his youth with a wife and father who care deeply for him and have kept his memory alive.

These are the qualities for which I myself can admire the heroes. At the same time, I admire the poems because they throw these qualities into relief, while also offering implicit critiques of traits and actions I would condemn. As a teacher, I try to keep these two perspectives in balance: the need to critique is urgent, especially today, but the need to admire is also great. I could not have studied and taught these works for forty years if I had not found much to admire in them. The *Odyssey* in particular has drawn and kept my attention for its interest in the relations between men and women and its celebration of the intelligence of both. Even its minor female characters are portrayed as perceptive and discreet, like Odysseus himself: thus queen Arete recognizes the clothing Odysseus is wearing but waits to question him until the other guests have gone home (7.229–39); thus Nausicaa manages to express her interest in Odysseus while anticipating and deflecting the possible censure of it (6.273–88).

This cleverness and subtlety are also traits of the epic narrator himself.[13] As I have argued elsewhere (Doherty, *Siren Songs* 161–77), the implicit identification of the narrator with Odysseus has the effect of confirming the hero's priority and credibility as a focalizer of the plot; this is largely responsible for the androcentric focus of the epic, with all of its troubling implications. Yet as I argued at the same time, actual audiences are capable of evading the epic's ideological net—which itself leaves "openings" for the imagination. One of the most striking of these is the relationship between the realism of the scenes in Ithaca and the fantastic quality of Odysseus's adventures. Paradoxically, the *false* tales Odysseus tells in Ithaca are more realistic than the true adventures he relates to the Phaeacians. And the epic narrator takes care to include details that confirm the truth of the adventures: thus he identifies an elderly Ithacan as the father of a crewman killed by the Cyclops (2.17–20) and a knot used by Odysseus as one taught to him by Circe (8.448).[14] In this case, the narrator's confirmation of his hero's veracity has, for me, a positive result: it makes the point that the marvelous version can be the truth.

In the translator's note to her version of the *Odyssey*, Wilson recalls her enchantment, as a child, with the features of the poem that also attracted me: its portrayal of "a world of magic and adventure" and "an individual's struggle to survive and return home" (Odyssey 81). As an adult, I have come to see it as a complex portrayal of the conditions and compromises through which its hero achieves success—a success that includes the reaffirmation of his relationships with his wife and father. I continue to believe in the positive value of these facets of the epic, not merely as bait to attract students but as an appropriate part of their education.

That even those of us who have lived with the poem for many years can continue to learn from it is demonstrated movingly by Daniel Mendelsohn in his book *An Odyssey: A Father, a Son, and an Epic*. The complexities of the father-son bond—and of that between husband and wife—are explored and illuminated by the discussions between Mendelsohn and his students, who include, exceptionally, his eighty-one-year-old father. The book shows by example how discussion of the epic among men and women of different generations can lead to unexpected insights and even to a deepening of the relationships among the people involved in these conversations.

It may be objected that any number of works can have this same effect. I agree, and I am glad to participate in efforts to increase the diversity of works taught in schools and universities. But I oppose efforts to cleanse the canon of any works that can be seen as endorsing or embodying illiberal ideologies. As long as these ideologies are prevalent, it is important to critique them. At the same time, it is important not to demonize complex works that include values we may wish to affirm. The study of literature may be framed in critical or celebratory ways. But a work like the *Odyssey* is valuable because it invites both approaches and shows that they are not incompatible.

NOTES

1. My book *Siren Songs* was mentioned in *Who Killed Homer?*, by Victor David Hanson and John Heath, as an example of the feminist critique that the authors believed was destroying students' interest in the field. My immediate, and enduring, reaction was that I am trying my best to keep Homer alive.

2. Translations are my own.

3. E.g., Bakker, *Meaning* 69–73; Loney; and Fahey's essay in this volume.

4. For an analysis of Achilles's speeches in the *Iliad* that includes this observation, see Friedrich and Redfield.

5. Translators usually render this in English as "Nobody" or "Noman"; a creative alternative used by Robert Fitzgerald is "Nohbdy" (9.397–400, corresponding to 9.366–69 in the Greek).

6. For the folktale origins of the Cyclops episode (with previous bibliography), see E. Cook, Odyssey 93.

7. The affinities between Odysseus and Ellison's "invisible man" have been described by Rankine. See also (among many possible examples) O'Meally on the *Odyssey* series by Romare Bearden.

8. As Rachel Lesser has reminded me in a personal communication, other females in the poem—Nausicaa, Arete, Calypso, Circe, even the Sirens, Scylla, and Charybdis—can also be seen (to different degrees) as independent and powerful.

9. See Murnaghan, "Penelope's *Agnoia*," for an exceptionally thoughtful treatment of the ways in which Penelope is and is not like Odysseus.

10. See Fahey's essay in this volume for the full simile and further discussion.

11. As this example shows, these interventions also benefit Odysseus. For a fuller treatment of the relationship between Athena and Penelope, see Doherty, "Athena."

12. Aristotle uses the term (sometimes translated as "discovery") more narrowly, to describe a character's coming to awareness of their own or another character's identity, as in the case of Oedipus (*Poetics* 1452a).

13. In a personal communication, Rachel Lesser added that "the narrative's complexity is itself a source of readerly engagement and pleasure."

14. A further confirming detail is the soliloquy in book 20, lines 18–21, where Odysseus himself recalls the endurance that got him out of the Cyclops's cave.

Epic Simile in the *Odyssey*: Figures of Journey and Homecoming

Maria Fahey

Amidst the pleasure of teaching Homer's *Odyssey* is the challenge of teaching an epic poem: How does one guide students' study of an epic in the limited time of a term? In this essay I suggest that focusing on the poem's epic similes promotes the kind of close reading that fosters a nuanced understanding of the poem at large. The *Odyssey*, which tells the story of Odysseus's return home after twenty years of war and travel, includes nearly forty epic similes, figures that repeatedly transport readers away from the main narrative to another time and place where a similar event occurs and invite them to recognize one thing (the simile's tenor) in the form of something else (the simile's vehicle).[1] The epic similes, which cast the poem's readers in the role of Odysseus navigating his way back home in a shape-shifting world, become particularly fertile sites for teaching Homer's poem of journey and homecoming.

In some similes, the events compared don't feel particularly distant from each other. For instance, when the narrator describes Odysseus making the raft on which he will leave Calypso's island, a simile compares Odysseus's raft-building skill to that of an expert shipwright: "As wide as a man marks off the hull's circumference / of a wide cargo ship, a man skilled in carpentry, / so wide did Odysseus make this raft" ὅσσον τίς τ' ἔδαφος νηὸς τορνώσεται ἀνὴρ / φορτίδος εὐρείής, εὖ εἰδὼς τεκτοσυνάων, / τόσσον ἔπ' εὐρεῖαν σχεδίην ποιήσατ' Ὀδυσσεύς (5.249–51).[2] Even though the simile transports us from the island where the marooned warrior-king has to make his own raft (the simile's tenor) to a place where a ship is crafted by a skilled shipwright (its vehicle), the journey is brief and the comparison of raft-building and shipbuilding close. Other similes, however, assert likenesses between worlds that feel separated by vaster distances. When, for instance, Odysseus tells the Phaeacians about how he clung to a fig tree waiting for the sea monster Charybdis to belch up his mast and keel, he compares the extraordinary moment when the remains of his wrecked ship reemerge from the monster's vortex to a mundane moment in civilized society: ". . . at last! At the hour when a man gets up from the agora to go to his dinner / after judging many quarrels of young men, / that was the time when those planks reappeared from Charybdis" . . . ὄψ'· ἦμος δ' ἐπὶ δόρπον ἀνὴρ ἀγορῆθεν ἀνέστη / κρίνων νείκεα πολλὰ δικαζομένων αἰζηῶν, / τῆμος δὴ τά γε δοῦρα Χαρύβδιος ἐξεφαάνθη (12.439–41). While Odysseus is using brute strength to escape a monster, we are transported to a civilized world where a man uses judgement to resolve young men's quarrels. However different, the men's work is similarly strenuous: Odysseus has been clinging to the tree's trunk since sunrise; the man "at last" goes home to eat, having spent the whole day judging quarrels. The explicit point of comparison is the time at which the planks of Odysseus's wrecked ship emerge, the same time at which the judge gets up to return home. Yet the distance traversed between the worlds with this common hour is disorienting.

However near or far the distance between tenor and vehicle, the transporting quality of a simile—its shuttling the audience of the poem away from the main narrative and back again—makes this figure key to teaching Homer's poem of delayed homecoming. Furthermore, even as a simile articulates a likeness (for instance, that the planks of Odysseus's wrecked ship will emerge at the same hour a judge goes home to eat), the details of the two joined stories rarely correspond neatly or fully and often evoke comparisons beyond those the speaker specifies. Inviting students to observe the similes closely thus helps them to grapple with the poem's complexities as they ponder questions raised by a simile's comparison. What is the effect, one might ask students, of being sidetracked to the quotidian world of a judge on his way home while the warrior-king literally is kept hanging? Are we reminded that young men's transgressions go unjudged in Ithaca as King Odysseus hangs above Charybdis's vortex? Does the simile emphasize the contrast between lawful human society and the lawless lands Odysseus visits on his journey? Or, in joining these two worlds, does the simile suggest that forceful and peaceful resolutions of conflict are not as distinct as we might think? Is there something about "home" that transcends the difference between the desire to return there at the end of a day of peacemaking and after twenty years of war and journey?

By relocating us from one place to another and asking us to recognize how they are alike, epic similes unsettle seeming dichotomies in the poem, including home and away, then and now, heroic and quotidian, civilized and monstrous, human and animal, male and female, young and old, self and other, victor and vanquished, divine and human, war and peace, *nostos* ("homecoming") and *kleos* ("fame"). After a brief introduction to epic simile, I shall demonstrate how pausing to consider the specific relation between a simile's tenor and vehicle can lead students to discover how such dichotomies are more vexed than the poem's narrators or characters may claim and can help students to explore the poem's deepest questions about conflict and homecoming. The dichotomies and groupings I include are meant to serve as examples of an approach to teaching the poem's similes, not as a comprehensive reading of them or of the poem.

A Brief Introduction to Epic Simile

Definitions of simile and its relation to metaphor vary, but philosophers from Aristotle to Quintilian to Christine Brooke-Rose identify simile as a figure that names both parts of a likeness or comparison and that signals the comparison with a marker such as *like* or *as*. Aristotle specifies that although similes can "do the same thing" (ποιοῦσι . . . τὸ αὐτό) as metaphors, a simile is "less pleasing because longer and because it does not say that this *is* that" ἧττον ἡδύ, ὅτι μακροτέρως καὶ οὐ λέγει ὡς τοῦτο ἐκεῖνο (*On Rhetoric* 1410b). Quintilian similarly observes that "[o]n the whole *metaphor* is a shorter form of *simile*, while there is this further difference, that in the latter we compare some object to the thing which we wish to describe, whereas in the former this object is actually substituted for the thing" (8.6.8). Brooke-Rose excludes similes from her study *A Grammar of Metaphor* because, as she points out, they "do not present any syntactic problems: the formula 'A is like B' or 'B . . . , so A', however lengthened or developed, is always the same, and both terms are always given" (14).

Definitions of "epic" or "extended" simile also vary, but most note the presence of a second marker that signals the conclusion of the comparison. Catherine Addison, for instance, observes that similes "always state both of their terms; they also label their terms clearly by means of comparative tags" (498). Addison specifies that "[i]n longer similes, the singular vehicular tags, 'like' or 'as,' usually give way to the double markers, 'just so' and 'so' (and their cognates), to label and connect tenor with vehicle over significant textual distance" (498–99). Some scholars have found it productive to sort figures that work by comparison into narrower categories. Jonathan Ready, for instance, explores the "spectrum of degree of likeness between tenor and vehicle in the epics" and identifies three categories of Homeric figures: similes, comparisons, and likenesses. He demonstrates how the *Odyssey* poet "exploits the existence and nature of this comparative spectrum for thematic and rhetorical effects" (453). Addison similarly suggests that "a sliding scale of 'literalness' and 'figurativeness' can be used to classify different simile types on a continuum" (498).

For the purposes of teaching the *Odyssey*, I count as "epic" those similes whose vehicles are detailed enough to function as a short digression and that signal the return to the tenor with a marker such as "just so." Even though an epic simile's markers clearly signal a point of departure from and return to the main narrative, epic similes can be disorienting nonetheless: their mini-digressions relocate readers in an alternate world for long enough to divert them from their journey through the poem's main world. The digressive vehicle of an epic simile distracts readers from the tenor, at least momentarily.[3] Highlighting this distraction, Ziva Ben-Porat asserts, "The processing of a multiplied simile, even when it does not end in misunderstanding or unresolved ambiguities, is necessarily an interrupted cognitive process" (755). And Addison points out, "While the vehicle's world becomes more developed, so the reader's excursion becomes less of a flash and more of a sojourn" (500).

Critics perceive various effects of a simile's interruptions and sojourns. In her study of the *Iliad*, Susanne Wofford observes, "Being tropes of disjunction as well as relation, the similes . . . could in principle allow one to see the two parts of the epic distinctly: they open a space for a reading that could begin to identify, and even criticize, the poem's ideological claims by showing how an ethical system was constructed out of a resistant material by the operation of various poetic figures" (2). Wofford suggests, however, that "although many similes appear to bring an alternative system of values into the poem, they more often work to the contrary, to aestheticize and to naturalize the story of war, thereby rendering it poetically and culturally acceptable" (2). In contrast, Ben-Porat points out that "[a]mong the many devices which contribute to the equation of opposites, the simile has a privileged position." Ben-Porat argues that "the interpreter of the Homeric text, guided by the inconsistencies and abundant details, comes to see the identification of predator with prey, of hunger with satiation, . . . of brutal slayer of men with helpless bird" (759–60). In reading the similes, my students often discover that, like the Ithaca that is at first unrecognizable to Odysseus when he returns home, the detour of an epic simile can make the world of the main narrative seem less familiar, and its social order and values less certain.

Civilized and Monstrous, Human and Animal: Odysseus as a Lion

Asking students to look closely at the series of similes comparing Odysseus to a lion helps them consider what it means to be human in the world of the *Odyssey*. Although Odysseus's slaughter of the suitors can be understood as an act of justice, the similes blur the line between human justice and animal instinct and lead students toward a more nuanced understanding of Odysseus's return to Ithaca.

It is Menelaus who speaks the first epic simile in the poem when, outraged by Telemachus's report on the suitors at Odysseus's palace, he foretells Odysseus's return:

> As when a deer in the lair of a powerful lion
> lays down her newborn suckling fawns
> and searches hills and grassy valleys
> to feed, while the lion comes back to his den
> and brings disgraceful death to both the fawns,
> just such a death will Odysseus bring to those men.
>
> ὡς δ᾽ ὁπότ᾽ ἐν ξυλόχῳ ἔλαφος κρατεροῖο λέοντος
> νεβροὺς κοιμήσασα νεηγενέας γαλαθηνοὺς
> κνημοὺς ἐξερέῃσι καὶ ἄγκεα ποιήεντα
> βοσκομένη, ὁ δ᾽ ἔπειτα ἑὴν εἰσήλυθεν εὐνήν,
> ἀμφοτέροισι δὲ τοῖσιν ἀεικέα πότμον ἐφῆκεν,
> ὣς Ὀδυσεὺς κείνοισιν ἀεικέα πότμον ἐφήσει. (4.335–40)

Menelaus's simile imagines Odysseus returning to his palace as a lion returning to its lair and the suitors as newborn fawns deposited by their mother-deer who goes to look for pasture. The simile's explicit point of comparison is that Odysseus will kill the suitors just as certainly as the lion "brings disgraceful death" to the powerless fawns. It emphasizes how dangerously out of place the suitors are in Odysseus's home and how natural and certain it is that Odysseus will slaughter them.

However aptly this scene of lion and deer predicts Odysseus's slaughter of the suitors, it also raises questions about the human interactions that occur when Odysseus arrives home to Ithaca. What, you might ask students, is the effect of imagining the suitors as helpless, newborn fawns, unable to accompany their mother as she "searches hills and grassy valleys," where her grazing will give her the strength to suckle her young? If the simile implies a kind of foolish innocence in what the suitors are doing, what does it suggest about Odysseus's unwillingness to spare them? If the suitors are like fawns, is Penelope—or are the suitors' parents—like the deer who deposits them in the lion's lair? After students observe how the simile figures Odysseus's slaughter of the suitors as an act of animal territorial instinct rather than an act of human justice, they will be ready to consider questions such as the following: Does the simile justify Odysseus's slaughter of the suitors as part of the natural order or call it into question as inhuman? Students also benefit from being prompted to notice how the simile's comparison of Odysseus to the lone, powerful lion is not entirely fitting: although Odysseus does bring death to the suitors and is the only one strong enough to string his bow, he succeeds through cunning strategy and with human and divine assistance.

Later, once Odysseus has returned to Ithaca and is planning his attack on the suitors, we hear Menelaus's prophetic simile again: Telemachus quotes it when telling his mother about his visit to Sparta (17.126–31). Then, after Odysseus has killed the suitors, the simile echoes in the narrator's description of how Eurycleia sees her victorious master:

> She found Odysseus among the men he had killed,
> splashed with blood and filth like a lion
> who goes on his way after eating an ox at pasture;
> all his chest and his jowls on both sides
> are bloody, terrible to see face to face;
> so Odysseus was spattered, hands and feet.

> εὗρεν ἔπειτ᾽ Ὀδυσῆα μετὰ κταμένοισι νέκυσσιν,
> αἵματι καὶ λύθρῳ πεπαλαγμένον ὥς τε λέοντα,
> ὅς ῥά τε βεβρωκὼς βοὸς ἔρχεται ἀγραύλοιο·
> πᾶν δ᾽ ἄρα οἱ στῆθός τε παρήϊά τ᾽ ἀμφοτέρωθεν
> αἱματόεντα πέλει, δεινὸς δ᾽ εἰς ὦπα ἰδέσθαι·
> ὣς Ὀδυσεὺς πεπάλακτο πόδας καὶ χεῖρας ὕπερθεν. (22.401–06)

Although this simile echoes Menelaus's, it includes a noteworthy variation. Instead of likening Odysseus to a lion who returns to his lair where fawns have intruded, it likens Odysseus to a lion who attacks a domesticated animal. In contrast to Menelaus's simile, which figures Odysseus's slaughter of the suitors as prompted by territorial instinct, as an act of reclaiming his home where others have trespassed, the narrator's simile figures the slaughter as prompted by hunger, as an act of hunting for food while trespassing upon another's property. What does this variation, where Odysseus's return home is imagined as an intrusion upon another's property, add to our understanding of his homecoming?

Furthermore, in its images of bloody eating, the simile recalls the Cyclops Polyphemus, who rejects Odysseus's plea that he and his men are guests and suppliants who, Odysseus insists, should be granted gifts "as is proper for hosts and guests" ἥ τε ξείνων θέμις ἐστίν (9.268). When Polyphemus instead snatches two of Odysseus's men "like puppies" ὥς τε σκύλακας and smashes them "to the ground" ποτὶ γαίῃ before eating them (9.289), he is compared to a lion: "Then cutting them limb from limb he prepared his dinner; / he ate like a mountain-bred lion—leaving nothing—/ guts and flesh and marrow-filled bones" τοὺς δὲ διὰ μελεϊστὶ ταμὼν ὁπλίσσατο δόρπον· / ἤσθιε δ' ὥς τε λέων ὀρεσίτροφος, οὐδ' ἀπέλειπεν, / ἔγκατά τε σάρκας τε καὶ ὀστέα μυελόεντα (9.291–93). Here the men's powerlessness when facing the merciless giant is emphasized by Polyphemus's knocking them "like puppies" and being compared to "a mountain-bred lion" who eats every last morsel of his prey. This link between Polyphemus and Odysseus as lions engenders further comparison. Like the suitors in Ithaca, Odysseus and his men enter Polyphemus's home without having been invited and help themselves to his food. Like Polyphemus, Odysseus slaughters his uninvited guests, including Leodes, who supplicates and begs for mercy (22.310–29). In the main narrative, Odysseus emphasizes how different the Ithacans are from the Cyclopes, who, he points out, lack councils, common laws, tilled land, and ships that would enable them to visit other people (9.106–15, 125–29). But Odysseus's and Polyphemus's kindred roles in these similes reveal that they both act outside the norms of civilized human society, especially in their refusal to show mercy to suppliants and guests.[4] Asking students to trace the lion similes linking Odysseus and Polyphemus helps them to see how the distinctions between Ithacans and Cyclopes, civilized and monstrous, human and animal, are not as clear as Odysseus or the poem's narrator might claim and makes space for criticism of Odysseus's choice to exact justice through violence.

Immediately before returning to Ithaca, Odysseus lands on Scheria naked, famished, and alone, his raft having been destroyed by Poseidon. Here, where Odysseus is most like a hungry lion, he acts least like the animal to whom he is compared. Upon being awakened by girls playing ball, Odysseus wonders if he has heard the voices of nymphs or humans. The narrator describes Odysseus's approach to the girls:

> And he went like a mountain-bred lion who, trusting his strength,
> advances through rain and wind, and his two eyes
> blaze; and he comes after oxen or sheep
> or deer of the wilderness, and his belly bids him
> even to enter the close sheepfold to attack the sheep;
> thus with the fair-haired girls Odysseus meant
> to mingle, naked though he was; for need had come to him.

> βῆ δ' ἴμεν ὥς τε λέων ὀρεσίτροφος, ἀλκὶ πεποιθώς,
> ὅς τ' εἶσ' ὑόμενος καὶ ἀήμενος, ἐν δέ οἱ ὄσσε

δαίεται· αὐτὰρ ὁ βουσὶ μετέρχεται ἢ ὀΐεσσιν
ἠὲ μετ' ἀγροτέρας ἐλάφους· κέλεται δέ ἑ γαστὴρ
μήλων πειρήσοντα καὶ ἐς πυκινὸν δόμον ἐλθεῖν·
ὣς Ὀδυσεὺς κούρῃσιν ἐϋπλοκάμοισιν ἔμελλε
μίξεσθαι, γυμνός περ ἐών· χρειὼ γὰρ ἵκανε. (6.130–36)

Although in this moment Odysseus's need is much like that of the lion to whom he is compared, the simile ultimately calls attention to how Odysseus does not act like a lion when he approaches the girls. Not only does he not use force, he does not supplicate by touching Nausicaa's knees. Instead, he uses "pleasing words" ἐπέεσσιν . . . μειλιχίοισι (6.143): Odysseus foregoes even ritualistic touch for the uniquely human means of speech to satisfy his hunger and achieve his desire. His use of words rather than force in Scheria contrasts starkly with his refusal of all negotiation or reparations offered him once back in Ithaca.

Tracing these lion similes invites students to consider how Odysseus compares to a lion who attacks and eats its prey and how he compares to Polyphemus, a giant who lives alone and lacks many elements of culture. The similes compel students to think about the relation between human motivation for justice and animal instinct for food and territory, and they raise questions about where revenge fits on the human-animal spectrum. Particularly in the context of the allegedly civilized Ithacans and savage Cyclopes, the similes invite students to consider the nature of Odysseus's homecoming, the kind of order it reestablishes, and the costs of Odysseus's absence and return.

Home and Away: Odysseus as Mother Cow and Fatherland

Whereas the poem's similes figuratively transform men into animals, Circe does so literally. After Odysseus successfully avoids Circe's magic and persuades her to release his men from their pig forms, he returns to his ship to retrieve the men who had stayed behind. Odysseus describes his reunion with his distraught, weeping companions:

As when calves who live in the fields greet the cows of the herd
when [the cows] come home to the farmyard sated with grazing,
[and the calves] all together skip to meet them, nor can the pens
hold them, but lowing constantly they run, circling
their mothers; so those men, when they caught sight of me,
huddled around me weeping; it seemed to them in their hearts
as if they had come to their fatherland and the very town
of rugged Ithaca, where they were born and raised . . .

ὡς δ' ὅτ' ἂν ἄγραυλοι πόριες περὶ βοῦς ἀγελαίας,
ἐλθούσας ἐς κόπρον, ἐπὴν βοτάνης κορέσωνται,
πᾶσαι ἅμα σκαίρουσιν ἐναντίαι· οὐδ' ἔτι σηκοὶ

ἴσχουσ', ἀλλ' ἁδινὸν μυκώμεναι ἀμφιθέουσι
μητέρας· ὣς ἐμὲ κεῖνοι, ἐπεὶ ἴδον ὀφθαλμοῖσι,
δακρυόεντες ἔχυντο· δόκησε δ' ἄρα σφίσι θυμὸς
ὣς ἔμεν ὡς εἰ πατρίδ' ἱκοίατο καὶ πόλιν αὐτὴν
τρηχείης Ἰθάκης, ἵνα τ' ἔτραφεν ἠδ' ἐγένοντο . . . (10.410–17)

Without their leader, who they fear has perished, Odysseus's men are like calves left in their pens while their mother cows are out at pasture. Whereas Circe's magic transforms the men at her palace into pigs who weep once they are restored to men, Odysseus's simile transforms the men left weeping at the ship into calves who cluster around their mothers. What is the effect of imagining Odysseus venturing out on Circe's island as a mother cow feeding at pasture before returning to her young? Odysseus's simile comparing the men to calves is followed immediately by another that compares the men's experience of Odysseus's return to their own homecoming: "it seemed to them in their hearts / as if they had come to their fatherland" δόκησε δ' ἄρα σφίσι θυμὸς / ὣς ἔμεν ὡς εἰ πατρίδ' ἱκοίατο (10.415–16). If, as the comparison implies, the men feel like they are in a foreign land when their leader is absent and at home when he returns, to what extent does being at home depend on a person, rather than a place? The similes' inversions are twofold. First, the men, who have not left the temporary home of their ship, nonetheless feel away from home without their leader. Second, although Odysseus returns to the ship, the men remain far from Ithaca, a home to which they never return. Whereas Circe's drugs and magic transform Odysseus's men into pigs who forget their home and weep with Odysseus once they are restored to human form, Odysseus's simile transforms the men left at the ship into calves who remember home.

Instead of reembarking on the journey home to Ithaca, Odysseus brings his men to Circe's palace, where they spend a full year feasting. Not until his men urge, "It is time now: remember our fatherland!" ἤδη νῦν μιμνήσκεο πατρίδος αἴης (10.472), does Odysseus ask Circe to send them on their journey home. Although Odysseus had evaded being changed into animal form, and although he had persuaded Circe to restore the form of his men, feasting and sleeping with the goddess nonetheless result in his forgetting home—the very effect of Circe's drug he had resisted with Hermes's help. Are the bodily desires of sex, eating, and sleeping that lead to forgetting home more animal than human? And, if so, how do we understand that the men's "minds remain the same" (νοῦς ἦν ἔμπεδος ὡς τὸ πάρος περ [240]) even as the drug makes them "forget their homeland altogether" ἵνα πάγχυ λαθοίατο πατρίδος αἴης (236)? Although transformation of men into animals is linked to forgetting home, it is the farm animals in the similes who remember their mothers, who make them feel at home. The distinctions between human and animal are blurred throughout.

Indeed, when Odysseus finally does make it back to Ithaca, his old, neglected dog, Argos, wags his tail when he realizes that Odysseus is nearby (17.301–02). Whereas countless Ithacans fail to recognize the king, who has been transformed by Athena into an old beggar, Argos sees and acknowledges his master with his last strength before dying. Eumaeus's guard dogs have similarly keen abilities to see through disguise. Although Telemachus does not see Athena arrive, the dogs do, and, the narrator tells us, "they did not bark. / With a whimper they backed across the hut, struck with fear" καί ῥ' οὐχ ὑλάοντο, / κνυζηθμῷ δ' ἑτέρωσε διὰ σταθμοῖο φόβηθεν (16.162–63).[5] These animals see through corporeal form to recognize essence, a skill said to be characteristic of gods.[6] What, then, do these similes suggest about how identity is recognized in a world of disguise and shape-shifting? Do animals share some forms of perception with gods that humans do not share? To what extent does being home depend on a place? To what extent does it depend on a person? And what does it mean for a man or an animal to feel at home?

Victor and Vanquished: Odysseus as a Weeping Widow

As book 19 reveals, Odysseus's homecoming is dependent not only on his surviving and reclaiming his palace and kingship but also on his being recognized and acknowledged as Odysseus, the man who departed twenty years earlier. Had he died at Troy, he would have been recognized with a hero's funeral, but his journey home threatens an unsung death: along with his body, his identity could be buried at sea or forever hidden on Calypso's island. When, in book 5, Poseidon wrecks his raft, Odysseus cries out, "Three and four times blessed were those Greeks who died then, / in the broad land of Troy" τρισμάκαρες Δαναοὶ καὶ τετράκις οἳ τότ' ὄλοντο / Τροίῃ ἐν εὐρείῃ (306–07). Odysseus wishes he had died when the Trojans attacked him near Achilles's corpse and explains, "Then I would have received my funeral rites, and the Greeks would have spread my glory" τῷ κ' ἔλαχον κτερέων, καί μευ κλέος ἦγον Ἀχαιοί (311). Telemachus, aware that his identity is tied to his father's, complains to Athena (disguised as Mentor) that the gods have made his father "invisible" ἄϊστον (1.235) and explains that his dying at Troy would have been preferable: "All the Greeks would then have made a tomb for him, / and he would have won great glory for his son hereafter. / But now the storm winds have snatched him away: / he is gone, unseen, unknown . . ." τῷ κέν οἱ τύμβον μὲν ἐποίησαν Παναχαιοί, / ἠδέ κε καὶ ᾧ παιδὶ μέγα κλέος ἤρατ' ὀπίσσω. / νῦν δέ μιν ἀκλειῶς ἅρπυιαι ἀνηρείψαντο· / οἴχετ' ἄϊστος, ἄπυστος . . . (1.239–42). Such desired fame is earned by heroic acts of war that are represented in song. And yet Odysseus weeps when he hears that his feats in Troy have been memorialized.

Before revealing his identity to the Phaeacians, Odysseus asks Demodocus to sing the story about the wooden horse. The narrator describes Odysseus's reaction when the bard sings of how Odysseus, "like Ares" ἠΰτ' Ἄρηα (8.518), had helped sack Troy:

> Odysseus
> dissolved in tears that wet his cheeks beneath his eyelids.
> As a woman weeps, falling and embracing her dear husband,

who falls in front of his city and his people,
trying to ward off the pitiless day for his town and its children—
and she, seeing him dying and fighting for breath,
wails, throwing herself around him; and [the enemy], behind her,
striking with their spears her back and shoulders,
lead her away into slavery, to have toil and woe,
and her cheeks are wasted with the most pitiful grief—
even so did Odysseus weep pitiful tears.

αὐτὰρ Ὀδυσσεὺς
τήκετο, δάκρυ δ᾽ ἔδευεν ὑπὸ βλεφάροισι παρειάς.
ὡς δὲ γυνὴ κλαίῃσι φίλον πόσιν ἀμφιπεσοῦσα,
ὅς τε ἑῆς πρόσθεν πόλιος λαῶν τε πέσῃσιν,
ἄστεϊ καὶ τεκέεσσιν ἀμύνων νηλεὲς ἦμαρ·
ἡ μὲν τὸν θνῄσκοντα καὶ ἀσπαίροντα ἰδοῦσα
ἀμφ᾽ αὐτῷ χυμένη λίγα κωκύει· οἱ δέ τ᾽ ὄπισθε
κόπτοντες δούρεσσι μετάφρενον ἠδὲ καὶ ὤμους
εἴρερον εἰσανάγουσι, πόνον τ ἐχέμεν καὶ ὀϊζύν·
τῆς δ᾽ ἐλεεινοτάτῳ ἄχεϊ φθινύθουσι παρειαί·
ὣς Ὀδυσεὺς ἐλεεινὸν ὑπ᾽ ὀφρύσι δάκρυον εἶβεν. (8.521–31)

At the moment Odysseus hears that he has become the subject of song, and that his invasion of Troy has warranted comparison to the god of war, Odysseus weeps like a woman whose husband has been killed while defending their home against invaders. Paradoxically, the song is evidence that Odysseus's identity lives on, but it makes Odysseus feel like a woman being brutally stripped of her identity. Whereas at Troy Odysseus was a victor, like the man leading a war widow off into slavery, in the simile he is like the woman who has lost her husband, her freedom, and her home.[7] What has Odysseus lost? Still away after twenty years, does he feel that he too may have lost his home in the war he helped win? In joining the grief of the victorious war hero and the defeated war widow, the simile troubles the idea that achieving *kleos*, being recognized in the songs of bards for having lived the life of a hero, is an adequate substitute for *nostos*, being recognized by people at home while living an everyday life.[8] This simile's surprising comparison opens space for criticism of heroic values as it compels students to grapple with the losses of war.

Self and Other: Odysseus and Penelope as Shipwrecked Sailors

Similes that cast characters in unexpected roles, like Odysseus as a war widow, prompt students to contemplate the nature of identity and the relation between self and other. Asking students to observe and ponder an inversion in an epic simile helps them ask questions about seemingly fixed familial and social roles.

Consider, for, instance, the moment Odysseus, shipwrecked by Poseidon, sees Scheria's shore:

> and he saw land nearby,
> keeping sharp watch, lifted up by a great wave.
> As welcome to his children is the life
> of a father who lies ill, suffering strong pains,
> wasting for a long time, and a hateful divinity hounds him—
> [as welcome as that father's life] when the gods release him from harm,
> so welcome to Odysseus did the land and woods appear.

> ὁ δ᾽ ἄρα σχεδὸν εἴσιδε γαῖαν
> ὀξὺ μάλα προϊδών, μεγάλου ὑπὸ κύματος ἀρθείς.
> ὡς δ᾽ ὅτ᾽ ἂν ἀσπάσιος βίοτος παίδεσσι φανήῃ
> πατρός, ὃς ἐν νούσῳ κεῖται κρατέρ᾽ ἄλγεα πάσχων,
> δηρὸν τηκόμενος, στυγερὸς δέ οἱ ἔχραε δαίμων,
> ἀσπάσιον δ᾽ ἄρα τόν γε θεοὶ κακότητος ἔλυσαν,
> ὣς Ὀδυσῆ᾽ ἀσπαστὸν ἐείσατο γαῖα καὶ ὕλη. (5.392–98)

As the simile begins, Odysseus corresponds most directly to the father. Like the sick father who has been "hound[ed]" by a "hateful divinity," Odysseus, tormented by Poseidon, is barely alive, and like the children in the simile, Telemachus will feel great joy to see his father return alive. But eventually the simile interrupts these more obvious correspondences with its explicit comparison of the shipwrecked Odysseus's joy at seeing land to the children's joy at seeing their father's life restored. What do the shifting identities in this simile—from father to child—reveal about Odysseus's identity and his struggle to return home? Does the simile suggest that, although Odysseus is father and king, his identity nonetheless is dependent on those of others, as a child's identity is tied to his father's?

In book 23 identities shift again when the shipwrecked swimmer becomes the vehicle of the simile describing Penelope once she finally recognizes her husband:

> He wept, holding his loyal wife who fit his heart.
> As when land appears welcome to swimmers
> whose well-built ship on the sea Poseidon
> smashes, struck by wind and strong waves,
> and few escape from the gray sea to the land
> by swimming, and much brine encrusts their skin,
> gladly they step onto land, escaping harm,
> so welcome to her was her husband as she looked upon him,
> and she did not stop embracing his neck with her white arms.

> κλαῖε δ᾽ ἔχων ἄλοχον θυμαρέα, κεδνὰ ἰδυῖαν.
> ὡς δ᾽ ὅτ᾽ ἂν ἀσπάσιος γῆ νηχομένοισι φανήῃ,
> ὧν τε Ποσειδάων εὐεργέα νῆ᾽ ἐνὶ πόντῳ

ῥαίσῃ, ἐπειγομένην ἀνέμῳ καὶ κύματι πηγῷ·
παῦροι δ᾽ ἐξέφυγον πολιῆς ἁλὸς ἤπειρόνδε
νηχόμενοι, πολλὴ δὲ περὶ χροῒ τέτροφεν ἅλμη,
ἀσπάσιοι δ᾽ ἐπέβαν γαίης, κακότητα φυγόντες·
ὣς ἄρα τῇ ἀσπαστὸς ἔην πόσις εἰσοροώσῃ,
δειρῆς δ᾽ οὔ πω πάμπαν ἀφίετο πηχεε λευκώ. (232–40)

Once again, the correspondences the simile first evokes are eventually reversed. "Holding his loyal wife who fit his heart" suggests that Penelope is "as welcome" to Odysseus "as the land to swimmers." The details about the sailors—Poseidon wrecking their ship and their skin all caked with brine—likewise recall Odysseus's experiences. But then the simile reorients us and asserts that it is Penelope's gladness to see her husband that is like what the shipwrecked swimmers feel at the sight of land. As it starts, the simile suggests that Penelope will be like the shore upon which Odysseus has landed, but as it concludes, the simile instead identifies Penelope as the drowning sailor and Odysseus as the land. The simile eventually names Penelope, the wife in danger of losing her home and identity, as the shipwrecked sailor saved by her husband's return, but the simile's reversal hints that Odysseus's identity is likewise dependent on his wife. The blurring of their roles—who has been at sea and who on land, who at home and who away—suggests an interdependence from which both of their identities emerge.

To be home, these similes reveal, is paradoxically to be like and not like yourself. In the poem's first two lines, the poet asks the Muse to tell the story of the *polutropon* man, literally the "much turned" man or the man "of many ways." In his disguises and in the many tropes about him, Odysseus is indeed a man of many turns: child and father, man and woman, king and beggar, bard and subject of song. Homecoming turns out to be the process of recognition of some shared likeness that transcends social roles, however fixed those roles may be.

Hearing Demodocus's story restricts Odysseus to the role of audience to his identity, whereas arriving home allows him to experience his identity as the man he is comes into alignment with the stories about him. Like Odysseus, Penelope is not comforted by stories of her fame. When beggar-Odysseus tells her "your glory reaches the wide heaven" ἦ γάρ σευ κλέος οὐρανὸν εὐρὺν ἱκάνει (19.108), she counters, "If that man were to return and care for my life, / my glory would be greater and finer" εἰ κεῖνός γ᾽ ἐλθὼν τὸν ἐμὸν βίον ἀμφιπολεύοι, / μεῖζόν κε κλέος εἴη ἐμὸν καὶ κάλλιον οὕτω (19.127–28). Moreover, Penelope is wary of accepting Odysseus's physical form as a reliable sign. After the revenge, when Athena restores and enhances Odysseus's appearance (23.156–58), Penelope observes, "I know well what you were like / when you left Ithaca on your long-oared ship" μάλα δ᾽εὖ οἶδ᾽ οἷος ἔησθα / ἐξ Ἰθάκης ἐπὶ νηὸς ἰὼν δολιχηρέτμοιο (23.175–76), but she does not acknowledge her husband until he tells the story of their bed. For Odysseus and Penelope, to be home is to engage in the dangers and promises of mutability, to realign their histories and memories with their mutable corporeal shapes, to tell each other their stories, to recognize and be recognized through likeness and difference. This process, the poem suggests, rivals any fixed story of one's identity, however famous or immortal: it is what Odysseus chooses when he rejects Calypso's offer of immortality and instead risks obliteration to journey home.

The *Odyssey*'s epic similes provide students with an experience akin to Odysseus's dilatory homecoming: they repeatedly lead us away from the main world of the poem and back again, revealing surprising likenesses and disturbing differences.[9] The similes don't promise the Sirens' perfect knowledge or the bard's spellbindingly pleasurable song: they compel us, rather, to read the imperfect signs of an obscure world and to keep moving. They invite us to understand homecoming not as the end of a journey but rather as the process of discerning identities of self and other in a shape-shifting world. As the poem concludes, Odysseus will leave home again and journey to a distant place where the form of his oar will be misread as a winnowing fan. There, far from the sea, he will sacrifice to Poseidon. The poem's final line tells us that Athena has kept Mentor's form. The *Odyssey*'s similes prepare us to feel at home in a world of errant human understanding where we might just recognize the divine.

NOTES

I am thankful to the late Philip Schwartz for many years of conversation about the *Odyssey* and to Tommy Fagin, Mike Johnson, Laura Levine, Cara Murray, and Sarah Spieldenner for their discerning questions and suggestions about this essay.

1. The terms "tenor" and "vehicle" are adopted from I. A. Richards's terms for the two parts of a metaphor: the tenor is "the underlying idea or principal subject which the vehicle or figure means" (97). Some scholars instead use the terms "target part" and "base part" (e.g., Ben-Porat 739).

2. Translations in this essay are by Lillian Doherty.

3. As Erich Auerbach points out in his analysis of Eurycleia's discovery of Odysseus's scar, a Homeric digression "seeks to win the reader over wholly to itself as long as he is hearing it, to make him forget what had just taken place" (4).

4. I ask students to compare Odysseus's refusal to show mercy to a suppliant with an episode in the fictitious story he tells to Eumaeus—namely, that his life was spared by a merciful Egyptian king whom he had supplicated in the midst of battle. This comparison further calls into question Odysseus's refusal to grant mercy (14.278–84).

5. In contrast, many human beings fail to recognize Athena. For instance, in book 1 the suitors fail to recognize that it is Athena visiting in the form of Mentor, and in book 3, Nestor recognizes Athena only after she "flew away . . . / in the appearance of a sea eagle" ἀπέβη . . . / φήνῃ εἰδομένη (371–72).

6. As the narrator remarks of Hermes's arrival to Ogygia, ". . . nor did Calypso, radiant goddess, fail to recognize him at sight, / for the deathless gods are not unknown to each other, / even if one lives at a distance" . . . οὐδέ μιν ἄντην / ἠγνοίησεν ἰδοῦσα Καλυψώ, δῖα θεάων, / οὐ γάρ τ᾽ ἀγνῶτες θεοὶ ἀλλήλοισι πέλονται / ἀθάνατοι, οὐδ᾽ εἴ τις ἀπόπροθι δώματα ναίει (5.77–80).

7. Helene Foley remarks that this simile "perhaps suggests how close Odysseus has come in the course of his travels, and in particular on Calypso's island, to the complete loss of normal social and emotional function which is the due of women enslaved in war" ("'Reverse Similes'" 20). She argues that the poem's "reverse similes . . . seem to suggest both a sense of identity between people in different social and sexual roles and a loss of stability, an inversion of the normal" and suggests that "these similes can be interpreted as a significant part of a larger pattern of social disruption and restoration in the epic" (8).

8. I have found that directing students to Odysseus's underworld encounter with Achilles's spirit furthers their consideration of the desirability of *kleos*. Achilles's spirit rejects Odysseus's praise of him as the "greatest by far of the Greeks" μέγα φέρτατ᾽ Ἀχαιῶν (11.478) and asserts, "I would rather be above ground and work as a hired man for another, / a landless man with little livelihood, / than rule over all the dead who have perished" βουλοίμην κ᾽ ἐπάρουρος ἐὼν θητευέμεν ἄλλῳ, / ἀνδρὶ παρ᾽ ἀκλήρῳ, ᾧ μὴ βίοτος πολὺς εἴη, / ἢ πᾶσιν νεκύεσσι καταφθιμένοισιν ἀνάσσειν (11.489–91).

9. As Laura Slatkin observes, "The *Odyssey* represents the journey of return (*nostos*) not as a direct path between two discrete points but as a process of shifting back and forth among recollection, recognition, projection, and anticipation in which past, present, and future dovetail, are refracted in the imagination, and become reconfigured" ("Homer's *Odyssey*" 317). The epic similes repeatedly take the poem's audience on this journey in small.

Remaking Kinship: Reading the *Odyssey* after the *Iliad*

Bruce M. King

In courses that center on the Western humanities, the *Odyssey* is often read after the *Iliad*, and for many students it is with the *Odyssey* that the lineaments of something like a familiar social and emotional world begin to emerge. This sense of recognition is especially the case in the field of kinship: the relations of parent and child and of husband and wife, the psychological cross-currents and collective rituals of coming-of-age and of marriage, the relation of close kin to the social structures of household and community, and the resultant sense of a self that is defined by its various and often shifting social ties. In these aspects of the *Odyssey*, readers begin to discern a familiar and familial world, even as that world is—in poetry—being newly made out of the wreckage of the *Iliad*. One subsequent remit for teachers of the *Odyssey* is to recover and foreground that very newness, and with it the non-inevitability, and even the strangeness, of the particular structures of kinship and of patriarchy—familiar and overfamiliar—that are formed and (mostly) valorized over the course of the *Odyssey*. By focusing our readings from the *Odyssey* on the poem's thematic determinations about who is admitted to, and who is excluded from, kinship as a "mutuality of being,"[1] we can open up conversations about the cultural preconditions, choices, and representations that have come to constitute the seemingly familiar or, rather, the seemingly natural.

In the study of kinship, the work of culture is often mystified by claims of blood and generation, as if the making of "kin" stands apart from, or beneath, cultural form and signification and as if senses of "kin" that extend beyond the immediately familial are secondary or negligible. If we read instead for junctures in the text when a "mutuality of being" is widened or narrowed, offered or refused, when others are made kin—and so admitted to relations of positive reciprocity and to claims of standing and recognition—or not, then we may also come to see the creative force of the *Odyssey* in shaping collective ideas of community, as well as of exclusion. And so, too, in our classrooms we can then begin to recover something of the history, local scope, and malleability of the forms of kinship as well as their susceptibility to pressure, reimagination, and creative work. And in these conversations about the *Odyssey*, we may then also regain the attention and imagination, both historical and prospective, of students for whom the structures of patriarchy, if all too familiar, have come to seem less and less as inevitabilities.

The generative power of the *Odyssey* in the field of kinship comes into particular focus when set against the precedent narrative of the *Iliad*. This is not because the composition of the *Odyssey* is later than that of the *Iliad*. Both poems emerge from the same tradition of oral performance, and crucially, each has a complementary knowledge of the other; mutual avoidance is also mutual awareness—and competition.[2] The two poems do, of course, present a sequence—the fall of Troy and the westward return of the surviving heroes, preeminently Odysseus—though not a history, at least not a recoverable one. Rather, the two poems construct a contrast between two fundamental stances toward, or evaluations of, collective life itself. While the *Iliad* is no less engaged than the *Odyssey* in questions of kinship and forms of community, it is altogether warier of the claims of the social order to primary loyalty or to a privileged capacity to remediate division, whether within the community or within the individual. The *Iliad*'s thematic focus rests upon a warrior camp that is itself riven by conflict and whose sole purpose is the destruction of Troy; both camp and city are without futures. Achilles himself—the "best of the Achaeans"—subjects the governing allegiances of that camp to scathing, dismantling criticism and comes to be an enemy not only of the Trojans but also, in the period of his withdrawal, of the Achaeans; he is wholly and destructively apart from any "mutuality of being." In the *Iliad*, the figure of the wanderer, of the exile, consistently shadows and chastens the totalizing claims of social necessity.[3] From this point of view, the primary work of the *Iliad* is negation, both of the heroic social order and of its forms of praise and poetry. The charge of the *Odyssey*, then, is to reassemble, if in radically different form, the pieces—of the hero, of kinship, and of community—that the *Iliad* has scattered upon the Trojan Plain. In the set of readings that follow, I revisit some of the principal forms of Odyssean kinship by contrast and in response to the *Iliad* so as to see those forms in the making. We might then also see that the familiar patriarchal forms of the *Odyssey* are neither natural nor inevitable nor without alternative but are, rather, one response to the wreckage of the *Iliad*, brought to completion by the *Odyssey*'s active determinations about who is and who is not to be included within a system of kinship, within a "mutuality of being."

Perhaps the most sorrowful of Odysseus's encounters in Hades is with the shade of his mother, Anticlea. Elsewhere in his adventures, Odysseus is the hero who consistently turns defeat into victory; he is the comic trickster who invariably fulfills his desire, however outrageous, to gain, for example, both poles of a choice that had in the *Iliad* been absolute: he will have both fame and a long life. Odysseus's meeting with his mother, however, remains unredeemed, impossible to convert into victory or unqualified self-praise. The shade of Anticlea, after recounting Penelope's fidelity and Laertes's retreat to the country, where "he sleeps in the dust, with the slaves" εὕδει, ὅθι δμῶες ἐνὶ οἴκῳ / ἐν κόνι (*Odyssey* 11.190–91), narrates her own death (11.197–207):

> "[And I too, like Laertes, grieved for you] and I was undone and fell
>   to fate.
> Neither did the keen-sighted Arrow-shooter
> attack and kill me with her painless shafts in the palace,
> nor did any disease come upon me, which most often
> with terrible wasting takes life from the body,

> but longing for you, for your cleverness, brilliant Odysseus,
> and for your gentleness, carried off my honey-sweet life."
> So she spoke, and then I, anxious of heart,
> wanted to take hold of the spirit of my dead mother.
> Three times I rushed forward, and my impulse drove me to hold her,
> But three times from my hands, like a shadow or even a dream,
> she flew away, and the grief became all the sharper in my heart.[4]

> 'οὕτω γὰρ καὶ ἐγὼν ὀλόμην καὶ πότμον ἐπέσπον·
> οὔτ' ἐμέ γ' ἐν μεγάροισιν ἐΰσκοπος ἰοχέαιρα
> οἷς ἀγανοῖς βελέεσσιν ἐποιχομένη κατέπεφνεν,
> οὔτε τις οὖν μοι νοῦσος ἐπήλυθεν, ἥ τε μάλιστα
> τηκεδόνι στυγερῇ μελέων ἐξείλετο θυμόν·
> ἀλλά με σός τε πόθος σά τε μήδεα, φαίδιμ' Ὀδυσσεῦ,
> σή τ' ἀγανοφροσύνη μελιηδέα θυμὸν ἀπηύρα.'
> ὣς ἔφατ', αὐτὰρ ἔγωγ' ἔθελον φρεσὶ μερμηρίξας
> μητρὸς ἐμῆς ψυχὴν ἑλέειν κατατεθνηυίης.
> τρὶς μὲν ἐφωρμήθην, ἑλέειν τέ με θυμὸς ἄνωγε,
> τρὶς δέ μοι ἐκ χειρῶν σκιῇ εἴκελον ἢ καὶ ὀνείρῳ
> ἔπτατ'. ἐμοὶ δ' ἄχος ὀξὺ γενέσκετο κηρόθι μᾶλλον. (11.197–208)

Anticlea perished neither of disease nor of old age but of "longing"—πόθος (*pothos*; line 202)—for Odysseus and his "gentleness" (203). *Aganophrosunē*—the word that is here translated as "gentleness" ("kindness" also works)—appears only here in the *Odyssey* and connotes a quality otherwise little seen in its hero, whose return home requires rather the trickster's ruthlessness, a frequent and remorseless cutting of losses in the cause of individual return. Anticlea's recollection of Odysseus's *aganophrosunē*, reciprocal to her own "honey-sweet life" (203), bespeaks, if fleetingly, a realm of private converse and respite and perhaps, too, an Odysseus for whom the maternal tie is an affective center—an Odysseus, that is, at odds with the normative masculine voice and *telos* of the poem. Moreover, Anticlea's evocation of that other—gentle, maternally centered, and largely repressed—Odysseus elicits from Odysseus himself a response of escalating grief and guilt, enacted in his effort, three times repeated, three times in vain, to embrace his mother's shade. Odysseus's living journey to Hades is itself the trickster's surpassing feat, but the death of the mother, with the sense of responsibility and of guilt it provokes, as well as the depth charge of the relation otherwise repressed, proves irremediable, beyond the resignifying power of Odysseus's characteristic *mētis* (μῆτις), or "cunning." In the futile repetition of Odysseus's grasp, an audience sees something of the return of the repressed: a love for the mother that the patriarchal ends of the *Odyssey*—the (re)marriage of the faithful wife, the reunion with father and son—cannot ultimately accommodate, precisely because the bond of mother and son is without social correlate. There is neither house nor city in Greek experience that finds its foundation in the unbroken or unerased or unsuppressed relation between mother and son. Anticlea's very name, which means "Anti-Fame," would seem to register her oblivion in the remainder of the *Odyssey*, even as it limns a larger cultural forgetting of the mother, whether in the forging of heroic or of civic identity. But here in Hades, if briefly, the repression of the maternal—upon which so much of western kinship and community takes form—is registered and is a cause of grief. ". . . and the pain in my heart was all the sharper" . . . ἐμοὶ δ' ἄχος ὀξὺ γενέσκετο κηρόθι μᾶλλον (11.208).

Odysseus's attempt to embrace Anticlea's ghost bears comparison to the likewise futile attempt of Achilles to embrace the ghost of Patroclus late in the *Iliad*. Patroclus's *psukhē* ("spirit") appears to Achilles in a dream and asks that Achilles perform his burial rites, so that he might join the other spirits—"images of the weary dead" εἴδωλα καμόντων (23.72)—in Hades and, more poignantly, that Achilles ensure that the ashes of the two ultimately be joined in a single urn (23.83–92). Achilles assents to the ghost's requests (23.96), even as he would also embrace Patroclus's *psukhē*, as if to keep it within the upper world (*Iliad* 23.97–102):

> "But stand close to me; even if fleeting, let us embrace
> each other and take solace in the painful dirge."
> So Achilles spoke and reached out for him with his arms,
> but he did not grasp him; the spirit went below, like smoke,
> with an eerie cry . . .
>
> 'ἀλλά μοι ἆσσον στῆθι· μίνυνθά περ ἀμφιβαλόντε
> ἀλλήλους ὀλοοῖο τεταρπώμεσθα γόοιο.'
> ὣς ἄρα φωνήσας ὠρέξατο χερσὶ φίλῃσιν
> οὐδ' ἔλαβε· ψυχὴ δὲ κατὰ χθονὸς ἠΰτε καπνὸς
> ᾤχετο τετριγυῖα . . . (*Iliad* 23.97–101)

As Anticlea slips from the reach of Odysseus, so, too, does Patroclus from Achilles; the *psukhē* "is something"—ἦ ῥά τίς ἐστι—as an amazed and baffled Achilles says, but "there is no heart within" ἀτὰρ φρένες οὐκ ἔνι πάμπαν (*Iliad* 23.103–04). And as in the *Odyssey*, the inability to catch the *psukhē* of the beloved dramatizes a loss that is absolute and unrelieved. For Achilles, the loss of Patroclus brings a grief, and a guilt, that is without possibility of mitigation, whether in social ritual or in any more private or personal mourning. Achilles's loss, moreover, in contrast to Odysseus's loss of Anticlea, is of a beloved who is not blood kin; indeed, Achilles proclaims the loss of Patroclus to be beyond that of male kin:

> I can suffer nothing worse than this,
> not even if I should hear that my father is dead,
> who now, I think, somewhere in Phthia weeps,
> at the loss of the son I am, who now in a foreign land

fight Trojans for Helen, who rouses cold fear;
or the death of my own son, who is raised for me in Skyros,
if godlike Neoptolemus is still alive.

οὐ μὲν γάρ τι κακώτερον ἄλλο πάθοιμι,
οὐδ' εἴ κεν τοῦ πατρὸς ἀποφθιμένοιο πυθοίμην,
ὅς που νῦν Φθίηφι τέρεν κατὰ δάκρυον εἴβει
χήτεϊ τοιοῦδ' υἷος· ὃ δ' ἀλλοδαπῷ ἐνὶ δήμῳ
εἵνεκα ῥιγεδανῆς Ἑλένης Τρωσὶν πολεμίζω·
ἠὲ τὸν ὃς Σκύρῳ μοι ἔνι τρέφεται φίλος υἱός,
εἴ που ἔτι ζώει γε Νεοπτόλεμος θεοειδής. (*Iliad* 19.321–27)

For Achilles, the death of his father or his son had been the prior terminus of conceivable loss, but that limit is now exceeded by his grief for Patroclus. The death of father and son is imagined, but only so as to articulate the loss of the comrade who now lies dead before him. In the *Iliad*, the irrecoverable *psukhē* is the singular and beloved male companion: "I can suffer nothing worse than this." Further, the grief of Achilles for Patroclus is not repressed in the *Iliad*, but is explosively manifest in a demonic, killing rage that is the subject of the last third of the poem. The ghost of Patroclus, who asks Achilles to release him in ritual to Hades, asks, as it were, that he might join Anticlea, among the repressed, at a structurally safe distance from the communities of the living. And yet, though Achilles does perform the requested rituals of burial for Patroclus, he himself remains haunted by his sorrow (see, e.g., *Iliad* 24.3–12) and the *Iliad* itself finds only an uneasy closure, in which loss and lament stand at the fore—of Achilles, of Priam, and of Andromache, Hecuba, and Helen in the closing threnody.

My guiding claim in this comparison between the ghosts of Anticlea and Patroclus is that both figures—the mother and the male comrade who surpasses kin—stand at interrogative odds to patriarchal structure in ways that are illustrative of the differences between Odysseus and Achilles and their respective poems. In the *Iliad*, the relation between Achilles and Patroclus is one of *philotēs* (φιλότης), which can connote relations of mutuality grounded in hospitality, in kinship, in martial camaraderie, and in sexual union.[5] Achilles and Patroclus traverse, as it were, the full semantic range of *philotēs*, as the word moves from its sense of "camaraderie," which is primary within the martial camp, to a sense that is singular, exclusionary, erotic, and, as it moves from the homosocial to the homoerotic, deeply destabilizing; as the suppressed bonds of the martial camp are brought to the surface, so, too, do they become explosive (see especially *Iliad* 16.97–100). The relationship of Achilles and Patroclus is queer not because the *Iliad* explicitly dramatizes the pair as sexual partners but because their relation stands apart from societal norms of kinship and masculine identity—and, indeed, places those norms under critique.[6]

The *Odyssey* is not a queer poem. Or if it is, its queerness—incestuous families, nymphs and witches, hybrids, cyborgs, asocial isolatoes—is relegated to the polymorphous perversity of Odysseus's travels in books 9–12. Odysseus may be a trickster, but his masculinity is perhaps his least malleable, least disguised, and least ironized trait (irony is saved for Telemachus).[7] Rather, as I suggested above, the *Odyssey* takes up the various negations of the *Iliad*, including of gender roles and kinship, and seeks to reassemble newly the disjecta membra in such a way that emergent kin relations are reinscribed within a larger community and become the basis for a reestablished political order.

The *Odyssey* begins with both the household of Odysseus and the larger community of Ithaca in disarray. While Odysseus's shape-shifting—his strategic indeterminacy—is the means of his survival and eventual return to Ithaca, the city itself has become chaotic in his twenty-year absence: the roles of king, father, and son have been destabilized; the alignments of family, city, and natural order have been skewed. Within the palace, Penelope's own indeterminacy, maintained by her wily deferrals of the suitors, has stymied the system of bride exchange with its attendant social function of making kinship and solidarity between families. Penelope's cunning, moreover, raises the specter of the bride's obverse: a woman free of male rule. Just who has the power to give Penelope away in marriage remains unresolved.[8] Penelope's indeterminacy within the social web of marriage is the means of her remarkable freedom, even as the poem itself, taken as a whole, shrinks from the possibility of an aristocratic woman who is not under the control of father, husband, or son. Penelope may be free, but she is also (so the poet assures us) unhappy; the return of Odysseus restores her happiness, even as it curtails her freedom by reinscribing her within a legible system of kinship.[9]

For Telemachus, Penelope is a perplexity. Her freedom within the palace exacerbates a deep male fear about paternity and the inscrutability of maternal knowledge. In response to the observation of Mentor (the disguised Athena) that he looks "uncannily" αἰνῶς (1.208) like Odysseus and the subsequent question as to whether he really is the son of that very man, Telemachus accuses his mother of being an unreliable narrator: "My mother says that I am his, but I, / I don't know; nobody ever really knows his own begetting" μήτηρ μέν τέ με φησὶ τοῦ ἔμμεναι, αὐτὰρ ἔγωγε / οὐκ οἶδ᾽· οὐ γάρ πώ τις ἑὸν γόνον αὐτὸς ἀνέγνω (1.215–16). Telemachus's response to Mentor is funny for its tetchy impatience with Dad's over-assuming and overbearing old friends, even as it also articulates a central problem of the *Odyssey* itself: the twenty-year absence of Odysseus—king, husband, father—has weakened the reach of past forms of patriarchal transmission into the present. A lack of knowledge of Odysseus and of his generation—people nowadays, as Telemachus says, prefer the "latest song" ἀοιδὴν . . . ἥ . . . νεωτάτη ἀμφιπέληται (*Odyssey* 1.351–52)—has rendered chaotic the forms and procedures of governance (as we see in the debacle of the public assembly in book 2 of the *Odyssey*) and has, for Telemachus, generated a crisis of self-knowledge; unknown and unknowable parents engender a self-knowledge that is stalled. If Telemachus is emblematic of a generation, he stands between fading and irretrievable models of the past and a future that is, as yet, not wholly formed.

In Telemachus's rejoinder to Mentor, he marks the mother's knowledge of the child's birth and identity as true by nature, as if somehow prior to language, even as her subsequent speech is always suspected of duplicity. The male's lack of full control—full knowledge—of the woman's body and experience (might she have had a secret lover?) is acknowledged and is made into a cause of distrust; such is the "logic" of patriarchy. Telemachus's response is ironized by the poet (yes, Telemachus, Odysseus really is your father! Penelope has had no other lovers!), even as it is both psychologically and culturally diagnostic. The subsequent work of the *Odyssey*, beginning with Telemachus's journey in search of knowledge of Odysseus, is to replace, as it were, what is understood to be the natural (but untrustworthy) knowledge of the mother with a discursive, cultural knowledge of paternity. For Telemachus, it is stories of the father that promise to make the natural fact of birth both individually and socially legible, and it is this collective knowledge—call it kinship—that carries status and legitimates claims to inheritance and to power in the city. Telemachus's disavowal of Penelope, as well as Odysseus's forgetting of Anticlea, enact, if in different emotional and poetic registers, the same social dynamic. The imperative to affirm the tie to the father, with its concordant claims of legitimation, inheritance, and rule, supersedes the mother's experience and knowledge of the child, as well as her claims upon the child.

One signal aspect, however, of book 1 of the *Odyssey*, and in particular of Telemachus's awkward reckonings with his parents, is that it raises those same cultural tensions to the surface of the text—the present mother's natural but untrustworthy knowledge, the absent father's promise of a synoptic, cultural knowledge, which would then affirm the son's identity—and thus makes thematic those very rifts and contradictions. In that way, we can understand the text itself as counter-ideological: it thematizes precisely what a less unsettled, less intellectually and politically generative text would smooth over or naturalize. The adolescent, occasionally illogical floundering of Telemachus (in books 1 and 2 as well as in book 22, lines 154–56) and the terrible grief of Odysseus at not catching hold of Anticlea, each in its own way, whether comic or tragic, offer occasions—in our own readerly wrestling with the text as well as in our classroom discussions—to think about the emotional and epistemological costs in making a system of kinship in which the father is the privileged signifier.

At the same time, it remains the case that the organizing *telos* of the *Odyssey* is the reunion of sons and fathers. Following the reconsummation of his marriage to Penelope in their famously immovable bed, Odysseus sets out on the following morning to Laertes's farmstead on the outskirts of the city. The revelation of identity that follows unsettles for its initial rawness of emotion and is, again, shadowed by the *Iliad*. Though Laertes, unlike Anticlea, has not succumbed to his longing for his son, he has imposed upon himself an exile from the city, a self-denying, melancholic labor from which he takes no profit or pleasure—a Hades of his own making. Laertes's exile is, moreover, a social death: in his first speech to his father,

Odysseus says that though Laertes gives much expert care, *komidē* (κομιδή [24.245, 247]), to the plants of his garden, he is himself like to a slave who receives no care, *komidē* (κομιδή), from his master:

> Good care [*komidē*] does not hold you, but you hold a grievous old age,
> and you are uncared for, dressed in squalor and shame.
> It's not because you're lazy that your master doesn't care [*komizdei*]
> for you,
> nor is anything of a slave visible
> in your looks and stature; you look like a man who is a king . . .
> But come, tell me this and speak it precisely:
> Whose slave are you?
>
> αὐτόν σ' οὐκ ἀγαθὴ κομιδὴ ἔχει, ἀλλ' ἅμα γῆρας
> λυγρὸν ἔχεις αὐχμεῖς τε κακῶς καὶ ἀεικέα ἕσσαι.
> οὐ μὲν ἀεργίης γε ἄναξ ἕνεκ' οὔ σε κομίζει,
> οὐδέ τί τοι δούλειον ἐπιπρέπει εἰσοράασθαι
> εἶδος καὶ μέγεθος· βασιλῆι γὰρ ἀνδρὶ ἔοικας . . .
> ἀλλ' ἄγε μοι τόδε εἰπὲ καὶ ἀτρεκέως κατάλεξον,
> τεῦ δμῶς εἰς ἀνδρῶν; (24.249–53, 256–57)

Laertes's care ensures the evident flourishing of the orchard, while his self-wounding carelessness of himself—"he was wearing a goatskin cap, so as to increase his sorrow" αἰγείην κυνέην κεφαλῇ ἔχε, πένθος ἀέξων (24.231)—blurs the meaning of his own appearance: though Odysseus says that Laertes, even in his abjection, has the physical presence of a king, he opts, finally, to address him as the slave of a careless master. All signifying connection between the body of the old king and his social status has been effaced by Laertes's melancholic despair at the loss of his son. The fall from king to slave is one articulation of the tragic life—"look to the end, for the god, having given a glimpse of happiness to many, overthrows them root and branch" σκοπέειν δὲ χρὴ παντὸς χρήματος τὴν τελευτὴν κῇ ἀποβήσεται (Herodotus 1.33)—which is here set in motion not by a generational curse or by a transgressive act but rather by the son who fails to return home and to protect the father.

Laertes's embodiment before the eyes of his son of the tragic consequence of a lack of filial care evokes the desolation of Achilles at the end of the *Iliad*. There, Achilles laments to Priam that he will never again see his father Peleus: "I give Peleus / no care [*komizdō*] as he grows old, . . . / since I sit here at Troy and make cares for you [Priam] and your sons" οὐδέ νυ τόν γε / γηράσκοντα κομίζω, . . . / ἧμαι ἐνὶ Τροίῃ, σέ τε κήδων ἠδὲ σὰ τέκνα (*Iliad* 24.540–42). Achilles's words are the *Iliad*'s concluding and most devastating formulation of the hero's life: without the possibility of extending active, positive care for one's own, the hero only makes negative cares for others.[10] Laertes's exilic, bereft existence is

Achilles's imagining of his father Peleus made manifest, while the "master" who has failed to care for Laertes is Odysseus himself—the son who will both protect and revive the father, even as he peaceably succeeds him.

But the turn from wanderer to kinsman and from tragedy to comedy is only achieved with considerable textual difficulty and friction. The prologue to the self-revelation of Odysseus to Laertes has often troubled readers: why does Odysseus remain in disguise before his father, when he is now, after the killing of the suitors, out of any immediate danger? Why does he insist on "testing" his father, whose misery is apparent and who surely conceals no danger to Odysseus, with yet another false story of wandering? Odysseus presents himself as "Tester" (*Epēritos*; 24.306) from the "Land of Wandering" (*Alubas*; 24.304).[11] Is lying—otherwise known as storytelling—so elemental to Odysseus's character that he simply cannot stop his own verbal invention, even when, as here, his listener, his own father, takes the story to imply his son's death, which in turn brings Laertes to the very threshold of death? Remarkably, the lines that describe the response of Laertes are the same as those that, in the *Iliad*, describe the response of Achilles to Patroclus's (actual) death:

> [Antilochus/Odysseus] spoke, and a black cloud of sorrow covered him
> [Achilles/Laertes];
> with both hands he [Achilles/Laertes] took up the sooty ash
> and poured it down over his head . . .
>
> ὣς φάτο, τὸν δ' ἄχεος νεφέλη ἐκάλυψε μέλαινα·
> ἀμφοτέρῃσι δὲ χερσὶν ἑλὼν κόνιν αἰθαλόεσσαν
> χεύατο κὰκ κεφαλῆς . . . (*Odyssey* 24.315–17; *Iliad* 18.22–24)

The mourning gestures of Laertes in response to the "death" of Odysseus are the same as those by which Achilles mourns Patroclus. So, too, as I noted in my discussion of book 11, lines 205–06, of the *Odyssey*, is Odysseus's attempt to embrace Anticlea in Hades the same as Achilles's attempt to embrace the *pshukhē* of Patroclus in book 23 of the *Iliad*. In each example, the Odyssean difference is that grief for blood kin—for mother, for son—replaces grief for the beloved, who is not kin. While the *Iliad* finds some of its most charged moments of beauty and challenge in the articulation of a love that eludes the social, the *Odyssey* valorizes the loves that are found within the *oikos* ("household"). Achilles's claim that the death of Patroclus is more grievous than that of father or son is contested: the great loves of the *Odyssey* are familial loves, neither metaphoric nor at odds with the social.

Perhaps it is the extremity of this turn to the comic, to kinship and to identity centered on the *oikos*, that accounts for the unsettling force, even the violence, of Odysseus's deception of Laertes and his subsequent revelation of self, which follows immediately upon Laertes's mourning for Odysseus and for himself:

The spirit roused in Odysseus, and now in his nostrils
a painful onslaught of breath rushed, when he saw his own father,
and he sprang on him and grappled him close and kissed him, then said,
"Here I am, father, this very one whom you seek;
I have come to my fatherland in the twentieth year."[12]

τοῦ δ' ὠρίνετο θυμός, ἀνὰ ῥῖνας δέ οἱ ἤδη
δριμὺ μένος προὔτυψε φίλον πατέρ' εἰσορόωντι,
κύσσε δέ μιν περιφὺς ἐπιάλμενος ἠδὲ προσηύδα·
'κεῖνος μέν τοι ὅδ' αὐτὸς ἐγώ, πάτερ, ὃν σὺ μεταλλᾷς,
ἤλυθον εἰκοστῷ ἔτεϊ ἐς πατρίδα γαῖαν.' (*Odyssey* 24.318–22)

The sight of Laertes's near-death—his catastrophic response to Odysseus's lies—knocks Odysseus out of his trickster-poet persona; he will not be responsible for Laertes's death, as he was for Anticlea's. The bodily intensity of Odysseus's response, like that of an adrenaline-driven warrior, attests to the very difficulty of that transformation. Odysseus is convulsed into a new life, from the careless wanderer who brings grief to all he encounters to a kinsman, bound in place by the reciprocities of familial and social structure. Odysseus's extraordinarily emphatic assertion of identity in book 24, line 321—"This one here . . . this very one I am"—following upon the physical shock provoked by Laertes's near-death, might be heard as a response to Achilles's negation of the value of the heroic life: "I give no care to my own, I only make cares for others" (*Iliad* 24.540–42). Odysseus's end will not be like that. His claiming of an ego, now lodged in the fatherland, comes only after, or is coterminous with, his overwhelming and painful recognition of care for the father. "No one really knows his own father," says Telemachus (*Odyssey* 1.216); but perhaps Odysseus does come to know his, if in a way that illuminates just how hard-won, just how near-tragic, that knowledge is: the father is, as it were, killed before he is rejuvenated; he is, in good psychoanalytic fashion, killed (in thought) by the son before he can be known by the son. Odysseus is Oedipus without the tragedy.[13]

As the *Odyssey* moves toward completion, the barely suppressed violence of the recognition of Odysseus and Laertes is set aside and the poem rushes toward its *telos* of patriarchal reunion and foundation. In the final mortal speeches of the poem, as Odysseus, Telemachus, and Laertes ready themselves for battle with the relatives of the suitors, each adds to a crescendo of challenge, boast, and affirmation:

"Telemachus, this now you'll know, as you go to the attack,
where the best of fighters distinguish themselves in battle:
Do not shame the blood-line of your forefathers, who in the past
in strength and in manhood excelled through all the earth."

In turn, thoughtful Telemachus answered back:
"Beloved father, you will see, if you really want, how in the fullness of this heart of mine
I will in no way shame your blood-line, as you expound."
So he spoke, and Laertes rejoiced:
"Beloved gods, what a day this is for me! I am overjoyed:
My son and the son of my son contest in courage."

'Τηλέμαχ', ἤδη μὲν τόδε γ' εἴσεαι αὐτὸς ἐπελθὼν
ἀνδρῶν μαρναμένων ἵνα τε κρίνονται ἄριστοι,
μή τι καταισχύνειν πατέρων γένος, οἳ τὸ πάρος περ
ἀλκῇ τ' ἠνορέῃ τε κεκάσμεθα πᾶσαν ἐπ' αἶαν.'
τὸν δ' αὖ Τηλέμαχος πεπνυμένος ἀντίον ηὔδα·
'ὄψεαι, αἴ κ' ἐθέλῃσθα, πάτερ φίλε, τῷδ' ἐνὶ θυμῷ
οὔ τι καταισχύνοντα τεὸν γένος, ὡς ἀγορεύεις.'
ὣς φάτο, Λαέρτης δ' ἐχάρη καὶ μῦθον ἔειπε·
'τίς νύ μοι ἡμέρη ἥδε, θεοὶ φίλοι; ἦ μάλα χαίρω·
υἱός θ' υἱωνός τ' ἀρετῆς πέρι δῆριν ἔχουσι.' (24.506–15)

Laertes's exultant recognition of the solidarity of fathers and sons—especially as enacted in martial competition—completes the *Odyssey*'s reconstruction of male kin. Laertes's delight and his now complete revivification are immediately affirmed by Athena (in her guise as Mentor), who extends the patriarchal line yet another generation by addressing Laertes with the patronymic "son of Arkeisios" Ἀρκεισιάδης (24.517) and by urging him to be the first to cast a spear in the battle with the suitors' kin. Laertes then strikes down Eupeithes (24.522–25), who is the father of Antinoos, the principal of Penelope's suitors and the first to be killed by Odysseus (22.8–21). For Eupeithes the loss of Antinoos is an "unforgettable sorrow" (*alaston penthos*; ἄλαστον πένθος [24.423]), which sets in motion an ineluctable desire for revenge. For all Laertes's joy in the reconstitution of his patriarchal line, that same narrow solidarity of kinship ensures irresolvable conflict: the loss that is "unforgettable" is also "unforgetting," as it compels the mourner to avenging violence.[14] The end of the *Odyssey* is, then, shadowed by the vengeful grief of others and by a correlative prospect of ever renewing violence; the triumph of Laertes can provide neither a stable future for Ithaca nor an end to the poem itself. Rather, the violent reciprocities of a community structured by loyalties of close blood kin provoke an extra-human intervention. It is Zeus's plan—and eventually his thunderbolt—that ultimately shapes the resolution of the poem:

Since brilliant Odysseus has taken vengeance on the suitors,
let them swear trustworthy oaths and let Odysseus be king forever,
and as for the deaths of their sons and brothers
let us now set down a forgetting; and let them be *philoi* to each other,
just as before, and let there be abundant prosperity and peace.

> ἐπεὶ δὴ μνηστῆρας ἐτίσατο δῖος Ὀδυσσεύς,
> ὅρκια πιστὰ ταμόντες ὁ μὲν βασιλευέτω αἰεί,
> ἡμεῖς δ' αὖ παίδων τε κασιγνήτων τε φόνοιο
> ἔκλησιν θέωμεν· τοὶ δ' ἀλλήλους φιλεόντων
> ὡς τὸ πάρος, πλοῦτος δὲ καὶ εἰρήνη ἅλις ἔστω. (24.482–86)

The unforgettable, unforgetting sorrows of the suitors' kinsmen are to be forgotten after all—though such a forgetting is at the very limits of mortal possibility and only follows upon the threat of a yet more devastating violence from Zeus (24.539–40).[15] This divinely ordained and mortally sanctioned forgetting of the deaths of male kin makes possible peace and prosperity, and also, I would suggest, augurs new and more expansive forms of kinship.[16] The men of Ithaca are to become *philoi* ("brethren," "comradely," and "loyal") to each other, though not, now, in the sense of blood kin but as constitutive, mutually sworn members of the same community—as, perhaps, citizens of the polis soon to come. In political kinship, they need love each other not as blood kin (nor as lovers) but as trustworthy, reciprocating members of a single heterogeneous community. From another, complementary point of view, the end of the *Odyssey* brings the mythical time of the epic as close as possible to the historical transformations of the late eighth century, including the development of the polis, within which ties of citizenship come to contest and sometimes surpass those of blood kin. But that history remains just over the horizon of the *Odyssey*'s end, adumbrated though not depicted. The poem itself, even as it looks to new, more expansive forms of kinship, also claims that Odysseus is to be king "forever" and that the bonds of kinship and loyalty of the Ithacans will be "just as before" ὡς τὸ πάρος (24.486). The *nostos*-poem insists, as a condition of its own genre, that Odysseus's return is a restoration, even as the *Odyssey* looks beyond its own enabling fictions of return and of temporal distance to the revolutionary transformations of kinship and state that mark its own historical moment.

The *Odyssey* conjoins the return of its hero with the reconstitution of close bonds of patriarchal kinship; the comic hero revives his father, even as he succeeds him without strife. But the poem also, in its closing measures, keenly registers the dangers of the endlessly reciprocating violence inherent in a kinship that is defined too narrowly. It is finally the forgetting—divinely ordained, mortally adjudicated—of prior male kin that makes peace possible and that points forward to more expansive, more productively political ideas of kinship. That final, full turn of the *Odyssey* to the claims of community is remarkable: forgetting is anathema to the traditional poet, whose art is predicated upon the memory of past heroes and their lineages. And in that turn from heroic tradition to Ithaca and to peace, we may also see a last general contrast to the *Iliad*, in which Achilles values the life of Patroclus beyond those of fathers and sons (see above, on *Iliad* 19.321–27), and the loss of Patroclus, the nonkin beloved, leads to Achilles's avenging, unforgetting rampage: to the very end of the *Iliad*, Achilles continues to remember and weep for Patroclus (24.3–9, 511–12). Moreover, Achilles's love for Patroclus claims a realm of singular value apart from the exchanges of the community—apart, at least in thought, from the norms and suasions of culture itself. For Achilles the loss of Patroclus puts the lie to the pretension that culture is sufficient to desire or to consciousness itself. Over the course of the *Iliad*, Achilles comes to inhabit, as it were, *Alubas*, the "Land of Wandering" (*Odyssey* 24.304)—the very place that Odysseus disavows in his final revelation of self to his father and his concordant location of that self in the "fatherland" (above, on 24.318–22). For Odysseus, paternal genealogy and place finally fix an identity, even as his poem then concludes with oaths that cast the prior solidarities of fathers and sons into oblivion; the past is to be forgotten for the sake of a newly made community, a new political possibility. The *Odyssey*, that is, looks not for places of refuge or vantage points apart from culture (Odysseus's wanderings in books 9–12 are uniformly, paradigmatically negative) but rather sets its concluding focus on community itself and on newly imagined forms of political kinship, on potentially more expansive "mutualities of being." Despite Zeus's assertion, Odysseus will not be king "forever" (24.483)—and that's a good thing. To gain such an end, the *Odyssey* seems even willing to cast its own tradition, its own fathers, into oblivion.

In reading and discussing the *Odyssey* with our students, the question of which works and which legacies of the Western tradition we might consign to oblivion—in the service of more expansive "mutualities" of collective life—has renewed force. The end of the *Odyssey* perhaps anticipates our own anxieties about how the intractable memory of, and the false nostalgia for, prior structures of kinship and community stifle our present aspirations for a collective life that more fully acknowledges the claims of all its members, including Anticlea and her sisters. For despite Zeus's best efforts to instill forgetfulness, the *Odyssey* remains very much with us, both as patriarchal charter and, perhaps more frequently than we sometimes think, as critique of the charter; at a minimum, I think we need to acknowledge that it is a tradition of conservative and sentimental interpretation we often castigate, rather than the poem itself, which delights in a regular subversion of the misapprehension that one signifier—"father"—brings unity and coherence to societies and to selves. Moreover, there also remains a crucial pedagogic value in working to show that kinship and patriarchy have histories, humanly made and remade, for better and for worse. We read the *Odyssey* for its abundant narrative pleasures, but also, and simultaneously, for its junctures of narrative unsettlement, where the underlying tensions of the poem rise to the surface, where the text itself is both most troubled and most resistant to easy closure. Those are often the junctures where kinship is, as it were, in the making—and where we might also apprehend that it might be made differently. When we read the *Odyssey* with the *Iliad*, we may enter into dialogues that spur us to articulate not only our own expectations of the political but our own senses of those values and those desires that elude cultural capture and form.

NOTES

1. Kinship as "mutuality of being" is a definition that I take from Sahlins, esp. 2, 2–6, and 18–37. In general, Sahlins prosecutes a compelling and uncompromising argument for understanding kinship wholly as cultural practice, apart from any notions of nature. Other work on kinship that underlies this essay includes Clastres 101–28; Pitt Rivers.

2. In Homeric studies, "Munro's law" holds that the *Odyssey*, though replete with references to the Trojan War, "never repeats or refers to any incident related in the *Iliad*" (Munro 325). The implications of Munro's law have been much discussed: see, e.g., Nagy, *Best* 15–25, on a "poetics of interaction"; Pucci 17–18, with notes; and more recently, Marks, "Epic Traditions." Pucci's book remains the most generative of studies of the relation between the *Iliad* and the *Odyssey*.

3. On the figure of the wanderer in the *Iliad*, see King. See Martin, "Hesiod's Metanastic Poetics," for an especially stimulating discussion of the figure of the *metanastēs* ("exile").

4. Translations throughout are my own.

5. On *philotēs* (φιλότης), see Chantraine, s.v. φίλος; Benveniste 1: 339–58; Landfester; Sinos.

6. See King and Kozak 41–45 for the full polemic.

7. Even when Odysseus has been reduced by the storm that follows him out of Fantasy Land to (in a simile) a "seed of fire" σπέρμα πυρός (5.490), he then reemerges, amongst the Phaiakian maidens, as a threateningly naked man, whose attempt to cover his genitals with a leaf and a "heavy hand" only draws further attention to that which is "hidden" (6.129, with the following simile of the hungry mountain lion).

8. See Katz 33–36 on the question of the *kurios* ("guardian") of Penelope.

9. Amongst much work on Penelope, see Katz; Felson; Zeitlin. On gender in the *Iliad* and the *Odyssey* more generally, see Felson and Slatkin as well as Rachel Lesser's essay in this volume.

10. On the centrality of care in the *Iliad*, see the study of Lynn-George, especially 16–19 on the passage cited here.

11. The name *Epēritos* (Ἐπήριτος) has a punning relation to the verbal root *peir-* (πειρ-), meaning "to test" or "to try out." The name appears in book 24 of the *Odyssey* (lines 216, 221, and 240), where it indicates Odysseus's intention to "test" Laertes. *Alubas* is built from the root *al-* (ἀλ-), which connotes "to wander."

12. In my translation I have tried to preserve some of the striking martial connotations of the language: the verbs *protuptō* (προτύπτω [319]) and *ephallomai* (ἐφάλλομαι [320]) are frequently used of the warrior in battle, as is the adjective *drimus* (δριμύς [319]), which is also used of the pain of childbirth (*Iliad* 11.270). The phrase τοῦ δ' ὠρίνετο θυμός ("his spirit within was roused" [318]) is used in the *Iliad* (9.595) when Meleager hears of the disasters that will afflict his kin and city if he does not fight—which he then rises to do. According to Heubeck and colleagues, "[T]he intensity of Odysseus' reaction . . . on seeing his father weeping with despair is described in words that are almost untranslatable" (3: 24.318–19).

13. In Barthes's words, "Death of the father would deprive literature of many of its pleasures. If there is no longer a father why tell stories? Doesn't every narrative lead back to Oedipus? Isn't storytelling always a way of searching for one's origin, speaking one's conflicts with the Law, entering into the dialectic of tenderness and hatred?" (47).

14. The adjective *alaston* (ἄλαστον) can connote both "unforgettable" and "unforgetting"; the former sense reflects the word's etymology as a privative derived from the verbal theme *lath-* (λαθ-), "to forget"; the latter sense connects the word to *alastōr* (ἀλάστωρ), an agent noun for an "avenging spirit," familiar from tragedy. Chantraine, s.v. ἀλάστωρ, discusses both senses and their interrelation.

15. The word for "forgetting" in line 485—*eklēsis* (ἔκλησις)—appears only here in Homer, while the word for "peace"—*eirēnē* (εἰρήνη)—also appears, rather tellingly, only here in the *Odyssey*; "prosperity"—*ploutos* (πλοῦτος)—appears only once elsewhere in Homer. The unique diction signals, I contend, a prolepsis or a prophecy of a new political settlement (see below). The *horkia*, the "oaths," of line 483 are sworn at line 546, in the poem's concluding sentence.

16. See Marks, *Zeus* 62–82 (especially 75–78) for other suggestive ways of reading the "forgetting" or "oblivion" imposed by Zeus at the end of the *Odyssey*.

Gender in the *Odyssey*: Significance and Ideology

Rachel H. Lesser

Gender is essential to the meaning of the *Odyssey*. The epic's first word is "man," and one of its projects is to set out ideals of heroic masculinity as performed successfully by Odysseus and unsuccessfully by most of the other men in the poem (Goldhill 1–2, 24). At the same time, women and goddesses are key players in the narrative, and the reconstitution of Odysseus's marriage with his wife, Penelope, is the epic's main goal; the nature of the female as represented in the *Odyssey* both explains Odysseus's driving desire for this reunion and determines his methods for achieving it. Insofar as gender is at its center, the *Odyssey* communicates a specific set of ancient Greek ideas about men and women and about gender roles, norms, and hierarchy,[1] which may be usefully compared with modern constructions of gender and gendered social organization. This essay is therefore designed as an aid for two kinds of undergraduate courses: literature courses that include the *Odyssey* and courses on the history of women, gender, and sexuality. I imagine students who are reading the *Odyssey* progressively over several class periods, and so I suggest inquiries aimed at successive portions of the epic and consider how gendered meanings and gender ideology come to light diachronically as the plot unfolds.

In its opening lines, the *Odyssey* introduces us to a man who has wandered much and suffered much after sacking Troy and who is now being detained by the goddess Calypso even as he "yearns for homecoming and his wife" νόστου κεχρημένον ἠδὲ γυναικός (1.13).[2] The epic's first four books go on to show what exactly Odysseus is missing and why he misses it through depiction of the human social world from which he is detached, not only the world of his son, Telemachus, and wife, Penelope, at his home in Ithaca, struggling to manage the unwanted suitors, but also the world of Nestor at Pylus and Menelaus at Sparta, where Telemachus journeys for news of his father and advice. These books (known collectively as "the Telemachy") therefore offer an essential introduction to the roles and occupations of Homeric men and women of various social classes and to their importance within the *Odyssey*'s narrative. Students may be divided into four groups to identify and report back on the activities and prerogatives of and expectations for elite men, non-elite men, elite women, and enslaved women and on the epic's relative interest in each of these categories of people.

At the top of the social hierarchy and at the center of narrative attention are elite men, whom Homer sometimes calls "heroes," including Odysseus, Telemachus, the suitors, the Ithacan gentry, Nestor and his sons, and Menelaus. They are landowners, who may have herds of cattle, sheep, goats, pigs, and even horses. They are also warriors and sailors, and if they were the right age or kings of their lands, they fought in the Trojan War. When not fighting, they spend their time playing games, feasting, conversing, and enjoying song and dance. They also visit other elite households, including for the purpose of courtship, and entertain high-status male guests in their own homes. On occasion, they gather formally in public to deliberate matters of interest to the community, as when Telemachus calls an assembly of the Ithacan men to complain about how the suitors abuse the household of Odysseus, the country's erstwhile king, and to ask for support in his search for news of his father (2.6–259). Finally, they take the lead in relating to the divine and in turn receive the gods' primary consideration: the elder Ithacan hero Halitherses is a seer who interprets the flights of birds (2.157–76); Nestor and his sons sacrifice and pray to Poseidon and Athena (3.5–9, 36–61, 178–79, 418–63); Telemachus is guided and watched over by Athena in his dealings with the suitors and in his travels.

Whereas Homer focuses his epic on the doings of the men of highest status, non-elite men exist in the poem only in their function of serving the elites. Thus, in the Telemachy, they are merely mentioned in passing, never starring in their own stories. They are heralds and attendants (*therapontes*) who facilitate the feasting, hospitality, and assembly of the elite; entertainers, such as the Ithacan bard Phemius (1.325–27) and the singer and acrobats who perform in Menelaus's palace (4.17–19); craftsmen, such as the goldsmith Laerces who gilds the horns of a sacrificial cow at Nestor's palace (3.425–38);[3] and enslaved individuals, such as Penelope's servant Dolius, who tends the orchard and whom the queen considers sending with a message to Odysseus's father Laertes (4.735–41). What non-elite and elite men share is occupation of public and semipublic spaces (such as the palace entrances and the banquet hall) and license to move between the home and the outside world.

Homeric (mortal) women, by contrast, stay inside the house in the Telemachy, except when participating in religious ritual. The Ithacan queen Penelope's first appearance in the narrative (1.328–64) is programmatic for establishing the appropriate place, activities, and power of elite women—and women in general—in Homeric society. On hearing Phemius singing in the banquet hall of the Greeks' baneful homecoming from Troy, Penelope, modestly chaperoned by enslaved women and veiled, descends from upper chambers to bid the bard to sing a different song that will not painfully remind her of her lost husband Odysseus. Telemachus, however, objects to Penelope's request and gives her the following order:

> going back into the house, take care of your own work,
> the loom and the distaff, and command your female attendants
> to busy themselves with their work; discourse [*muthos*] will be the concern of men,
> all of them, but me especially, for mine is the power in the house.

> εἰς οἶκον ἰοῦσα τὰ σ' αὐτῆς ἔργα κόμιζε,
> ἱστόν τ' ἠλακάτην τε, καὶ ἀμφιπόλοισι κέλευε

> ἔργον ἐποίχεσθαι· μῦθος δ᾽ ἄνδρεσσι μελήσει
> πᾶσι, μάλιστα δ᾽ ἐμοί· τοῦ γὰρ κράτος ἔστ᾽ ἐνὶ οἴκῳ. (1.356–59)

According to Telemachus, elite women are meant to keep quiet, stay sequestered in the inner, private parts of the home, and devote themselves to textile production and the supervision of the work of those whom they enslave, leaving authoritative speech to the men who exercise control over the household. Mary Beard (3–9) has analyzed this passage as the first witness of the ideological and real suppression of the female public voice that continues through the present day.[4]

The epic endorses this view of women's place by celebrating Penelope's compliance. The queen takes the "astute" (πεπνυμένον) command of her son to heart and returns without comment to her upper chambers to weep for Odysseus until Athena puts her to sleep (1.360–64). The narrator then immediately describes the suitors' prayers to lie next to her, establishing her as an object of desire—and validating Odysseus's own yearning for her—in the context of her adherence to the female gender norms laid out by Telemachus. Later we learn that Penelope's main activity for the past four years has been weaving and unweaving a shroud for her father-in-law Laertes in order to delay her remarriage to a suitor (2.93–110); by engaging in normative feminine labor, she has cleverly kept faith with Odysseus. After describing this "trick" (δόλον [2.93], δόλῳ [2.106]), the suitor Antinous praises her as surpassing all other women in weaving, wits, and wiles and recognizes that her deferral of the suitors, though depleting the household's resources, is bringing her "great fame" (*mega kleos*; 2.116–26).

Yet it turns out that Telemachus's articulation of female norms is more prescriptive than descriptive. The elite women that he encounters in his travels are less publicly silent and secluded than Penelope. Nestor's daughters, daughters-in-law, and wife Eurydice are present at the Pylians' sacrifice to Athena and raise a ritual ululation (3.450–52). Nestor's youngest daughter, Polycaste, helps care for their guest, washing, anointing, and dressing Telemachus (3.464–67). Most notably, Menelaus's wife, Helen, emerges from her bedchamber with her distaff and wool basket to join her husband in the Spartan banquet hall where he is entertaining Telemachus, and, as Menelaus is considering whether to inquire about his guest's identity, she speaks first to guess rightly who he is (4.116–46). Unlike Penelope, she remains with the men for the rest of the evening; furthermore, she drugs everyone with a medicine that makes one forget all evils and then continues the "discourses" (*muthoi*) with a story about how she assisted Odysseus when he came as a spy to Troy (4.219–64). Her drug keeps her auditors from objecting to this speech about the grievous past "when for the sake of me, dog-faced, the Achaeans / came to Troy" ὅτ᾽ ἐμεῖο κυνώπιδος εἵνεκ᾽ Ἀχαιοὶ / ἤλθεθ᾽ ὑπὸ Τροίην (4.145–46). Helen is an authoritative speaker who occupies a semipublic space and hosts a foreign guest together with her husband—and who once abandoned her husband and home to follow another foreign guest to Troy.

The problematics of her behavior are indicated not only by her self-abuse as "dog-faced"[5] but also by Menelaus's answering speech, in which the king provides a counternarrative of Helen's activities at Troy. He describes how she nearly derailed the Greek sack of Troy by standing outside the wooden horse with the Trojan prince Deiphobus and calling to the warriors hidden inside with the voices of their wives, trying to elicit a response (4.265–89). Here Menelaus suggests that Helen was a traitor to the Greek cause and points to the danger of her uncontrolled movement and speech, both of which are linked to her sexuality. We are left wondering whether Helen in Troy was a valuable aid to the Greeks, as she claims, or almost their undoing. Helen establishes the dual potential of women to be helpers or hurters of men, and introduces the difficulty of correctly identifying to which category a woman belongs (Wohl 34–37).

Whereas both Helen and Penelope are fully realized characters who receive considerable narrative attention, enslaved women, like non-elite and enslaved men, appear only in relation to the elites. Unnamed enslaved women provide service in the public areas of the palaces: they fetch water and prepare and serve food (1.136–40 = 4.52–56, 3.427–29); they bathe, anoint, and clothe guests (4.49–50); and they make up beds for them (4.296–301). Others accompany elite women wherever they go as attendants (1.331–35, 4.121–25, 4.760). Odysseus's and Telemachus's old nurse Eurycleia is one of the few named enslaved women in the Telemachy and has the most important responsibilities: she serves the master of the house, helping Telemachus to bed (1.427–42), and she is the steward of the palace storeroom who provisions Telemachus for his journey (2.337–80).

While the demands of enslavement keep most enslaved women from achieving the ideals of femininity laid out by Telemachus, Eurycleia's special status seems to be justified by her approximation of these ideals. She appears exclusively in the private areas of the house, and, though she dares to advise Telemachus against his voyage, she accepts his decision to persevere without protest and, on his command, commits herself to silence regarding his journey by swearing and keeping an oath not to tell Penelope that he has departed (2.361–78, 4.745–49). Thus Eurycleia, like Penelope, represses her opinion and voice (Fletcher 82–89), rating obedience to the male master above solidarity with the female mistress.[6]

Also like Penelope, she is sexually "chaste." Laertes, who bought Eurycleia with possessions worth twenty oxen "and honored her equally to his cherished wife" ἶσα δέ μιν κεδνῇ ἀλόχῳ τίεν, did not have sex with her in order to avoid angering his wife (1.430–33); now she is an old woman, implicitly beyond the age of sexual desirability. The narratorial commentary on Laertes's self-restraint—exercised to preserve marital harmony rather than for the sake of Eurycleia herself—reveals that it is the exception to the rule of masters' sexual exploitation of the women whom they enslave (Thalmann, "Female Slaves" 29; Wilson, "Slaves" 26–27); indeed, when Telemachus arrives in Sparta, the royal household is celebrating the marriage of Menelaus's son Megapenthes, who was born to him by an enslaved woman (4.10–12).

In sum, then, the human world of the *Odyssey* is an aristocratic patriarchy. The non-elite and enslaved of both genders serve the aristocracy, who direct their movements and activities. Regardless of class, women are contributors to the household and sexual objects, and are valued as such, the more so if they keep quiet, excel at their work, and channel their sexuality according to the wishes of the men who claim authority over them.

Elite men are at the center of the Telemachy's narrative: these books tell the story of Telemachus's maturation into a man capable of defending his household against the encroachment of other male aristocrats. Once the Homeric social structure and norms for female behavior have been apprehended, students may be asked to consider the negative and positive models of elite masculinity that are presented to Telemachus and the epic's external audience in this opening section of the *Odyssey*.

We are first confronted with examples of elite masculinity to avoid—Aegisthus and his counterparts on Ithaca, the suitors. Near the beginning of the epic, Zeus complains that mortals suffer "through their own recklessness" σφῇσιν ἀτασθαλίῃσιν (1.34), describing how Aegisthus married Agamemnon's wife and killed him on his homecoming despite the gods' warning, and then was himself killed in retribution by Agamemnon's son Orestes (1.32–43). The suitors likewise woo an absent man's wife and plot to murder his heir and surrogate, Telemachus (4.663–74). Telemachus resents them as disrespectful guests who have overstayed their welcome and are consuming his inherited wealth, specifically Odysseus's herds of sheep, goats, and cattle; the goddess Athena in disguise confirms his assessment, calling them "exceedingly insulting" ὑβρίζοντες ὑπερφιάλως (1.227) and wishing them dead (1.265–66). Finally, though the suitors kill and eat animals, they never sacrifice or pray to the gods. In the Telemachy and elsewhere, the suitors are repeatedly described as "arrogant" (*agēnores*) and "overbearing" (*huperēnoreontes*), terms that incorporate the stem for "man" (*anēr*) and can be more literally translated as "excessively manly" and "engaging in hyper-masculine behavior," respectively; that is, they demonstrate "lack of manly restraint" and "fail to take into account the needs and rights of other men" (Graziosi and Haubold, "Homeric Masculinity" 73–74)—or of the gods. In other words, the suitors' masculinity is toxic.

Surrounded by such poor role models, Telemachus needs outside guidance to learn how to be a proper man. His first teacher is Athena, disguised as Odysseus's Taphian guest-friend Mentes and then as the Ithacan elder Mentor; once he leaves Ithaca, he receives further direction from Nestor and Menelaus, his father's old friends, whose successful homecomings from Troy testify to their masculine excellence. Athena's initial lesson for Telemachus is to exercise his masculine prerogative of speaking: call an assembly and bid the suitors to depart and his mother to return to her father's house if she wishes to be remarried (1.272–78). Athena reiterates this lesson at Pylus when she urges Telemachus to approach Nestor directly for advice and allays his concern that he is not experienced enough in "discourses" (*muthoi*) to address his elder (3.14–28). Telemachus's second lesson—introduced by Athena and then echoed by Nestor—is to act boldly like Orestes: once he has learned his father's fate, he should devise and execute a plan to kill the suitors (1.294–302, 3.193–200). That is, Telemachus should utilize both speech and action to gain control over his household and eliminate his enemies. Ultimately, then, Telemachus must emulate Odysseus, who, according to Athena, "would set his hands on the shameless suitors" ὅ κε μνηστῆρσιν ἀναιδέσι χεῖρας ἐφείη (1.254). The goddess explains further: "Telemachus, you will not hereafter be cowardly or lacking understanding / if your father's excellent drive has been instilled in you, / such was he to bring both deed and word to fruition" Τηλέμαχ', οὐδ' ὄπιθεν κακὸς ἔσσεαι οὐδ' ἀνοήμων, / εἰ δή τοι σοῦ πατρὸς ἐνέστακται μένος ἠΰ, / οἷος κεῖνος ἔην τελέσαι ἔργον τε ἔπος τε (2.270–72). Odysseus is thus positioned as a paradigm of heroic masculinity.

At Sparta, Telemachus learns more about what it means to be like Odysseus when the royal couple tell stories about their experiences with his father. Helen describes an Odysseus who used disguise to spy on and kill the Trojans, and who did not trust her until she had sworn oaths not to reveal his identity (4.244–56): he is crafty—a quality emphasized by his signature epithet *polymētis*, "much-scheming"—and wary, skilled at ambush and a master of self-restraint. Menelaus highlights these same traits of Odysseus in his story of how the hero kept the Greek warriors from betraying themselves in the wooden horse when Helen mimicked their wives' voices (4.271–89). Moreover, he prefaces his account by affirming Odysseus's masculine exemplarity:

> I have come to know the resolve and disposition
> of many heroic men, and I have traveled over much land;
> but never have I seen with my eyes
> such a heart as belonged to Odysseus, steadfast in mind.
>
> ἤδη μὲν πολέων ἐδάην βουλήν τε νόον τε
> ἀνδρῶν ἡρώων, πολλὴν δ' ἐπελήλυθα γαῖαν·
> ἀλλ' οὔ πω τοιοῦτον ἐγὼν ἴδον ὀφθαλμοῖσιν
> οἷον Ὀδυσσῆος ταλασίφρονος ἔσκε φίλον κῆρ. (4.267–70)

Menelaus's own return from Troy was dependent on his performance of similar craftiness and endurance: he had to hide in the skin of a seal in order to catch the sea-god Proteus and then hold firm while the god changed shape in order to learn his way home (4.384–480). But Odysseus is not only cunning but also good in a fight: echoing Athena, Menelaus later asserts that Odysseus would destroy the suitors like a lion killing a doe and her fawns, remembering how the hero threw down his opponent in a wrestling match (4.333–46).

Nestor and Menelaus together teach Telemachus one final lesson in heroic masculinity: ensure that you have the gods on your side. Nestor instructs by example: on Telemachus's arrival, he is sacrificing to Poseidon, and after Athena's epiphany, he sacrifices to her and asks for "fame" (*kleos*; 3.380). His narrative of the Greeks' fraught homecoming from Troy is a cautionary tale of what happens when you have offended the gods; only once Nestor has sought an omen and sacrificed to Poseidon does he have smooth sailing and a quick return (3.132–85). Similarly, Menelaus recounts how the gods kept him in Egypt after he failed to offer them perfect sacrifices (4.351–53). When he first converses with Telemachus, Nestor wishes the young man the same favor that Athena had shown his father Odysseus, asserting that then the suitors would forget about marriage (3.218–24); after Athena reveals herself as Telemachus's guide, Nestor exclaims that this divine support augurs well for Telemachus's future (3.375–76).

When considering the next section of the *Odyssey*, the narrative of Odysseus's travels (books 5–12), one may begin by asking students how Homer reinforces in these books the ideals of elite masculinity presented in the Telemachy. We discover that when Odysseus and his companions fail to live up to these ideals, they suffer or die, whereas when Odysseus correctly performs this heroic masculinity, he triumphs over his enemies and moves closer to homecoming. The Cyclops episode in book 9 is a case in point. Odysseus gets himself and his men trapped in the man-eating Polyphemus's cave after he greedily remains as a guest in the Cyclops's home, like the rapacious suitors in his palace in Ithaca. Nevertheless, through a cunning and bold ambush of words (the "Noman" lie) and deeds (secretly fashioning a stake, drugging the Cyclops with wine and blinding him, then hiding under sheep), Odysseus manages to defeat Polyphemus and escape with half of his original party. Yet when the hero drops his guard and boastingly reveals his true identity, the Cyclops nearly scuttles Odysseus's ship; more seriously, he is enabled to call down a curse on Odysseus, setting his father Poseidon against the hero and drastically prolonging his grievous wanderings.[7]

The same pattern recurs in other episodes. For example, on Circe's island, Odysseus's companions get themselves turned into pigs after they openly approach the goddess's home, accept her invitation to enter, and eat her drugged food (10.220–43). While the survivor Eurylochus is ready to escape without these men, Odysseus sets out bravely to confront Circe and, with Hermes's help, tricks the goddess and forces her to guarantee his safety on oath, then liberates his men, earning Circe's extended hospitality and guidance in his journey home (10.261–574). Later, when Odysseus and his companions are stranded on Helius's island, the hungry men—again acting like the suitors—slaughter and eat the sun god's forbidden cattle after Odysseus has relaxed his vigilance and fallen asleep. On account of this impious transgression, allowed by Odysseus's failure of fortitude, Zeus causes shipwreck, bringing about the death of all of Odysseus's men and leaving the hero himself marooned on Calypso's island (12.260–453). In the end, Odysseus learns his lesson: when he finally makes it to the Phaeacians' land through the intervention of Hermes and the aid of Calypso and Ino, he employs the utmost caution to earn the hospitality of the princess Nausicaa, queen Arete, and king Alcinous, and waits until he has secured promises of conveyance home before he reveals who he is; lastly, Odysseus cements his hosts' goodwill with his enthralling story of his adventures at sea.

During his wanderings in books 5–12, Odysseus encounters a multitude of female characters—goddesses, mortal women, ghosts, and monsters—who together create a complex but largely consistent portrait of the female and her function in the *Odyssey*. I recommend examining a selection of these female figures in turn with students, asking in each case what messages she communicates about femininity and what her role is in the poem.

First, in book 5 we meet Calypso, whose name means "Concealer." She is nurturing: she rescued Odysseus from the sea and has taken care of him for seven years. She is also alluring: she sings and weaves (5.61–62), and is more beautiful and taller than Penelope (5.211–18). She offers the hero eternal (sexual) pleasure, but it comes at the cost of his mortal identity and homecoming, and she is more powerful than Odysseus, keeping him hidden on her island and in her bed against his will as he tearfully yearns for wife and home "since no longer was the nymph pleasing to him" ἐπεὶ οὐκέτι ἥνδανε νύμφη (5.153). She cannot, however, defy the will of the divine patriarch Zeus and ultimately helps Odysseus build a raft and sail away. Calypso represents the female as both caretaker and seductress, who not only nourishes but also threatens to distract and obscure the male with her sexuality; her considerable power can thwart Odysseus's will or be harnessed for his advantage.

Nausicaa (book 6) is a mortal and thus a less independent—and threatening—variant of Calypso. She, too, cares for Odysseus after he is shipwrecked and is interested in marrying him if he remains on the island (6.244–45). She, too, is desirable: like a goddess in beauty and height (6.16), she is twice compared to Artemis (6.102–09, 6.151–52), and the best Phaeacian young men woo her (6.34–35). Odysseus acknowledges Nausicaa's marriageability and the benefits of a good marriage by praying:

> May the gods grant you whatever you long for in your heart,
> a husband and home and like-mindedness [*homophrosynē*];
> for nothing is stronger and better than
> when two who are like-minded [*homophroneonte*] in their thoughts have a household,
> husband and wife; this causes many pains for those who hate them,
> but joys for those who love them; and they themselves are most famous.
>
> σοὶ δὲ θεοὶ τόσα δοῖεν ὅσα φρεσὶ σῇσι μενοινᾷς,
> ἄνδρα τε καὶ οἶκον καὶ ὁμοφροσύνην ὀπάσειαν
> ἐσθλήν· οὐ μὲν γὰρ τοῦ γε κρεῖσσον καὶ ἄρειον,
> ἢ ὅθ' ὁμοφρονέοντε νοήμασιν οἶκον ἔχητον
> ἀνὴρ ἠδὲ γυνή· πόλλ' ἄλγεα δυσμενέεσσι,
> χάρματα δ' εὐμενέτῃσι· μάλιστα δέ τ' ἔκλυον αὐτοί. (6.180–85)

Odysseus, however, already has a wife waiting at home, and, unlike Calypso, Nausicaa is too modest (6.273–88)—and not powerful enough on her own—to compel his sexual companionship. After the hero follows Nausicaa's advice to gain the favor of her influential mother Arete, who, along with Helen and, as we shall see, Clytemnestra, represents how ruling women have significant capacity to determine the fate of men, the Phaeacians bring him home to Ithaca. Both princess and queen are beneficent helpers of Odysseus, yet Nausicaa's sexuality, like Calypso's, would subsume Odysseus—ending his story and precluding future glory or return to his previous family and kingship—if he were to give in to her attractions and accept her father Alcinous's proposition for him to stay in Scheria and marry her, gifted with a house and possessions (7.311–15).

The goddesses and female monsters whom Odysseus describes meeting in his tale to the Phaeacians are far more sinister versions of Calypso and Nausicaa. The daughter of the Laestrygonian king directs Odysseus's men to her father's palace, where they find her mother to be a fearsome ogress and her father a cannibal, who rallies his giant subjects to kill and eat the men from eleven of Odysseus's twelve ships (10.103–32). As we have seen, the beautiful goddess Circe (book 10) entices half of his remaining companions into her palace with her singing and weaving, only to transform them into pigs; Odysseus must use a divine antidote to resist her decivilizing, dehumanizing magic and threaten her with his sword—a symbol of sexual dominance—to sleep with her safely (Wohl 24–25). Though she ultimately nurtures Odysseus and his crew and sends them on their way, the (alimentary and sexual) pleasures of her company make Odysseus forget himself for a full year on her island. Finally, the females in book 12 are pure peril: the Sirens, like Circe, lure men with their irresistible singing and keep them spellbound until they die, while the doggishly yelping monster Scylla and vaginal whirlpool Charybdis actually consume them. As Seth Schein observes, in the cases of all these females, "their menace is literally or symbolically sexual—specific instances of the general danger of being swallowed, engulfed, concealed, or obliterated" ("Female Representations" 19).[8]

At this point, one may ask students to consider how Athena, as she appears in the *Odyssey*'s first half, compares to the goddesses, women, and monsters previously discussed. Uniquely for a female, she repeatedly disguises herself, often in masculine form,[9] and unlike other goddesses, she acts with the mandate of Zeus, her father and the divine king; thus, Athena has an androgynous, male-identified aspect. As a virgin goddess, she is the only entirely asexual female in the poem, and—like the elderly Eurycleia, who is no longer a sexual object—she is unambiguously helpful to Odysseus and Telemachus in realizing themselves and achieving heroic fame (*kleos*), engineering the former's homecoming and the latter's maturation. Yet she is also typically feminine in directing her great intelligence, power, and agency exclusively at Odysseus (or his son) and existing in the *Odyssey* solely in relation to him and his adventures. Despite the *Odyssey*'s myriad female figures, the epic is androcentric, and focused particularly on Odysseus, its paradigmatic man. We see this androcentrism perpetuated even in the case of Odysseus's account of the famous women who he claims told him their stories as ghosts in the underworld (11.225–329): he introduces them as "all who were the best men's wives and daughters" ὅσσαι ἀριστήων ἄλοχοι ἔσαν ἠδὲ θύγατρες (227), and their narratives are entirely about their submission to a man or god in marriage (or rape) and the glorious sons that they bore (Doherty, *Siren Songs* 108–09).

Whereas Odysseus portrays these wives and mothers in a predominantly positive light, probably in a clever ploy to win his auditor Arete's favor (Doherty, *Siren Songs* 66–68, 95–99), his next interlocutor in the underworld, the ghost of Agamemnon, voices the epic's most explicit characterization of the sexualized female as mortally dangerous. He recounts how he was murdered on his return home by Aegisthus and his own "dog-faced" (κυνῶπις) wife Clytemnestra, who killed his enslaved concubine Cassandra over his body and did not even deign to close his eyes and mouth (11.409–26). Agamemnon goes on to assert that Clytemnestra, in contriving her husband's murder, has "poured down shame also on women to come, even the one who does good" κατ' αἶσχος ἔχευε καὶ ἐσσομένῃσιν ὀπίσσω / θηλυτέρῃσι γυναιξί, καὶ ἥ κ' εὐεργὸς ἔῃσιν (11.433–34), and he warns Odysseus not to disclose everything to Penelope despite her good character (11.441–46) and to arrive in Ithaca secretly "since no longer are women to be trusted" ἐπεὶ οὐκέτι πιστὰ γυναιξίν (11.456).

In the second half of the *Odyssey*, Odysseus, acting on Agamemnon's advice and now performing the epic's ideals of heroic masculinity to perfection, makes a clandestine homecoming through disguise, lies, and Athena's aid, and then, together with Telemachus and his loyal swineherd and cowherd, successfully takes his revenge on the suitors through a daring ambush in the banquet hall of his palace. In the last scene of the epic, Laertes, Odysseus, and Telemachus—hegemonic patriliny reconstituted—together bravely fight an armed mob of the dead suitors' kinsmen until Athena mediates a peaceful resolution (24.496–548).

Earlier, after the slaughter of the suitors, Odysseus finally reveals himself to Penelope and they enjoy a protracted night of sex, storytelling, and sleep in a culminating episode of narrative resolution (23.241–343). Penelope, in her cleverness and self-control in fending off the suitors and remaining faithful to Odysseus, has made possible these triumphs and pleasures and shown herself to be a "like-minded" match for her husband;[10] together, they have indeed become "most famous."[11] Yet the epic also raises questions about Penelope's desires and intentions, validating Odysseus's decision to keep his wife in the dark about his return, in three complex and critically contested scenes in books 18, 19, and 23. I suggest dividing students into small groups, assigning one scene to each group, and asking them to try to determine, with reference to their scene, Penelope's attitudes towards the suitors and Odysseus, and her agenda, and to compare her with other Odyssean females.

In the first scene (18.158–303), Athena inspires Penelope to appear before the suitors, "so that she might especially open up / the hearts of the suitors and become honored / more than before by her spouse and son" ὅπως πετάσειε μάλιστα / θυμὸν μνηστήρων ἰδὲ τιμήεσσα γένοιτο / μᾶλλον πρὸς πόσιός τε καὶ υἱέος ἢ πάρος ἦεν (160–62). Though Penelope seems bemused by her sudden urge to show herself, after Athena puts her to sleep and beautifies her, she goes downstairs, inspires the suitors' "desire" (*erōs*; 212), announces that she is ready to be remarried since Telemachus is grown, criticizes the suitors' consumption rather than provision of household goods, and then receives gifts from them while the disguised Odysseus observes everything with delight. Some interpret Penelope here as an unwitting pawn of Athena, being used to entrap the suitors and enrich Odysseus's household (e.g., Lesser 112–18), while others believe that she is guilefully manipulating the suitors to part with some of their wealth, using her feminine charms in the hope or knowledge of Odysseus's return (e.g., J. Winkler 147).[12] Most but not all agree that she is truly averse to the suitors: one scholar suggests that this scene represents Penelope's "resurgence of sexual interest in men" and parallels Nausicaa's sexual awakening vis-à-vis Odysseus (Van Nortwick 272–76; cf. Zeitlin 140).[13] In any case, it highlights Penelope's capacity to allure men (like Circe or the Sirens) as she indicates for the first time that she is willing to marry a suitor.

In the second scene (19.509–99), Penelope speaks to the disguised Odysseus during a private audience in the banquet hall after dinner. She describes her uncertainty about whether or not to remarry, and then asks her guest to help interpret her dream about how an eagle killed her pet geese, then identified himself as Odysseus and the geese as the suitors. The disguised Odysseus confirms her husband's imminent return, but Penelope doubts the dream's authenticity and announces her intention to hold a bow contest the next day and marry the victorious suitor. In her dream, Penelope weeps over the slaughter of the geese, which may represent positive feelings towards the suitors or ambivalence about Odysseus's return. It has been suggested that she sets the bow contest because she recognizes Odysseus and is colluding with him to kill the suitors (e.g., J. Winkler 154–55; Levaniouk, "Penelope" 24), or as another tactic to delay remarriage, or because she truly means to marry the suitor who proves himself Odysseus's equal for her own sake or Telemachus's (Felson 16–17; H. Foley, "Penelope" 102–04). Whatever the reason, by definitively planning remarriage in her husband's absence despite repeated indications of his impending arrival, Penelope invites comparison of herself to the unfaithful Helen.

In the third scene (23.1–232), Penelope refuses at first to acknowledge Odysseus after he has killed the suitors; her coldness provokes Telemachus's reproach and recalls the character of Clytemnestra (Katz 164). To prove Odysseus's identity, she tests him, craftily suggesting that their marriage bed—a metaphor for the integrity of their relationship—is no longer fixed in place; she thus not only elicits an indignant Odysseus's proprietary account of how he made the bed around a living olive tree but also brings up the possibility that she has been unfaithful (Zeitlin 122). After accepting Odysseus as her husband, Penelope defends her hesitant recognition by contrasting her circumspect reception of a foreign man with Helen's heedless elopement with the Trojan prince Paris. Though to all appearances Penelope has acted differently than Helen, her invocation of their similar circumstances makes the specter of infidelity loom large, and some understand her to be excusing Helen's adultery (e.g., Zeitlin 144; cf. Fredricksmeyer 489–91).

In these scenes, Homer gives no explicit account of Penelope's interiority and many opposing interpretations of her behavior are available (Murnaghan, "Penelope's *Agnoia*" 104). Her "indeterminacy" (as Katz describes it in the title of her book) suggests the unknowability of even "good" women and, consequently, their inherent untrustworthiness. Therefore, while Penelope represents the importance of the normative, devoted wife and mother for the aristocratic family, she is also portrayed as an uncertain exception to the rule of the perilous female, justifying male hegemony. Her superlative beauty and cunning intelligence make her desirable and valuable, but also all the more dangerous in her capacity to seduce and deceive men. The hero's dependence on his wife for achieving fame is thus shown to be a liability; women's threat must be neutralized by "depriving them of power" (Murnaghan, "Penelope's *Agnoia*" 108), as Odysseus does when he withholds his identity from Penelope. In this respect, the masculine heroic ideals of wiliness and wariness that the *Odyssey* promotes may be understood as a necessary corollary to the epic's view of women.

Finally, one may ask students how Telemachus's hanging of the twelve palace enslaved women "who poured shame on my head / and my mother, and slept beside the suitors" αἳ δὴ ἐμῇ κεφαλῇ κατ' ὀνείδεα χεῦαν / μητέρι θ' ἡμετέρῃ παρά τε μνηστῆρσιν ἴαυον (22.463–64) informs the epic's gender ideology. In one reading, these women are Penelope's doubles and foils, lower-class scapegoats who, because of their sexual association with the suitors, receive the punishment that "all of the unfaithful or potentially unfaithful women of the poem" deserve—thus allowing, conversely, for the unproblematic celebration of the elite Penelope's virtue (Fulkerson 346–47; see also Doherty, *Siren Songs* 159). Through their deaths, the danger of the sexually promiscuous woman is contained, and their example serves as a warning to all women to control themselves and maintain allegiance to their proper masters. However, Homer is reticent about the degree to which these enslaved women exercised any agency in their sexual liaisons; Odysseus even asserts to the suitors, "and you slept beside my slave women forcibly" δμῳῇσιν δὲ γυναιξὶ παρευνάζεσθε βιαίως (22.37). Moreover, the narrator compares the hanging women to ensnared birds and describes their deaths as "most pitiful" οἴκτιστα (22.468–72; Wilson, "Slaves" 30–34). From this perspective, the enslaved women are victims of Odysseus's and Telemachus's desire to regain control over their household and purify it of the memory of the suitors' dishonoring presence. In the midst of Odysseus's triumph, we are forced to confront how Homeric patriarchy denies women full autonomy and perpetrates violence (sexual and deadly) on their bodies, especially on those of the most disempowered—the enslaved.

NOTES

1. Cristiana Franco elucidates how Homeric epic transmits "cultural conceptions" concerning women and gender rather than being a reliable source for historical realities ("Women" 54–57).

2. Translations in this essay are my own.

3. The special narrative attention given to Laerces may reflect his professional identification with "cunning intelligence" (*mētis*; Detienne and Vernant), a quality that defines the epic's hero, Odysseus, who is also an excellent craftsman (woodworker). Additionally, since both craftsmen and bards are "public workers" (*demiourgoi*) welcome throughout the land (17.383–86), the *Odyssey* poet may see in Laerces a reflection of himself.

4. Beard's essay is well-suited as a secondary reading with the *Odyssey* in a course on the history of women and gender. On this exchange between Penelope and Telemachus, see Fletcher 78–80.

5. Franco argues that with this self-insult, Helen evokes the "dog as traitor" that has been enticed from its master by someone else offering treats, unable to restrain its desires properly (*Shameless* 151–55), and also the fawning dog that conceals a dangerous intent to bite (204–05).

6. Eurycleia is especially identified with the men of the house, while the similar enslaved woman Eurynome, who appears first in book 17, is Penelope's own servant; as Pedrick shows, Eurycleia gives good advice to Penelope, while Eurynome subtly advocates dishonorable behavior, initiating a patriarchal trope about the danger that the female confidante poses to a heroine's virtue. When discussing female speech in the *Odyssey*, I find it profitable to ask students whether the epic satisfies the Bechdel-Wallace test: Does it feature at least two women who talk to each other about something other than a man?

7. Heroes in the *Iliad*, the other great Homeric epic, regularly boast triumphantly over defeated opponents on the Trojan battlefield, thus promoting their own fame (*kleos*). By showing Odysseus's boast to be terribly misguided here, the *Odyssey* rejects this Iliadic model (Newton 11n20) and asserts self-restraint and dissimulation as new ideals of masculinity. On rivalry between the *Iliad* and *Odyssey* traditions in the area of male heroic ethics, see Edwards; Pucci.

8. On the sexual pleasure offered by the Sirens' song, see Schein, "Female Representations" 21.

9. In fact, Athena is the only other character in the poem besides Odysseus to take on a disguise (Doherty, "Athena" 34).

10. Penelope's comparison to a shipwrecked sailor reaching shore as she joyfully recognizes Odysseus (23.233–39) recalls Odysseus's own experiences at sea and indicates their "like-mindedness," as do other "reverse similes" in which she is compared to a lion (4.791–92) and to a good king (19.108–14) and Odysseus is compared to a bereaved wife (8.521–31). On these, see H. Foley, "'Reverse Similes.'" Doherty compares Penelope with both Odysseus and his divine patron Athena ("Athena").

11. Near the end of the *Odyssey* (24.196–98), Agamemnon's ghost attests to Penelope's "fame" (*kleos*), which the *Odyssey* itself disseminates together with that of Odysseus.

12. For extended discussion of the scene's ambiguity, see Katz 78–93.

13. When Penelope emerges earlier in the day to greet Telemachus, she is described as "like Artemis and golden Aphrodite" Ἀρτέμιδι ἰκέλη ἠὲ χρυσέῃ Ἀφροδίτῃ (17.37), recalling Nausicaa's comparison to the virgin goddess Artemis, while also linking the queen with the goddess of desire and sex, who, in one song of the Phaeacian bard Demodocus, cheats on her husband Hephaestus with Ares (8.266–366).

Polyphemus and Postcolonialism: The Island of the Cyclopes in the *Odyssey*

Kirsten Lodge

I currently teach the *Odyssey* at Midwestern State University Texas, as part of a course adapted from a required first-year introduction to great books course I taught at Columbia University, known as Literature Humanities. Because this is an introductory course, I do not spend much time on literary theory, but I endeavor to teach students to read against the grain by focusing not only on broader themes but also on close reading. I situate Homer's epic within the broader context of Greek colonialism, and I point out the exclusion of others' voices in Odysseus's adventure stories, considering that they are narrated entirely from Odysseus's point of view.

I harness students' natural enthusiasm at the beginning of each semester and have them read the *Odyssey* in full. In general, I problematize Odysseus's narration of his own epic adventures, considering that the truthfulness of his story is not guaranteed by the Muses; he is known to be cunning and deceitful, and he has to tell a good story in order to please the Phaeacians, who in turn will reward him with gifts and a ride home. I also encourage students to question Odysseus's motivations and ethos throughout the epic, although at the same time I emphasize that the Greek hero frequently acts immorally, in contrast to what we expect of those considered heroes today.

It is especially rewarding to question Odysseus's story in the Polyphemus episode. In teaching Odysseus's encounter with the Cyclopes in book 9, I take a postcolonial and deconstructive approach to emphasize how Odysseus perceives and treats Polyphemus. I call my approach "postcolonial" insofar as it emphasizes power relations between two peoples, one of which attempts to denigrate and subjugate the other, and "deconstructive" because it undermines the binary of civilization and barbarism that Odysseus himself sets up from the very beginning of this story. Insensitivity toward the other, and particularly the foreign other, remains common to this day, and the negative example of Odysseus's conduct suggests the necessity of getting to know other peoples' beliefs and traditions rather than trying to impose our own cultural systems on them, assuming they are inferior to us, and asserting authority over them. This is a provocative reading, because Odysseus's skillful narration makes it seem that he is a great hero, while Polyphemus is nothing more than a monster. It is important to note, however, that it is Odysseus who wields the power of discourse, and he alone shapes the audience's view of both himself and the other. The other may speak in his narrative, but he does so mostly through Odysseus's voice (except when Odysseus quotes him, as when he speaks to his ram). In this story it is ultimately not Odysseus who is "Nobody," but the voiceless Polyphemus, who is represented only through the discourse of the notoriously unreliable Odysseus.

Carol Dougherty has discussed the Polyphemus adventure in the context of the shift in Archaic Greek society that began in the eighth century BCE toward increased overseas expansion and emphasis on profit (*Raft* 122–42). Awareness of this context facilitates a close reading of the episode. As soon as Odysseus arrives on the Cyclopes' island, he ponders its potential value as a colony: he thinks men with ships could make it "well settled" νῆσον ἐϋκτιμένην ἐκάμοντο (9.130) and able to "bear all crops in season" φέροι δέ κεν ὥρια πάντα (131) and that it could provide a "harbor good for mooring" ἐν δὲ λιμὴν εὔορμος (136).[1] He also notes that it possesses rich meadowlands, vineyards, and "smooth land for plowing" ἐν δ' ἄροσις λείη (9.132–35). It is evident that he is contemplating how advantageous it would be to take possession of the island, whose fertility contrasts sharply with the rocky landscape of his native Ithaca. One would think that the Cyclopes' easy life in their island idyll, blessed by the gods, would suggest that they are still living in Hesiod's golden age, and therefore could be considered superior to men of the Iron Age, such as Odysseus and his companions. Oddly, however, Odysseus instead interprets their tranquil lifestyle as a sign of barbarism. In fact, Odysseus characterizes Polyphemus as "not like / a man who eats bread, but like a wooded peak of the high mountains" οὐδὲ ἐῴκει / ἀνδρί γε σιτοφάγῳ, ἀλλὰ ῥίῳ ὑλήεντι / ὑψηλῶν ὀρέων (9.190–92), thus completely identifying him with nature and monstrosity while denying him any semblance of humanity. As these passages illustrate, Odysseus rationalizes his colonizing vision by assuming that the Cyclopes are inferior to the Achaeans.

Odysseus announces outright that the Cyclopes are barbarous because they do not plow, have no institutions, and do not build ships for travel (9.108, 112, 125–29), ignoring the fact that they work as shepherds, which could be considered a civilized occupation. He also says that they do not care about one another, but this statement is proven untrue when we see the Cyclopes come running in response to Polyphemus's anguished cries, asking him what is wrong. In addition, that Polyphemus himself is capable of affection can be seen in his address to his ram. Furthermore, Odysseus's first words to Polyphemus are strikingly presumptuous and narcissistic: he introduces himself as a follower of Agamemnon and a sacker of Troy, assuming that Polyphemus is not only aware of the Trojan War and its leader but also supportive of the Achaeans. He thus immediately attempts to compel the Cyclops to recognize his authority based on military superiority. Moreover, he apparently does not realize that introducing himself and his men as sackers of a great city might be seen as a veiled threat to their potential host. The Greek warrior then demands presents, declaring they are "what is due to strangers" ἥ τε ξείνων θέμις ἐστίν (9.268), in accordance with *Greek* custom. He never stops to consider that the Cyclopes may not be aware of Greek culture or that they may have customs of their own of which he has no knowledge. Although he considers the Cyclopes to be savages, he nonetheless expects them to adhere to Greek norms.

Although Odysseus demands recognition of the sacred custom of *xenia* ("mutual hospitality"), he and his men violate it without a second thought when they invade Polyphemus's cave in his absence and help themselves to his cheeses. Odysseus's violation of *xenia* is particularly ironic because it parallels what the suitors are doing in his own home. Moreover, Polyphemus's cave is in fact comparable to the dining hall in which Odysseus eventually slaughters the feasting suitors. Odysseus must have appeared as horrifying to them as Polyphemus had to him, but while he is certain that he has the moral right to kill the offenders, he denies it to Polyphemus when the Cyclops kills Odysseus's men. As both Homer's epics make clear, violation of *xenia* is one of the worst possible crimes in the Greek world, and yet the audience does not question it here, as Odysseus skillfully glosses over his own wrongdoing. It is telling that Zeus, who severely punishes those who violate the law of hospitality, does not accept the sacrifice that Odysseus offers him immediately after his adventure on the island of the Cyclopes, but instead, Odysseus assumes, considers how best to destroy Odysseus and his crew (9.550–55).

Whether or not students concede that Polyphemus is less barbarous than Odysseus wishes his listeners to believe, we go on to discuss various reasons that Odysseus might want to define him as such and then to find parallels with Odysseus's sense of superiority in our own world. First, Odysseus characterizes Polyphemus as a cannibal. Ancient Greek culture considered cannibalism a marker of extreme barbarism, a view that persisted in Western culture well into the Age of Exploration. (One may think of Michel de Montaigne's essay "On Cannibals" as a deconstructive interpretation of that bias.) Moreover, to promote imperialism as a just mission, oppressors have often appealed to the philanthropic need to spread "civilization" to barbarous lands populated by violent and even subhuman peoples, projecting the aggression of colonization onto the colonized. Napoleon, for instance, justified his imperialist wars as spreading the world's greatest civilization to all humanity, and King Leopold II of Belgium appealed to "the sacred mission of civilization" and "the sanction of right" to justify Belgian atrocities in the Congo (119). Odysseus's discourse similarly constructs the Cyclopes as "lawless" ἀθέμιστοι and "insolent" ὑπερφίαλοι (9.106) and himself and the Greeks as the epitome of civilization. However, he is no less cruel and violent than Polyphemus, as evidenced by his description of the blinding.

Odysseus describes the mutilation of the giant in grisly and sadistic detail, taking pleasure not only in the barbarous act itself but also in his narration of it. Comparing the act to the work of a shipwright boring a plank, he tells the Phaeacians:

> Just so, taking the fire-sharpened log, in his eye
> we whirled it, and the blood flowed out around the hot point.
> The breath of fire singed all his eyelids and eyebrows
> as the eye was burning, and its roots crackled with the heat.
>
> ὣς τοῦ ἐν ὀφθαλμῷ πυριήκεα μοχλὸν ἑλόντες
> δινέομεν, τὸν δ' αἷμα περίρρεε θερμὸν ἐόντα.

> πάντα δέ οἱ βλέφαρ' ἀμφὶ καὶ ὀφρύας εὗσεν ἀϋτμὴ
> γλήνης καιομένης· σφαραγεῦντο δέ οἱ πυρὶ ῥίζαι. (9.387–90)

The violent act seems all the more barbarous because Odysseus repeatedly refers to civilization in describing it. He compares himself and his men first to a shipbuilder boring timber (9.383–86) and then to a blacksmith plunging a hot iron blade into cold water, which sizzles like the eye of the Cyclops (391–94). These metaphors collapse the distinction between civilization and barbarism on which the narrative is purportedly founded, particularly since Odysseus identifies shipbuilding with civilization at the beginning of this episode, and it is in large part the seafaring expertise of his Phaeacian audience that makes them an extraordinarily civilized colonial settlement.

Reading the story against the grain, as it were, we realize that Polyphemus may be literally blind by the end of the episode, but Odysseus is figuratively blind throughout the entire adventure. His cultural blindness affirms the thesis of the postcolonial theorist Abdul R. JanMohamed that "the colonizer's invariable assumption about his moral superiority means that he will rarely question the validity of his own or his society's formation and that he will not be inclined to expend any energy in understanding the worthless alterity of the colonized" (18). The tendency to look down upon other civilizations as inferior and the drive to assert power over them has proven to be an integral part of our history, and it invariably leads to cruelty and injustice.

Herodotus's *Histories* raises similar issues. Some readers may object that Polyphemus is undeniably monstrous because he devours Odysseus's men; however, a rebuttal to that argument may be found in Herodotus's cultural relativism. Although to some extent Herodotus cannot help but see other cultures through the lens of Greek culture, he nonetheless strives to value diverse customs. In a famous passage he writes that "each group regards his own [tradition and religion] as the best" νομίζουσι πολλόν τι καλλίστους τοὺς ἑωυτῶν νόμους ἕκαστοι εἶναι (*Histories* 3.38), and he goes on to contrast the treatment of the dead by the Greeks and the Callatiae, an Indian tribe. Darius I, king of Persia, he claims, summoned representatives of the two peoples to exchange views through an interpreter. Herodotus emphasizes the presence of the interpreter, as if to stress the removal of the language barrier that is inevitably the first obstacle to communication and understanding. The Callatiae are horrified to learn that the Greeks burn their dead parents, whereas the Greeks are appalled to learn that the Indian tribe eats theirs. This passage illustrates that even cannibalism, one of the strictest taboos in Greek society, may be a respected tradition in other cultures.

One may also legitimately object that Polyphemus is not human, and if this is so, he cannot rightly be called a cannibal. It could therefore be considered hypocritical to fault him for killing and eating animals that he considers inferior to himself, as humans themselves are carnivorous. Odysseus and his men approaching Polyphemus could be compared to a flock of chickens approaching a man, and in such a situation we would not hold it against the man if he slaughtered them for food.

This approach to Odysseus's first adventure stimulates discussion among students, who usually come to class thinking that Odysseus is a great hero and Polyphemus is a terrible monster. As we discuss the episode, they start to question their initial assumptions. Once students recognize the condescension in Odysseus's encounter with the Cyclopes, they are able to apply their insight to their own experience and, hopefully, learn to take a more sympathetic view of the other. In addition, they begin to realize that discourse always shapes our perception not only of the other but also of every aspect of reality.

My approach to the *Odyssey* is typical of how I encourage my students to read other classical works in the course. For example, when we read *Medea*, most students come to class thinking that she is crazy and monstrous. I make the argument that Medea is actually not all that different from Odysseus and may be considered a hero in her own right, given her circumstances. (I do not tell students that some Greeks did consider her a hero [Maurizio 509–10], because I want them to come to their own conclusions.) I also argue that the work may be considered proto-feminist. When we read Vergil's *Aeneid*, I encourage students to read between the lines and to see the work not as plagiarism of Homer and not as propaganda for Augustus but rather as subtly critical, especially with its emphasis on the suffering caused by war. This approach to reading helps students develop close reading and critical thinking skills, and it also bolsters their interest in all the works we read.

NOTE

1. Translations of Homer are by Lillian Doherty.

Maps, Movement, and "the Man": Cultural Exchange and Migration in the *Odyssey* and Today

Jennifer R. Ballengee

As funding for departments of Greek and Latin classics has continued to decline in recent decades, along with student enrollment in the major, classicists and others who work on ancient texts have sought ways to foreground the field's relevance, particularly in an educational climate that tends toward the devaluation of the humanities in general. Moreover, the trend toward globalization in politics and in higher education may tend to destabilize fields like classics and English, which have traditionally been situated as foundational to the "Western world." Yet, as Kwame Anthony Appiah has pointed out, the idea of "Western civilization" is misleading, a social construction of sameness and difference that doesn't bear out either in history or in the present.

My approach to teaching Homer's *Odyssey* reflects upon Appiah's point, with an acute awareness that the course in which I teach the epic poem—Introduction to Classical Mythology—is offered by an English department (at a state university with no dedicated classics department) that is likely to have conceived of this class in the first place as integral to the English curriculum, undoubtedly as a testament to the very foundations of the "Western tradition," which Appiah critiques, and to which many English departments continue to adhere.

My approach, by contrast, seeks to broaden students' conception of the *Odyssey*, moving beyond the valorizing European frame that has so often inflected the discipline of classics for us since the eighteenth and nineteenth centuries and resituating the poem within the geographic exchanges and "protocolonial" concerns of its historical period (Malkin 14). Our careful exploration of the *Odyssey* within its own cultural, geographic, and historical context—rather than approaching the poem only within the frame of a "Western tradition"—illuminates the poem's frequent reflections upon Mediterranean exchange, providing a literary space that allows us to address the ancient poem *and* its reception, generating consideration of issues that dominate our current political and social conversation: refugees, race, and the contrapuntal forces of globalization and nationalism.[1]

Our own current moment, in the early twenty-first century, features the highest number of displaced people ever on record in history, as a result of war, inequality, and climate change—consequences of the unfolding of history. While allowing current circumstances to inflect a reading of an ancient poem might be dismissed as "presentist," François Hartog suggests that the "omnipresent presence" of the present remains an inescapable aspect of the work of recounting history.[2] Indeed, as we shall see, the co-incidence of the past (and future) within the present emerges as a prominent theme in the *Odyssey*. This telescoping of time in the diegesis of the poem may be productively imitated in the reading of it—in an echo of Pierre Vidal-Naquet, who demonstrated in the years following World War II how the value of ancient study at times also lies in its capacity to give depth to our experience or understanding of the present.

As literature often can do, the human story of the challenges that Odysseus confronts in his *nostos*, or "homecoming," brings home the urgency of mortal peril both then and now. After all, the poem is first and foremost the story of a "man," an *anēr*—literally, since it is the first word of the poem, whatever else the translation my students are reading might imply. As this essay demonstrates, examining the cultural and historical significance of ὁ πολύτροπος ἀνήρ ("the complicated man," to use Emily Wilson's straightforward rendering [1.1]) foregrounds the sociocultural and geographic network that determines the variable and complex meanings of "the man" at the time of the poem's composition in the eighth-century-BCE Mediterranean world—and perhaps even today.

Reading the poem closely within its ancient context organically fosters a discussion of Mediterranean exchange in the past as well as in the present while also prompting exploration of how the reception of the *Odyssey*, and of ancient Greek culture in general, has been complicated by problems of nationalism, national boundaries, and identity. Specifically, by considering the identity of Odysseus as it takes shape through *nostos*, we see how this epic hero without a battlefield is constructed in terms of time and space—that is, through narrative and through movement, an aggregate of the people and places that comprise the journey home.

Time and the Man

When I teach the *Odyssey*, I begin by spending significant class time discussing the proem, which communicates to the poem's audience the primary concerns of the work as a whole. Contrasting the first word of the *Odyssey*, *andra* ("man"), with the first word of the *Iliad*, *mēnin* ("rage"), we draw out the differences between the two poems. As we move forward through the proem (typically lines 1–10), we start to explore what the poem as a whole means by "man," beginning with the adjective that modifies the noun: *polutropon*.[3] A broad range of potential meanings of the word *polutropos* are elaborated by Daniel Mendelsohn in his memoir, *An Odyssey: A Father, a Son, and an Epic*, which interweaves his own approach to teaching the poem with a sensitive account of his evolving relationship with his aging father (see esp. 3–43). I emphasize Mendelsohn's memoir here as I note it for my students, encouraging them to consider the word *anēr* not as an impersonal term but as a very significant designation: in the patriarchal ancient Greek world, the status of an *anēr* is connected to his father primarily and then woven into a broader social and kinship network. This is certainly the case for Odysseus in the *Odyssey*, which begins with the story of the son Telemachus at the cusp of manhood and ends with a truncated fight scene in which grandfather, father, and son occupy the front lines: the three generations—past, present, and future—standing together.[4]

In this sense, *polutropos* stands in for many potentials of the man: literally "many-turned," the adjective may refer to Odysseus's resourcefulness, his craftiness, or his complexity; his many facets as he moves through time;[5] his generational potential; or the circuitous nature of his stories or of the epic narrative as a whole. Or, as we shall see, *polutropos* may describe his "many long wanderings" through space (μάλα πολλὰ / πλάγχθη [1.1–2]): he is a man of "many ways" (Lattimore, Odyssey [1967] 1.1) or of "twists and turns" (Fagles, Odyssey [Penguin Classics] 1.1), a well-traveled man, or a man who has been around, as they say. Indeed, as the proem continues, sacking the sacred citadel of Troy is followed for Odysseus by a host of wanderings on the sea, in which he "sees the towns and learns the minds of many people" πολλῶν δ'ἀνθρώπων ἴδεν ἄστεα καὶ νόον ἔγνω (1.3) as he suffers and struggles to save his life and those of his companions, each striving toward their own *nostos*. Yet in another insight into human motivation, the proem tells us that the companions are "ruined by their own recklessness" αὐτῶν γὰρ σφετέρῃσιν ἀτασθαλίῃσιν ὄλοντο (1.7), their *atasthalia*: an irrational urge that stands in tension with Odysseus's successful return home.

As I point out to my students, recklessness driven by hunger, desire, or greed emerges repeatedly in the *Odyssey* as a threat to reason and a potential destroyer of *nostos*—in other words, as a threat to memory and the hero's related goal: a good, coherent reputation, or *kleos*.[6] In lieu of a reputable death in war, the warrior's *kleos*, once established on the battlefield, must be secured in the successful return home. Thus, as Elton Barker and Joel Christensen suggest, "*nostos* signifies both a homecoming and a *song about* homecoming" (85–86). Absent that homecoming, memory and reputation remain unsecured and subject to forgetting. This lesson is painted in broad strokes by the behavior of the suitors, who act in contrast to established social rules because Odysseus's whereabouts and possible demise remain unknown.[7]

The dangers of a delayed or unsuccessful *nostos* are indicated more pointedly at the outset of the epic by Odysseus's son, Telemachus. In book 1, Telemachus expresses doubts about his long-absent father. Not surprisingly, some of his doubt focuses on whether Odysseus is alive or dead. For example, he notes that the suitors are eating up the resources of "a man whose white bones rot in the rain / somewhere on the mainland, or roll in the salty ocean swells" ἀνέρος οὗ δή που λεύκ' ὀστέα πύθεται ὄμβρῳ / κείμεν'ἐπ' ἠπείρου, ἢ εἰν ἁλὶ κῦμα κυλίνδει (1.161–62). But Telemachus expresses uncertainty about not just where but also who his father is: for example, in book 1, lines 215–16, when he says to Athena (who is disguised as Mentes), "Mother tells me I am his, but I / don't know: no one ever yet knew his father" μήτηρ μέν τ' ἐμέ φησι τοῦ ἔμμεναι, αὐτὰρ ἐγώ γε / οὐκ οἶδ'· οὐ γάρ πώ τις ἑὸν γόνον αὐτὸς ἀνέγνω. These nagging doubts must be assuaged by the stories of Odysseus's heroism and travels that he hears from Nestor and Menelaus.

The visits to Pylos and Sparta in books 3 and 4 provide Telemachus and the poem's audience with reminders of Odysseus's distinctive character, as illustrated in tales of several of his exploits and of general heroic events at Troy. The episodes also demonstrate good guest-host relations (*xenia*), in contrast to the transgressive behavior of the suitors back in Ithaca; they warn of the dangers that might accompany a homecoming (in the oft-repeated accounts of Agamemnon's death at the hands of his wife's lover); they present Telemachus with models for his own development as a hero (as both Nestor and Menelaus praise Orestes's success in avenging his father's murder); and they offer reflections upon the importance of the *nostos* in the context of reputation, or wandering in the context of identity. Not coincidentally, most of these lessons and tales are exchanged at the table, as the characters break bread together. As is commonly understood, not only hospitality but also the act of eating itself is full of significance in the *Odyssey*.[8]

Eating is related to memory and being remembered. The poem demonstrates in books 3, 4, and 8–13 how the ritual of eating is a social behavior: repeated phrases mark the ritual each time it occurs (as in the *Iliad*), the ritual happens in the context of *xenia*, and it is at banquet that heroic tales are told (as in the case of Nestor and Menelaus in books 3 and 4 and Odysseus in books 9–12) or sung (as Odysseus's bard Phemius does in book 1, or Demodocus in book 8).[9] To eat properly is to participate in rituals of social relation, which in their repetition merge past, present, and future. Likewise, the ritual of eating, linked as it is to the repeated stories sung by the bard while men feast, provides a means for establishing and remembering a coherent, narrative reputation. Indeed, despite their transgressive consuming of Odysseus's stores of food and wine, even the suitors still have Phemius sing of the Achaeans' troubled homecoming from Troy while they dine in Odysseus's palace in Ithaca (1.325–27).

By contrast, to be eaten is to be forgotten, consumed into obscurity and denied the coherence and reinvigoration of memory that comes with mourning and burial. The person serving as fodder for another is stripped of humanity in the bestial urgency of sating an appetite—horrifying and gruesome obliterations we see in the episodes of the Cyclopes, Scylla, and the Laestrygones, all of which are narrated by Odysseus. Likewise, improper eating can lead to oblivion for the eater: thus the recklessness, the *atasthalia*, of Odysseus's men in the proem serves as a warning against the dangers of gluttony—the threat of losing one's control, moderation, or reason in the pursuit of desires, causing the coherence of one's life story (*kleos*) to be lost as well.

The drug proffered by Helen in book 4 lies somewhere in between the possibilities of eating and being eaten. Telemachus, Pisistratus (Nestor's son), and Helen join Menelaus in communal weeping for loved ones lost in battle—until Helen rises and mixes a drug of forgetfulness into their wine, so that they may drink and eat in peace, sharing the food placed before them. On the one hand, in curing the sadness of mourning, Helen's drug causes forgetfulness, in opposition to the value of remembering *kleos*. On the other hand, however, the drug enables the ritual of eating—and the stories that accompany it—to resume, with two stories about Odysseus. That the drug's provenance is Egypt emphasizes the ambivalence of Mediterranean exchange in general—it has both positive and negative potential—and reflects its similarity to the overtly dangerous drugs that erase the desire for homecoming in Odysseus's later account to the Phaeacians: the Lotus and Circe's potion.

The correspondence of consuming (food or drugs) or being eaten with the conservation or loss of coherent memory or reputation emphasizes how both function in direct response to human mortality. My class would have already approached these themes in an earlier reading of Hesiod's *Theogony*. Much as Hesiod's Muses refer to mortal men ("shepherds of the field") as "mere bellies" ποιμένες ἄγραυλοι, κακ' ἐλέγχεα, γαστέρες οἶον (*Theog.* 26), Odysseus emphasizes his mortal need to eat, adopting the disguise of a beggar in book 17 and commenting to Eumaeus:

> There's no hiding the ravenous belly,
> cursed thing, which gives many troubles to men,
> and on account of which the well-benched ships cross
> the barren sea, bearing evils to enemies.
>
> γαστέρα δ'οὔ πως ἔστιν ἀποκρύψαι μεμαυῖαν,
> οὐλομένην, ἣ πολλὰ κάκ' ἀνθρώποισι δίδωσι,
> τῆς ἕνεκεν καὶ νῆες ἐΰζυγοι ὁπλίζονται
> πόντον ἐπ' ἀτρύγετον, κακὰ δυσμενέεσσι φέρουσαι. (17.286–89)

The burden of hunger, inescapable in humans, signals mortality; to move beyond this limit, the epic poem (and ancient Greek culture in general) offers values such as *kleos*, the reputation that allows a mortal man to live on at least in song, and *xenia*, the social practice guaranteed by Zeus that enables mortal men to travel around the Mediterranean with the expectation that their mortal need to eat will be met by the hospitality of others. The teleological course of narrative echoes the teleological course of a life: in each case, the coherent passage of time must be sustained by eating.

Space and the Man

Menelaus makes the mortally necessary function of *xenia* clear when he reprimands Eteoneus for questioning initially whether or not to receive their visitors: "Surely we two have been nourished by many host-gifts / from other men before returning here" ἦ μὲν δὴ νῶϊ ξεινήϊα πολλὰ φαγόντε / ἄλλων ἀνθρώπων δεῦρ' ἱκόμεθ[α] (4.33–34). It is not surprising that Menelaus would emphasize their own reliance upon *xenia* for survival, given the many wanderings he and his own men had before returning to Lacedaemon. Indeed, it is not long after they are seated together at banquet that Menelaus recounts in detail the places he traveled before arriving home: wandering to Cyprus and Phoenicia, then encountering Egyptians,

Ethiopians, Sidonians, Erembi, and Libyans (4.81–89). Significantly, the adventures that Odysseus narrates to the Phaeacians and the *nostoi* that he tells in disguise as "Cretan" Odysseus in books 13–19 have in common a geographic organization that echoes the much briefer tale of Menelaus's *nostos* in book 4.[10] These homecoming stories, which reference particular places and place-names around the Mediterranean (Crete, Egypt, Libya, etc.), reflect a broad awareness of the Mediterranean world on the part of the poet, the storytellers and the audiences within the poem, as well as audiences that would have heard the epic performed, sung by the hearths of palaces in the eighth century BCE.[11]

The broad geographic knowledge of actual places and people around the Mediterranean reflected in the *nostoi* ("homecomings") of Menelaus and "Cretan" Odysseus attests to the prominence of trade and settlement around the Mediterranean at the time. As Malkin notes, "Between the eleventh and the eighth century Greeks migrated and established settlements in the eastern Aegean and Asia Minor; between the second half of the eighth century and the sixth, they founded cities in what we know as mainland Greece, along the coasts of the Black Sea, and almost throughout the Mediterranean" (10). Carol Dougherty (*Raft* 108–11) offers an extensive bibliography of works attesting to trade between ancient Greece and the Levant prior to the dating of the *Odyssey*.[12] While scholars debate an unbroken era of trade from the twelfth century BCE forward, there is ample evidence showing trade between Greece and the Near East dating to around 950 BCE at least. The evidence indicates a lively mineral trade in addition to Greek exploration of the Levant to establish commercial contacts and outposts. There was exchange not only of goods but also of people (and thus of culture), as witnessed, for example, by the diffusion of pottery styles and of the alphabet. Noting this history, Dougherty asks rhetorically, "Is it an accident that the *Odyssey* is especially interested in the worlds beyond Greek shores, interested in exploring the nature of relationships (commercial and colonial) between Greeks and people overseas, at exactly the moment when its audience is settling those shores and establishing trade contacts throughout the Mediterranean?" (11; see also Vidal-Naquet 37–38). The narrative of the *Odyssey*—and the multiple narrative *nostoi* within the poem—provides a space within which to work out the possibilities and potentials for such geographic, economic, and cultural exchanges.

Tracing a narrative map of the Mediterranean, the *nostoi* told by Menelaus and the disguised "Cretan" Odysseus reflect real geographic landmarks; examining maps in class, students see that these places are, as Malkin describes, "human and topographical." By contrast, in the narrative tales that Odysseus relates to the Phaeacians "the geographical dimension is monstrous": the "real world" turned surreal, the stuff of nightmares (151). For what is striking about surreal art, or what is terrifying about nightmares, is not their absolute foreignness but rather their uncanny, disconcerting similarity to what we know very well. In this sense, Odysseus *polytropos*, in his travelling *nostos* and in his narrative *nostoi*, functions as a mediator, tracing out the negative and positive possibilities of geographic trade and exchange. Malkin suggests, "What Odysseus reflects is the ambivalence implied in exploration and protocolonization: hope of discovering a magnificently rich land mixed with fear that its inhabitants might be Cyclopes" (4).

After all, while Odysseus suspects the Cyclopes have "good knowledge neither of laws nor customs" οὔτε δίκας εὖ [εἰδότας] οὔτε θέμιστας (9.215), when Polyphemus asks the identity of his intruders (Odysseus and his men), Odysseus's response shows that he clearly assumes the Cyclopes know of the heroic war with Troy and respect the practice of *xenia* (9.259–71). Polyphemus answers by calling Odysseus a fool for imagining that he would care about the law of Zeus and then promptly and brutally smashes two of Odysseus's men on the ground and eats them. While this is undoubtedly far from Achaean custom, the poem notes that, rather than simply gobbling them up after hurling them onto the cave floor, Polyphemos "[cuts] them limb from limb and prepares [the men] for his dinner" τοὺς δὲ διὰ μελεϊστὶ ταμὼν ὁπλίσσατο δόρπον before eating them (9.291). The phrase indicating that he "prepares" dinner is repeated each following time he dines on Odysseus's men (ὁπλίσσατο δεῖπνον [9.311] and ὁπλίσσατο δόρπον [9.344]).[13] While Polyphemus undoubtedly appears brutal in Odysseus's tale, he also displays some semblance of civilized behavior: civilized enough for Odysseus to assume that they share some customs (*xenia*) and civilized enough for Polyphemus to milk his sheep and process the milk and to prepare his dinner before eating it. In other words, rather than a monstrous Other, Polyphemus represents an exaggerated, nightmarish, monstrous version of mortal man: compelled by hunger to eat but moderating (slightly) that urge to gorge with the ritual of preparing the meal.

The cannibalism of the Laestrygones follows a similar pattern: Odysseus and his men arrive at a land that seems to reflect the familiar customs Odysseus knows. A maiden meets the scouts and points the way to her father's palace, a pattern quite clearly paralleled in Odysseus's own introduction to Alcinous and Arete through Nausicaa. Yet, in a sly moment of metanarrative, the poem has the character Odysseus regale his Phaeacian hosts with an account of the worst possible welcome. For instead of practicing *xenia*, the Laestrygonian king Antiphates snatches up one of Odysseus's three scouts to eat for dinner (the other two manage to escape). Like Polyphemus, however, he doesn't simply take the man and gobble him down, but rather "immediately taking hold of one of my companions, he prepared him for dinner" αὐτίχ' ἕνα μάρψας ἑτάρων ὁπλίσσατο δεῖπνον (10.116). Later, as the rest of the men struggle to leave the narrow opening of the bay, they are beset by swarms of the giant Laestrygones, who throw boulders at Odysseus's men and, "piercing them like fish, carry them away for their joyless feast" ἰχθῦς δ' ὣς πείροντες ἀτερπέα δαῖτα φέροντο (10.124). While this is certainly a different sort of banquet than those enjoyed by Menelaus, Nestor, and the other Achaeans and Phaeacians, the term designating the monstrous banquet, δαῖτα, is the same. Similar to Polyphemus, then, while the Laestrygones brutally kill and consume Odysseus's men, this carnage is framed with the echoes of the customs Odysseus expects: a palace, a king and queen, and the process of preparing dinner and of having a feast, albeit a joyless one.

Given the correlation of eating and the preservation of memory, the episodes with Polyphemus and the Laestrygones suggest the worst that might happen in the process of Mediterranean exchange: not an encounter with a radical other being but a reminder of the vulnerability of mortal life and memory, which motivates the compelling need for *nostos*. The creatures that populate the (not-yet-completed) *nostos* that Odysseus tells the Phaeacians demonstrate often grotesque exaggerations of mortal qualities, from the gulping feminized mouth of Charybdis to the seductions of Circe (whose feminine temptations bring out the beast in men) to the encounters with those in the underworld in book 11, where the ghostly figures seem so human that Odysseus tries and fails three times to hug his mother's shade.

Recognizing the vague similarities that the nightmarish creatures of books 9 through 12 have to Odysseus, his men, and all mortals enables us to recognize the manner in which Odysseus *polutropos*, the complicated man, demonstrates the extent to which "telling" "the man" (that is, exploring the identity of the human) is achieved by means of tracing his contours in time and space (that is, by means of the *nostos*). As Joel Christensen suggests, "A *nostos* is also a return to *self*. What kind of self this may be is a central issue" (*Many-Minded Man* 7).[14] The nature of this "self" emerges in the course of the *nostos*.

Christensen argues that the self in the *Odyssey* is constructed by means of both the *experience* of the *nostos*, the homecoming, and the corresponding narrative *account* of it; as he puts it, Homeric identity is composed of "social roles, speech, and action" (*Many-Minded Man* 7). The encounter with the Laestrygones, in which the land itself forms a consuming mouth, shows us that place is also internalized as part of the experience constitutive of the self. Here Odysseus narrates a *nostos* that is as much about his interaction with the land as with its people. The episode begins with Odysseus's description of the mouth of the bay—which in his account takes on the shape of a human mouth: "We entered the glorious harbor, / which was encircled by a high unbroken cliff / and promontories jutting out on either side / at the mouth, and there is a narrow entrance" ἐς λιμένα κλυτὸν ἤλθομεν, ὃν πέρι πέτρη / ἠλίβατος τετύχηκε διαμπερὲς ἀμφοτέρωθεν, / ἀκταὶ δὲ προβλῆτες ἐναντίαι ἀλλήλῃσιν / ἐν στόματι προὔχουσιν, ἀραιὴ δ' εἴσοδός ἐστιν (10.87–90). An enormous stony mouth, the harbor reflects the form of the action. Odysseus lingers at the lip of the bay like words waiting to emerge from the mouth of the poet. Indeed, by remaining at the bay's and the mouth's opening, Odysseus survives to narrate this episode of his *nostos*. The consuming mouth of the bay echoes the consuming mouths of the Laestrygones, a haunting repetition of Odysseus's traumatic survival.

In this sense, the *andra* of which the *Odyssey* sings is an aggregate composed by means of the *nostos* narrative and the *nostos* homecoming—an identity constructed over time (through narrative) and through space (wandering around the Mediterranean). My students come to realize as we move through the poem in this way that Odysseus's encounters reflect the positive and negative possibilities of Mediterranean exchange—possible gain encountered in known cities and towns and possible losses figured in monstrous distortions of those people and places.[15] The character Odysseus *polutropos* is a reflection of these myriad possibilities, coursing through narrative time and geographic space. He is a wanderer and a witness, a traveler-observer whose movements and encounters trace a "complicated," aggregate self. The encounters he survives reflect the best possible outcome for an identity that is constructed in space and time—a person who goes away and hopes to come back, rather than being lost, his fate unknown.

Colonization versus Protocolonization

While the informed knowledge of the broader Mediterranean world demonstrated in the *Odyssey* won't feel surprising to a well-trained classicist, it can be revelatory for students from a range of majors in an introductory classical mythology class. Most of the students in the class will have read some excerpts of the *Odyssey*—often only the monster-filled stories Odysseus tells the Phaeacians in books 9–12—in middle or high school and will have learned in that process the traditional reading of the poem, in which Odysseus the clever hero encounters all sorts of uncivilized creatures in his efforts to finally reach home and establish civilized behavior again there. Or at least this is what my students typically report having learned about the poem already, before we begin our study of it. The distinct categories of civilized versus uncivilized reflected in students' earlier encounters with the poem are significant here, reflecting as they do the traditional European and American approach to ancient Greek literature and culture that students in the United States have inherited.

Yet as we have seen, the received notion of the *Odyssey* as a poem of civilized versus uncivilized, a proto-European story of colonization of the exotic other, doesn't quite work. For one thing, a modern notion of colonization misrepresents the earlier practice of settlement of the ninth century BCE and earlier, a practice Malkin categorizes as "protocolonization" to distinguish it from the practice of colonization that emanated from distinct *poleis* beginning at the end of the eighth century BCE. In the wandering tales of the *Odyssey*, Malkin suggests, we find something more like "finding a 'land good to settle' as Odysseus calls the offshore island facing the land of the hostile Cyclops" (Malkin 14 [quoting 9.130]). Protocolonization in this sense reflects an exploration of land and possibility, even an exchange of culture and people, rather than the domination intended to "civilize" an other that we typically associate with colonization (whether ancient or modern).[16]

Such a concept of the other, or the foreign, François Hartog and others suggest, isn't a formulation found as early as the eighth century BCE. In *Memories of Odysseus*, Hartog quotes Thucydides to argue that, while the idea of the Barbarians eventually arose as antithetical to the Greeks—that is, used in a dialectical fashion by the Greeks to construct an idea of themselves in opposition to the Barbarians—in the Homeric world this distinction didn't exist: "In his Archaeology, Thucydides observes that in the Homeric poems, which described the struggle between the Achaeans and the Trojans, there was no such division: 'He [Homer] does not even use the term "Barbarians" and this, in my opinion, is because in his time the Hellenes were not yet known by one name, and so marked off as something separate from the outside world'" (*Memories* 80 [quoting Thucydides 1.3.3]). Only later, once the fifth-century-BCE encounters with the Persians begin to suggest the idea of a barbarian other, does such a clear delineation arise.

Rather than reflecting a domain of uncivilized versus civilized peoples and places, the *Odyssey* with its various *nostoi* describes a diverse world of Mediterranean trade and exchange, offering both negative and positive possibilities for the construction and preservation of life and identity. Exploring the difference between the "traditional" reading and one that recognizes the poem's participation in Mediterranean exchange involves considering the manner in which the poem has been received for the past two centuries: drawing students' attention to the manner in which the poem—and the ancient Greek world in general—became framed in a certain way (Western, European, even white) by European nations seeking to found their own traditions and self-image upon a particularly delimited notion of ancient Greece.[17] The *Odyssey* provides an excellent way of talking about this—especially when combined with other texts over the course of the semester. For example, in Introduction to Classical Mythology, I have taught the epic alongside Euripides's *Medea*, which provides a good example of the later Greek notion of barbarian or other, or Euripides's *Bacchae*, which can serve as part of a unit on Dionysus, whose mythical biography has him wandering around the Mediterranean and as far east as India. Showing the students images of the various appearances of Dionysus in ancient art and mosaics scattered around the Mediterranean, including in North Africa, and noting for them Herodotus's claim that the Egyptian god "Osiris is, in the Greek language, Dionysus" Ὄσιρις δέ ἐστι Διόνυσος κατὰ Ἑλλάδα γλῶσσαν (*Histories* 2.144) provides a vivid illustration of the complexities and ambiguities of Mediterranean cultural exchange. A class period spent interpreting the metopes of the Parthenon and Athenian myths of autochthony presents yet another opportunity to consider how and why Greek notions of the Other developed—as well as a discussion of the later appropriation of Periclean Greece by Europe in the name of Western heritage and nationhood.

This kind of approach destabilizes not only the past but also the present, encouraging students to reconsider their notions of race, refugees, who counts as "human," and what kinds of social structures humans need (and therefore have a right to). For Odysseus, like an ancient refugee, wanders the edges of the known Greek world, uprooted by war and wandering homeless for years before achieving a homecoming and, in a sense, reestablishing his identity. Gregory Feldman, who in his book *We Are All Migrants* traces a connection between Odysseus and the current refugee situation, suggests that "to become fully human in the ancient world, one needed access to a public space where one could appear in word or deed as a distinct person. Freedom *to* appear and freedom *from* migrant-hood were opposite sides of the same coin" (43). Exploring this comparison, I trace not only geographic connections between the past and present, through maps and images, but also thematic connections, prompting students to consider how borders—national and otherwise—and political entities shape our understanding of ourselves and others. I allow the *Odyssey* to become a catalyst for considering homelessness in the past and in the present and for reshaping our idea of what it means to be human, then and now. In this manner, students begin to see how the poem really is about "the complicated man" and about the complicated human: how human life is caught up in the social system, in reputation and story, and in the space of exchange. In this way, the classroom becomes its own community, a social system in which students feel prompted to recognize, through confronting epic representations of what is not really so other-than-human, the Other that is constitutive of the aggregate human identity, in strangers as well as in themselves.

NOTES

1. McCoskey's *Race: Antiquity and Its Legacy* explores how the discipline of classics has been framed by nineteenth-century racial ideologies, one of several recent considerations of race in antiquity (see esp. 5–34).

2. One example Hartog notes is illustrated in the *Odyssey* when Odysseus hears the bard Demodocus singing Odysseus's own exploits at Troy: the hero dissolves into tears, Hartog argues, because he is tormented at that moment by the tension of experiencing himself simultaneously as both past and present (*Regimes* 8, 50).

3. This noun and adjective pair (like *mēnin* in the *Iliad*) are in the accusative case, the object of the vocative command to the Muse: ἄνδρα μοι ἔννεπε, Μοῦσα, πολύτροπον, which in typical English word order often becomes, "Tell me, Muse, about the *polutropon* man." The nominatives are *anēr* and *polutropos*. Translations are my own unless otherwise indicated.

4. On kinship and masculinity, see also King in this volume.

5. That is, through his own teleological life history, in the sense of life as a temporal journey, as C. P. Cavafy suggests in his 1911 poem "Ithaca."

6. For more on the importance of a successful *nostos* in the construction of a coherent self-narrative, see Christensen, *Many-Minded Man* (esp. 4–5).

7. That death on the battlefield establishes a reputation—and that *kleos* lives on after death—emerges with clarity in the underworld scenes of books 11 and 24.

8. The correspondence of eating versus being eaten and remembering versus being forgotten is widely recognized (so much so that it is included in *SparkNotes* and *CliffsNotes*); it is a reading I absorbed as a graduate student teaching assistant for Peter Bing, Bracht Branham, and Sandra Blakely. I thank them for their enduring and positive impact on my teaching. (The flaws are mine.)

9. For more on the relation between occasion and topic for the poetic singer, see Dougherty, "Phemius' Last Stand."

10. In noting this distinction among the several *nostoi* in the poem, I follow Barker and Christensen; Malkin; Vidal-Naquet; Dougherty, *Raft*; and others. Nagy draws fascinating connections between the "Cretan" Odysseus's tales and the space of Minoan-Mycenean culture and mythology through the Cretan empire: see Nagy, *Homer*, "Cretan *Odyssey*, Part 1" and "Cretan *Odyssey*, Part 2."

11. For earlier Bronze Age knowledge of the Mediterranean world, see Romm.

12. For cultural exchange across the Mediterranean and its impact on Homeric epic, see Louden, *Homer's* Odyssey (esp. 11–12). Archaeological evidence tracing the development of seagoing ships enabling contact between Mediterranean peoples dates back at least to the third millennium BCE, moving from the Minoans of Crete to the Mycenaeans and then the Phoenicians, with crucial advances happening in the second millennium BCE, including the development of internal bracing and the sailing rig (Casson 30–43). Wallinga notes the characterization of Homeric ships as twenty-oared ships that were apparently broader than average, to increase cargo space; he connects this development with increasing trade in the eighth century BCE (43).

13. The poem also notes that Polyphemus builds up his fire as part of his process of preparing for dinner, though there is no clear indication of cooking.

14. Thus the narration of his *nostos* to the Phaeacians begins with his name: "I am Odysseus, son of Laertes, known to all men for craftiness, / and indeed my reputation goes to the heavens" εἴμ' Ὀδυσεὺς Λαερτιάδης, ὃς πᾶσι δόλοισιν / ἀνθρώποισι μέλω, καί μευ κλέος οὐρανὸν ἵκει (9.19–20).

15. The ambivalent possibility of travel and trade is illustrated, too, by Menelaus's *nostos*, particularly his encounters in Egypt (4.81–91), including the drug that Helen proffers.

16. For a contrasting view from a postcolonial perspective, see Lodge in this volume.

17. Also examining the limiting "Western" tradition that has framed our reception and conception of the ancient Mediterranean, López-Ruiz examines how the impact of the Phoenicians upon the ancient Mediterranean world has been inadequately recognized or considered (see esp. 23–89).

RECEPTION

Dante's Canto of Ulysses and Reception History

Julie Van Peteghem

Instructors wanting to incorporate artistic responses to the *Odyssey* in their courses have no shortage of choices in the literary, visual, and performing arts. This essay introduces the possibilities and advantages of using comparative and reception studies approaches in teaching the *Odyssey* through the case study of canto 26 of the *Inferno*, the so-called canto of Ulysses, by the medieval Italian poet Dante Alighieri.

Dante is the poet I teach most often, but I find several reasons for teachers who are not Dante specialists to consider this artistic response for their *Odyssey* courses or units. The *Inferno* is a poem that students might encounter or have already encountered in other courses. In a survey or great books course, for example, the *Inferno* may well be on the reading list weeks after the *Odyssey*. From a practical and organizational point of view, canto 26 of the *Inferno* is a short additional reading of 142 verses that easily stands on its own. Because of the large number of outstanding open access materials on Dante's poem and his world, this activity does not require much additional preparation, nor the need to create new teaching materials.[1]

Moreover, the success of this activity does not depend on a complete reading of the Homeric poem. Students can appreciate the comparison between Homer's and Dante's poems even if they are only reading a selection of books and passages from the *Odyssey*. In fact, Dante himself did not have to read a single verse of Homer to create his Ulysses, whom W. B. Stanford in *The Ulysses Theme* called "next to Homer's . . . the most influential in the whole evolution of the wandering hero" (178). Dante was impressively well read, but, like his Italian contemporaries, did not read Greek. To craft his "Ulisse"—the Italian name for Ulysses—Dante relied on the ways classical and medieval Latin writers had rendered the Greek hero. That in the reception history of a literary text there rarely exists a straight line from the original work to the artistic response is an important lesson to instill.

In fact, before reading a single verse of the *Odyssey*, I suggest presenting the following questions to students: Who is Ulysses? What do you know about him? And where do you know this from? Since for some students the answer will be "nothing," it helps to add matter-of-factly that this one-word answer is as informative as a more detailed one. Digital word cloud generating tools such as Mentimeter or WordClouds can visualize their responses to the whole class. One student may bring up James Joyce's *Ulysses*, another the movie *Troy*, or the hero's other name, Odysseus. The texts and contexts where students have encountered Ulysses could also be placed on a timeline. This activity takes up some class time but will lay the foundation for thinking about our reading of the *Odyssey* today as part of a long history of reading the Homeric poem. Through their different responses, students may start to see how literary characters like Ulysses can take root in both the literary and popular imagination and become "known" culturally without a precise source or a thorough reading of the original literary texts. This exercise also illustrates that every reader brings different experiences to the text.

After this initial presentation, there is no one right time to place the *Inferno* in conversation with the *Odyssey*. When I taught a first-year seminar on masterpieces of Western literature with both the *Odyssey* and the *Inferno* on the reading list, the moment for textual comparison presented itself naturally. When I teach Dante's *Inferno*, I introduce the Homeric poems early in the course: Homer is a character in canto 4 of the *Inferno*, and looking at the proems of the *Iliad*, the *Odyssey*, and Vergil's *Aeneid* helps students identify epic conventions in Dante's opening cantos. Depending on the class scope and schedule, these activities can be introduced at various points. Given the focus of this volume on teaching the *Odyssey*, I consider the Homeric poem the starting point of all activities.[2]

As I hope to illustrate, the use of comparative and reception studies offers various pedagogical advantages and is an effective way to show how diverse and complex interpretation can be. Reading and analyzing creative responses to the *Odyssey*, which often focus on a particular character (Ulysses first and foremost, of course, but also Penelope and Circe),[3] can offer opportunities for creativity and invention on the part of the students. Close readings of the artistic responses, furthermore, can enrich their understanding of the original text and vice versa.

Now let us turn to canto 26 of Dante's *Inferno*. Students will need to know that Dante wrote the *Inferno* in Italian during the early fourteenth century and that the poem details his journey through the nine circles of hell accompanied by the Roman poet Vergil (Virgilio).[4] We are thus encountering Ulysses in a medieval Christian poem and context. To aid student comprehension, ensure that students have access to a good English-language map of Dante's hell (for instance, by Christian Paniagua or Suloni Robertson) together with the text of the canto. On the *Digital Dante* and *The World of Dante* websites students can read the English translation of Allen Mandelbaum alongside the Italian text; the translation of Robert and Joan Hollander is available on the *Princeton Dante Project*.[5]

A helpful pre-class reading assignment for this canto—and any canto in Dante's *Divine Comedy* for that matter—is to ask students to break it down into narrative units.[6] Paying attention to its formal aspects is an accessible entry point into the text. In my experience, this is more effective than immediately assigning questions on content or interpretation, which some students, especially when just introduced to Dante, may find difficult because of their (perceived) lack of knowledge about the poem, author, and period. Students' encounter with medieval literature, as with the Homeric *Odyssey* itself, can provoke a sense of unsurmountable distance between the text and their own world and experiences (Forde 15–16).

Canto 26 of the *Inferno* has four main narrative units: an invective against Florence (lines 1–12), a description of the eighth *bolgia*, or "ditch" (13–48), the introduction of Ulysses and Diomedes (49–84), and Ulysses's speech (85–142). Students will undoubtedly come up with other descriptors for these units and will perhaps even further divide them or do so differently. That is all fine; the idea is to direct their focus to the structure of the poem and to Dante's artistic choices. Another way to set up this pre-class exercise is to share a list of common elements found in the nine circles of Dante's *Inferno*: a description of the atmosphere and architecture of the circle; a definition of the sin punished there; a list of the sinners found in that circle; a description of the punishment; the presence of guardians; conversations with particular sinners; and apostrophes or addresses to the poem's readers, to places, or to personified abstractions. Students may then be asked to identify which of these elements can be found in canto 26.

Nested within Ulysses's speech (lines 85–142) is a brief second speech (112–20). Since this speech-within-a-speech—his *orazion picciola*, or short oration (122)—is a main focus of our time in class, I include a second pre-reading question to set up the discussion. Students who are familiar with the main plot elements of the *Odyssey* are asked to identify any verses in Dante's canto that mention events from Homer's poem.[7] The relatively few references to the Homeric story—the stay with Circe (90–93), the longing for his son (94), father (94–95), and wife Penelope (95–96)—already signal that Dante is putting forward something different in his portrayal of the protagonist of the *Odyssey*.

Class starts with the discussion of the students' answers. First, we compare our findings on the narrative divisions of the canto. Discussion of the first fifty verses or so can be brief: as the students' structural analysis will show, most of the canto is dedicated to the encounter with Ulysses and Diomedes.[8] A similar conclusion will be reached if instead students have been asked to identify common features in Dante's circles of hell: again, students will see that the "conversation with particular sinners" (in this case, Ulysses) takes up a large portion of the canto.[9] Next we discuss which plot elements from the *Odyssey* made it into Dante's account. Especially when marking up these passages together in Dante's text, it should become clear that very few verses in canto 26 are actually story lines from the *Odyssey*. Some students may mention the Trojan horse (lines 58–60), tricking Achilles into participating in the war (61–62), and the theft of the Palladium (63), but these events appear only briefly in the *Odyssey* or are not mentioned at all. Students may also bring up the final journey of Ulysses and his companions that led to their deaths (121–42), another narrative element in the *Inferno* that they will not recognize from their reading of the *Odyssey*. At this point, the questions asked at the beginning of the course should be applied to Dante: What did Dante know about Ulysses? And where did he know this from?

I start answering these questions by directing our attention to Dante's unnamed "guide" ("duca"; lines 15, 46, 77) and "master" ("maestro"; 49, 65) in the canto.[10] As shared with the students before, this guide is Virgilio, Dante's fictionalization of Vergil. It is Virgilio, and not Dante, who speaks with Ulysses and Diomedes. "Let me talk to them" ("Lascia parlare a me"; 73), Virgilio tells Dante, deviating from the normal scenario in which Dante engages with the punished souls in hell. Canto 26 is very effective in illustrating how Virgilio serves as master and cultural mediator to both Dante the protagonist of the *Inferno* and Dante the poet.[11] I refer back to their first encounter in the opening canto of the *Inferno*, where Dante calls Virgilio "my master and my author" ("lo mio maestro e 'l mio autore"; 85). Virgilio guides Dante through hell, and, as a fellow denizen of the Classical world, is better positioned to address the Greek heroes Ulysses and Diomedes than Dante, the Italian-speaking man of the Middle Ages. Vergil was indeed an important author to Dante: in particular, book 6 of the *Aeneid*, which narrates Aeneas's descent into the underworld, is a significant intertext for Dante's *Inferno*. Vergil's account of Ulysses in book 2 of the *Aeneid* was one of Dante's main sources for canto 26. Just as in canto 26 the character Dante is kept from engaging directly with the Greek heroes, Dante the poet did not read Greek and knew about Ulysses from Latin sources only. And just as the character Virgilio is the intermediary between the medieval Italian Dante and the Greeks in the canto, the historical Vergil drew on various elements from the Homeric poems in his *Aeneid*, connecting the Greek and Roman worlds in its narrative.

At this point I provide some more information on Dante's sources and reading practices. In the *Aeneid*, Vergil portrays Ulysses as a real con man—the invention of the Trojan horse, the tricking of Achilles into war, and the theft of the Palladium are all mentioned in book 2. But this negative portrayal of Ulysses in Vergil's poem was not Dante's only Latin source. In Cicero's *De finibus bonorum et malorum* (*On the Ends of Good and Evil*), Dante found a positive characterization of the Greek hero as someone desiring knowledge. The Homeric poems were further known to Dante through medieval Latin sources incorporating these classical references to Ulysses. There is no need to look at specific passages from these sources in class—the main point to be made is one about cultural translation and mediation.[12] Without direct access to Greek literature and thought, medieval Italian readers and writers relied on what Latin authors translated, adapted, and passed on. In the case of the Homeric poems, Dante's knowledge about the Trojan War and its aftermath came from Latin texts; in other instances, such as Aristotle's philosophy, Dante's understanding was mediated through Arabic translations and commentaries of the Greek philosopher's works, which in their turn had been translated into Latin. This brief overview will provide some context to "reading the *Odyssey*" in the Italian Middle Ages, but will also make a wider point about the role of translation and adaptation in the reception of a literary text and of a character. At the same time, it is important to underline that while some elements from the abovementioned sources made their way into canto 26 of the *Inferno*, the hero's final voyage—a storyline that is not only absent from, but contradicts what we read in the *Odyssey*—is Dante's creation.

A closer look at the map of hell is helpful at this point. Students will see that Ulysses is found in the eighth circle of hell, where simple fraud is punished; that is, the betrayal of people without a special bond of trust. To betray someone who knows and trusts you is considered the gravest sin in Dante's hell and is punished in the ninth and final circle. As the map further shows us, this part of hell, called Malebolge, consists of ten ditches (*bolge* in Italian), and in the eighth *bolgia* we find the "fraudulent counselors." Instructors may point out that this descriptor comes from canto 27, where Dante mentions how another punished soul gave "fraudulent counsel" ("consiglio frodolente"; line 116). Finding Ulysses and Diomedes so close to the bottom of hell underscores the seriousness of their sin in Dante's eyes.

After providing this information, I center the class discussion around the following questions: first, whether Dante depicts Ulisse as a "fraudulent counselor," and, if not, what his sin really is, and, second, how Dante judges the character. For both questions I give students some time to write down their thoughts, and I ask them to refer to specific passages in the text to support their answers. To that end, I also read aloud Ulysses's entire speech (lines 85–142) in class.[13] These questions lend themselves well to a think-pair-share activity: students first think about their answers alone, then pair up with a peer to discuss their answers, and finally share with the entire class (Lightner and Tomaswick).

I always get a wide range of responses to these questions. Responses to the second question can be placed on a scale ranging from a negative portrayal of Ulysses (as in Vergil) to a positive assessment (as in Cicero) and anything in between. The following questions may be helpful if students need more guidance: Is Dante agreeing with Vergil and only considering Ulysses a trickster? Does Ulysses's "fraudulent counsel" refer to the Trojan horse, the tricking of Achilles, the theft of the Palladium, or to the short speech with which he convinced his companions to undertake one more journey? Are there traits in Ulysses that Dante seems to admire or condemn? In discussing students' answers, it is useful to note that Dante's portrayal of Ulysses in canto 26 has sharply divided Dante scholars as well: some see the passage as Dante's expression of pure admiration for Ulisse, while others find that Dante presents him as a transgressor like Adam in the garden of Eden. Teodolinda Barolini provides a short summary of this critical divide, which instructors might look at with students (pars. 23–33). Definitely share Barolini's conclusion:

> Dante is most often a both/and writer, rather than an either/or writer. So much of his language is susceptible to multiple meanings, not in the banal sense of allegory but in the living sense of language that goes in multiple directions, all psychologically true and real to life. In *Inferno* 26 Dante weaves together both the deceptive Ulysses of the *Aeneid* and the lover of knowledge praised by Cicero in the *De Finibus*. Dante's brilliance is to capture both strands in a polysemous whole. (par. 33)

Like Homer's Ulysses, Dante's Ulisse is a "complicated man" (Wilson, Odyssey 1.1).

Each group of students is different, but I have found that the following passages in Dante's canto most often draw their attention. These are all passages that underscore Barolini's point about Dante's language being "susceptible to multiple meanings." First, there is the mention of Ulisse's "desire . . . to become experienced of the world and of human vices and virtue" ("l'ardore / . . . a divenir del mondo esperto / e de li vizi umani e del valore"; lines 97–99), which was stronger than his feelings for his son, father, and wife (94–96). The precise sentiments associated with the unnamed Telemachus ("fondness"; "dolcezza") and Laertes ("devotion"; "pieta"), and with Penelope ("love owed"; "debito amore") can generate some rich discussion, especially when connected to our reading of the *Odyssey*. Then there is Ulisse's short speech to his old and tired companions (112–20), convincing them to undertake one more journey to unexplored territories. Again, the notions of experience and knowledge are central: to see the "world without people" is an experience they "should not want to deny themselves";[14] they were, after all, created to "follow virtue and knowledge" ("per seguir virtute e canoscenza"; 120), concludes Ulisse. Students doubting the sincerity of these words may point to Ulisse's description of the same undertaking further on as a "mad flight" ("folle volo"; 125). And then, at the end of the canto, comes the final reckoning. The exploration of Ulysses and his companions ends with a shipwreck, which we learn was willed by God, the "other" intended in the final verses:

> Three times [the whirlwind] made our ship turn around with all the water,
> at the fourth time it made the stern go up
> and the prow go down, as it pleased another,
> until the sea closed again over us.
>
> Tre volte il fé girar con tutte l'acque;
> a la quarta levar la poppa in suso
> e la prora ire in giù, com' altrui piacque,
> infin che 'l mar fu sovra noi richiuso. (139–42)

What does it mean to be punished for wanting to go where no human has gone before?

Reflecting on these questions could be the conclusion of a unit on Dante's Ulisse, but I have recently added a creative coda. I asked students to revisit our discussion and distill their interpretation of Dante's canto in a blackout poem or found poem based on canto 26 that captures the essence of Dante's Ulisse. First, I ask them to read short definitions of blackout, erasure, and found poetry—terms that are often used interchangeably (for definitions of "erasure" and "found poem," see "Erasure"; "Found Poem"). I also provide a few examples, including Twila Newey's "my heart weaving," four poems created by erasing with stitches of thread most of the words on a page of Emily Wilson's translation of book 19 of the *Odyssey*. In her appended artist statement, Newey describes these erasures as "an attempt to uncover another possible voice, what Penelope might have sung had the song been hers." The examples not only highlight different approaches and materials that can be used but also show how little is needed to create such poems: one can simply encircle or black out words. Some students, of course, will welcome the possibility of adding drawings and designs or experimenting with materials. In an artist statement to be included with their poem (Newey's is a good example: short but to the point), they will briefly explain the "what," "how," and "why" of their poems, offering a final opportunity to reflect on their readings of Homer and Dante.[15]

Dante's Ulisse became an inspiration in his own right to many readers as well as to writers, like Jorge Luis Borges and Primo Levi, and to visual artists, from illuminators rendering scenes of canto 26 in medieval manuscripts to contemporary artists such as Salvador Dalí, Robert Rauschenberg, and Tom Phillips. Works by any of these artists could further supplement this unit. In works of reception such as these, the wanderings of Ulysses have never ended.

As I hope to have shown, Dante's Ulisse delivers a high return on a minimal investment: it is a short additional reading, for which excellent open access pedagogical resources are available. But for instructors who select a different text or artifact to compare with the *Odyssey*, these are the general features of my approach. First, ask students what they know about Ulysses and where they know this from. Then, while or after reading as much of the *Odyssey* as the course schedule allows, introduce an artistic response to the *Odyssey*. In providing some preliminary context, refer back to those two initial questions: What could the artist have known about Ulysses, and where could they know this from? Ask students to engage in a comparative exercise, identifying elements from Homer's poem that shaped the artistic response and what new or different meanings Ulysses takes on. Give students time to think, write, and discuss in pairs and then with the class, always asking them to connect their interpretations to the texts or visual artifacts. Acknowledge that Ulysses was a complicated man and that critical analysis can be quite complicated too. Consider concluding the unit with a creative assignment that summarizes students' interpretations of both the *Odyssey* and the related text or artifact. Such an exercise permits students to participate in the ongoing artistic "wanderings" of Ulysses.

NOTES

1. All resources for teaching the *Inferno* included in this essay are created by Dante scholars and are freely available online.

2. I have used Richmond Lattimore's and Emily Wilson's translations of the *Odyssey*.

3. Forde has more suggestions for short poems on each of these characters (18). See also Murnaghan in this volume.

4. Montemaggi et al. is an excellent short introduction to Dante's *Divine Comedy*.

5. I assign different translations depending on the kind of course. If I want the translation to support students in their reading of the original text, I select a more literal translation, such as Robert Durling's translation of the *Inferno*. If we read the poems in English, I use the more poetic translations mentioned above.

6. Several editions of the *Inferno* include such brief outlines at the beginning of each canto, with varying attention to detail.

7. A different and broader formulation of this question would be, What is "Homeric" about Dante's canto? This question invites students first to reflect on their interpretation of Ulysses in the *Odyssey* and then to think about the relationship between the two texts.

8. I include a few pointers on those first fifty verses. The opening verses (lines 1–12) give students a sense of Dante's complicated relationship with his native Florence; the description of the canto's environment (13–48), rich in similes, is a good sample of Dante's style.

9. These are the elements from the abovementioned list present in canto 26 of the *Inferno*: an apostrophe or address to a place, a description of the atmosphere and architecture of the circle, a description of the punishment, conversations with particular sinners.

10. I cite the Italian text of Dante's *Divina Commedia* edited by Giorgio Petrocchi, which is available on *Digital Dante*, *World of Dante*, and the *Princeton Dante Project*. These three websites include facing English translations of Dante's poem. All translations in this essay are my own.

11. In Italian the name of both the historical poet Vergil and the fictional character in Dante's *Divine Comedy* is Virgilio. It is conventional in anglophone Dante criticism to use the English name Vergil to refer to the historical figure and Virgilio for the character in the poem.

12. For a brief overview with citations from the texts, see Barolini (pars. 17–22).

13. While I always encourage students to read Dante's poetry aloud, here I prefer to read myself so that they can focus on the text. It is very easy to find recordings (audio or video) of readings of this canto in Italian, but it is not so easy to find them in English.

14. Writing at the beginnings of Atlantic explorations, Dante imagined Ulisse would find the open sea and unpopulated territories beyond the Pillars of Hercules at the entrance of the Strait of Gibraltar. The full sentence reads, "You should not want to deny yourselves the experience of what lies behind the sun, of the world without people" ("non vogliate negar l'esperïenza, / di retro al sol, del mondo sanza gente"; lines 116–17).

15. For the precise assignment instructions and some of my students' poems, see Van Peteghem et al.

Reading the *Odyssey* with Modern Lyric

Sheila Murnaghan

Over the past several decades I have developed and taught an undergraduate course on the reception history of the *Odyssey* entitled The *Odyssey* and Its Afterlife. This is a classical studies course open to students of all backgrounds, majors, and levels of preparation at a four-year private university. The semester is divided into three distinct segments. We begin with a monthlong close reading of the *Odyssey* in English translation. This is followed by a chronological survey of the poem's reception, which typically includes selections from Vergil's *Aeneid*, Lucian's *True History*, and Dante Alighieri's *Inferno*; Alfred, Lord Tennyson's "Ulysses" and "Lotos-Eaters"; selections from James Joyce's *Ulysses* and Ralph Ellison's *Invisible Man*; an essay by June Jordan; Derek Walcott's *The* Odyssey*: A Play*; Margaret Atwood's *Penelopiad*; and Louise Glück's *Meadowlands* (for a full list of course readings, see the appendix). The final weeks of the course are devoted to presentations by students of works responding to the *Odyssey* that they themselves have identified and find especially interesting; these can come from any period, cultural context, or medium, and every time I teach the course I am introduced to new and surprising manifestations of the *Odyssey*'s inexhaustible afterlife.

I begin the course by devoting a good deal of time to the *Odyssey* itself for several reasons. There are some students who have never encountered the *Odyssey* before, although those tend to be in the minority, and I want all of them to have enough time to realize just how subtle and sophisticated a poem it is: it is too easy for students of modern reception to treat ancient works reductively, assuming, for example, that it takes a modern reteller to introduce psychological depth or narrative complexity to a simpler ancient model (forgetting that the ancient model was modern and even revisionary in its day). I also want sufficient time to situate the *Odyssey* in its original context, bringing out the distinctively Greek values and forms of social organization that pertained at the outset of the poem's long historical arc.

While I aim to transmit a good grasp of the *Odyssey*'s afterlife as it developed historically, especially within the western European classical tradition, I also resist chronology—honoring a central tenet of reception studies, that the dialogue between ancient works and their later reworkings goes in both directions. I want to avoid a strict segregation between original text and derivative reworkings, and to get students thinking right away about the nature of reception in general and about their own reading of the poem as itself an instance of reception. With these goals in mind, I pair each reading assignment in the *Odyssey* with one or more brief modern lyric poems.

Modern lyrics work especially well for my purposes because they so often foreground a speaker's subjectivity and situated perspective. This is usefully thematized in the poem that I pair with the first assignment from the *Odyssey*, which involves books 1 and 2: Linda Pastan's "Rereading *The Odyssey* in Middle Age" (the second poem in a seven-poem cycle with the same title, published in 1988). This poem takes its bearings from the famous episode—recalled several times in the *Odyssey* and first in book 2, lines 93–110—of Penelope weaving and unweaving a shroud for her father-in-law, Laertes, as a delaying tactic. The speaker wonders why Penelope was weaving a shroud for her father-in-law but also "why have I thought for years / it was a shawl she made" (24). The shawl she misremembers would have been wrapped around Penelope's shoulders on cold, windy nights by one of her young suitors. Pastan's opening questions instantly get across the point that a single work looks different to different readers or even to the same reader at different stages of life, depending on their preoccupations: for a younger reader (closer to the age of my students), Penelope's story is about the romance of being desired; for a middle-aged one, about the family obligations of a daughter-in-law responsible for an aging older generation. This opening also evokes the element of surprise involved in encountering or reencountering old books—something that resonates with the experiences of students, both those who have read the *Odyssey* before, often quickly and with a particular emphasis (for example, in a history course that stressed hospitality as a Greek value), and those who are meeting it for the first time and finding that it does not necessarily match their expectations of a venerable ancient classic. The individual experience of rereading at a specific time of life serves as a telling model for reception in general: the return to a text already freighted with assumptions from the vantage of a particular point in time.

The responses of this speaker's earlier and current selves draw attention to what the *Odyssey* chooses to leave out or play down and raise questions about the blurry distinction between free invention and the reading between the lines that is required to make sense of any narrative. The younger reader's vignette of the suitor with the shawl can be seen as a transformative reworking of the *Odyssey* or as an expansion on indications that Penelope actually enjoys the suitors' company, which the *Odyssey* includes but also mutes. This same reader's concern with Penelope's age brings to the surface questions about the age and the ongoing desirability of the poem's middle-aged protagonists that students often puzzle over but that the poem addresses only obliquely (largely through magical transformations).[1]

The speaker's present puzzlement about why Penelope was weaving a shroud leads to the further question of whether she actually meant to finish it and from there to further speculation about her motives: "could that mean / she wished Laertes dead?" (24). Pastan here exploits—and so points to—one of Homer's most conspicuous silences: the absence of clear indications of what Penelope is thinking through much of the poem, even when she plays a decisive role in the plot. I encourage students to consider why the poet leaves this subject unexplored and to recognize the opportunity this silence has provided for women poets like Pastan to fill in what is missing, drawing on their own experiences and using what Penelope thinks but does not say as a way of acknowledging and challenging her role as a dutiful wife and mother.

When we get to the later sections of the *Odyssey*, in which Penelope is especially featured, we read other examples from the extensive archive of such poems.[2] Many of them were written by mid-twentieth-century writers influenced by second-wave feminism, but not by any means all of them. One I often include, "Penelope's Musings," was found in a diary entry for 1875 by a Midwestern American woman, Jemimah Makepiece Sturt. Sturt deftly reconstructs Penelope's thoughts as an unspoken address to Odysseus at the point in the epic when she is unsure whether to recognize him or not (23.93–110). She begins, "I know thee not, yet know thee well," but this Penelope's knowledge of her husband goes beyond recognition of his identity to rueful thoughts about his waywardness, infidelity, and unreliability: "Thine eyes have seen the deeps of Hell. / Thy limbs have lain in witches' arms," she adds, and she concludes, "Stay with me if you must a'while . . . I know I'll be alone at death." More recently, in "Penelope Writes" (1982), Katha Pollitt, like Pastan, develops the rebellious potential of Penelope's unweaving, but in an angrier register:

> No one imagines
> how almost lovingly
> with what delight each night I make destruction.
> I rip and slash. My fingers bleed. And then
> I dream in my abandon
> I am tearing my whole house down. (15)

Odysseus's narrative of his adventures (books 9–12) can be paired with modern poems that give greater voice and interiority to numerous characters whose point of view the *Odyssey* glosses over, such as the "other women," Circe and Calypso, who figure in the poem primarily as obstacles or accomplices in Odysseus's project of homecoming.[3] A challenging poem by Margaret Atwood, "Siren Song" (1974), cleverly exposes the calculated appeal to male vanity that makes the Sirens such a threat to heroic journeys like his. These unenchanted evocations of marginalized women's perspectives are especially instructive for revealing how the poem, for better or worse, adopts an Odysseus-centric perspective, aligning its values with his aspirations and treating the satisfaction of his desires as necessary and laudable.

Some modern poets comment explicitly on this skewing of the *Odyssey*'s universe. Pollitt's Penelope ruefully imagines what Odysseus's perennial good fortune must feel like to him:

> Husband, on your long oceans
> islands rise up to save you, sudden, blue,
> miraculous as dolphins.
> And each time you think, "Why not? I'm young! I'm young!
> It is right that such things happen." (14)

A relatively recent addition to the syllabus, Honorée Fanonne Jeffers's "Blues: Odysseus" (2020), expresses a similar ambivalence about the poem's privileged and protected hero through the story of Odysseus's rescue by the sea nymph Eidothea (*Odyssey* 5.333–53):

> I want to be happy that Homer imagined
> a sea housing pretty, forgiving Nymphs—
> while somewhere else, a wheel dances
> and someone else drowns.
> Sharks should pass Odysseus by,
> never imagining his taste.
> The gods shouldn't pull at his fate—
> now angry, now benevolent.
> I try hard not to blame that man:
> We all deserve our Maker's love.

Jeffers's poem introduces a further layer of complexity because she reads that episode from the *Odyssey* in conjunction with one of the *Odyssey* collages of the early-twentieth-century Harlem artist Romare Bearden, "Odysseus Rescued by Sea-Nymphs,"[4] and she recalls, as Bearden's image does, "*The Zong* slave ship massacre of 1781, when at least one hundred and thirty enslaved Africans were murdered when the ship's crew threw them overboard." This means that her poem anticipates several other themes of the course: the significant role of intermediary works of reception in shaping later ones and the distinctive traditions of reception through illustration.

Whether or not the issue of the storyteller's partiality is explicitly articulated, as in these two examples, later writers' attempts to animate characters given minor roles in the *Odyssey* help students read with greater sensitivity to the inevitable biases of narrative and recognize the omissions that result as openings to later retellings. As Pastan puts it in a later poem in her *Odyssey* cycle, "There is always a story / that no one bothers to tell" ("Suitor"); here she has in mind a young, gentle, unimportant member of the band of Penelope's suitors.

As Pastan's young suitor indicates, not all the poems I use foreground women; and some focus on Odysseus himself. When we get to the reunion of Odysseus and Telemachus in book 16, I assign Joseph Brodsky's "Odysseus to Telemachus" (1972), in which a still-wandering Odysseus apostrophizes Telemachus, expressing uncertainty about whether they will ever meet and suggesting that his own absence might not be such a bad thing for his son:

>   away from me
> you are quite safe from all Oedipal passions,
> and your dreams, my Telemachus, are blameless.

The explicit concerns of Brodsky's Odysseus, expressed in modern Freudian terms, highlight the hints of tension and competition present under the surface as Homer's Odysseus does return and reinhabits his son's life (*Odyssey* 16.192–212, 21.113–39, 24.505–15). Another angle on Odysseus's story is provided by Robert Graves's "Ulysses" (1933), in which all the hero's experiences are simply a series of repetitive sexual conquests:

> To the much-tossed Ulysses, never done
> With woman whether gowned as wife or whore,
> Penelope and Circe seemed as one:
> She like a whore made his lewd fancies run,
> And wifely she a hero to him bore.

This serves especially well to illustrate the way that reading from a specific standpoint is reductive as well as incisive.

Although most of the short poems I incorporate into this part of the syllabus come from England and America of the last three centuries, I also have students read the pastoral poem known as "The Cyclops," by the Hellenistic Greek poet Theocritus (ca. 300–250 BCE) alongside book 9 of the *Odyssey*. In Theocritus the Cyclops appears a lovelorn shepherd, pouring out a song with which he tries to woo an unresponsive sea nymph. This might seem to be a complete departure from the *Odyssey* if the poem did not include some pointed foreshadowing of the events of book 9. This text not only directs students' attention to the elements of pathos in Homer's Cyclops but also testifies to the long time span of antiquity itself (five hundred years separate Theocritus from Homer), which students generally foreshorten, and shows that the transformation of earlier texts was already a feature of the ancient world.

Through this series of pairings, I offer my students an early preview of the recent and contemporary understandings and uses of the *Odyssey* that are the endpoint of a chronologically arranged syllabus that begins in the distant past. These brief poems provide them with a foundation for the longer works on which we focus in the next section of the course. Having already learned from Theocritus's vision of the Cyclops that the portrayal crafted by Odysseus in book 9 need not be definitive, they are well prepared to see this figure variously reimagined as the myopic patriot of Joyce's *Ulysses*, the drunken white racists of Ellison's *Invisible Man*, the watchful authoritarian strong man of Walcott's *The* Odyssey: *A Play*, and the passive victims who think no one is to blame when they are exploited and oppressed in June Jordan's essay "Problems of Language in a Democratic State." With its evocation of Bearden and the Zong massacre, Jeffers's poem establishes connections between Odysseus's seafaring and the African diaspora that Walcott develops more fully in his stage version of the *Odyssey*. Having experienced the ways in which, in poems by Pastan, Sturt, and Pollitt, Penelope serves as a self-centering vehicle for a modern poet's sensibility, students are well positioned to see how that potential is expanded and complicated when Penelope's voice is presented as one of several in longer works: Louise Glück includes poems spoken by a Penelope figure who is also a poet in her extended *Odyssey*-based cycle *Meadowlands* but makes that figure rigorously self-critical and juxtaposes her voice with those of other characters from the epic, including a skeptical Telemachus; in *The Penelopiad*, Margaret Atwood constructs a counterpoint between an unillusioned Penelope, who speaks in prose, and her twelve hanged enslaved women, who are given a lyric voice and who haunt her to the point of compassion fatigue. Finally, in addition to setting up specific thematic connections and variations, I aim through these brief lyrics to prepare students to read with a more sophisticated understanding of reception in general: with awareness of some of the particular ways in which the *Odyssey* itself invites revision and a sharper sense of reception as (in many cases) a selective, pointed, and personally inflected enterprise.

NOTES

1. On the *Odyssey*'s magical reversals of time, including the presentation of Odysseus's true age as merely a disguise, see Murnaghan, *Disguise* 5, 10–11.
2. For the rich tradition of poems exploring Penelope's thoughts and experiences, see Murnaghan and Roberts, "Penelope's Song"; Doherty, "Figure"; Hurst.
3. For poems exploring the perspectives of the *Odyssey*'s "other women," see Murnaghan and Roberts, "Forecast."
4. For an image of "Odysseus Rescued by Sea-Nymphs," see "Romare Bearden."

APPENDIX: COURSE READINGS

Individual Poems

Atwood, Margaret. "Siren Song." *Selected Poems, 1965–1975*, by Atwood, Houghton Mifflin, 1976, p. 195.

Brodsky, Joseph. "Odysseus to Telemachus." Translated by George L. Kline. *A Part of Speech*, by Brodsky, Farrar, Straus and Giroux, 1980, p. 58.

Graves, Robert. "Ulysses." *Collected Poems*, by Graves, Cassell, 1975, p. 56.

Jeffers, Honorée Fanonne. "Blues: Odysseus." *The Age of Phillis*, by Jeffers, Wesleyan UP, 2020, p. 23.

Pastan, Linda. "Rereading *The Odyssey* in Middle Age." *The Imperfect Paradise*, by Pastan, W. W. Norton, 1988, pp. 24–25.

———. "The Suitor." *The Imperfect Paradise*, by Pastan, W. W. Norton, 1988, p. 31.

Pollitt, Katha. "Penelope Writes." *Antarctic Traveler*, by Pollitt, Knopf, 1983, pp. 14–15.

Sturt, Jemimah Makepiece. "Penelope's Musings." *Homer in English*, edited by George Steiner, Penguin, 1996, p. 187.

Theocritus. "Cyclops." *Theocritus: Idylls and Epigrams*, translated by Daryl Hine, Athenaeum, 1982, pp. 42–44.

Longer Works of Reception*

Atwood, Margaret. *The Penelopiad*. Canongate, 2005.

Dante. *Inferno*. Translated by Robert Pinsky, Farrar, Straus and Giroux, 1994.

Dulac, Edmund. *Sinbad the Sailor and Other Stories from the Arabian Nights. Project Gutenberg*, 2024, www.gutenberg.org/ebooks/47285.

Ellison, Ralph. *Invisible Man*. Vintage, 1995.

Glück, Louise. *Meadowlands*. Ecco, 1996.

Jordan, June. "Problems of Language in a Democratic State." *On Call: Political Essays*, by Jordan, South End Press, 1985, pp. 27–36.

Joyce, James. *Ulysses*. Vintage, 1986.

Lucian. *The True History*. Translated by Paul Turner, Indiana UP, 1974.

Mason, Zachary. *The Lost Books of the* Odyssey. Farrar, Straus and Giroux, 2007.

Tennyson, Alfred. "The Lotos-Eaters." *Homer in English*, edited by George Steiner, Penguin, 1996, pp. 133–38.

———. "Ulysses." *Homer in English*, edited by George Steiner, Penguin, 1996, pp. 138–40.

Vergil. *The Aeneid*. Translated by Sarah Ruden, Yale UP, 2021.

Walcott, Derek. *The* Odyssey: *A Play*. Farrar, Straus and Giroux, 1993.

* These are read in the second part of the course, after the *Odyssey*. Some are excerpted, and not all are read in every iteration of the course. The translations of Dante, Lucian, Sinbad the Sailor, and Vergil listed here are ones that I have found to be accessible for students encountering the works for the first time, but in each case there are other translations available that may suit particular instructors as well or better.

2001 Space Odysseys: Teaching the *Odyssey* with Pop Culture

Brett M. Rogers

In popular culture, Homer's *Odyssey* lurks nearly everywhere. Its ongoing and widespread popularity partly derives from the many distinctive elements it offers to creators of new narratives: its journey and homecoming (*nostos*) story patterns, its many encounters with the strange or other, its menagerie of supernatural beings and creatures, its revenge plot, and its heterosexual love reunion. Moreover, for many modern storytellers and artists, the *Odyssey*'s status as an ancient myth lends it authority, evoking a feeling that such themes and stories are somehow "timeless" or "universal." Thereby the *Odyssey* has become a trusted resource for the purpose of creating new stories that feel old, familiar, even comfortable—and therefore are more likely to resonate with audiences. The widespread popularity of the *Odyssey* has been such that audiences are often familiar with the poem's basic plot even if they themselves have never read it.[1] One such audience, a thirteenth-century Florentine fanboy named Dante Alighieri, did not have access to the *Odyssey* itself and only knew it indirectly, yet still managed to work content derived from Homeric mythos into his own work (*Inferno* 26.52–27.3).[2] Much like the poem's protagonist, then, the pervasive influence of the *Odyssey* may be detected even in its seeming absence.

And yet, as storytellers have brought this ancient story into their own contemporary contexts, the *Odyssey* has offered a productive space for experimentation and innovation. Take, for example, the case of science fiction, wherein various authors have refigured the *Odyssey* to conduct experiments on the construction and limits of human knowledge. Already in the second century CE, Lucian of Samosata drew upon several elements of the then-millennium-old *Odyssey* for his *True Narratives*, also translated as *The True History* (arguably the first science fiction text), in order to ask what it means to (not) tell a true story and, more importantly, what the techniques are for producing false narratives. A comparable thought experiment is found in Matt Fraction and Christian Ward's comic book series *Ody-C*, which uses the *Odyssey* to test assumptions about sex, gender, and warfare: set in a visually psychedelic version of outer space, their gender-flipped *Ody-C* explores the problem of male supremacy by asking what would happen if (almost) all males ceased to exist and all the heroes of Greek myth were women or transgender.[3] This thought experiment opens up questions both epistemological and ethical: Does removing males remove warfare? Does it remove sexual hierarchies and consequently sexual oppression? Admittedly, *True Narratives* and *Ody-C* are not perfectly designed thought experiments, so we may question whether their male creators' androcentric worldviews just lead to confirmation bias. (For example, both texts delight in a kind of titillation that seems to reflect not the *Odyssey*'s own sexism but forms of sexism contemporary to those reception texts.) Nevertheless, *True Narratives* and *Ody-C* indicate that the ancient poem has been perceived as a renewable and transformable resource for the creation of strange, new narratives and the exploration of our processes for constructing knowledge about that which is, or is not, human.

As scholars and teachers, we can thus harness the *Odyssey* and its receptions as valuable and versatile tools for examining the processes by which storytellers transform the ancient past into modern cultural products, as well as the social, ethical, epistemological, and political dimensions of such work. Teaching the *Odyssey* in tandem with popular culture can be effective with students for a variety of reasons. Students sometimes grasp a point or problem in the *Odyssey* more clearly when it is refracted through a modern or familiar perspective.[4] Students are often animated in their work when they see texts or media with which they may already be familiar. Furthermore, students are often excited to think about creative and playful ways to use ancient texts to make new narratives or works of art—which is especially helpful for activating different kinds of thinking and, perhaps more importantly, reaching students who struggle with traditional academic work. For example, my introductory myth class ends with a myth interpretation project that essentially functions as an art exhibition and festival of songs and sketches: each student is asked to create a work of art and explain briefly their choices for making this particular work. In this assignment, I have seen some thought-provoking *Odyssey* paintings, board games, folk songs, and even a stunning Scylla and Charybdis cake. I have seen all these student responses when teaching the *Odyssey* and its receptions—especially receptions that derive from popular culture—in a wide variety of classroom contexts over the past two decades.[5] In these varied contexts, and given my own research on classical receptions, I have tried to develop clear and intentional techniques for students to explore the spaces where the ancient *Odyssey* and its modern receptions come together. In this essay I discuss some of the particular techniques and exercises I have devised to help students engage productively with the *Odyssey* and its popular cultural receptions.

Comparison and Cultural Companions

At the very least, we might see the *Odyssey* and a modern popular cultural text as "cultural companions" who shed light on one another.[6] From this perspective, it may be enough to do a simple compare-and-contrast activity, setting the *Odyssey* alongside a modern popular text and seeing what students do with the comparison through discussion, writing, or creative activity. This can be done in class on a small scale or a large scale.

For a small-scale version of such comparative work, for example, I might invite students to read the *Odyssey* in translation over the course of two weeks in class, then spend a class session comparing the ancient epic with a popular cultural text, either something that obviously cites its relationship to the *Odyssey* (e.g.,

2001: A Space Odyssey, the Franco-Japanese cartoon series *Ulysses-31*, or Fraction and Ward's *Ody-C*) or something that does not cite the *Odyssey* but is clearly concerned with the same themes (e.g., the films *Big Fish* or *Cold Mountain*, which are both engaged with themes of homecoming and hospitality).[7] One might scale up this activity to a week of classes: for example, in a course entirely dedicated to receptions of the *Odyssey*, we watched *Big Fish* and *Cold Mountain* along with *O Brother, Where Art Thou?* to ask a larger, sustained question about why the *Odyssey* and its themes seem particularly prominent in popular films about the American South at the turn of the twenty-first century.

For a large-scale version of this comparative approach, I do something more ambitious in my course titled Theories of Myth. As the title indicates, the course is focused on tracing the theoretical schools that have dominated how we interpret myth, with an emphasis on theories since the discovery of (what we now call) Proto-Indo-European in the late eighteenth century. Since the course requires students to engage with a wide array of theories, I choose only one ancient text, to which students apply each theory: I use the *Odyssey* since there is ample scholarship about the epic belonging to all the major theoretical schools discussed in the class.[8] In the final weeks of the class, I ask students to compare the *Odyssey* with a modern American *nostos* tale that has recently undergone a similar transition from text to myth and that has been subjected to an array of receptions and theory-based interpretations: L. Frank Baum's *The Wonderful Wizard of Oz*. For this particular exercise, I ask students to focus on a series of *Oz* texts: for example, Baum's novel, films such as *The Wizard of Oz* and *The Wiz*, Shelley Jackson's hypertext novel *Patchwork Girl*, the Broadway recording or recent film adaptation of the musical *Wicked*, and the science fiction series *Tin Man*. The students, who have just spent the previous twelve weeks working closely on the *Odyssey*, invariably compare the *Odyssey* and *Oz* in terms of plot, theme, narrative structure, and even the way both texts transform over time from discrete texts into traditional tales. In exploring the *Odyssey* alongside the *Oz* texts as cultural companions, students come to recognize more easily how texts operate in a still-emergent mythic tradition and to think more critically about other media they consume.

Refining First Principles and Goals

The comparative approach to teaching and studying classical receptions in popular culture has been a tried-and-true approach for some time and is the basis of much scholarship in reception studies. We can and should use popular culture texts strategically, with the same care in design that we bring to any text or activity we build into our courses. Certainly, it is easy to be excited to share every new popular manifestation of the *Odyssey* or to read it alongside some new text we love. If this is done carelessly, however, teachers run the risk of either engaging in a kind of scopophilia—as if indulging in the pleasure of seeing the *Odyssey* manifest in a modern popular cultural text is sufficiently "scholarly"—or promoting a pernicious colonizing attitude, as if to claim, "Since I study the *Odyssey*, everything is about the *Odyssey*." It is important to be intentional about which texts we use and how we deploy them in discussions, papers, or other projects. To this end, whenever I create a new reception-based assignment, I reflect on the following questions:

> What kind of media (film, television, comics, illustration, etc.) do I want students to encounter in this teaching moment? (Am I trying to vary the kind of text with which students are engaging? Am I trying give them a break from reading dense text?)
>
> Do I want the assignment to emphasize the ancient "source" text (e.g., the *Odyssey*)? The modern "reception" text (e.g., *Ody-C*)? Both equally? How much space do I need to leave for this work?
>
> Do I want students to focus on author-oriented criteria (e.g., choices the author made in the reception) or audience-oriented criteria (i.e., reader response)?
>
> Do I want students to produce critical work (such as a scholarly essay)? Creative work (such as a play or painting)? Some combination of both?
>
> What skills do students need for this work that will transfer to interpreting other reception texts and especially to their subsequent encounters with popular culture (whether as consumers or creators) outside of class?

In the process of answering these questions, the contours of a given assignment or series of assignments may emerge.

Popular Culture

It is also important for teachers and students to reflect on what it means to describe some texts as "popular culture." Any instructor who sets ancient texts alongside modern texts—especially "popular" texts or "popular culture"—is bound to raise questions about what it means to set these different texts in dialogue. For example, some readers may find jarring the casualness with which I have in this essay set the *Odyssey* and Dante's *Inferno*, both "classic" texts, alongside Lucian's *True Narratives* (an "ancient" text, but not always "canonical") and Fraction and Ward's *Ody-C* (a "modern" work of "popular culture"). Similarly, in my introductory myth class, I invite students to consider books 9–12 of the *Odyssey* alongside book 10 of Plato's *Republic* (the myth of Ur), Theocritus's *Idyll* 11 (Polyphemus's love song to Galatea), book 6 of Vergil's *Aeneid* (the underworld), and Fraction and Ward's *Ody-C* (Lotus-Eaters, Cyclops, and Aeolus narratives). In moving across time (Classical Greek, Hellenistic, Roman, and American) and genres (philosophy, bucolic, epic, and sci-fi comics), these juxtapositions invite students to reflect on what it means to define some texts as "high art" or "literary" and others as "popular art" or "popular culture." After all, are not all these works in a sense *Odyssey* fan fiction? Why do we use the terminology and draw the boundaries that we do? What are the stakes?

In support of this work, I find it useful to have students read something like Jesse Weiner's essay "Classical Epic and the Poetics of Modern Fantasy," in which Weiner examines the modern notions of "high art" and "popular art" as aesthetic categories developed only in the past two centuries. Weiner usefully details the aesthetic and classist assumptions that underlie these two categories: for example, texts that are categorized as "high art" are regularly described as "avant-garde," "classic," "serious," "sophisticated," or "transcendent," while "popular art" tends to be described as "romantic," "light," "entertaining," "commercial," or even "formulaic" (41–44). Students are prone to making similar aesthetic distinctions without necessarily being conscious they are doing so, and it is important to interrogate these assumptions at the beginning of our classwork. Why is the *Inferno* "serious" and "transcendent" but *Ody-C* "light" and "entertaining"?

Such concerns become especially important when we engage with the *Odyssey*. Is it meaningful or even useful to describe the *Odyssey* as "high art" or "popular art"? After all, the *Odyssey* is a "serious" "classic" (often taught in classics departments), yet it is also "romantic," "accessible," and quite literally "formulaic" (in that the poem was originally composed in performance out of formulaic poetic language). How do we productively navigate this paradox that confounds the aesthetic categories students bring into the classroom? Since the *Odyssey* itself confounds our modern aesthetic categories, we can use this opportunity to enable students to develop more nuanced and more productive critical lenses through which they may read the ancient epic and its receptions in "popular culture."

Critical Vocabularies

While I am advocating for dismantling categories that reinforce unproductive and alienating (classist, sexist, racist, etc.) biases, it is still important to introduce students to other, productive critical vocabularies in order to guide their encounters with the *Odyssey* and its receptions in popular culture. This is an especially pressing concern since much modern popular culture relies upon a seeming blurring of boundaries that gives way to the worst excesses of (a caricature of) postmodernism. As Benjamin Eldon Stevens and I argue in an essay on classical receptions in science fiction:

> We therefore believe it is important for Classicists in particular to acknowledge that in more recent SF (as well as other genres) "the classics" have been transformed into something like "reliably esoteric, public-domain material for popular cultural ironization." In this way "the classics" are being made into vivid signifiers neither of the ancient past, nor even of professional knowledge of antiquity, but of a present moment: an advanced postmodern moment marked by recomposition of past cultural products

> that is omnivorous and, from a scholarly perspective, generally uncritical. These "classics," as it were cobbled and stitched together into a new monstrum, constitute an imagistically vivid but ontologically indistinct entry in an advanced postmodern encyclopedism that is, in its own view, not hierarchical but associative and, so, willfully apolitical about its cultural recompositions. (Rogers and Stevens 131)

In other words, if we accept the premise that classical receptions are cultural productions that may have social, cultural, and political ramifications—no matter how entertaining or accessible or willfully apolitical the reception text appears to be—then we need to empower students to recognize the workings, power, and effects of classical receptions. More simply, if we want to help our students be more sensitive readers and more cautious consumers of text—if, as Ben Stevens and I are wont to say, we want to build a better geek—then we need to give students some tools and methods to do so.

To this end, I include in some courses activities that introduce students to (still-emergent) critical vocabularies for studying classical receptions. I have found three works of scholarship to be both accessible and particularly helpful for introducing students to critical vocabularies: Lorna Hardwick's *Reception Studies*, whose introduction offers a thumbnail sketch of how reception studies works and provides useful author- or creator-oriented critical vocabulary (9–10); Tony Keen's important blogpost "The 'T' Stands for Tiberius," which offers an audience-oriented critical vocabulary that draws examples from classical receptions in science fiction;[9] and C. W. Marshall's essay "Odysseus and the *Infinite Horizon*," which offers an audience-oriented framework comparable to Keen's vocabulary but with some differences worth exploring with students (19–23).[10]

Once I introduce students to this critical vocabulary, I use it regularly and encourage students to do the same in our discussions and short assignments, so that we can learn how to use these tools and test their interpretive value and limits. In support of this work, I build into every session of my Sci-Fi, Fantasy, and Antiquity course a low-stakes activity called "Spec Fic Show n' Tell," with the following prompt:

> Speculative fiction—that is, science fiction and fantasy—is ever-increasing in its scope, including the constant production of books, magazines, films, television programs, comic books, games, action figures, household goods, etc. Any course I could possibly design on classical receptions in science fiction and fantasy will *a priori* be woefully insufficient in scope. Thus, in order to broaden our scope, you will bring into class for presentation one item for Show n' Tell—that is, a film or television clip, a book or comic or magazine that contains some kind of classical reception in speculative fiction. You will have ten minutes to describe and contextualize the item for us, discuss its significance for you and for broader audiences, and offer analysis using the various theories we have discussed.

"Spec Fic Show n' Tell" has several advantages. It encourages students to practice using critical vocabulary. It centers student voices and interests at the beginning of each class session. Affectively speaking, it reduces (inevitable) complaints about the science fiction or fantastic texts that I have omitted from the course, allowing each student to contribute to our collective knowledge. And it stimulates student thinking about the independent research papers they will produce at the end of the course.

The course midterm paper (five to seven pages in length) then builds on the work of "Spec Fic Show n' Tell." Again, I require students to use this critical language, giving them a prompt with the following directions:

> First, choose one ancient text and one science fiction text [from a list of readings that I provide]. Then, make a sustained argument about the relationship between your two chosen texts. Consider the following questions: How does your science fiction text "receive" the ancient text? To what use does the science fiction text put the ancient text? What might the ancient text make possible for or reveal about the science fiction text? In turn, what might the science fiction text reveal about the ancient text?
>
> In answering these questions, use the terminology provided by Hardwick, Keen, Marshall, or all three. You may also borrow any useful concepts from other articles we have read. Clearly define any terminology or concepts you use.

For example, in my Sci-Fi, Fantasy, and Antiquity course, students will have read ancient texts such as books 9–12 of the *Odyssey* as well as various passages from Hesiod, Plato, and Ovid, and they will have encountered science fiction texts such as Lucian's *True Narratives*, Fraction and Ward's *Ody-C*, Mary Wollstonecraft Shelley's *Frankenstein*, Stanley Weinbaum's "Martian Odyssey," *2001: A Space Odyssey*, and the film *Alien: Resurrection*. We will have explored each text in depth during class discussions—the unit on the *Odyssey* and incredible voyage runs during weeks 5 to 7—so this midterm paper is meant to be both summative and formative. In other words, the goal here is to make sure students have a command of a discrete corpus of critical vocabulary and see what they discover as they practice its use. I deliberately limit the scope of what students may write about so as to keep the paper from getting unwieldy. That said, as the scare quotes around the word "receive" in the prompt indicate, I also invite students to challenge what it means to talk about "reception" and whether the terminology adequately describes or explains what may be taking place between the ancient and modern texts. In the prompt I also encourage students to reverse the stream ("In turn . . .") so that we do not think about "tradition" or "reception" or even "transformation" as linear or diachronic processes but consider how modern texts might affect or reveal things about ancient texts.[11]

Introducing students to critical vocabulary for reception studies is a helpful prelude or accompaniment to the primary source readings for a variety of reasons. First, it helps students understand that popular culture is no less an object of serious scholarship than any other cultural product and thus works to dismantle the distinction between high art and popular art. Second, introducing students to this critical vocabulary demonstrates that method and theory are important tools, so that students understand this work not as mere enthusiasm or fandom but as subject to critical processes comparable to those found in other established academic disciplines. (Since students are prone to confuse identity and fandom with expertise, I sometimes illustrate this principle with a pair of examples: I am Jewish, but that does not make me a Jewish studies scholar; I am not an ancient Greek, but I am an ancient Greek scholar.) In classes that use popular culture, it becomes important to emphasize the processes of ongoing scrutiny, evaluation, and transformation that are also the foundation for other disciplines (such as chemistry, anthropology, philology, etc.). Since classical reception studies in modern popular culture is a fairly recent discipline, and we may eventually reject or replace the particular critical vocabularies offered by, for example, Hardwick, Keen, or Marshall, students need to recognize the importance of trial, error, and peer review.

Finally, introducing students to these critical vocabularies is important for their ability to pursue independent research papers on their own chosen topics at the end of the term (and, hopefully, for projects beyond the course). There is a superabundance of popular cultural receptions, so we need our students to feel ready to contribute to the ongoing interrogation of classical receptions in popular culture—so that we might resist the uncritical and willfully apolitical tendencies of many modern texts and their consumers and instead produce better conversations and behaviors informed by careful methodologies and some degree of quality control.

Odyssean Histories and Genealogies

The paper assignment on critical vocabularies is predicated on perhaps the simplest way to introduce students to reception studies: compare and contrast modern text A with ancient text B. In classes for which my goal with the modern popular culture text is to help students see the lasting influence of ancient texts and incite their imaginations, I tend to use a simple version of this exercise. ("Let's read the *Odyssey* and then watch *O Brother, Where Art Thou?*") However, focusing on comparisons can wrongly imply that the two texts are directly related—that the creator or creators of modern text A knew or had access to ancient text B. (For example, the Coen brothers famously claimed in interviews that they had not read the *Odyssey*, despite claiming in the credits that the film is based on Homer [Romney].) Simply comparing a modern text with an ancient text skips the often-complicated stemmata or genealogies that chart the historical movement of a given reception from antiquity to modernity. Recall the earlier example of Odysseus in Dante's *Inferno*: we know that Dante had never read the *Odyssey* since the ancient Greek epic had disappeared from Italy, so how did the homecoming narrative of a character from an absent text make its way into the Italian poem? In the case of Dante, Odysseus's homecoming narrative makes its way into *Inferno* through Latin literature—Dante knows Odysseus from Vergil, Ovid, and the like. We should thus be asking our students to wonder about the various texts and historical events that may have an impact on a given classical reception, so that we are careful about whose Odysseus we may be encountering in a given modern popular reception.

A caveat is important here. I started this essay with the claim that Homer's *Odyssey* lurks everywhere in modern popular culture; in his history of the reception of the *Iliad* and *Odyssey*, Alberto Manguel makes this point more eloquently:

> A book's influence is never straightforward. Common readers, unrestricted by the rigours of academe, allow their books to dialogue with one another, to exchange meanings and metaphors, to enrich and annotate each other. In the reader's mind, books become entwined and intermingled, so that we no longer know whether a certain adventure belongs to Arsilaous or to Aquiles, or where Homer ends Ulysses' adventures and the author of Sinbad takes them up again. (88)[12]

We might substitute the words "authors" or "creators" for Manguel's "common readers": the creative process is often a slippery combination of tradition, influence, and innovation. So we must encourage students to be careful with the scope of any given claim they make about a given reception taking place in a work of popular culture.

I nevertheless find it important to encourage students to attempt to track an aspect of reception from the eighth-century-BCE *Odyssey* to a twentieth- or twenty-first-century popular cultural reception. To this end, for the second paper in a reception-focused course I devised an assignment I call "The Monster Genealogy Project," which includes the following prompt:

> Choose one "monstrous" character from those who appear in books 9–12 of the *Odyssey* (e.g., the Lotus-Eaters, Polyphemus, Aeolus, the Laestrygonians, Circe, Scylla, Charybdis, the cattle of Helius, or Calypso). First, research that character and construct a list of every appearance of it. In other words, construct a history or genealogy of the different versions of that monster from Homer's *Odyssey* to today. Then, examine your genealogy to identify some of the different uses to which that monstrous figure has been put throughout its history. Are there any particular patterns that appear? Or are there moments in which a receiving author reshapes "the monster," altering it iconically? And, in constructing a genealogy, how can we tell which version of the "monster" influenced certain later versions?

Students quickly realize that this paper is a serious challenge—and, frankly, an impossible task for a five-to-seven-page undergraduate paper during one month of a semester-long course. When I hand out this prompt two to three weeks ahead of the due date, a student might raise concerns about its feasibility, and I steer the class into a discussion about the challenges and process of studying Odyssean receptions. I gently emphasize that I do not expect them to find everything—I direct them to the words "that you can find" in the prompt—but I want them to undertake the process of *attempting* to do so. One week later I ask how the paper is going, at which point some students will have figured out how hard it is to track all the occurrences of a given monster and to make claims about the source text or texts that influence a given appearance of a modern monster. Conversation soon follows about scholarly books on Homeric reception, mythology compendia, the *Lexicon Iconographicum Mythologiae Classicae* (*Dictionary of Iconography of Classical Mythology*), and even our frenemy *Wikipedia*. Students nevertheless find the process highly instructive, and the skills they develop in trying to track a monster transfer over into later projects in the same class—that is, they realize how much work goes into making claims carefully and how tendentious it can be to claim a historical or genealogical relationship between an Odyssean monster and its seeming modern counterparts.[13]

There's No Place Like Home(r)

The *Odyssey* is a rich source text whose numerous receptions in popular culture, from *The Wizard of Oz* to *2001: A Space Odyssey* to its prominent role in season 2 of the Netflix adaptation of *The Umbrella Academy*, merit our careful attention in the classroom. Given the proliferation and wide accessibility of popular culture—and with it, the appearance of strange and hitherto unimagined versions of the *Odyssey*—it is imperative for educators to help students recognize and critically analyze these classical receptions. If we can empower our students to become more thoughtful and cautious consumers, interpreters, scholars, and producers of narrative, then even greater (space) odysseys may yet lie ahead for us all.

NOTES

I extend my gratitude to Benjamin Eldon Stevens and Jesse Weiner for helpful feedback on this essay.

1. See the brief discussion of the Coen brothers and *O Brother, Where Art Thou?* below in this essay.

2. See Stevens; see also Van Peteghem in this volume.

3. In the first narrative arc of the comic (issues 1–5), the only human bio-males known to survive are He, a male Helen of Troy, and Odyssea's son, Telemachus. On gender in *Ody-C*, see Rogers, "Postmodern Prometheus" 219–21.

4. Sometimes an aspect of the *Odyssey* may even become more emotionally recognizable. For example, the pathos of the death of Odysseus's dog Argus (17.290–327) is vividly evoked in the heartbreaking final sequence in the *Futurama* episode "Jurassic

Bark," in which the protagonist's loyal dog, Seymour Asses, waits a decade and a half for his absent master until Seymour finally dies of old age. See Rogers, "Cyber-Dogs," especially 54.

5. I have taught the *Odyssey* in introductory undergraduate courses on Greek culture and myth, introductory and advanced Ancient Greek language courses, an intermediate course on classical receptions focused exclusively on the *Odyssey*, an advanced undergraduate course on classical receptions in science fiction, and as the central text in an advanced undergraduate course on theories of myth.

6. For the term "cultural companion" in the context of classical reception, see James 239.

7. Charles Frazier's novel *Cold Mountain*, on which the film is based, in contrast does explicitly cite the *Odyssey*. This example may be instructive for showing students how key information that verifies the modern author's intentional engagement with an ancient source text can be lost as the modern narrative is translated across media.

8. I thus assign students a series of short papers that require them to perform, for example, nineteenth-century-style comparatist, Freudian psychoanalytic, or Lévi-Straussian structuralist readings of the *Odyssey*.

9. Prior to Keen's blogpost, the only works of scholarship that aimed to theorize classical receptions in science fiction with respect to the genre (and not narrowly focused on a case study) were Fredericks, "Greek Mythology" and *Future*. On Lucian's *True Narratives* as a work of science fiction, see also Fredericks, "Lucian's *True History*." See Keen, "More 'T,'" for reflections on and minor revisions of that blogpost.

10. For a 2017 workshop I co-organized at the Center for Hellenic Studies, I created a chart that compares these three critical vocabularies; the portion of this chart comparing the schemata of Keen and Marshall may be found in Keen, "More 'T'" 12. Instructors who are seeking further discussions of reception studies may wish to consult, for example, Hardwick and Stray; Shane Butler; Willis; or Baker et al.

11. In addition to viewing the film *Alien: Resurrection*, I ask students to read Rogers, "Hybrids," which treats the *Odyssey* as a cultural companion with *Alien: Resurrection* and whose final section explores how the film's interest in ethical hybridity illuminates Archaic Greek heroes and Odysseus's slaughter of the suitors.

12. Arsilaous is Achilles's name in Arabic; Aquiles is his name in Spanish.

13. I use a similar assignment in my introductory myth class: I ask students to read a book most of them have already read, *D'Aulaires' Book of Greek Myths* (D'Aulaire and D'Aulaire); then, after we read a series of cosmogonic and theogonic myths from ancient sources, I ask them to return to one story in *D'Aulaires' Book of Greek Myths* and track it through the ancient versions of the myth to try and figure out which version or versions the D'Aulaires were drawing upon and to what end.

CLASSROOM CONTEXTS

Navigating the *Odyssey* with Ninth Graders

Patricia Vreeland

Perhaps you, like me, have experienced two kinds of journeys: the kind where someone else leads you around and the kind that requires you to study the maps and schedules and make the plans yourself. Both can be rewarding, but I would suggest that the second has benefits beyond seeing a new place; it develops residual skills. I want the latter kind of experience for my students in their reading. In other words, I want them to engage in the kind of "interactive instruction" described by Fred M. Newmann, Anthony S. Bryk, and Jenny Nagaoka in which "students are often asked to formulate problems, to organize their knowledge and experiences in new ways and to solve them, to test their ideas with other students, and to express themselves using elaborated statements, both orally and in writing" (10–11). To learn how to navigate a difficult text like the *Odyssey*, my ninth-grade students use the tools of navigation—logs, charts, and action—not only to study this particular text but also in preparation for future journeys and texts.

These three navigation tools are used concurrently and consistently throughout our journey. Student journals—which I prefer to have students keep handwritten in a composition book—are used for the log to trace virtual landmarks, such as names and places, events, significant cultural values, ideas in the text, and impressions in response to prompts presented in class. Charts, also included in the journal, involve students generating a number of visual aids—maps, graphics, and timelines—to clarify concepts. And the action part of our study engages students in improvisation of scenes that they have read in the text. Ultimately, each of the journal entries and the improvisations serve both as formative assessments and as the basis for the summative assessments: a traditional test and an essay examining evidence for the values expressed in the text.

Instead of students learning *about* the *Odyssey*, I want students to *read* the *Odyssey*; as Timothy Shanahan reminds us:

> Part of the point of the CCSS [Common Core State Standards] (and of "close reading") is that text must play the central role in reading and cannot profitably be ignored. . . . Instead of preparing students so thoroughly that they confront no problems in understanding a text, briefer introductions simply get students started. Any interpretive problems that may ensue can be dealt with along the way. (8–9)

Hence, I do not give students prepared lists, summaries, or definitions ahead of reading; instead, my introduction is very brief. Because their studies of ancient Greece in middle school focused on the Classical period (fifth to fourth centuries BCE), students may need a bit of clarification regarding historical background, so I make a quick timeline differentiating the periods of the Trojan War, the probable date of the composition of the epic, and the Classical period. Then we read book 1 together in a close reading that involves interaction between reader and text, careful observations and interpretations, and rereading (Lehman and Roberts 4). This reading and recurring note-taking in the journal is the primary vehicle of study throughout the epic. Admittedly, a lot of direction is needed on the part of the instructor to initiate this routine, so in what follows I describe the reading for book 1 in some detail.

Log: Using the Journal

We read book 1 of the *Odyssey* together, using close reading, asking questions, noting cues for story frames, acting out scenes, and reading conversations aloud in character roles. Book 1, in Fagles's translation, is titled "Athena Inspires the Prince."[1] Adapting from the reliable reading comprehension method known as "SQ3R," which consists of five steps—survey, question, read, recite, and review (Robinson), I pose this title as a set of questions to be asked as we read: Who is Athena? Who is the prince? How do they inspire him? I read aloud lines 1–15 of Fagles's translation (1–13 in the Greek)[2] once; I then like to slam the book down and say with disgust, "Spoiler alert! We know the whole story now!" Truly, the epic has already given us the outline of its story. I ask students to revisit these lines and ask them what happened. We then initiate the log; I help them set up one of many "closet organizers" (i.e., note-taking guides to organize the information they are gathering), because, as Neil Mercer writes, "[i]nformation can be accumulated, but knowledge and understanding are only generated by working with information, selecting from it, organizing it, arguing for its relevance" (qtd. in Zwiers and Crawford 18). The first "cubbyhole" in this "closet" is a character list. In the composition book set aside exclusively for this text, students enter the heading and the names we have encountered so far—Muse, Sungod, Zeus—and supply a short identifier for each name. I model this on the board. They should reserve about four pages for this character list. We continue with lines 16–24 (13–21), which provide us with more information and names to add to our list. This is also a good time to set up our first chart—a timeline—with a horizontal line extending over two full pages. Unlike the way the story is told, this timeline is chronological.[3] Near the far-left side, we enter "Trojan War." About two-thirds of the way toward the far-right side, we enter "home in Ithaca." As reading continues, students add names to the character list and events to the timeline. We share these entries regularly to check for understanding and formative assessment, but more importantly, in the long run these become learning strategies that students can incorporate into their toolkits for reading any text.

One of the reasons the *Odyssey* is challenging is its inclusion of references to earlier and later events (in narratological terms, *analepses* and *prolepses*). An example occurs as early as book 1, lines 24–36 (22–31), with the gods assembled in the present and Zeus telling a story from the past; therefore, it is important that students learn to recognize the change by noting words like "remembering" μνήσατο (1.34; 1.29) and "recalling" ἐπιμνησθείς (1.36; 1.31). After continuing through line 52 (43), I ask students what Zeus is angry about and then give them a brief version of the Clytemnestra story. (My exaggerated expression of shock and dismay at this scandal goes a long way in convincing students that this book might be worthy of their attention.) I model adding the character names from the earlier event and a notation on the timeline shortly after the start. Returning to the question "Do we know anything about Athena and the Prince yet?," we get back to the main story with lines 53–95 (44–79). Adding to our character list, it's important to note the description of Odysseus (78–79; 65–67), the character of Polyphemus the Cyclops, and the interference of Poseidon in Odysseus's attempt to return home.

Another challenge for students is differentiating single events from recurring values. The latter is the more important aspect of our study, and in fact the summative essay is based on one of the cultural values demonstrated in the book. By finding evidence as we are reading, we not only attend better to the important attributes of this culture but also learn how to provide patterns for reading and how to support propositions in writing. As the first example of cultural values, we set up a page to record instances of intervention of the gods, on which we note Poseidon's interference (1.88–90; 1.74–75) as well as the plan to dispatch Hermes with a message to Calypso (1.100–02; 1.84–86) and Athena's intention to visit Telemachus (1.104–05; 1.88–89). Since students will need to refer to these notes later, I model adding book and line numbers after each entry.

Following up on the question initially posed by Fagles's title of book 1, we finally get some idea of Athena's plan and appearance, the identity of "the Prince," the situation in his home, and his despair over his father's absence. Likewise, we encounter instances of another value that reverberates throughout the text. The suitors are abusing the hospitality they have demanded (1.124–31; 1.106–12). At the same time, a positive example of hospitality is supplied by Telemachus, who is "mortified" νεμεσσήθη (1.140; 1.119) that a guest is kept waiting. It's worth calling up volunteers to act out this scene as the teacher reads aloud lines 138–68 (118–43), as it encapsulates the many instances throughout the epic of a value highly esteemed by the Greeks. So we set up a page for hospitality and enter these two examples: one negative and one positive. Continuing aloud, I ask several people to demonstrate Athena's "sparkling" eyes—γλαυκῶπιν Ἀθήνην (1.182; 1.156)—and pause to let them skim back and forth to find other descriptions of her eyes: for example, "glinting" (1.206; 1.178). With attention to style (and later, interpretation of origins), we set up a page for epithets, the first entry being Athena's sparkling eyes, followed by the line references. To this list, as the epic progresses, students can add "Dawn with her rose-red fingers" ῥοδοδάκτυλος Ἠώς (Fagles, Odyssey [Penguin Classics] 2.1; 2.1) and the other epithets.

With the conversation between Athena and Telemachus, we initiate two more recurring activities—action or oral activities (e.g., dramatization or improvisation) and short written responses (quickwrites)—as well as continuing to add note-taking categories. Two students can dramatize this conversation, and after they have read lines 180–311 (155–269), other students retell Athena's cover story and the news she imparts. At this juncture, we can see the interplay between oral communication and another use of the log. I ask students to set up a page for quickwrites, write the date, and pose this problem for the first entry: "There's something really bad going on at your house that you can't handle by yourself. What can you do?" To answer the prompt, students usually come up with the idea of contacting neighbors, relatives, or friends to help, and so when reading continues with lines 311–60 (269–313), Athena's suggestions make sense. When we read of Penelope's arrival, we note how her face is veiled, she is crying, and she can't even bear to listen to the song. We add Penelope's name to the character list, and we also add a new category of values: gender roles. Students enter their observations (with references) characterizing Penelope's role. Having two students read aloud the conversation in lines 387–414 (337–59) dramatizes another insight into cultural values. When the newly enlivened Telemachus assumes "the power in the house" τοῦ γὰρ κράτος ἔστ' ἐνὶ οἴκῳ (1.414; 1.359)[4] and dismisses his mother to her room, we add this evidence.

We have already instituted a page for examples of intervention of the gods, but it's also useful to designate a page for fate; on that page we include those lines that portray the belief that one's path is preordained. Often, this fate seems subject to the will of the gods, as when Athena, disguised as Mentes, tells Telemachus, "But this is in the lap of the gods" ἀλλ' ἦ τοι μὲν ταῦτα θεῶν ἐν γούνασι κεῖται (1.309; 1.267) and again when Telemachus tells his mother, "But I suppose Zeus is to blame, who gives / whatever he wishes to every man who works for a living" ἀλλά ποθι Ζεὺς αἴτιος, ὅς τε δίδωσιν / ἀνδράσιν ἀλφηστῇσιν ὅπως ἐθέλῃσιν ἑκάστῳ (1.401–02; 1.348–49). To the character list, after lines 420–78 (365–419), we add Antinous's and Eurymachus's names and identifications. After Eurycleia is introduced as Telemachus's "devoted nurse" κεδνὰ ἰδυῖα / Εὐρύκλει[α] (Fagles, Odyssey [Penguin Classics] 1.488; 1.428–29), we add her name, noting that while she is accepted as a member of the household, she is enslaved, evidence of the class hierarchy in the ancient Greek culture. As we finish notations for book 1, we add a section on summaries, and students are asked to formulate a short summary of this first book. As I ask students for their preliminary summary statements for book 1, I combine the best of what they offer and write a model as an exemplar for future entries. Generally these should be a sentence or two, and sometimes I need to emphasize that it is a summary, not a complete retelling.

At this point in our close reading of book 1, we have established those tools that will guide us through the rest of the epic, as notes are continually added, checked, and discussed, with varying daily activities. We have also initiated the journal; all the major characters of Ithaca have been identified; we have a timeline, several categories of cultural values (intervention of the gods, hospitality, gender roles, fate), and one example of an epithet that will be repeated throughout the story. I frequently ask students to identify aloud these note-taking categories and reading strategies, so that they become aware of them as tools that they can use to their benefit—as opposed to just another thing a teacher says to do. Student notebook entries are important formative assessments; they are scanned and checked daily throughout the unit, and at the end of the unit, they are given point credit. These entries also provide material for test review and for essay writing.

Using the Log for Class Discussion

As students continue reading the *Odyssey*, some of the reading takes place in class, but students are also assigned reading (along with updating their notes) for homework. Our time in class becomes a forum for sharing some of the reading but also for sharing our understanding, asking questions, checking for comprehension, and writing to short in-class prompts. In addition to the content, we address some of the potential reading challenges. At appropriate times, we note more phrases that warn us of time shifts, as we did in book 1. For example, there are important markers of stories-within-stories in book 8, which might be confusing if students haven't yet learned to recognize them; Alcinous calls for dancers and for Demodocus the bard (8.284–89; 8.250–55), and the dancers dance to a song about yet another unfaithful wife. The shift is recognizable with "Next [the bard], accompanying himself on the lyre, began a beautiful song / about the love of Ares and garlanded Aphrodite" αὐτὰρ ὁ φορμίζων ἀνεβάλλετο καλὸν ἀείδειν / ἀμφ᾽ Ἄρεος φιλότητος ἐϋστεφάνου τ᾽ Ἀφροδίτης (8.300–02; 8.266–67) and clearly ends with "That was what the famous harper sang" ταῦτ᾽ ἄρ᾽ ἀοιδὸς ἄειδε περικλυτός (8.411; 8.367). Near the end of book 8, there is an important transition, as Alcinous asks Odysseus, "But come, tell me this and recount it exactly: / what places you were driven and what countries you reached" ἀλλ᾽ ἄγε μοι τόδε εἰπὲ καὶ ἀτρεκέως κατάλεξον / ὅππῃ ἀπεπλάγχθης τε καὶ ἅς τινας ἵκεο χώρας (8.641–44; 8.572–73). Thereafter, books 9 through 12 are Odysseus's account of his adventures since leaving Troy, told in flashback as he sits at the table with Alcinous and his household in Phaeacia. This story-within-a-story is clear at the start of book 9: "Odysseus, the great teller of tales, launched out on his story" (Fagles's expansion of the formulaic line τὸν δ'ἀπαμειβόμενος προσέφη πολύμητις Ὀδυσσεύς [9.1]) and adopts a more chronological sequence of the story starting with, "The wind, carrying me from Ilium [Troy] . . ." Ἰλιόθεν με φέρων ἄνεμος . . . (9.44; 9.39). I point out this story framing at the end of book 8 and start of book 9, since there are multiple implications for students' understanding the overall structure. We also update the timeline accordingly, placing the events in books 9–12 in the appropriate chronological sequence.

Using the Log for Writing

Much of the writing that we do in our study is informal. As William Zinsser writes, "Writing organizes and clarifies our thoughts. Writing is how we think our way into a subject and make it our own. Writing enables us to find out what we know—and what we don't know—about whatever we're trying to learn" (16). While the note-taking and summaries that we set up in our journals tend to summarize the text, it is equally important to provide opportunities for writing as a tool students can use for exploring and processing. Indeed, "[m]ost of the research suggests that students benefit by writing in all content areas—that it enhances critical thinking; allows students to take greater responsibility for their own learning; promotes reflective thinking and questioning; and helps students make connections between events, people, and ideas" (Urquhart and McIver 3). As mentioned above, we created a space for quickwrites in our journals and did one on the first day of reading. Throughout the reading of the epic, I continue to give short writing prompts. In one instance, students make a T-chart (a two-column table) to track Circe's warnings in the first part of book 12 and the outcomes in the remainder of the book. Another type of prompt asks students to apply a situation to their own lives, as when I ask them to identify their own "siren songs" (12.172–217; 12.158–200)—distractions from their goals—and ways to overcome them. Others involve shifts in the point of view, such as when I ask students to retell a section in the voice of one of the characters. A way of revisiting and reviewing the scene, retelling also encourages identification with a character. Another prompt asks students how relationships between the characters correspond with their own experience; for example, after Odysseus has successfully met Penelope's challenge in book 23, students write concerning a shared memory that they might ask about to prove the identity of someone close to them who had been away. Throughout, these short writings create personal connections and help students to focus on specific aspects of the text.

Another journal entry provides an impetus to consider social and personal aspects of the text. I ask all students, near the end of our reading, to address this prompt:

> Some bestsellers have presented advice for business or personal development based on literary authors or characters. Examples include *The*

> *Leadership Secrets of Genghis Khan, The Management Style of Jesus, The Leadership of Judith,* and *The Tao of* [*Winnie the*] *Pooh.* Write the start of your book, to be placed in the Business Management or Self-Help section, based on a character in the *Odyssey.*

After some talk in pairs to generate ideas, students write a short entry in their journals. The management style of Odysseus is a popular topic, but others write about the Telemachus complex (boys with absent fathers); Penelope offers advice as a single mother; Athena on being the woman behind the man; Circe's view on learning to let go, and "wasting time on mortal men" by Calypso. Such writing allows students not only to revisit the text but also to link personal and literary experiences and to explore "the complexity of the emotions, the social dynamics, the ethics, the characterizations, the shifting narrative points of view" (Krebs and Wilson 4). Later, some students opt to get extra credit by expanding this particular quickwrite into a full page or more.

Charts: Visualization and Drawing

Another method of re-presenting the text highlights visualization skills, which are necessary for reading comprehension. Inouk E. Boerma, Suzanne E. Mol, and Jelle Jolles summarize much of the research on this approach: "Understanding a story text requires the reader to form a mental representation, or situation model, of that story. . . . Students who are not inclined to make mental images in general while reading were found to show poor reading performance, whereas students who are used to making mental images tended to be more proficient readers" (2). Building, then, upon these studies, I incorporate informal opportunities for students to draw pictures and thus to strengthen their visualization skills. I clarify that their pictures are not judged on artistry but on faithfulness to the text; I easily demonstrate this low standard with my own drawing. Sketching helps the reader visualize the scene; even one student's simple sketch of clouds, sleep Z's, musical notes, and flowers to reflect the story of the Lotus-Eaters (9.91–117; 9.82–104) tells me that they understand the scene. Another type of graphic organizer is a map. Since even experts disagree, I don't expect students to pinpoint exact locations, but I do give them a very simple outline of Greece and Troy flanking the Aegean Sea and ask them to fill in islands with pictures of different episodes. Some depictions are simple but knowing: Calypso surrounded by little hearts, Aeolia with many wisps of expressed air coming from a bag nearby, and the menacing underworld where everyone has *X*'s for eyes. Some years students have done more art work, such as an accordion book of the adventures that are portrayed in books 9 to 12. For the most part, however, drawing remains informal, a way of helping students visualize and concentrate: "Drawing shouldn't be about performance, but about process. . . . Think of it as a way of observing the world and learning, something that can be done anytime, like taking notes, jotting down a thought, or sending a text. . . . At its core, drawing is a problem-solving tool" (Quito 4).

In addition to drawing for comprehension, students, by creating and interpreting their own graphics, learn to identify the attributes of the epic form. One consistent graphic throughout our reading is the timeline, representing events not as they are told in the epic but as they would have occurred in chronological order. It is helpful to record Odysseus's activities (e.g., living with Calypso) above the line and the events in Ithaca (e.g., Athena meets with Telemachus) below the line to get a sense of what is happening in different places simultaneously. It is also helpful to add a book number along with events. Thus it becomes graphically clear, when we examine the timeline around book 13, that many of the events told in books 9–12, for example, occurred before the telling of the epic even starts, with the meeting of the gods in book 1. After students conclude, then, that the epic is told not chronologically but beginning in the middle of things, I give them the formal term: *in medias res*. For some time, I use the word *epic* generously without really defining it (but recoiling at their misuse of it to describe anything exciting, like a skateboard trick). In fact, however, they have been cataloging the elements that define an epic as they have been reading. With a few questions (e.g., Do you remember how the first book started?), we can generate a list of epic conventions: invocation of the muse, beginning in medias res, descent to the underworld. Essential epic characteristics have more to do with the purpose and beliefs demonstrated in the epic, and again a little prompting (e.g., Is it long or short?) and looking at notes generates the following: a long narrative poem about a hero on a quest who gets supernatural help. From the lists of values we have traced, we conjecture that the epic is entertaining but that it also illustrates values that are important to the culture, like hospitality. Thus students have constructed the definition from their own observations.

This fundamental understanding of the epic form is an important goal of the ninth-grade curriculum, as a foundation for the future study of literature from other times and cultures. Using a graphic is particularly helpful in reconstructing the epic hero's journey. We start to reconstruct the hero's journey around book 13, which begins, "His tale was over now. The Phaeacians all fell silent" ὣς ἔφαθ', οἱ δ' ἄρα πάντες ἀκὴν ἐγένοντο σιωπῇ (13.1).[5] This reminds us that books 9–12 were stories that Odysseus was telling about the past (with the brief exception of 11.378–436; 11.333–84) and that we are now sitting at the table in Phaeacia. After the Phaeacians take him home—and are punished by Poseidon—"Odysseus woke / from sleep in his own fatherland" ὁ δ' ἔγρετο δῖος Ὀδυσσεὺς / εὕδων ἐν γαίῃ πατρωΐῃ (13.213; 13.187–88). This is a good time to ask, "So, is it over?" The answer is obviously no, but it provides an entrée into tracking the journey in a way that puts the elements into perspective. I have found that students themselves have developed some sense of the hero's journey since their earliest reading and watching, from Maurice Sendak's *Where the Wild Things Are*; to Disney films such as *Mulan* and *Frozen*, wherein the heroines perform brave acts in order to save society; to Harry Potter, the young wizard who must battle evil; to the *Lord of the Rings* trilogy; to the *Star Wars* trilogy, which George Lucas admits was intended to reflect mythological principles (Henderson 10). So we can construct much of this by using students' prior knowledge to assist in their reading of the epic. I use a simplified circular, clockwise illustration of the journey and—with an enlargement on the screen and printed copies at their desks [illegible] ask students to start telling me the incidents in the *Odyssey* that seem to correlate. (They might not talk about these steps in order; it may be easier, for example, to place the underworld in its place at the bottom of the circle and work from there.)

Because the movie was actually inspired by Joseph Campbell's monomyth of the hero, some students find it useful to consider the journey of Odysseus in relation to that of Luke Skywalker in *Star Wars,* though of course there is wide latitude in this comparison. For Odysseus's "call to adventure" we decide on leaving Troy, which corresponds with Campbell's observation that the call to adventure

> signifies that destiny has summoned the hero and transferred his spiritual center of gravity from within the pale of his society to a zone unknown . . . always a place of strangely fluid and amorphous beings, unimaginable torments, superhuman deeds, and impossible delight. . . . [He] may be carried or sent abroad by some benign or malignant agent, as was Odysseus, driven about the Mediterranean by the winds of the angered god, Poseidon.
> (*Hero* 58)

Similarly, students might note that Princess Leia's message on the telescreen is the "call to adventure" in *Star Wars*. So we go on to negotiate—sometimes in whole class discussion, sometimes in small groups—which episodes in the *Odyssey* illustrate the steps on the template, and students may choose to supplement with examples from *Star Wars* or other sources if that assists them: supernatural aid (Athena / the Force), threshold (leaves Troy / leaves Tatooine), helper (crew, Hermes / Chewbacca and Han Solo), mentor (Circe / Obi-Wan Kenobi), abyss, death and rebirth (Kingdom of the Dead / trash compactor).

Campbell tells us, "The ultimate aim of the quest, if one is to return, must be neither release nor ecstasy for oneself, but the wisdom and power to serve others" (*Myths* 234). As we continue reading from Odysseus's arrival in Ithaca, then, we continue to add to the cycle. These stages might include atonement (reconciliation with Telemachus, Penelope, Laertes) and return (establishes justice). I also remind students that they will encounter this journey schema in other texts.

Action: Improvisations

In our reading of what was initially a collection of oral tales, we use multiple instances of oral language along with reading: asking and answering questions, negotiating identifications, reading conversations in roles, improvising scenes, making connections. We continue to elaborate upon oral language strategies, since, as Zwiers and Crawford note, "[o]ral language is a cornerstone on which we build our literacy and learning throughout life" (7). They also note that not only does oral language tend to be neglected in high school, but with the increased use of text-messaging, games, online social networks, and email, face-to-face communication is also decreasing. Robert Putnam, noting that diminishing participation in social spheres contributes to a loss of social capital, urges us to renew "social connectedness in the twenty-first century" (28). Developing skills in oral communication builds social capital and creates a stronger social identity; students who can talk about what they are learning "reported feeling smarter and more capable" (Zwiers and Crawford 24).

We use various forms of improvisation to build oral language skills while reviewing the text. Often we revisit a book by making someone take the "hot seat": that is, assume the role of a character and answer questions about the book. For example, after reading book 3, I might put one student in the role of Nestor, and I initiate the questions—for instance, "So, Telemachus is visiting you. How did you know his father Odysseus, anyway?"—but students quickly take over. In line with Viola Spolin, the originator of theater games, "[t]he student audience is not to sit by and be entertained, nor are they to protect or attack the players" (27). In fact, the person in the "hot seat" can ask for help when necessary, so everyone has to be attentive to the interaction.

Students identify with much of book 8, as it is devoted to partying and sports. After Alcinous's citizens prepare the boat for Odysseus, they proceed to Alcinous's palace for hearty eating, drinking, and listening to the bard "sing the deeds of heroes" ἀειδέμεναι κλέα ἀνδρῶν (8.87; 8.73)—the last an image of the process by which the *Odyssey* was composed. There follow a footrace, wrestling, discus throwing, archery, spear-throwing—all suitable for improvisation—and some superb examples of mad-dogging and taunting, also suitable for improvisation. Students enjoy playing the roles of Laodamas, Broadsea (Euryalus), and Odysseus in the scene in which the Phaeacian bullies challenge Odysseus (8.165–215; 8.145–85). When Broadsea says, "You don't look like an athlete" οὐδ' ἀθλητῆρι ἔοικας (8.190; 8.164), Odysseus has a comeback: "Stranger, what you say isn't proper; you seem like a reckless man. / So the gods don't give pleasing qualities to all / men—in body, mind, or speech" 'ξεῖν', οὐ καλὸν ἔειπες· ἀτασθάλῳ ἀνδρὶ ἔοικας. / οὕτως οὐ πάντεσσι θεοὶ χαρίεντα διδοῦσιν / ἀνδράσιν, οὔτε φυὴν οὔτ' ἄρ φρένας οὔτ' ἀγορητύν' (8.191–94; 8.166–68). Oh, snap!

An extension of the "hot seat" is the talk show approach, in which multiple students assume the roles of characters but are asked questions by the host. These questions might come from a single student, or could be devised ahead of time in groups so that the scenes are revisited in multiple ways. From the time that Odysseus awakes on Ithaca (13.213; 13.187) through the end of book 19, several scenes provide fruitful material for either improvised dialogues (e.g., Athena and Odysseus, Eumaeus and the disguised Odysseus, Odysseus and Telemachus), or for including the larger cast of suitors in a talk show format. Of course, with the suitors, there is potential for the taunting and violence of book 17, making it appear more like *Jerry Springer* than *Oprah*, but that's acceptable as long as students understand that they are evaluated on remaining true to the character (e.g., Antinous is irascible, but Odysseus is reserved).

Another form of improvisation occurs when a narrator does a voice-over of a story; in other words, "[t]he story-teller relates the story to the actors on stage, and they follow his direction" (Spolin 313). In its simplest form, the narrator reads a section of text and characters act it out. For a greater challenge, the narrator can give a short prompt to the cast to recreate a scene. From the last part of book 12 (282–452; 260–419), for instance, they would start by saying, "Odysseus warns the crew," without supplying actual dialogue. Obviously, I don't expect verbatim quotations from the book; I'm looking for "Odysseus's" recall that it's the cattle of Helius that need to be avoided—and so on to the end of the episode (complete with slaughter of the cows, feasting, and destruction of the ship and crew).

Students particularly enjoy recreating the events in books 20 to 21, in which Odysseus reveals himself. We do a little more preparation for these scenes; students, who have already read the two books, work in groups of four to put into the correct sequence a list of events (ten from book 20, eighteen from book 21) that I have listed and scrambled, with the names of characters in bold font. After they have worked for about fifteen minutes, I start distributing index cards with the names of characters from the events list, as well as additional designations such as other suitors and maids. Students draw a card without seeing the name. Students then check their events sequence against a key that I post, and they correct any errors. Then we start with Odysseus and Athena "on stage." A designated student director is responsible for getting people up and into action at appropriate times. In such a crowded scene, we follow Spolin's advice: "never have individuals in mobs make incoherent sounds. They should all speak . . . full meaningful remarks" (167).

Throughout the use of improvisation, I generally assign roles blindly, through handing out index cards with characters' names on the back. Students may briefly consult their own notes (but not the text), so keeping updated notes is rewarded. They also have one opportunity to ask for a substitute, and they may ask for coaching from the class. I keep track of who has participated and mark a simple plus or minus on my checklist to show whether the student seems to have recalled the material and stayed true to the character.

Assessment

Given that my goal for students is not just content knowledge but also the accumulation of transferable skills (close reading, note-taking, use of graphic organizers, visualization, recognizing time shifts, oral communication, drawing conclusions from their notes, re-presenting the text in different ways such as improvisation and drawing, writing in various forms, making personal connections) that will guide them in being more effective readers in the future, assessment actually includes all of the activities in which we engage. As Grant Wiggins and Jay McTighe explain, "Effective assessment is more like a scrapbook of mementos and pictures than a single snapshot. . . . This continuum of assessments includes checks of understanding (such as oral questions, observations, dialogues); traditional quizzes, tests, and open-ended prompts; and performance tasks and projects" (152), pointing out that these assessments may vary in scope, time frame, setting, and structure. My students know that "everything counts," so I give credit for everything in the log (character lists, notes, summaries, practice citations, and journal entries) with a quick daily stamp and then evaluate completeness with checklists at intervals. I also give credit for improvisations (using a checklist to be sure everyone has participated at some point) and for other activities.

I do, however, also give short quizzes and a final multiple-choice test on the basics of the story and important terminology. The quizzes might be as simple as my asking ten oral questions (for example, after every two to four books) and having students write one-word answers, usually the names of important characters (e.g., "Who is the goddess who appears to Telemachus to give advice?"). In another instance, I give a matching quiz with thirteen names and descriptors from books 11 to 15, along with one short-answer question about Pisistratus, the son of Nestor. This latter format reinforces names and events without demanding total recall.

As a summative assessment, students write a three-to-five-page essay for which they write drafts, get peer feedback, make revisions, edit, and submit for a grade. All our activities have been directed toward this product, in the language of backward planning: "Toward what performance goals do this reading and these discussions head, so that I might focus and prioritize my studies and note taking?" (Wiggins and McTighe 15). The topic for the essay is chosen from among the cultural values on which we have note-taking categories, and the citations have been collected along the way, as part of students' notes. To clarify expectations, as part of the assignment we study the SAT scoring guide, and this same rubric will be used for grading. On the due date, students must bring hard copies, and we follow a process of review that includes self-scoring, peer comments, and a statement of intended changes. After I have read the drafts, I plan an editing lesson by collecting common errors from student essays, printing a page with these excerpts, and having students make the corrections. Finally, students submit their revised essays along with earlier drafts and statements of changes.

Over many years I have realized that the *Odyssey* is much more meaningful as a journey if students have a way to understand not just the destinations (the facts of the story) but also the itinerary (the means of getting there). I am convinced, with Robert Probst, that "meaning lies in that shared ground where the reader and text meet—it isn't resident within the text, to be extracted like a nut from its shell" (38). The *Odyssey* is a difficult book, but I want my ninth graders to know they can engage with this book—or any hard book—rather than just try to remember what a teacher (or website) told them about it. So my methods in teaching the *Odyssey* have evolved over several years in an effort to construct situations in which students can make meaning from text, develop their own skills, and relate to the work in ways that would inspire rather than stultify. By using their logs with summaries, character lists, quickwrites, and values evidence; their charts with timelines, maps, and drawings; and action in the form of spoken improvisations, they have learned how to encounter challenges and find their way through them, to collaborate with others, and to achieve goals. Students' final metacognitive self-evaluations of the strategies involved convince me that they now possess skills that enable them to navigate not just this text but also other challenging texts.

NOTES

1. The book titles are Fagles's invention.

2. Throughout this essay, when two sets of line references are given, the first set refers to Fagles's translation; the second refers to the Greek text.

3. In narratological studies, *story* refers to the order in which the fabula, or the underlying sequence of events, is told. Our timeline is in effect an outline of the fabula.

4. From here on, unless otherwise noted, with the exception of individual words, translations from the Greek are by Lillian Doherty. The first set of line numbers refers to the passage in Fagles's translation; the second, to the Greek text.

5. The translation is Fagles's; the line number is the same as in the Greek.

The Emerging Outline: Character Analysis and the *Odyssey*

Henry Alley

I have taught the *Odyssey* in translation for over three decades, as the first book in a three-course series covering literature from ancient times to the present. The undergraduates, most of them in their first year, arrive fresh from high school and the summer, ready to enjoy the seminar style, with its emphasis on writing and discussion. At the same time, however, it might be easy for them to feel overwhelmed, arriving in our honors college expecting themselves to understand what "sophisticated literary criticism" might look like. I have come to assume, based on what earlier students have told me, that when approaching the first book in their literature sequence, they are looking for solid, step-by-step guidance. To make matters simple, I emphasize character—its components, how it changes in the course of the epic, and how the various dramatis personae connect with one another under common themes. Such an emphasis helps launch a campaign I promote throughout the entire year: much of narrative literature is best approached through a consideration of character and the ambiguities surrounding it. As Evan Kindlay writes, "[I]n my experience the desire to understand characters is merely one on-ramp for the reader, one way to access all of the other valuable things a literary text might be able to give."

Some teachers may still carry the legacy of the skepticism launched by the formalists of the early part of the twentieth century, as advanced and developed by the spokespeople for the New Criticism that followed: the view that it is self-delusional to speak of characters in literature as though they were living beings. Subsequent trends in literary criticism, from structuralism and narratology to the different forms of post-structuralism, have either de-emphasized the study of character or even attacked it as ideologically suspect.[1] However, studies such as Amanda Anderson, Rita Felski, and Toril Moi's *Character: Three Inquiries in Literary Studies* and Robert Alter's *The Pleasures of Reading in an Ideological Age* point out that readers can be moved by the inhabitants of novels and plays while being quite aware, consciously or subconsciously, of the fictive nature of these creations. As Anderson, Felski, and Moi write, "[P]erhaps it is the fictional qualities of characters that make them real: figures in novels and films are alluring, arresting, alive, not in spite of their aesthetic dimensions, but because of them" (19). With regard to those who wish to see literature as merely a collection of signs, Alter writes, "What is left out in such a view is the powerful capacity of the literary work to refer its readers to a complex order of moral, emotional, and psychological realities" (76).

Homer's *Odyssey*, in fact, allows the students and the teacher to rejoice in the simultaneously compelling and artifactual nature of character, since the fictional beings belong to the world of myth and distant history. This discussion can serve as a launching point for examining Homer's own success in the *Odyssey* in projecting a sense of a character as "one being" whose changes are still remarkable. The critic Richard P. Martin can be particularly helpful here, for he shows how the medley of epithets that are applied, for example, to Telemachus "lets us construct a three-dimensional picture of the hero" ("Telemachus" 233). Martin points out that the epithets belonged to a tradition of "folk epic performance" (223), which demanded that the audience keep seeing them in different ways as the narrative contexts changed within what Alter calls "the mimetic enterprise of literary tradition" (76). To emphasize this Protean nature of the descriptors in the classroom would also emphasize that we are not dealing with characters as beings living just down the block but as Homeric constructions that are built over the course of the epic by the inventive use of conventional elements.

Having established this context, our classroom can now turn to the actual text of the *Odyssey*, and here I would put on the board a list of the major characters as they appear in basic book groupings: for example, books 1–3 (Ithaca and Pylos), Telemachus, Athena, Nestor, Penelope; books 4–5 (Sparta and the Isle of Calypso), Menelaus, Helen, Calypso; books 6–8 (Phaeacia), Nausicaa, Alcinous, Arete; books 9–12 (the Great Wanderings), Agamemnon, Anticleia, the Cyclops, and Circe. For the first half of the epic, the groupings would be smaller; for the second half, whose setting would be Ithaca, I would have a larger set of characters all under books 13–24: the suitors, Eumaeus, Laertes, and Eurycleia as well as Penelope, Telemachus, and Odysseus.

At the start of the course, this presentation helps orient everyone in time and space. I then select, for practice, a single character and have us talk about that character's traits, being careful to discuss the difference between an emotion and a trait. (For example, anger would be an emotion; irascibility a trait.) Let us take the Cyclops Polyphemus. Here definitely is an artifactual creation; his very grotesque nature would demand it. Having acknowledged this, we can put in front of us self-centeredness, brutality, suspicion, impiety, gullibility. We can then engage in the interesting process of finding a surprise characteristic, such as, in the case of the Cyclops, a sense of nurture, as we see in his treatment of his sheep and goats. Such a complexity we would need to back up with quotations from Odysseus's adventure with his men in the cave, a process we would emphasize in illustrating all of the characteristics. By the time we have a list on the board, we actually have, in rough outline, a character analysis. With a little background in how to generate an overall outline for a literary essay, it becomes clear that each trait can be treated as a topic sentence. In a separate handout, I take students through the scatter outline (the product of brainstorming), which evolves into the idea outline, which then evolves into the topic sentence outline. The traits fit nicely into the topic sentence outline. We then talk about moving the traits around, as though on a magnetic board, so that a presentation of each one leads naturally into another. Underneath each trait we would put the quotations that illustrate it. We can subsequently balance this sequence against the important rhetorical plan of going in order of ascending interest and complexity. In this case, we would have brutality, suspicion (both rather prominent and obvious), then impiety (a kind of defiance of the gods, hence moral blindness); hence the narrow view belonging to gullibility, hence a kind of natural and surprising innocence, which we might connect to a form of pastoral life. Notice, for example, "he lit his fire and then set about milking his glorious / flocks, each of them in order, and put lamb or kid under each one" καὶ τότε πῦρ ἀνέκαιε καὶ ἤμελγε κλυτὰ μῆλα, / πάντα κατὰ μοῖραν, καὶ ὑπ' ἔμβρυον ἧκεν ἑκάστῃ (Lattimore, Odyssey [1967] 9.308–09).[2] Notice also Polyphemus's comic and rather heartbreaking talk with his ram once he is blinded.

An X-ray vision into a single character can help focus a discussion and aid students, with the support of linked study questions, in finding a road map through exciting but sometimes baffling territory where names and locales come rushing past. In looking at the Cyclops episode, I also have us listen to Anthony Quayle's extraordinary reading of Richmond Lattimore's translation (Lattimore, Odyssey [Quayle]), a performance that brings up not only all the menace of the Cyclops's character but also the pathos and comedy of his self-pity and narcissism. With this blueprint in front of us, we look at how the essay—of which this list of qualities is a projection—is going to begin and end. Such a stance is extremely helpful in this very primary teaching of outlines for papers, since I have rarely had a student come up with a thesis paragraph or a conclusion before the student has considered the body of the paper. First illustrations, then topic sentences, then beginning and end—that is, moving from the center out.

After being sure we have sufficiently illustrated each of the traits through a representative sample of quotations, with students, perhaps, reading some passages aloud, we can, in planning a concluding paragraph, reexamine the outlined character analysis of the Cyclops and ask what theme or themes he represents in the epic. Here we have the advantage of starting to talk about how each character is related to a host of other characters, because by theme, we mean a short declaration from the author that would apply to the entire cast. This end goal can help students get past the misconception that the conclusion of an essay should merely repeat its thesis and beginning. In this case, we could talk about the consequences of inhospitality or the repugnant nature of unmitigated self-interest. It is then imperative that we show how other characters throughout the epic come under the umbrella of such themes—for example, in this case, Circe, the suitors, or even Odysseus himself. Once we have determined what the concluding paragraph might look like, we ultimately come up with a thesis statement that will serve as an introduction to all that we have written, something that has its own power and is not a mere anticipation of the conclusion we are moving toward.

In the context of this collective work, students can break out into smaller groups, where they are assigned individual characters as candidates for analysis and for similar practice write-ups. In open discussion, we can look at controversial approaches to the characters in the *Odyssey*—for example, whether Penelope is crafty, indefatigably artless, or somehow both. We can question why Odysseus, cunning and wily though he is, shouts his name at the Cyclops while he is escaping, thereby creating years of toil and destruction for himself and his men. Hence another collection of complex characteristics that include not only hubris but also *kleos*, or the rather admirable quest for fame, so that Odysseus does not remain a "Nobody."[3]

When it comes to assigning the actual first paper of the course, I find it important to give students a blueprint like this one for writing a character analysis, but I allow them to select the character themselves. I have found over the years that so much of motivation for the writing student depends on personal investment. Here some students will be drawn to the ambiguity of Penelope's motives, to the combined sense of treachery and hospitality associated with Circe, or to the combined naivete and pluckiness of Telemachus. I always emphasize that their thesis paragraph should justify, in some way, why out of all of these characters in the epic, this particular one was chosen.

Let us consider the handout I give students for writing this paper, using Telemachus as the subject. Over the years, the three-page guideline uses sample prose that both I and my students have written. The sample thesis paragraph begins by justifying its choice—Telemachus's understatedness as a hero stands out in a poem generally devoted to a showier, larger-than-life protagonist, namely his father. We then enumerate the traits—considerate, reverent, naive, hospitable, resourceful, perceptive. We will have the interesting job of making "perceptive" go along with "naive," but we can frame these within the epic's sense of evolving character—another great attraction of the poem. The Telemachus we see at the beginning is not the same as the one we see at the end. Such a group of facets can also open the door to the sense of comedy that surrounds the opening of the poem. For example, we can show how the rather bitter and scathing dialogue between Helen and Menelaus, in the aftermath of her escape with Paris and her supposed complicity with the Trojans, goes completely unnoticed by Telemachus, who after talking with them in book 4 calls for simply going to bed. A trait like "perceptive" seems out of line here, but it allows us to debate the ambiguity as to whether Telemachus early discovers who the mysterious visitor, Mentes, really is: "But Telemachus, walking along the sea beach away from the others / washed his hands in the gray salt water and prayed to Athene: 'Hear me, you who came yesterday, a god into our house'" Τηλέμαχος δ' ἀπάνευθε κιὼν ἐπὶ θῖνα θαλάσσης, / χεῖρας νιψάμενος πολιῆς ἁλός, εὔχετ' Ἀθήνῃ· / Ἱκλῦθί μοι, ὃ χθιζὸς θεὸς ἤλυθες ἡμέτερον δῶ' (Lattimore, Odyssey [1967] 2.260–02). Further, a trait like "hospitable" allows us to examine a major theme of the epic. We can present Telemachus as "scandalized / that a guest should still be standing at the doors" νεμεσσήθη δ' ἐνὶ θυμῷ / ξεῖνον δηθὰ θύρῃσιν ἐφεστάμεν (Lattimore, Odyssey [1967] 1.119–20) and emphasize that he treats the disguised Athena with the respect that any stranger should receive in the ancient Greek tradition.

In writing the conclusion, we can come back to our original intent in choosing Telemachus as a subject in the first place—he and his father form a contrast. The thesis we come up with can then extend not only to the main hero but also to other members of the supporting cast:

> Telemachus illustrates the heroism of the underdog. He helps shed light on such easily passed over characters as Nausicaa and Eumaeus. Nausicaa, although just a maiden in a kingly household, is actually responsible for saving Odysseus's life. Indeed, he acknowledges, "my life was your gift" σὺ γάρ μ'ἐβιώσαο, κούρη (Lattimore, Odyssey [1967] 8.468). Eumaeus, a simple swineherd, also becomes a key figure for understanding the code of hospitality in the epic.

The end result is an essay with a sense of direction, one that can ultimately surprise with an unexpected characteristic and can lead into an understanding of what Homer was trying to give as a thematic message. The approach can be enriched in a variety of ways. For example, in an adult education course, I supplemented the discussion with two classic translations of the poem, George Chapman's and Alexander Pope's, to show how they can enhance our sense not only of character but also of the perspective of each translator on his particular milieu. A case in point happens when, speaking of the Cyclopes as a group, Chapman calls them "loiterers" (9.168)—a perfect opportunity to discuss the work ethic in the epic. Pope's presentation of Alcinous's garden as a neoclassic enterprise, all in regimented rows, can tell us a great deal about the eighteenth-century need for order.

Ultimately, the assignment is a simple approach to a complex poem, and like all good writing assignments, it is directly linked to the class discussion and to the controversies as they come up between students. Homer has given us a rich range of perceived personalities, which even include the persona of the narrator, which can be treated with the same method, starting with the question of whether that "Homer" who narrates comes across as a man or woman or as something less binary, and, additionally, whether the narrator seems a tragedian with a sense of humor or a comic author with a strong sense of the tragic notes struck by the post-Troy experience. This is a storyteller with an enormous understanding of the human psyche, who even uses the conventional devices of simile and oral formulaic epithet as tools of characterization. As Aubrey de Sélincourt writes, we are in a world where qualities are celebrated, as though we were looking at them for the first time. We are continually invited to look at objects and beings anew (291–92). And so the characters stand before us in all their facets, many of which we had not considered before. As Virginia Woolf concludes, "Penelope crosses the room; Telemachus goes to bed; Nausicaa washes her linen; and their actions seem laden with beauty" (39)—a wonderful starting point for any course in the humanities.

NOTES

1. See, e.g., the resume and critique in Alter 51–53.

2. Here and throughout, line numbers in Lattimore's translation are the same as in the Greek.

3. Odysseus's use of the pseudonym "Nobody" is discussed in Doherty's essay in this volume.

Odysseus, Masculinity, and the Paradox of Domesticity

Jamie L. Brummer

Here's the challenge: transport a classroom of high school boys back in time, across vast oceans and towering mountain ranges; grapple with an array of cultural, historical, and linguistic differences; and hope, in the process, to connect in an intellectually honest and meaningful way with Homer's epic poem the *Odyssey*. The obstacles seem insurmountable at times, and my students and I have, at times, almost given up. But when we persevere, when we come closest to bridging the historical and cultural divides, we do so by focusing on a specific aspect of the epic. We turn the lens away from Odysseus in the heat of battle, or floundering on the high seas, or cunningly outwitting both mortals and immortals and instead redirect our attention to perhaps the most terrifying obstacle our hero actually faces: the domestic space. When the monsters and myths of ancient Greece seem most foreign to us, we are reminded that the promise and peril of home are eminently relatable. Even if my students are not consciously aware of it, they know what *nostos* ("homecoming") means, and Odysseus's journey home will animate their own journey.

Like most (male) heroes we have inherited in Western culture, Odysseus seems most at home when he's away from home. The Trojans, the Cyclops, the Lotus-Eaters, Scylla, and Charybdis—these are foes Odysseus is happy to vanquish; indeed, he seems most himself when surrounded by other men, apart from the responsibilities of being a spouse and a father, acting out the fantasies of endless adolescence. Students come to appreciate how none of these adversaries most threaten Odysseus; rather, the home front presents the most existential threat to his sense of self and, by extension, to a dominant sense of masculinity that has evolved without ever going away. Leslie Fiedler once claimed that "our classic literature is a literature of horror for boys" (29), a perpetually adolescent literature dominated by boys seeking to maintain their innocence or perhaps safeguard it from the temptations of women. Though Fiedler's focus was American literature, the argument applies in many ways to the *Odyssey*. Situating the epic in this manner challenges students to reconsider the strengths and weaknesses of one of Western literature's most famous male figures.

Much has been written of late regarding a crisis in masculinity. In addition to Fiedler's *Love and Death in the American Novel*, students examine arguments in E. Anthony Rotundo's *American Manhood*, Michael Kimmel's *Manhood in America*, and even Chris Hedges's *War Is a Force That Gives Us Meaning*. When I teach the *Odyssey*, my students and I reference these modern constructions of masculinity and the growing evidence that PTSD makes seamless reentry into domestic life far more difficult than previously imagined[1] as we search for gestures back to the roots of Western culture. From the distant past, Odysseus's aspirations and fears mirror those of my students as they transition from the world of adolescence to adulthood. Focusing our reading on issues of domesticity in the poem not only allows us to understand Homer's work on a deeper level but also encourages these young men of the twenty-first century to reevaluate their own conceptions of masculinity just as they are about to embark on their own epic adventure.

Who Holds the Reins of Power in the House?

Two things are obvious as the *Odyssey* begins: first, the poem's narrative arc will return our hero to his home; second, it won't be easy. The word *homecoming* (in Greek, *nostos*) appears repeatedly in the poem's opening lines, and Athena's insistence that the gods issue an "infallible decision: / the *nostos* of Odysseus, that he return home" νημερτέα βουλήν, / νόστον Ὀδυσσῆος ταλασίφρονος, ὥς κε νέηται (1.86–87)[2] neatly emphasizes the poem's central tensions. After years of fighting and struggle, those comrades of Odysseus's fortunate enough to escape "sheer destruction" αἰπὺν ὄλεθρον (1.11) at the hands of the gods "were at home" οἴκοι ἔσαν (1.12). One man alone remains in exile. Thus the dramatic focus emerges immediately: the hero, after countless trials and tribulations, must find his way home. We then accompany Athena as strangers to the gates of Odysseus's palace in Ithaca for a foretaste of what lies in store for him upon his fated return.

In his absence a power vacuum threatens to destroy Odysseus's household and by extension his kingdom. The political stakes are only magnified by Telemachus's relative youth and inexperience and the fact that the suitors who so threaten the palace "were just a little older than Telemachus when he [Odysseus] left for Troy. They were boys and Telemachus was still a baby" (Gottesman 37). Issues of gender, authority, ownership, and the right to rule all hang in the balance as the young prince bemoans the suitors who are "consuming [his] house" τρύχουσι δὲ οἶκον (1.248): "And my mother neither refuses a hateful marriage, nor is she able / to make an end, while they are eating / me out of house and home. Soon they will crush me too" ἡ δ'οὔτ' ἀρνεῖται στυγερὸν γάμον οὔτε τελευτὴν / ποιῆσαι δύναται· τοὶ δὲ φθινύθουσιν ἔδοντες / οἶκον ἐμόν· τάχα δή με διαρραίσουσι καὶ αὐτόν (1.249–51). The reader is situated in much the same position as Telemachus: fearfully awaiting the hero's return, questioning Penelope's options and agency, and unsure if the boy-prince can muster the courage and support to hold on. As Athena, still in disguise as Mentes, bluntly tells Telemachus: "you must not hold on to your childish ways, / since you are a child no longer" οὐδέ τί σε χρὴ / νηπιάας ὀχέειν, ἐπεὶ οὐκέτι τηλίκος ἐσσί (1.296–97). Robert Fagles makes explicit a conflation of gender and authority in his translation of line 297, a conflation that is implicit in the Greek: "It's time you were a man!" (342). The suitors, particularly Antinous, take every opportunity to emasculate Telemachus, reminding him of his youth, his orphaned state, and the power that his mother, Penelope, wields in his stead. The poem insists that the domestic space—the palace (and by extension Telemachus's entire universe)—needs a man to protect it. The driving question then becomes, Can Telemachus assume the role until his father returns?

The epic gives priority to the domestic space from its opening pages as the palace becomes a microcosm for the poem's central themes. Presenting a home front under attack by outsiders who call into question the normative roles of father, mother, and son, books 1 and 2 of the *Odyssey* challenge my students to reassess the importance of domestic spaces in a story they too readily associate with exotic locales, foreign assailants, and mythical creatures. In many ways, Penelope rules in Ithaca just as Calypso holds power in Ogygia. What does it mean for the hero to cede power to women in these domestic spaces? Perhaps the real threats, and the real heroes, are much more mundane and much closer to home.

Husband and House, but Lasting Harmony?

Before we meet Odysseus himself in book 5, I ask students about their prior knowledge of the epic. What associations do they have with the famous hero? Why should his tale among countless others have stood the test of time? Invariably, they mention his exploits in battle, his physical prowess, his craftiness, and his awesome ability to vanquish man and beast. They have heard of the Cyclops Polyphemus, of the Sirens, of Scylla and Charybdis; they may mention raging giants and vengeful gods. They have heard of the Trojan horse. But no one mentions Ogygia.

They are surprised, therefore, to first meet our hero not on the field of combat or using brain and brawn to overcome one in a series of mythical nemeses but near a lustrous cave, where "a great fire burned on the hearth and from far off / the smell of split cedar wood filled the island / as it burned . . ." πῦρ μὲν ἐπ' ἐσχαρόφιν μέγα καίετο, τηλόθι δ' ὀδμὴ / κέδρου τ' εὐκεάτοιο θύου τ' ἀνὰ νῆσον ὀδώδει / δαιομένων . . . (5.59–61). Instead of bloodshed and battles, we find luxuriant woods, teaming meadows, ripe vines, a home where "even one of the immortals coming to that place / would wonder at the sight, and be pleased at heart" ἔνθα κ' ἔπειτα καὶ ἀθάνατός περ ἐπελθὼν / θηήσαιτο ἰδὼν καὶ τερφθείη φρεσὶν ᾗσιν (5.73–74). We soon see Odysseus weeping and groaning in anguish as he longs to return to Ithaca and his family, but an important motif has again been amplified: the home front, or a divine facsimile thereof, often poses a greater threat to Odysseus than the battle scenes and challenges with which he is typically associated. What greater temptation for any hero than to set aside endless conflict, suffering, and pain of death to rest? Calypso's home represents profound risk to Odysseus: luxury, companionship, immortality, and sex. Of course, Ogygia is Calypso's realm, her seat of power not his; perhaps Odysseus also experiences the nascent fear of a kind of boredom, "rust[ing] unburnish'd," as Alfred, Lord Tennyson, would put it ("Ulysses" [*Poetry Foundation*]), and not shining in use. Students are quick to point out that the man who claims to want nothing more than to return to his home and his wife, the man who will readily fight all who stand in his way, doesn't seem to put up much of a fight against the nymph. The text may say "By night, he would sleep with her by constraint / in the hollow cave . . ." νύκτας μὲν ἰαύεσκεν καὶ ἀνάγκῃ / ἐν σπέσσι γλαφυροῖσι . . . (5.154–55), but students don't buy it. They point to a passage a few pages later when we find that "the two, entering the depths of the hollow cave, / took their pleasure in love, remaining beside one another" ἐλθόντες δ' ἄρα τώ γε μυχῷ σπείους γλαφυροῖο / τερπέσθην φιλότητι, παρ' ἀλλήλοισι μένοντες (5.226–27). Students remember these scenes and call out Odysseus for his hypocrisy in contrast to long-suffering Penelope, whose fidelity to her husband makes possible his triumphant return.[3] But they also remember that our first glimpse of Odysseus, like our first glimpse of Telemachus, finds him embroiled in the promise and peril of a domestic drama.

With divine assistance Odysseus escapes Calypso's temptations and, after twenty days of peril adrift at sea, washes ashore in Phaeacia, where he meets the princess Nausicaa, pleads for her aid and compassion, and, in doing so, gives poignant voice to one of the epic's central themes:

> Pity me, princess, for after suffering much
> to you first I have come, and of the others I know none,
> who hold this land and city.
> Show me the town, and give me a rag to clothe myself,
> if perhaps you had some wrapping for clothes when you came here.
> And may the gods give you all that you long for in your heart,
> a husband and a home, and may they grant like-mindedness,
> a good thing; for there is nothing better and stronger than this,
> when a husband and wife keep house in harmony of mind:
> much grief to those who wish them ill, but joy to those who wish them well,
> and they themselves know best what it means.
>
> ἀλλά, ἄνασσ', ἐλέαιρε· σὲ γὰρ κακὰ πολλὰ μογήσας
> ἐς πρώτην ἱκόμην, τῶν δ' ἄλλων οὔ τινα οἶδα
> ἀνθρώπων, οἳ τήνδε πόλιν καὶ γαῖαν ἔχουσιν.
> ἄστυ δέ μοι δεῖξον, δὸς δὲ ῥάκος ἀμφιβαλέσθαι,
> εἴ τί που εἴλυμα σπείρων ἔχες ἐνθάδ' ἰοῦσα.
> σοὶ δὲ θεοὶ τόσα δοῖεν ὅσα φρεσὶ σῇσι μενοινᾷς,
> ἄνδρα τε καὶ οἶκον καὶ ὁμοφροσύνην ὀπάσειαν
> ἐσθλήν· οὐ μὲν γὰρ τοῦ γε κρεῖσσον καὶ ἄρειον,
> ἢ ὅθ' ὁμοφρονέοντε νοήμασιν οἶκον ἔχητον
> ἀνὴρ ἠδὲ γυνή· πόλλ' ἄλγεα δυσμενέεσσι,
> χάρματα δ' εὐμενέτῃσι· μάλιστα δέ τ' ἔκλυον αὐτοί. (6.175–85)

In his benediction to the princess, Odysseus expresses his own heart's desire and something of his fear as well. Reduced to rags, floundering and alone, Odysseus's deepest longing is also his greatest threat. Students are surprised to find that lasting glory is gained not only on the battlefield, in the plunder of cities, or in the amassing of treasure but also in harmony, in relationships, and in the home.

They are even more surprised to discover that these deepest desires carry with them their own potential for destruction.

You Can't Go Home Again

By the time we reach the final scenes of the epic, we are primed to pay careful attention to the details and circumstances of Odysseus's homecoming. Instead of pomp and circumstance, the loving embrace of family and friends, the comforts of home and hearth, Odysseus finds chaos and bloodshed. Athena declares:

> But come, I will make you unknowable to all mortals;
> for I will wither the fine flesh on your supple limbs
> and take the fair hair from your head; with rags
> I will clothe you, to repel anyone who sees you,
> and make dim your eyes, formerly so handsome,
> so you will appear shabby to all the suitors
> and to your wife and son, whom you left in your halls.
>
> ἀλλ᾽ ἄγε σ᾽ ἄγνωστον τεύξω πάντεσσι βροτοῖσι·
> κάρψω μὲν χρόα καλὸν ἐνὶ γναμπτοῖσι μέλεσσι,
> ξανθὰς δ᾽ ἐκ κεφαλῆς ὀλέσω τρίχας, ἀμφὶ δὲ λαῖφος
> ἕσσω ὅ κε στυγέῃσιν ἰδὼν ἄνθρωπος ἔχοντα,
> κνυζώσω δέ τοι ὄσσε πάρος περικαλλέ᾽ ἐόντε,
> ὡς ἂν ἀεικέλιος πᾶσι μνηστῆρσι φανήῃς
> σῇ τ᾽ ἀλόχῳ καὶ παιδί, τὸν ἐν μεγάροισιν ἔλειπες. (13.397–403)

These lines, a thread in the web Athena and Odysseus spin to catch the suitors and regain the throne, suggest a more fundamental transformation, one not so easily cast off when the time is right. What if the trials and temptations of the hero's extended exile have irrevocably changed him? What if, in some sense, it is impossible to go home again? Perhaps the inability of even Odysseus's closest loved ones to recognize him is not simply a function of Athena's artful disguise but also indicative of just how much he has changed. Perhaps wily Odysseus, so skilled in guile and trickery, has fallen victim to his own conceits. When, as Aethon, he tells his story to Penelope, the narrator reminds us that "he knew how to tell many falsehoods that were like the truth" ἴσκε ψεύδεα πολλὰ λέγων ἐτύμοισιν ὁμοῖα (19.203). This is shaky ground on which to rebuild relationships and rule once more. The attributes that serve Odysseus so well while away—violence, deception, pride—now complicate his ability to reintegrate into the domestic sphere. How, for example, can harmony be restored after a scene such as the following?

> And they,[4] like birds of prey with hooked claws and beaks
> coming down from the mountains swoop after smaller birds;
> these flee over the field, cowering,

while the predators pounce on them and destroy them; there is no help
for them or escape, and men enjoy [watching] the hunt.
Just so, swooping after the suitors in the hall
they struck right and left, and ugly groans were heard
as heads were struck and the whole floor ran with blood.

οἱ δ᾽ ὥς τ᾽ αἰγυπιοὶ γαμψώνυχες ἀγκυλοχεῖλαι
ἐξ ὀρέων ἐλθόντες ἐπ᾽ ὀρνίθεσσι θόρωσι·
ταὶ μέν τ᾽ ἐν πεδίῳ νέφεα πτώσσουσαι ἵενται,
οἱ δέ τε τὰς ὀλέκουσιν ἐπάλμενοι, οὐδέ τις ἀλκὴ
γίγνεται οὐδὲ φυγή· χαίρουσι δέ τ᾽ἀνέρες ἄγρῃ·
ὣς ἄρα τοὶ μνηστῆρας ἐπεσσύμενοι κατὰ δῶμα
τύπτον ἐπιστροφάδην· τῶν δὲ στόνος ὄρνυτ᾽ ἀεικὴς
κράτων τυπτομένων, δάπεδον δ᾽ ἅπαν αἵματι θῦε. (22.302–09)

Odysseus undoubtedly loves his wife and son, his father, and his aged dog, but he loves the hunt as well. This tension between how Odysseus defines himself outside the home and his sincere desire to find his place within the home is central to the entire epic. In a work famous for soaring scenes of adventure and conquest, the poem boils down to this quiet, poignant interchange between husband and wife:

and he against the tall pillar
sat looking down, waiting to see if she would address him,
his loyal wife, when she saw him with her eyes.
And she sat long in silence, her heart struck with amazement:
sometimes, as she looked in his face, she thought she knew him;
sometimes she failed to know him in his ragged clothes.

ὁ δ᾽ ἄρα πρὸς κίονα μακρὴν
ἧστο κάτω ὁρόων, ποτιδέγμενος εἴ τί μιν εἴποι
ἰφθίμη παράκοιτις, ἐπεὶ ἴδεν ὀφθαλμοῖσιν.
ἡ δ᾽ ἄνεω δὴν ἧστο, τάφος δέ οἱ ἦτορ ἵκανεν·
ὄψει δ᾽ ἄλλοτε μέν μιν ἐνωπαδίως ἐσίδεσκεν,
ἄλλοτε δ᾽ ἀγνώσασκε κακὰ χροῒ εἵματ᾽ ἔχοντα. (23.90–95)

The great hero has returned home at last. But tribulations, suffering, violence, and loss have followed him. The prophet has declared that the only way for Odysseus to find "a gentle death" in his homeland (θάνατος . . . ἀβληχρός [23.281–82]) will be to leave his home and family once more, to travel among strangers, beyond the call of the sea, fearing that neither he nor his wife will have any joy of it (οὐ μέν τοι θυμὸς κεχαρήσεται· οὐδὲ γὰρ αὐτὸς / χαίρω . . . [23.266–67]). Reading the *Odyssey* with a focus on domesticity reveals a troubling paradox: the definitive traits that prove so essential to the hero's success while conquering the world may make him incapable of settling down when he returns home.

Students note that this paradox, so central in one of Western literature's seminal texts, persists in modern storytelling as well. How many Hollywood cowboys, grizzled detectives, or Marvel superheroes return home from their worldly exploits to well-adjusted family lives?

"I Am Become a Name"

Because we are encountering the *Odyssey* for the first time, I hesitate to introduce an array of secondary material in our study of the epic. Surely the hero's exploits, his triumphs and failures, are enough. Yet I make one exception. When we near the end of the poem, when the hero has returned from decades of suffering and struggle only to find himself tested once more in his own home, we read Tennyson's "Ulysses." Robert Fagles titles the final book of the epic "Peace," yet it's a strange sort of peace at best, where fathers barely recognize their sons, where Laertes is moved to say that his heart "quakes with fear that all the Ithacans / will come down on us in a pack, at any time" νῦν δ' αἰνῶς δείδοικα κατὰ φρένα μὴ τάχα πάντες / ἐνθάδ' ἐπέλθωσιν Ἰθακήσιοι (Fagles, Odyssey [Penguin Classics] 24.393–94; 24.353–54), and where in the poem's final lines the men must again be commanded as follows:

> "Hold back from painful battle, Ithacans,
> So you may be parted at once without bloodshed."
> So spoke Athena, and pale fear seized them;
> in their fear all their weapons flew from their hands,
> and fell upon the ground as the goddess was speaking.
>
> 'ἴσχεσθε πτολέμου, Ἰθακήσιοι, ἀργαλέοιο,
> ὥς κεν ἀναιμωτί γε διακρινθῆτε τάχιστα.'
> ὣς φάτ' Ἀθηναίη, τοὺς δὲ χλωρὸν δέος εἷλε·
> τῶν δ' ἄρα δεισάντων ἐκ χειρῶν ἔπτατο τεύχεα,
> πάντα δ' ἐπὶ χθονὶ πῖπτε, θεᾶς ὄπα φωνησάσης. (24.531–35)

And in many ways, the poem ends where it began. Within this context, Tennyson's poem provides a telling bridge from Homer's age to our own. It manages to both idolize and ironize the masculine hero's fate, that of a man obsessed with returning home only to find "how dull it is to pause, to make an end, / To rust unburnish'd, not to shine in use!" ("Ulysses" [*Poetry Foundation*]). The epic's final scene reveals three generations of men—grandfather, son, and grandson—"[striking] with swords and double-edged spears. / And now they would have killed them all and deprived them of homecoming, / if Athena, daughter of Zeus of the aegis, / had not called out . . ." τύπτον δὲ ξίφεσίν τε καὶ ἔγχεσιν ἀμφιγύοισι. / καί νύ κε δὴ πάντας ὄλεσαν καὶ ἔθηκαν ἀνόστους, / εἰ μὴ Ἀθηναίη, κούρη Διὸς αἰγιόχοιο, / ἤϋσεν φωνῇ . . . (24.527–30). Odysseus has returned home. His wife and son are safe. His throne has been restored. Now his battles begin.

NOTES

1. My students reference narratives of heroic quests in popular films like *American Sniper* and *The Hurt Locker.*

2. Translations are by Lillian Doherty unless otherwise noted.

3. As Doherty argues, "While both males and females help and hinder Odysseus, the poem portrays differences in the *ways* in which they do so. In particular, the poem's female characters are described as more fully invested in, and defined by, their helping or hindering capacities" ("Athena" 43).

4. "They" refers to Odysseus, Telemachus, and the two herdsmen helping them.

The Odyssey Project: Teaching the *Odyssey* to Incarcerated Students

Michael Morgan and Olga Faccani

One of the underlying messages of the *Odyssey* is that "human life is always in process: to live as a mortal is to suffer and to change, and to keep learning about both men and gods" (Segal 513). Every time Odysseus lands safely on a foreign shore, unexpected challenges and hurdles come in the way of his happy *nostos*, or "homecoming," further separating him from his family and intensifying his nostalgia, his pain of being far away from home. This idea of a homecoming process informs our approach to teaching the *Odyssey* to incarcerated youth as part of The Odyssey Project. In our teaching we embrace the inevitable challenges of working in carceral spaces with disenfranchised youth and engage in ongoing assessments of our approach and our positionality. In artistic endeavors that claim an activist intention, the facilitators must often expose the shortcomings of such endeavors, since much of the work is not about reinforcing a status quo but about opening a new opportunity to rebuild lives and communities. Therefore, while introducing The Odyssey Project, we also scrutinize its efficacy in supporting young people as they develop a sense of their worth and see the world as a place where their voices count.

Michael created The Odyssey Project in the summer of 2011 as a course that brings together undergraduate students from the University of California, Santa Barbara, and incarcerated youth from the Santa Barbara Department of Youth Probation's Los Prietos Boys Camp, a minimum security detention facility, to develop a prison theater program using Homer's *Odyssey*. The goal of the course was to situate ancient Greek literature in dialogue with the experiences of marginalized populations in order to revitalize a canonical text through a contemporary and activist lens. By using the template of Homer's epic, participants explore Odysseus's journey back home as mirrored in their own lives, reconstructing the poem in their voices. In 2019 we partnered with the Ventura Youth Correctional Facility, a maximum security detention center, to facilitate the retelling of the *Odyssey* in the form of a staged performance held at the facility. The examples discussed in this essay are borrowed from this collective experience, spanning a six-week class and rehearsal process, during which the ensemble engaged in writing and spoken word exercises, mask making, choreography, and acting. This six-week engagement between university students, incarcerated youth, and local artists culminated in a public performance, which included a postshow discussion with the ensemble and community members.

Odysseus's journey offers a paradigm for exploring the arduous process from conflict and imprisonment to homecoming and reentering society within a structure that invites reflections about identity and displacement, considerations about how to return home, and provocations about what home is. For these reasons, we found that the text of the *Odyssey* particularly resonated within the prison context among conflict-affected youth, who often experienced gang violence and physical and emotional trauma. The first part of this essay discusses the process of teaching the *Odyssey* to incarcerated youth using theater modalities. The second part focuses on the themes of the course and the participants' experience re-interpreting the epic. Finally, the third part centers on some challenges inherent in teaching within a carceral space and ethical considerations about our role as facilitators in this program.

We have written this essay in a personal voice, filtering through our accounts the process of teaching the *Odyssey* to incarcerated youth; at the same time, we attempt to go beyond accounts of personal experience and write with an awareness that "prisons are not only material institutions but also equally a state of mind. . . . They contain emotions, memories, and lives spent" (Lockard and Rankins-Roberts, "Prison Writing" 3). One of our goals is to honor the emotions, memories, and experiences of each participant as they re-interpreted Homer's heroic poem while negotiating the tension "between expressive freedom and absence of physical freedom" (4). To safeguard the privacy of every participant, any example borrowed from class material is offered in an anonymous form, and we omit any references to personal details.

Process

The incredible power of ancient Greek texts as a medium to explore questions of trauma, oppression, and displacement, from Greek performance to epic, has been variously noted by scholars and practitioners. In his volume *Odysseus in America*, the clinical psychiatrist Jonathan Shay suggested that the performance of Athenian plays served as a form of cultural therapy that helped reintegrate combat veterans returning to civilian life. Theater projects such as Peter Meineck's Aquila Theatre and Bryan Doerries's Theater of War Project have recently demonstrated the suitability of texts from Greco-Roman antiquity as frameworks for discussing on modern stages issues of overcoming trauma and surviving violence. Likewise, The Odyssey Project started as an effort to bridge the educational divide between conflict-affected youth in correctional facilities and academic institutions while leveraging the story of Odysseus as a paradigm for discussing issues of violence, class, identity, race, and gender. In doing so, it also offers a platform for participants to discuss the conditions of incarceration in the United States, which has the world's largest prison population and disproportionately incarcerates Black and Latinx people.

The project begins with reading parts of the *Odyssey* in translation and exercises aimed at helping the participants rewrite the ancient text as an original play. Then, students take on the role of Odysseus and think about what it means to return home, what "home" means, and what may be the obstacles to their journey of self-discovery within and outside prison. The program employs writing, drawing, acting, singing, rapping, improvisatory movement, choreographed dancing, and devised theater practices—teaching students how to move on stage and occupy space while also ruminating on what it means to have a space to occupy. In this way the project also constitutes an artistic intervention by the incarcerated youth, interrogating the relationship between education and conflict and examining how education can be a unifying force in the dehumanizing context of prison.

The Odyssey Project aims to provide a space where participants can take as much power as they need for their creative work. Since the process begins with rewriting a canonical text and reframing the journey of Odysseus through a personal starting point, it relies heavily on reading and writing as means of self-expression and growth. The project is also highly collaborative and involves the participation of not only University of California students and faculty members but also choreographers, mimes, mask makers, martial artists, costume designers, and animation and rap artists to guide participants as they explore these disciplines. The teaching artists come to the project to bring art modalities and resources to the young participants, and their professional expertise is there to support the youths' visions. In this way, the participants take over and determine what they want the outcome of the project to be. This process builds up to a performance for the public that includes incarcerated peers, if the facility allows them to attend. We strive to invite people in power: lawmakers and policymakers who can make a difference in the lives of these young people. The audience also includes family and friends who have the opportunity to see participants in a new, uplifting light.

Live theater achieves a "balance between intimacy and distance" (Snyder-Young 3), and the presence of an audience at the final performance that concludes the project brings out the "immediacy of real humans connecting in the same time and in the same space . . . , and perhaps serves as an antidote to the invisibility and isolation that constitute the prison experience" (Rada and Rocchio 171–72). In a context where incarcerated youth are often viewed from a generalizing perspective, performance implicates "the real through the presence of living bodies" (Phelan 148) and, in doing so, blurs the boundaries between prison students and university students and opens the prison walls to "allow participants to be seen" (Rada and Rocchio 175). Moreover, wearing a mask on stage—during rehearsal and during the final performance—becomes an opportunity for participants to ponder issues of identity, vulnerability, and masculinity. As part of the project, incarcerated and nonincarcerated students create personalized masks that encapsulate their heroic persona as informed by Athena in supplication to Zeus for a safe homecoming. For the participants, wearing masks is not an escape from their true selves or a "lesson in patriarchal masculinity" (hooks 153) but rather a way to step into their humanity in a collective exercise of vulnerability that is both intimate and communal.

While the project ends in a public performance at the facility, as teachers and artist-activists we are aware that the gravitational forces that brought these young people to detention centers are still in place when they exit the prison and return to their communities. As a six-week theater program, The Odyssey Project makes no claims of dramatically transforming the participants' lives. We do not embed rehabilitative impulses into our pedagogy since we do not share the belief that participants enter the program to become "better citizens." In facilitating the project, we strive instead to provide a network of support with social service and educational institutions beyond the program's life. In staging the final performance, we hope to ignite a cultural dialogue encompassing the social realities that create prisons.

Personal Odysseys

As part of The Odyssey Project, participants contemplate Homer's epic, from Telemachus's wanderings in search of the truth about whether his father is alive or dead to Odysseus's return to Ithaca. The *Odyssey* allows students to explore "the fundamental nature of justice, whether or not individuals (rather than governments or divine powers) are responsible for dispensing justice, and whether or not the existence of a just world is a real possibility" (Lamont Hill 22). Through textual analysis and written exercises, students grapple with questions of justice, otherness, conflict, and more, and they provide their interpretations of specific episodes explored as part of the program. For example, students reflect on how Odysseus is remembered as a hero of Greek myth and what the word *hero* means in the narrative poem and in our contemporary society. Ancient Greek heroes "were men of pain who were both needed by their people and dangerous to them" (Shay, *Odysseus* 2), exemplified by Odysseus failing to lead his crewmates to safety in his journey to Ithaca. Participants in the project identify their heroic qualities in reaction to reading the epic and choose a heroic name and persona for themselves as they trace their journeys of homecoming after prison. These are some of the accounts shared by students as part of the journey of authenticating their ability to define or redefine themselves: "My heroic name is Treasure. To my understanding, I am the treasure never found. My mission in life is to bring a treasure of happiness to my mother and sister. Also, living the life I was born to live becomes my own treasure"; "Atticus Lincoln, the knight, the activist, the fighter, the wolf, the righteous. I'm here to break stereotypes of a Mexican culture, prove that it can happen—Sí puedo.—Encounter the obstacles"; "I am a survivor of Abuse when others called it Discipline."

Students observed that, to Odysseus, home was synonymous not only with family and safety but also with danger and violence: Odysseus had to defeat the suitors in a confrontation that ended in bloodshed before reuniting with his wife and son. In his work with veterans returning to civilian society, Jonathan Shay observed that "looking beneath the surface to what Odysseus, the master of disguise, has hidden in the stories he tells the civilians, we see not only the '*what*' of real experiences, but the '*why*' of a veteran's need to disguise his experiences at all. What is '*home*' anyway?" (*Odysseus* 4). Similarly, incarcerated youth often have complex relationships with their homes and family, and looking backward to where their journey began becomes an essential part of looking forward to their future. One student reflected on his home and past and shared that his Odyssean journey began when he was in middle school, when he first experimented with tobacco, alcohol, sex, and other rites of passage associated with entering adolescence. The student noted that, at that time, he began to change not only his wardrobe and circle of friends but also, eventually, his physical appearance and identity. In his writings, the student chronicles the climax of drugs and substances that led him from middle school to a juvenile detention center and camp and that progressively created a bigger and bigger gulf between him and his friends. The vivid account of the student's journey to prison ends with the police department forcibly incarcerating him one night and with the student waking up the next morning as if from a dream, thinking he was still back home, until he realized he was confined within the claustrophobic white walls of his cell.

Within the context of prison, incarcerated youth are often seen through stereotypes of the criminalized other; for this reason, the episode of Odysseus's arrival in the land of the Cyclopes can generate rich discussions about the meaning of terms such as *other*, *outcast*, or *monster*. Homer characterizes the Cyclopes as "lawless brutes" and Polyphemus as "a savage deaf to justice, blind to law" (Fagles, Odyssey [Penguin Classics] 9.120, 240). However, the text of the *Odyssey* prompts a deeper examination of the responsibility of Odysseus and his crewmates when they enter Polyphemus's home, as men "who cast [their] lives / like dice, and ravage other folk" (Fitzgerald 9.256–57). The participants in the project leveraged the Cyclops episode as a lens to examine myths of society's monsters, people who are considered outcasts and throwaways. They rewrote the episode from the perspective of Polyphemus as a misunderstood outsider, infusing the episode with deeply felt personal narratives. For example, one student reflected on his identity as an African American male and on the societal stereotypes he endured. In his writings, the student noted that society perceives him as violent and uncivilized, but he is more than chaos and rage, and the feelings he internalized made him high as a tree and tough as a wall. The student denounced the demonization of his character through societal stereotypes, and the fact that he was taught to hate and curse even when, in reality, his disposition is kind and caring. Another student responded to the Polyphemus passage in the epic by composing an original piece of rap that traced the student's life journey and experience with rejection and discrimination. The student remembered the many voices throughout his life in the inner city that repeated to him that he would not amount to anything and that he was no good and did not belong in this country. He denounced the system for portraying him like a monster.

Like many literary works of Greco-Roman antiquity, the *Odyssey* has been and continues to be a normative locus for Western discourses of oppression, discrimination, and class supremacy. In rewriting the *Odyssey* as a personal homecoming journey, the participants exposed hegemonic structures embedded in the text for critical and artistic purposes, often recalling their experiences with oppression and societal rejection. At the same time, while rewriting the *Odyssey* becomes an occasion to identify and critique discourses of power and supremacy, these conversations necessarily occur within the confines of the authoritarian and dehumanizing space that is prison.

Challenges

As facilitators of The Odyssey Project, we are acutely aware of the lack of parity between teachers and students: the experiential chasm between incarcerated students and university students, and between incarcerated students and instructors or facilitators. To work in carceral spaces is to acknowledge one's positionality and to address the fact that "to walk in and out of a prison before and after classes manifests class privilege" (Lockard 24). We believe that hand in hand with this awareness is the fundamental question "Education for what?"—a question that is often answered with the goal of rehabilitating the incarcerated population through the tools of pedagogy. As noted by Joe Lockard, "Education has been conscripted as a tool for perennially ineffective efforts to prevent the systemic problem of recidivism rather than as a means to engage with root social causes of incarceration that would challenge a circumscribed focus on personal responsibility" (11–12). With our work as part of The Odyssey Project, we do not claim to create a learning environment where fundamental differences between incarcerated and nonincarcerated students are erased. Instead, because writing and performing are acts of expressive production, the artistic journey of each participant is a testament to the fact that "within every prison reside multitudes of skilled artists and writers, possessing greater or lesser degrees of aptitude, and countless cultural producers" (Rada and Rocchio 181). We see our role in The Odyssey Project much like the role of Paulo Freire's teacher who is "taught in dialogue with the students, who in turn while being taught also teach" (80). We see ourselves as "being with" the creative products of the participants and facilitating their process of rewriting the *Odyssey*.

One of the legacies of ancient Greek literature throughout millennia is the concept of nobility, and its endurance is attested to by our current fascination with contemporary series like *The Crown*. Educators and practitioners such as Freire, Bertolt Brecht,[1] Augusto Boal, and others have contested the notion of nobility and the social and political systems in which it develops, pointing to its dichotomous nature in the fact that, for example, "Queen Elizabeth was one of the greatest debtors of the English banks" (Boal 53). As facilitators who synthesize canonical masterpieces with narratives from incarcerated voices in our own time, we similarly acknowledge the dangers of oversimplification and straining to make analogies, and we recognize the necessity of looking at the disconnects. For example, we look at Odysseus as a "nobleman"[2] in the social and historical context of the *Odyssey* who at the same time displays pivotal faults that humanize him and allow for critical reflections. By pairing Odysseus with marginalized others, often living in poverty, with limited access to education and mobility, the project challenges prescribed notions of nobility, posing the question, "What does it mean to be noble?" In this way the project seeks to stimulate a deep core of identity where inner nobility may reside through honoring one's courage in survival, resourcefulness, and perseverance.

Even though performances by incarcerated people are often disparaged as a form of entertainment that is either perceived as not deserved by the incarcerated artists or seen as meaningless since it originates within confinement, The Odyssey Project proceeds from the practical application of idealism predicated on the agency of youth. We see teaching as a noble calling, and since the teaching is always mutual, the project is rooted in the highest standards of service, personal investment, cooperative mission, and vision in recognizing the pursuit of youthful potential to define a voice and make that voice heard.

NOTES

1. For more on Brecht, see Willett.
2. The Greek equivalent would be *agathos* or *aristos*, the second of which is the basis of the English word *aristocrat*. Yet like *noble*, they are also words with ethical implications.

NOTES ON CONTRIBUTORS

Henry Alley is professor emeritus of literature and a writing specialist at the University of Oregon's Clark Honors College. He is a winner of the Faculty Achievement Award for Distinguished Teaching. His publications include *The Quest for Anonymity: The Novels of George Eliot*, six novels, a short story collection, a handbook on teaching creative writing, and articles on the work of Virginia Woolf, Oscar Wilde, and E. M. Forster. His shorter fiction, which has appeared since 1969, has been nominated for the O. Henry Prize and the Pushcart Prize. He teaches in the University of Oregon's Osher Lifelong Learning Institute.

Jennifer R. Ballengee is professor and chair of the Department of Languages, Literatures and Cultures at Towson University. She is the author of *The Wound and the Witness: The Rhetoric of Torture* (2009) and coeditor, with David Kelman, of *Trauma and Literature in an Age of Globalization* (2021). Her other publications, which have appeared in a range of academic and nonacademic journals and newspapers, focus on the conjunction of politics and the humanities. Ballengee regularly teaches undergraduate and graduate courses on critical theory, Ancient Greek language and literature, human rights, and related topics.

Jamie L. Brummer is the principal at Christian Brothers High School in Memphis, Tennessee, where he also teaches English and coaches soccer. His dissertation explored issues related to masculinity in Cormac McCarthy's Western novels. In addition to conference presentations, he has contributed to the journals *Callaloo*, *The Cormac McCarthy Journal*, *The Explicator*, and *Gothic Studies*; the MLA series Approaches to Teaching World Literature (*Approaches to Teaching the Works of Cormac McCarthy* and *Approaches to Teaching Dostoevsky's* Crime and Punishment); and the books *Bonds of Brotherhood in* Sons of Anarchy: *Essays on Masculinity in the FX Series* and *The African American Novel in the Early Twenty-First Century*.

Lillian E. Doherty is professor emerita of classics at the University of Maryland, College Park. Most of her scholarship has been on the Homeric *Odyssey* and its reception. She is the author of *Siren Songs: Gender, Audiences, and Narrators in the* Odyssey (1995) and *Gender and the Interpretation of Classical Myth* (2001); with Bruce M. King, she edited *Thinking the Greeks: A Volume in Honour of James M. Redfield* (2019). She has been active in the Women's Classical Caucus and served a term as associate editor for Greek of the *American Journal of Philology*.

Casey Dué is professor and director of classical studies at the University of Houston. She is the author most recently of *Achilles Unbound: Multiformity and Tradition in the Homeric Epics* (2019). Other publications include *Homeric Variations on a Lament by Briseis* (2002), *The Captive Woman's Lament in Greek Tragedy* (2006), and (with Mary Ebbott) Iliad *10 and the Poetics of Ambush* (2010). She is associate editor of *The Cambridge Guide to Homer* (2020).

Olga Faccani oversees the professional development of teaching assistants through the Office of Teaching and Learning at the University of California, Santa Barbara, where she also earned her PhD in classics. Drawing from psychotherapy, trauma studies, and affect theory, her dissertation examined disorientation stemming from death and change in the works of the Athenian playwright Euripides. She is passionate about the public humanities, and she maintains an active collaboration with The Odyssey Project.

Maria Fahey is a member of the faculty at Friends Seminary, where she teaches English to middle and high school students. She is the author of *Metaphor and Shakespearean Drama: Unchaste Signification*, which was short-listed for the 2012 Shakespeare's Globe Book Award, and "Transporting Florimell: The Place of Simile in Book III of *The Faerie Queene*," published in *Spenser Studies*.

Marya Fisher is a member of the classics department and head of high school at the Pierrepont School in Westport, Connecticut. Prior to teaching at Pierrepont, Fisher taught at Vassar College and New York University and has participated in fieldwork throughout the Mediterranean, including in Polis Chrysochous, Cyprus (Princeton University); in Selinunte, Sicily (Institute of Fine Arts at New York University); and at the Sanctuary of the Great Gods in Samothrace (American School of Classical Studies at Athens).

Bruce M. King teaches ancient literature and its reception at the Brooklyn Institute for Social Research, where he is the director of the Language Learning and Critique program. His research interests include Homeric poetry, pre-Socratic philosophy, Attic tragedy, and religious and philosophical histories of Magna Graecia as well as comparative, psychoanalytic, and queer readings of antiquity. His book on the *Iliad*, *Akhilleus All-Unheroic*, is forthcoming.

Rachel H. Lesser is associate professor of ancient Greek and Roman studies at Gettysburg College. Her research and teaching focus on women, gender, and desire in ancient Greek literature, especially Homeric epic. Her first book is *Desire in the* Iliad*: The Force That Moves the Epic and Its Audience* (2022), and she has also published articles on the *Odyssey*, Sappho's lyrics, and the reception of Homer.

Kirsten Lodge is professor of humanities and English and the humanities program coordinator at Midwestern State University Texas, where she teaches courses in great books, world cultures, world literature, comparative literature, literary theory, and the humanities. She has translated classics of Russian literature, including Dostoevsky's *Notes from the Underground* and Tolstoy's *"Death of Ivan Ilyich" and Other Stories*, among others. She is the translator and editor of *Solitude, Vanity, Night: An Anthology of Czech Decadent Poetry*; the translator of *A Gothic Soul*, by Jiří Karásek; the editor and cotranslator of *The Dedalus Book of Russian Decadence: Perversity, Despair, and Collapse*; and the author of *Translating the Early Poetry of Velimir Khlebnikov*.

Michael Morgan teaches voice and applied theater at the University of California, Santa Barbara. He has also taught at the Yale School of Drama; Temple University; Brussels Theatre Conservatorium; Liege Royal Conservatoire; Arena Stage; the University of Hawaiʻi; the University of California, San Diego; Cal Arts; Shanghai Theatre Academy; and Athens Theatre of Changes. He has appeared in plays, films, and TV shows. Morgan is the founder of The Odyssey Project, which has received an NEA grant. His essay "A Poetics of Performance Liberation: A Conversation about The Odyssey Project," cowritten with Zachary Price, appeared in *Classics and Prison Education in the US*.

With Catherine Fitzmaurice, he is the author of *Fitzmaurice Voicework: Embodying the Holistic Voice* (2025).

Sheila Murnaghan is Alfred Reginald Allen Memorial Professor of Greek at the University of Pennsylvania. She works on ancient Greek poetry, especially epic and tragedy; gender in Greco-Roman culture; and classical reception. She is the author of *Disguise and Recognition in the* Odyssey, coeditor of *Odyssean Identities in Modern Cultures: The Journey Home*, and coauthor of *Childhood and the Classics: Britain and America, 1850–1965*. She has published Norton Critical Editions of new translations of Euripides's *Medea* and Sophocles's *Antigone*. She has a forthcoming collection of essays on the tragic chorus, *Sharing in the Action: The Choral Plot of Classical Athenian Tragedy*, and is currently working on an edition with commentary of Sophocles's *Ajax*.

Brett M. Rogers is professor and chair of Greek, Latin, and ancient Mediterranean studies at the University of Puget Sound. His research interests include Greek epic and drama, ancient education, classical myth, and the reception of antiquity in modern media and popular culture. He has coedited four volumes on classical receptions in science fiction and modern fantasy, including, most recently (with Benjamin Eldon Stevens), *Once and Future Antiquities in Science Fiction and Fantasy* (2019). In 2021 he received the Award for Excellence in the Teaching of Classics at the College and University Level from the Society for Classical Studies.

Laura M. Slatkin is Gallatin Distinguished Professor at New York University and visiting professor in the Committee on Social Thought at the University of Chicago, where she regularly offers courses on early Greek poetry. She is the author of *The Power of Thetis and Selected Essays* (2011) as well as other essays on epic, tragedy, and comparative poetics.

Julie Van Peteghem is associate professor of Italian at Hunter College, City University of New York, and a doctoral faculty member in comparative literature and the Interactive Technology and Pedagogy program at the Graduate Center, City University of New York. Her research and teaching focus on thirteenth- and fourteenth-century Italian literature, classical reception, and Italian language and translation. She is the author of *Italian Readers of Ovid from the Origins to Petrarch* (2020) and various essays on medieval Italian poetry. She is managing editor of the scholarly site *Digital Dante* and editor of *Intertextual Dante*, an interactive digital tool that allows users to read Dante's *Divine Comedy* alongside its sources.

Patricia Vreeland has taught English in grades 7 to 12 in San Diego–area schools; supervised aspiring educators from the University of California, San Diego, and the University of San Diego; presented at the convention of the California Association of Teachers of English; and contributed to the NCTE journal *Voices from the Middle*. She was an assessor for the National Board of Professional Teaching Standards and the Measures of Effective Teaching (Gates Foundation and Stanford University). She is affiliated with the San Diego Area Writing Project.

SURVEY RESPONDENTS

Henry Alley, *University of Oregon*
Brian Armstrong, *Augusta University*
Lisa Arter, *Southern Utah University*
Erin Ashworth-King, *Angelo State University*
Diane Ayer, *Lyman Memorial High School*
J. Bair, *Christian Heritage School*
Courtney Baklik, *Lyme-Old Lyme High School*
Jennifer R. Ballengee, *Towson University*
Cristina J. Baptista, *Sacred Heart School*
Alissa Becker, *Woodland Regional High School*
Jamie L. Brummer, *Christian Brothers High School*
Gretchen Busl, *Texas Woman's University*
Ellen Caldwell, *Clarkson University*
Richard Caputo, *Farmingdale State College, State University of New York*
Amee Carmines, *Hampton University*
Mária Cipriani, *John Jay College, City University of New York*
Steven Colburn, *University of South Florida*
Raymond Cormier, *Longwood University*
Jason Courtmanche, *University of Connecticut*
Susan Crisafulli, *Franklin College*
David Currell, *American University of Beirut*
Lisa Darien, *Hartwick College*
Angelina Del Balzo, *University of California, Los Angeles*
Jessica Duga, *Manchester High School*
Iris Jamahl Dunkle, *Napa Valley College*
Nikolai Endres, *Western Kentucky University*
Ann W. Engar, *University of Utah*
Maria Fahey, *Friends Seminary*
Roger Fox, *National Park College*
Sharon M. Gallagher, *Penn State University, Erie-Behrend*
Robert Gambles, *University of Utah*
John Garrison, *Grinnell College*
Virginia Gilbert, *Alabama A&M University*
Alexandre Gontchar, *Harvard University*
David Gorman, *Northern Illinois University*
Sean Hadley, *Trinitas Christian School*
Eric Ashley Hairston, *Elon University*
Wendy Halsey, *Montville High School*
Meghan Hatch-Geary, *Woodland Regional High School*
Spencer Hawkins, *University of Notre Dame*
Thomas Hendrickson, *Stanford Online High School*
Md. Amir Hossain, *IBAIS University*
Anne Hruska, *Stanford Online High School*

Ann A. Huse, *John Jay College, City University of New York*
R. Mark Jackson, *Angelo State University*
Glenn Jellenik, *University of Central Arkansas*
Allan Johnston
Cynthia A. Jones, *University of Missouri, Kansas City*
Rajender Kaur, *William Paterson University*
Thomas V. Kenney, *Briarcliff Manor High School*
Robert Kilgore, *University of South Carolina, Beaufort*
Meghan King
Doug Kirshen, *Brandeis University*
Allyson Lambert, *Notre Dame High School*
Brooke Lenz, *Saint Mary's University of Minnesota*
Ernesto Livorni, *University of Wisconsin, Madison*
Kirsten Lodge, *Midwestern State University Texas*
Richard Mace, *Pace University*
Liesder Mayea, *University of Redlands*
Jen McConnel, *Queen's University*
Rhonda McDaniel, *Middle Tennessee State University*
Stephanie McKenna, *Wethersfield High School*
Corinna McLeod, *Grand Valley State University*
Peter J. Miller, *University of Winnipeg*
Salam Mir, *Lasell College*
Andrew Mossin, *Temple University*
Kristen Mucinskas, *Wethersfield High School* and *University of Connecticut Early College Experience*
William Nelles, *University of Massachusetts, Dartmouth*
James Nohrnberg, *University of Virginia*
Yoandy Cabrera Ortega, *Texas A&M University*
Regina O'Sullivan, *Granby Memorial High School*
Gavin Paul, *University of British Columbia*
Mark Pearsall, *Glastonbury High School*
Gail D. Pells, *Woodland Regional High School*
Peter Ponzio, *Loyola University*
Donna Prejean-Kalloch, *Tri-County Technical College*
Evan Radcliffe, *Villanova University*
Paul Reiff, *Libertyville High School*
Rebecca Resinski, *Hendrix College*
Barry Sarchett, *Colorado College*
Veronica Schanoes, *Queens College, City University of New York*
Lauren Shafer, *Granby Memorial High School*
Gail Berkeley Sherman, *Reed College*
Christine Shugrue, *Shepaug Valley School*
Alissa Simon, *Harrison Middleton University*
David Morgan Spitzer, *Binghamton University, State University of New York*
Scott Stewart, *Weilenmann School of Discovery*
Jan Susina, *Illinois State University*
Michelle Szetela, *Copper Hills High School*

Carlos Torres, *Casady School*
Julie Van Peteghem, *Hunter College, City University of New York*
Meghan Vicks
Patricia Vreeland, *University of San Diego*
Jeff W. Westover, *Boise State University*
Julia M. Wiellette, *Avon High School, Connecticut*
Adam Williams, *Oak Hall School*
Timothy Wutrich, *Case Western Reserve University*

WORKS CITED

Addison, Catherine. "'So Stretched Out Huge in Length': Reading the Extended Simile." *Style*, vol. 35, no. 3, fall 2001, pp. 498–516.

Agrimbau, David. *Homer's The* Odyssey*: A Graphic Novel*. Illustrated by Smilton Roa Klassen, Capstone Press, 2017.

Ahlberg-Cornell, Gudrun. *Herakles and the Sea-Monster in Attic Black-Figure Vase-Painting*. Paul Åströms Förlag, 1984.

Alien: Resurrection. Directed by Jean-Pierre Jeunet, 20th Century Fox, 1997.

Alighieri, Dante. *La Divina Commedia*. Edited by Giorgio Petrocchi, 1975. *Digital Dante*, digitaldante.columbia.edu/dante/divine-comedy.

———. *Inferno*. Edited and translated by Robert M. Durling and Ronald L. Martinez, Oxford UP, 1997.

———. *Inferno*. Translated by Robert Hollander and Joan Hollander, Doubleday, 2000. *Princeton Dante Project*, dante.princeton.edu/pdp/.

———. *Inferno*. Translated by Allen Mandelbaum, Bantam, 1982.

Allen, Thomas W., and D. B. Monro, editors. *Odysseae Libros I–XII*. 2nd ed., Oxford UP, 1917. Vol. 3 of *Homeri Opera*.

———, editors. *Odysseae Libros XIII–XXIV*. 2nd ed., Oxford UP, 1922. Vol. 4 of *Homeri Opera*.

Alter, Robert. *The Pleasures of Reading in an Ideological Age*. W. W. Norton, 1996.

Ameis, Karl Friedrich, et al., editors. *Homers* Odyssee. 1908–20. A. M. Hakkert, 1964. 2 vols.

Anderson, Amanda, et al. *Character: Three Inquiries in Literary Studies*. U of Chicago P, 2019.

Apollodorus. *The Library*. Translated by James G. Frazer, vol. 2, Harvard UP, 1921.

———. *The Library of Greek Mythology*. Translated by Robin Hard, Oxford UP, 1997.

Appiah, Kwame Anthony. "There Is No Such Thing As Western Civilization." *The Guardian*, 9 Nov. 2016, theguardian.com/world/2016/nov/09/western-civilisation-appiah-reith-lecture.

Arentzen, Wout. "An Early Examination of the 'Mask of Agamemnon.'" *L'antiquité classique*, vol. 70, 2001, pp. 189–92.

Aristotle. *On Rhetoric: A Theory of Civic Discourse*. Translated by George A. Kennedy, 2nd ed., Oxford UP, 2007.

———. *Poetics*. Translated by Malcolm Heath, Penguin Classics, 1997.

Armitage, Simon. *Homer's* Odyssey. Faber and Faber, 2006.

———. *The* Odyssey. Narrated by Tim McInnerny et al., audiobook ed., BBC Audio, 15 Apr. 2005. *Audible*, audible.com.

Arnold, Matthew. *On Translating Homer*. 1861. Chelsea House, 1983.

Athanassakis, Apostolos, translator. *The Homeric Hymns*. 3rd ed., Johns Hopkins UP, 2020.

Atwood, Margaret. *The Penelopiad.* Canongate, 2005.

———. "Siren Song." *Selected Poems, 1965–1975*, by Atwood, Houghton Mifflin, 1976, p. 195.

Auerbach, Erich. "Odysseus' Scar." *Mimesis*, by Auerbach, Princeton UP, 1953, pp. 3–23.

Autenrieth, Georg. *A Homeric Dictionary for Schools and Colleges.* Translated by Robert Porter Keep, Harper and Brothers, 1891. *Perseus Digital Library*, www.perseus.tufts.edu/hopper/text?doc=Perseus:text:1999.04.0073.

Baker, Patrick, et al., editors. *Beyond Reception: Renaissance Humanism and the Transformation of Classical Antiquity.* De Gruyter, 2019.

Bakker, Egbert, editor. *Homer:* Odyssey *Book 9.* Cambridge UP, 2025.

———. *The Meaning of Meat and the Structure of the* Odyssey. Cambridge UP, 2013.

———. *Poetry in Speech.* Cornell UP, 1997.

Bakker, Egbert, and Ahuvia Kahane. *Written Voices, Spoken Signs.* Harvard UP, 1997.

Barker, Elton T. E., and Joel P. Christensen. "Odysseus's *Nostos* and the *Odyssey*'s *Nostoi*: Rivalry within the Epic Cycle." *Philologia Antiqua*, vol. 7, 2014, pp. 85–110.

Barolini, Teodolinda. "*Inferno* 26: The Epic Hero." *Digital Dante*, Columbia University Libraries, 2018, digitaldante.columbia.edu/dante/divine-comedy/inferno/inferno-26.

Barthes, Roland. *The Pleasure of the Text.* Translated by Richard Howard, Farrar, Straus and Giroux, 1975.

Baum, L. Frank. *The Wonderful Wizard of Oz.* George M. Hill, 1900.

Beard, Mary. "The Public Voice of Women." *Women and Power: A Manifesto*, by Beard, Liveright Publishing, 2017, pp. 1–46.

Beetham, Frank. *Beginning Greek with Homer: An Elementary Course Based on* Odyssey V. Bristol Classical Press, 1998.

Ben-Porat, Ziva. "Poetics of the Homeric Simile and the Theory of the (Poetic) Simile." *Poetics Today*, vol. 13, no. 4, winter 1992, pp. 737–69.

Benveniste, Emile. *Le vocabulaire des institutions indo-européennes.* Éditions de Minuit, 1969. 2 vols.

Bernabé, A., editor. *Poetarum Epicorum Graecorum.* 1987. Teubner, 1996.

Bierl, Anton, and Joachim Latacz. *Homer's* Iliad*: The Basel Commentary.* Translated by Benjamin W. Millis and Sara Strack, edited by S. Douglas Olson, De Gruyter, 2000–. 11 vols.

Big Fish. Directed by Tim Burton, Sony Pictures, 2004.

Black-figure Little Master cup with Herakles and Triton. *Classical Art Research Centre*, U of Oxford, 2003–25, www.carc.ox.ac.uk/record/1FB4F4C9-756B-4092-8881-F0DD68A8B8C1.

Blackwell, Nicholas G. "Making the Lion Gate Relief at Mycenae: Tool Marks and Foreign Influence." *American Journal of Archaeology*, vol. 118, no. 3, 2014, pp. 451–88.

Blakolmer, Fritz. "Images and Perceptions of the Lion Gate Relief at Mycenae during the Nineteenth Century." *Cogitata tradere posteris: The Representation of Ancient Architecture in the Nineteenth Century*, edited by Francesca Buscemi, Bonanno Editore, 2010, pp. 49–66.

Bloom, Harold, editor. *Homer's The* Odyssey. Chelsea House, 2008.

Boal, Augusto. *Theater of the Oppressed*. Pluto Press, 1970.

Boardman, John. "Symbol and Story in Geometric Art." *Ancient Greek Art and Iconography*, edited by Warren G. Moon, U of Wisconsin P, 1983, pp. 15–36.

Boar's tusk helmet with cheek guards. *Heraklion Archaeological Museum*, heraklionmuseum.gr/en/exhibit/boars-tusk-helmet-with-cheek-guards/. Accessed 18 June 2025.

Boeotian black-figure skyphos with Odysseus. *Classical Art Research Centre*, U of Oxford, 2003–25, www.carc.ox.ac.uk/record/F609979C-BB9D-4E50-9A9C-1734DEFE85A7.

Boerma, Inouk E., et al. "Reading Pictures for Story Comprehension Requires Mental Imagery Skills." *Frontiers in Psychology*, vol. 7, 2016, https://doi.org/10.3389/fpsyg.2016.01630.

Bowie, A. M., editor. *Homer:* Odyssey *Books 13 and 14*. Cambridge UP, 2014.

Brodsky, Joseph. "Odysseus to Telemachus." Translated by George L. Kline. *A Part of Speech*, by Brodsky, Farrar, Straus and Giroux, 1980, p. 58.

Brooke-Rose, Christine. *A Grammar of Metaphor*. Secker and Warburg, 1965.

Burgess, Jonathan. "Coming Adrift: The Limits of Reconstruction of the Cyclic Poems." Fantuzzi and Tsagalis, pp. 43–58.

———. "Recent Reception of Homer: A Review Article." *Phoenix*, vol. 62, nos. 1–2, 2008, pp. 184–95.

———. *The Tradition of the Trojan War in Homer and the Epic Cycle*. Johns Hopkins UP, 2001.

Burkert, Walter. *Greek Religion*. Translated by John Raffan, Harvard UP, 1985.

Butler, Samuel, translator. *The* Odyssey *of Homer, Rendered into English Prose*. 1900. *Project Gutenberg*, www.gutenberg.org/files/1727/1727-h/1727-h.htm.

Butler, Shane, editor. *Deep Classics: Rethinking Classical Reception*. Bloomsbury Academic, 2016.

Calder, William M., III. "Is the Mask a Hoax?" *Archaeology*, vol. 52, no. 4, 1999, pp. 53–55.

Campbell, Joseph. *The Hero with a Thousand Faces*. Princeton UP, 1973.

———. *Myths to Live By*. Bantam Books, 1972.

Canevaro, Lilah Grace. *Women of Substance in Homeric Epic: Objects, Gender, Agency*. Oxford UP, 2018.

Capettini, Emilio, and Nancy Sorkin Rabinowitz, editors. *Classics and Prison Education in the US*. Routledge, 2023.

Carson, Anne, translator. *If Not, Winter: Fragments of Sappho*. Knopf, 2002.

Casson, Lionel. *Ships and Seamanship in the Ancient World*. Princeton UP, 1971.

Cavafy, C. P. "Ithaka." *Poetry Foundation*, 2025, www.poetryfoundation.org/poems/51296/ithaka-56d22eef917ec.

Chantraine, Pierre. *Dictionnaire étymologique de la langue grecque: Histoire des mots*. Klincksieck, 1968–80. 4 vols. *Internet Archive*, archive.org/details/Dictionnaire-Etymologique-Grec.

Chapman, George, translator. *Chapman's Homer: The* Iliad, *the* Odyssey, *and the Lesser Homerica*. 1614–15. Edited by Allardyce Nicoll, 2nd ed., Princeton UP, 1967.

Christensen, Joel P. *The Many-Minded Man: The* Odyssey, *Psychology, and the Therapy of Epic*. Cornell UP, 2020.

———, editor. *The Oxford Critical Guide to Homer's* Odyssey. Oxford UP, 2026.

Clastres, Pierre. *Society against the State*. Translated by Robert Hurley, Zone, 1989.

Clay, Jenny Strauss. *The Wrath of Athena: Gods and Men in the* Odyssey. Princeton UP, 1983.

Clay, Jenny Strauss, et al., editors. *Panhellenes at Methone: Graphē in Late Geometric and Protoarchaic Methone, Macedonia (ca. 700 BCE)*. De Gruyter, 2017.

Cline, Eric H. *The Trojan War: A Brief Introduction*. Oxford UP, 2013.

Čolaković, Zlatan. "Avdo Međedović's Post-Traditional Epics and their Relevance to Homeric Studies." *Journal of Hellenic Studies*, vol. 139, 2019, pp. 1–48.

Cold Mountain. Directed by Anthony Minghella, Miramax Films, 2003.

Coldstream, J. N. *Geometric Greece, 900–700 BC*. 2nd ed., Routledge, 2003.

"Collection of Mycenaean Antiquities." *National Archaeological Museum*, 2025, namuseum.gr/en/collection/syllogi-mykinaikon-archaiotiton/.

Cook, Albert, editor and translator. *Homer: The* Odyssey. Norton Critical Edition, 2nd ed., W. W. Norton, 1993.

Cook, Erwin F. "Ferrymen of Elysium and the Homeric Phaeacians." *Journal of Indo-European Studies*, vol. 20, 1992, pp. 239–67.

———. *The* Odyssey *in Athens: Myths of Cultural Origins*. Cornell UP, 1995.

Cox, Fiona, and Elena Theodorakopoulos, editors. *Homer's Daughters: Women's Responses to Homer, 1914–2014*. Oxford UP, 2019.

Cox Gurdon, Meghan. "Even Homer Gets Mobbed: A Massachusetts School Has Banned 'The Odyssey.'" *The Wall Street Journal*, 27 Dec. 2020, www.wsj.com/articles/even-homer-gets-mobbed-11609095872.

Cribiore, Raffaella. *Gymnastics of the Mind: Greek Education in Hellenistic and Roman Egypt*. Princeton UP, 2001.

Crielaard, J. P. "Homer, History and Archaeology." *Homeric Questions: Essays in Philology, Ancient History and Archaeology, including the Papers of a Conference Organized by the Netherlands Institute at Athens*, edited by Crielaard, J. C. Gieben, 1995, pp. 201–88.

———. "Homeric Communities." Pache, pp. 227–44.

Cunliffe, Richard John. *A Lexicon of the Homeric Dialect*. 1924. Expanded ed., U of Oklahoma P, 2012.

D'Aulaire, Ingri, and Edgar Parin D'Aulaire. *D'Aulaires' Book of Greek Myths*. 1962. Delacorte Press, 1992.

Daumas, Michèle. *Cabiriaca: Recherches sur l'iconographie du culte des Cabires*. Boccard, 1998.

de Jong, Irene. *A Narratological Commentary on the* Odyssey. Cambridge UP, 2001.

———. *Narrators and Focalizers: The Presentation of the Story in the* Iliad. Bristol Classical Press, 1987.

Demakopoulou, Katie. "The Case for Authenticity." *Archaeology*, vol. 52, no. 4, 1999, pp. 57–58.

Derbew, Sarah. "Definitions and Representations of Race in Ancient Greek Literature." McCoskey, *Cultural History*, pp. 21–31.

———. *Untangling Blackness in Greek Antiquity*. Cambridge UP, 2022.

Desmond, Marilynn. "Homer and the Latin West in the Middle Ages." Pache, pp. 435–43.

Detienne, Marcel, and Jean-Pierre Vernant. *Cunning Intelligence in Greek Culture and Society*. 1978. Translated by Janet Lloyd, U of Chicago P, 1991.

Dickinson, Oliver. "The Face of Agamemnon." *Hesperia*, vol. 74, no. 3, 2005, pp. 299–308.

Doherty, Lillian. "Athena and Penelope as Foils for Odysseus in the *Odyssey*." *Quaderni Urbinati di Cultura Classica*, new series, vol. 39, no. 3, 1991, pp. 31–44.

———. "The Figure of Penelope in Twentieth-Century Poetry by American Women." *American Women and Classical Myths*, edited by Gregory A. Staley, Baylor UP, 2009, pp. 181–206.

———, editor. *Homer's* Odyssey. Oxford UP, 2009. Oxford Readings in Classical Studies.

———. *Siren Songs: Gender, Audiences, and Narrators in the* Odyssey. U of Michigan P, 1995.

Dougherty, Carol. "Phemius' Last Stand: The Impact of Occasion on Tradition in the *Odyssey*." *Oral Tradition*, vol. 6, no. 1, 1991, pp. 93–103.

———. *The Raft of Odysseus: The Ethnographic Imagination of Homer's* Odyssey. Oxford UP, 2001.

Draper, P. A., editor. *An* Odyssey *Reader: Selections from Homer's* Odyssey, *Books 1–12, with Notes and Vocabulary*. U of Michigan P, 2013.

Dué, Casey. "*Epea Pteroenta*: How We Came to Have Our *Iliad*." *Recapturing a Homeric Legacy: Images and Insights from the Venetus A Manuscript of the* Iliad, edited by Dué, Center for Hellenic Studies / Harvard UP, 2009, pp. 19–30.

Dué, Casey, and Mary Ebbott. Iliad *10 and the Poetics of Ambush: A Multitext Edition with Essays and Commentary*. Center for Hellenic Studies, 2010, nrs.harvard.edu/urn-3:hul.ebook:CHS_Due_Ebbott.Iliad_10_and_the_Poetics_of_Ambush.2010. Hellenic Studies 39.

Dunbar, Henry. *A Complete Concordance to the* Odyssey *of Homer*. Revised by Benedetto Marzullo, Georg Olms Verlag, 1962.

Edmunds, Lowell. "Helen's Divine Origins," *Electronic Antiquity*, vol. 10, 2007, pp. 1–45.

Edwards, Anthony. *Achilles in the* Odyssey: *Ideologies of Heroism in the Homeric Epic*. Anton Hain, 1985.

Eleusis neck amphora with blinding of the Cyclops. *Classical Art Research Centre*, U of Oxford, 2003–25, www.carc.ox.ac.uk/carc/resources/Introduction-to-Greek-Pottery/Keypieces/Protoattic/Eleusis.

Ellison, Ralph. *Invisible Man*. 1952. Vintage, 1995.

"Emily Wilson's *Odyssey* Translation, Book 1, Read by Emily Wilson." *YouTube*, uploaded by EmilyRC Wilson, 15 May 2020, www.youtube.com/watch?v=az0Qxcf_ms4.

"Erasure." *Academy of American Poets*, poets.org/glossary/erasure. Accessed 8 May 2025.

Ervin, M. "A Relief Pithos from Mykonos." *Archaiologikon Deltion*, vol. 18, 1963, pp. 37–75.

Evelyn-White, H. G., editor and translator. *Hesiod, Homeric Hymns, Epic Cycle, Homerica*. Heinemann, 1914.

Fagles, Robert, translator. *The* Odyssey*: Homer*. Penguin Classics, 1999.

———. *The* Odyssey*: Homer*. Narrated by Ian McKellen, audiobook ed., unabridged ed., Penguin Audio, 1999.

Fantuzzi, Marco, and Christos Tsagalis. *The Greek Epic Cycle and Its Ancient Reception: A Companion*. Cambridge UP, 2015.

Farron, S. G. "The *Odyssey* as an Anti-Aristocratic Statement." *Studies in Antiquity*, vol. 1, 1979–80, pp. 59–101.

Feldman, Gregory. *We Are All Migrants: Political Action and the Ubiquitous Condition of Migrant-Hood*. Stanford UP, 2015.

Felson, Nancy. *Regarding Penelope: From Character to Poetics*. Princeton UP, 1994.

Felson, Nancy, and Laura Slatkin. "Gender and Homeric Epic." Fowler, pp. 91–114.

Fiedler, Leslie A. *Love and Death in the American Novel*. Dalkey Archive, 1997.

Finkelberg, Margalit, editor. *The Homer Encyclopedia*. Wiley-Blackwell, 2011. 3 vols.

Finley, Moses I. *The World of Odysseus*. 1954. New York Review Books, 2002.

Finnegan, Ruth. *Oral Poetry: Its Nature, Significance, and Social Context*. Cambridge UP, 1977.

Fitzgerald, Robert, translator. *The* Odyssey*: Homer*. 1961. Farrar, Straus and Giroux, 1998.

Fletcher, Judith. "Women's Space and Wingless Words in the *Odyssey*." *Phoenix*, vol. 62, nos. 1–2, 2008, pp. 77–91.

Foley, Helene. "Penelope as a Moral Agent." *The Distaff Side: Representing the Female in Homer's* Odyssey, edited by Beth Cohen, Oxford UP, 1995, pp. 93–116.

———. "'Reverse Similes' and Sex Roles in the *Odyssey*," *Arethusa*, vol. 11, nos. 1–2, spring-fall 1978, pp. 7–26.

Foley, John Miles, editor. *A Companion to Ancient Epic*. Blackwell Publishing, 2005.

———. *Immanent Art: From Structure to Meaning in Traditional Oral Epic*. Indiana UP, 1991.

Forde, Shane. "Using Classical Reception to Develop Students' Engagement with Classical Literature in Translation." *Journal of Classics Teaching*, vol. 20, no. 39, 2019, pp. 14–23, https://doi.org/10.1017/S2058631019000035.

"Found Poem." *Academy of American Poets*, poets.org/glossary/found-poem. Accessed 8 May 2025.

Fowler, Robert, editor. *The Cambridge Companion to Homer*. Cambridge UP, 2004.

Fraction, Matt, and Christian Ward. *Ody-C*. Image Comics, 2014–.

Frame, Douglas. *Hippota Nestor.* Center for Hellenic Studies, 2009.

———. *The Myth of Return in Early Greek Epic*. 1978. *Center for Hellenic Studies*, nrs.harvard.edu/urn-3:hul.ebook:CHS_Frame.The_Myth_of_Return_in_Early_Greek_Epic.1978.

Franco, Cristiana. *Shameless: The Canine and the Feminine in Ancient Greece*. Translated by Matthew Fox, U of California P, 2014.

———. "Women in Homer." *A Companion to Women in the Ancient World*, edited by Sharon L. James and Sheila Dillon, John Wiley and Sons, 2012, pp. 54–65.

François Vase. *Classical Art Research Centre*, U of Oxford, 2003–25, www.carc.ox.ac.uk/carc/resources/Introduction-to-Greek-Pottery/Keypieces/blackfigure/francois.

Frazier, Charles. *Cold Mountain*. Atlantic Monthly Press, 1997.

Fredericks, Sigmund Casey. *The Future of Eternity: Mythologies of Science Fiction and Fantasy*. Indiana UP, 1982.

———. "Greek Mythology in Modern Science Fiction: Vision and Cognition." *Classical Mythology in Twentieth-Century Thought and Literature*, edited by Wendell M. Aycock and Theodore M. Klein, Texas Tech UP, 1980, pp. 89–106.

———. "Lucian's *True History* as SF." *Science Fiction Studies*, vol. 3, no. 1, 1976, pp. 49–60.

Fredricksmeyer, H. C. "Penelope 'Polutropos': The Crux at *Odyssey* 23.218–24." *American Journal of Philology*, vol. 118, 1997, pp. 487–97.

Freire, Paulo. *Pedagogy of the Oppressed*. 1970. Translated by Myra Bergman Ramos, Continuum, 2000.

Friedrich, Paul, and James Redfield. "Speech as a Personality Symbol: The Case of Achilles." *Language*, vol. 54, no. 2, 1978, pp. 263–88.

Fulkerson, Laurel. "Epic Ways of Killing a Woman: Gender and Transgression in *Odyssey* 22.465–72." *The Classical Journal*, vol. 97, no. 4, 2002, pp. 335–50.

Garvie, A. F., editor. *Homer:* Odyssey *Books 6–8*. Cambridge UP, 1995.

Glück, Louise. *Meadowlands*. Ecco, 1996.

Goldhill, Simon. *The Poet's Voice: Essays on Poetics and Greek Literature*. Cambridge UP, 1991.

Gottesman, A. "The Authority of Telemachus." *Classical Antiquity*, vol. 33, no. 1, 2014, pp. 31–60, https://doi.org/10.1525/ca.2014.33.1.31.

Grafton, Anthony. "Renaissance Readers of Homer's Ancient Readers." Lamberton and Keaney, pp. 149–72.

Graves, Robert. "Ulysses." *Collected Poems*, by Graves, Cassell, 1975, p. 56.

Graziosi, Barbara, and Emily Greenwood, editors. *Homer in the Twentieth Century: Between World Literature and the Western Canon*. Oxford UP, 2007.

Graziosi, Barbara, and Johannes Haubold. "Homeric Masculinity: ΗΝΟΡΕΗ and ΑΓΗΝΟΡΙΗ." *Journal of Hellenic Studies*, vol. 123, 2003, pp. 60–76.

———. *Homer: The Resonance of Epic*. Duckworth, 2005.

Green, John. "A Long and Difficult Journey, or the *Odyssey*: Crash Course Literature 201." *YouTube*, uploaded by CrashCourse, 27 Feb. 2014, youtube.com/watch?v=MS4jk5kavy4.

Green, Peter, translator. *The* Odyssey*: Homer.* U of California P, 2019.

Griffin, Jasper. *Homer: The* Odyssey. 2nd ed., Cambridge UP, 2004.

Griffith, R. Drew. "Sailing to Elysium: Menelaus' Afterlife (*Odyssey* 4.561–569) and Egyptian Religion." *Phoenix*, vol. 55, 2001, pp. 213–43.

Hainsworth, J. B. Review of *Concordantia Homerica, Pars 1*, by J. R. Tebben. *Journal of Hellenic Studies*, vol. 118, 1998, pp. 207–08.

Hall, Edith. *The Return of Ulysses: A Cultural History of Homer's* Odyssey. Johns Hopkins UP, 2008.

Hammond, Martin, translator. *Homer: The* Odyssey. Bristol Classical Press, 2000.

Hansen, William. *Ariadne's Thread: A Guide to International Tales Found in Classical Literature.* Cornell UP, 2002.

———. "Homer and the Folktale." Morris and Powell, pp. 442–62.

Hanson, Victor David, and John Heath. *Who Killed Homer? The Demise of Classical Education and the Recovery of Greek Wisdom.* Free Press, 1998.

Hardwick, Lorna. *Reception Studies.* Oxford UP, 2003.

Hardwick, Lorna, and Christopher Stray, editors. *A Companion to Classical Reception.* Wiley-Blackwell, 2008.

Harrington, Spencer P. M., et al. "Behind the Mask of Agamemnon." *Archaeology*, vol. 52, no. 4, July-August 1999, pp. 51–59, archive.archaeology.org/9907/etc/mask.html.

Hartog, François. *Memories of Odysseus: Frontier Tales from Ancient Greece.* Translated by Janet Lloyd, U of Chicago P, 2001.

———. *Regimes of Historicity: Presentism and Experiences of Time.* Translated by Saskia Brown, Columbia UP, 2015.

Hedges, Chris. *War Is a Force That Gives Us Meaning.* Random House, 2003.

Heimberg, Ursula. *Die Keramik des Kabirions. Das Kabirenheiligtum bei Theben III.* De Gruyter, 1982.

Henderson, Mary. *Star Wars: The Magic of Myth.* Bantam Books, 1997.

Herodotus. *Herodoti Historiae.* Edited by N. G. Wilson, Oxford UP, 2015. 2 vols.

———. *The Histories.* Translated by Robin Waterfield, Oxford UP, 1998.

Hesiod. *Theogony*. Edited by M. L. West, Clarendon Press, 1966.

Heubeck, Alfred, et al., editors. *A Commentary on Homer's* Odyssey. Oxford UP, 1988–92. 3 vols.

Hexter, Ralph. *A Guide to the* Odyssey*: A Commentary on the English Translation of Robert Fitzgerald.* Vintage, 1993.

Hinds, Gareth. *The* Odyssey. Candlewick Press, 2010.

"Homer, *Odyssey* Rhapsody 01 (Audiobook Spoken in Reconstructed Ancient Greek)." *YouTube*, uploaded by Podium-Arts, 9 May 2018, www.youtube.com/watch?v=UdyXlUmD3v4.

"*Homer's* Iliad*: The Basel Commentary.*" *De Gruyter Brill*, 2025, www.degruyterbrill.com/serial/homer%20e%20ed-b/html?lang=en.

hooks, bell. *The Will to Change: Men, Masculinity, and Love.* Washington Square Press, 2004.

Hurst, Isobel. "'We'll All Be Penelopes Then': Art and Domesticity in American Women's Poetry, 1958–1996." *Living Classics: Greece and Rome in Contemporary Poetry in English*, edited by S. J. Harrison, Oxford UP, 2009, pp. 275–94.

Hurwit, Jeffrey M. "The Dipylon Shield Once More." *Classical Antiquity*, vol. 4, no. 2, 1985, pp. 121–26.

"Indo-European Languages." *Britannica*, 14 Apr. 2025, britannica.com/topic/Indo-European-languages.

"Invitation to World Literature: The *Odyssey*." *Annenberg Learner*, 2025, learner.org/series/invitation-to-world-literature/the-odyssey/.

Jackson, Shelley. *Patchwork Girl; or, a Modern Monster by Mary/Shelly and Herself*. Eastgate Systems, 1995.

James, Paula. "Crossing Classical Thresholds: Gods, Monsters, and Hell Dimensions in the Whedon Universe." *Classics for All: Reworking Antiquity in Mass Culture*, edited by Dustin Lowe and Kim Shahabudin, Cambridge Scholars Publishing, 2009, pp. 237–60.

Jamison, Stephanie. "Penelope and the Pigs: Indic Perspectives on the *Odyssey*." *Classical Antiquity*, vol. 18, 1999, pp. 227–72.

Janko, Richard. *Homer, Hesiod, and the Hymns: Diachronic Development in Epic Diction*. Cambridge UP, 1982.

———. "πρῶτόν τε καὶ ὕστατον αἰὲν ἀείδειν: Relative Chronology and the Literary History of the Early Greek Epos." *Relative Chronology in Early Greek Epic Poetry*, edited by Øivind Andersen and Dag Haug, Cambridge UP, 2012, pp. 20–43.

———. Review of *A New Companion to Homer*, edited by Ian Morris and Barry B. Powell. *Bryn Mawr Classical Review*, vol. 9, no. 8, 1998, pp. 764–77.

JanMohamed, Abdul R. "The Economy of Manichean Allegory." *The Post-colonial Studies Reader*, edited by Bill Ashcroft et al., Routledge, 1999, pp. 18–23.

Jeffers, Honorée Fanonne. "Blues: Odysseus." *The Age of Phillis*, by Jeffers, Wesleyan UP, 2020, p. 23.

Jenkins, Thomas E. "From the Cinema to Beyond: Homer in Comics, Television, Apps, and New Media." Pache, pp. 541–43.

Jensen, Minna Skafte. *Writing Homer: A Study Based on Results from Modern Fieldwork*. Kongelige Danske Videnskabernes Selskab, 2011.

Joint Association of Classical Teachers. *The Triumph of Odysseus: Homer's* Odyssey *Books 21 and 22*. Cambridge UP, 1996. Reading Greek.

Jones, Peter. *Homer's* Odyssey*: A Companion Based on the Translation of Richmond Lattimore*. Bristol Classical Press, 1991.

Jordan, June. "Problems of Language in a Democratic State." *On Call: Political Essays*, by Jordan, South End Press, 1985, pp. 27–36.

Joyce, James. *Ulysses*. 1922. Vintage, 1986.

"Jurassic Bark." *Futurama*, created by Matt Groening, season 4, episode 7, Comedy Central, 17 Nov. 2002. *IMDb*, www.imdb.com/title/tt0584444/.

Kahane, Ahuvia, and Martin Mueller, editors. *The Chicago Homer*. Northwestern U Library, 7 July 2024, homer.library.northwestern.edu/.

Kanigel, Robert. *Hearing Homer's Song: The Brief Life and Big Idea of Milman Parry.* Knopf, 2021.

Katz, Marylin A. *Penelope's Renown: Meaning and Indeterminacy in the* Odyssey. Princeton UP, 1991.

Keats, John. "On First Looking into Chapman's Homer." *Poetry Foundation*, 2025, poetryfoundation.org/poems/44481/on-first-looking-into-chapmans-homer.

Keen, Tony. "More 'T' Vicar? Revisiting Models and Methodologies for Classical Receptions in Science Fiction." *Once and Future Antiquities in Science Fiction and Fantasy*, edited by B. M. Rogers and B. E. Stevens, Bloomsbury Academic, 2019, pp. 9–17.

———. "The 'T' Stands for Tiberius: Models and Methodologies of Classical Reception in Science Fiction." *Memorabilia Antonina*, 10 Apr. 2006, tonykeen.blogspot.co.uk/2006/04/t-stands-for-tiberius-models-and.html.

Kim, Lawrence. "Homer in Antiquity." Pache, pp. 417–34.

Kimmel, Michael. *Manhood in America: A Cultural History*. Oxford UP, 2006.

Kindlay, Evan. "The People We Know Best." *The New York Review of Books*, 1 Oct. 2023, nybooks.com/articles/2021/03/25/character-people-we-know-best/.

King, Bruce M. "Bellerophon and Akhilleus: Self-Destruction and World Destruction in the *Iliad*." *Being Alone in Antiquity: Greco-Roman Ideas and Experiences of Misanthropy, Isolation, and Solitude*, edited by Rafal Matuszewski, De Gruyter, 2022, pp. 305–18.

King, Bruce M., and Lynn Kozak. "#Patrochilles: Find the Phallus." *The Routledge Companion to the Reception of Ancient Greek and Roman Gender and Sexuality*, edited by K. R. Moore, Routledge, 2023, pp. 41–57.

Knox, Bernard. Introduction. Fagles, Odyssey [Penguin Classics], pp. 3–64.

Krebs, Paula, and Emily Wilson. "Translating Scholarship." *MLA Newsletter*, vol. 51, no. 2, summer 2019, pp. 4–5.

Kretler, Katherine. *One Man Show: Poetics and Presence in the* Iliad *and* Odyssey. Center for Hellenic Studies, 2020.

Kuhn, Adalbert. "Über die durch nasale erweiterten verbalstämme." *Zeitschrift für vergleichende Sprachforschung*, vol. 2, 1853, pp. 455–71.

Lamberton, Robert. "The Neoplatonists and the Spiritualization of Homer." Lamberton and Keaney, pp. 115–33.

Lamberton, Robert, and John Keaney, editors. *Homer's Ancient Readers*. Princeton UP, 1992.

Lamont Hill, M. "A World without Prisons: Teaching Confinement Literature and the Promise of Prison Abolition." *The English Journal*, vol. 102, no. 4, 2013, pp. 19–23.

Landfester, Manfred. *Das griechische Nomen "philos" und seine Ableitungen*. Georg Olms Verlag, 1966.

Latacz, Joachim. "Commenting on Homer: From the Beginnings to this Commentary." Olson, pp. 1–26.

Lattimore, Richmond, translator. *The* Iliad *of Homer.* 1951. U of Chicago P, 2011.

———. *The* Odyssey *of Homer.* 1967. Harper Perennial, 2009.

———. *The* Odyssey *of Homer.* Narrated by Anthony Quayle, vinyl ed., abridged ed., Caedmon Records, 1969. *The Internet Archive,* archive.org/details/1-odyssey-book-ix-lines-19-436-the-sacking-of-the-kilkonians-the-lotus-eaters-th.

Lawrence, T. E., translator. *The* Odyssey *of Homer.* 1932. Oxford UP, 1991.

Lehman, Christopher, and Kate Roberts. *Falling in Love with Close Reading.* Heinemann, 2014.

Leopold II. "The Sacred Mission of Civilization." *Joseph Conrad: Heart of Darkness,* edited by Paul B. Armstrong, Norton Critical Edition, 4th ed., W. W. Norton, 1991, pp. 119–20.

Lesser, Rachel. "The Pandareids and Pandora: Defining Penelope's Subjectivity in the *Odyssey.*" *Helios,* vol. 44, no. 2, 2017, pp. 101–32.

Levaniouk, Olga. "Did Sappho and Homer Ever Meet? Comparative Perspectives on Homeric Singers." Ready and Tsagalis, pp. 178–202.

———. "Penelope and the Pandareids." *Phoenix,* vol. 62, 2008, pp. 5–38.

Lexicon Iconographicum Mythologiae Classicae. Artemis, 1981–2009. 8 vols.

Lightner, J., and L. Tomaswick. "Think, Pair, Share." Center for Teaching and Learning, Kent State U, 2017, www.kent.edu/ctl/think-pair-share.

"Lion Gate at Mycenae: Late Helladic IIIB." *JSTOR,* www.jstor.org/stable/community.9116482.

Lobel, Edgar, and Denys Page. *Poetarum Lesbiorum Fragmenta.* Oxford UP, 1955.

Lockard, Joe. "Prison Writing Education and US Working-Class Consciousness." Lockard and Rankins-Robertson, *Prison Pedagogies,* pp. 11–31.

Lockard, Joe, and Sherry Rankins-Robertson, editors. *Prison Pedagogies: Learning and Teaching with Imprisoned Writers.* Syracuse UP, 2018.

———. "Prison Writing in a Dark Time." Lockard and Rankins-Robertson, *Prison Pedagogies,* pp. 1–10.

Lombardo, Stanley, translator. *Homer:* Odyssey. Hackett Publishing, 2000.

———, translator and narrator. *Homer:* Odyssey. Audiobook ed., unabridged ed., Parmenides Publishing, 2007.

Loney, Alexander C. *The Ethics of Revenge and the Meanings of the* Odyssey. Oxford UP, 2019.

López-Ruiz, Carolina. *Phoenicians and the Making of the Mediterranean.* Harvard UP, 2021.

Lord, Albert B. *The Singer of Tales.* 1960. 2nd ed., edited by Stephen Mitchell and Gregory Nagy, Harvard UP, 2000, nrs.harvard.edu/urn-3:hul.ebook:CHS_LordA.The_Singer_of_Tales.2000.

Louden, Bruce. *Homer's* Odyssey *and the Near East.* Cambridge UP, 2011.

———. *The* Odyssey: *Structure, Narration, and Meaning.* Johns Hopkins UP, 1999.

Lucian. *The True History.* Translated by Paul Turner, Indiana UP, 1974.

Ludwig, Emil. *Schliemann: The Story of a Gold-Seeker.* Little, Brown, 1931.

Lynn-George, Michael. "Structures of Care in the *Iliad.*" *Classical Quarterly*, vol. 46, 1996, pp. 1–26.

Malkin, Irad. *The Returns of Odysseus: Colonization and Ethnicity*. U of California P, 1998.

Mandelbaum, Allen, translator. *The* Odyssey *of Homer.* Bantam Classics, 1990.

Manguel, Alberto. *Homer's the* Iliad *and the* Odyssey*: A Biography*. Grove Press, 2007.

Marks, Jim. "Epic Traditions." Pache, pp. 49–52.

———. *Zeus in the* Odyssey. Harvard UP, 2008.

Marshall, C. W. "Odysseus and *The Infinite Horizon*." *Son of Classics and Comics*, edited by George Kovacs and Marshall, Oxford UP, 2016, pp. 3–31.

Martin, Richard P. "Hesiod's Metanastic Poetics." *Ramus*, vol. 21, 1992, pp. 11–35.

———. *The Language of Heroes*. Cornell UP, 1989.

———. "Telemachus and the Last Hero Song." *Colby Quarterly*, vol. 29, no. 3, Sept. 1993, pp. 222–40.

Mask of Agamemnon. *Ministry of Culture and Sports*, 2007, odysseus.culture.gr/h/4/eh430.jsp?obj_id=4503.

Mason, Wyatt. "The First Woman to Translate the *Odyssey* into English." *The New York Times Magazine*, 2 Nov. 2017, www.nytimes.com/2017/11/02/magazine/the-first-woman-to-translate-the-odyssey-into-english.html.

Maurizio, Lisa. *Classical Mythology in Context*. Oxford UP, 2016.

Mavroudi, Maria. "Homer in Greece from the End of Antiquity I: The Byzantine Reception of Homer and His Export to Other Cultures." Pache, pp. 444–72.

McCaughrean, Geraldine, adapter. *The* Odyssey. Puffin Books, 1997. Originally published by Oxford UP, 1993.

McConnell, Justine. *Black Odysseys: The Homeric* Odyssey *in the African Diaspora since 1939*. Oxford UP, 2013.

McCoskey, Denise, editor. *A Cultural History of Race in Antiquity*. Bloomsbury Academic, 2021. Vol. 1 of *A Cultural History of Race.*

———. *Race: Antiquity and Its Legacy*. Oxford UP, 2012.

Mendelsohn, Daniel, translator. *The* Odyssey. U of Chicago P, 2025.

———. *An Odyssey: A Father, a Son, and an Epic*. Knopf, 2017.

Mercer, Neil. *The Guided Construction of Knowledge: Talk amongst Teachers and Learners.* Multilingual Matters, 1995.

Merry, W. Walter, et al., editors. *Homer's* Odyssey. Clarendon Press, 1886. *Perseus Digital Library*, perseus.tufts.edu/hopper/text?doc=Perseus%3Atext%3A1999.04.0055%3Abook%3D1%3Acommline%3D1.

Miller, Madeleine. *Circe*. Little, Brown, 2018.

Mitchell, Jack. *The Odyssey of Star Wars: An Epic Poem*. Abrams, 2021.

Montaigne, Michel de. "On Cannibals." *Essays*, by Montaigne, translated by J. M. Cohen, Penguin Classics, 1958, pp. 105–19.

Montemaggi, Vittorio, et al., editors. "Introducing Dante: The *Commedia*." Leeds Centre for Dante Studies, U of Leeds / Devers Program in Dante Studies,

U of Notre Dame, 2025, ahc.leeds.ac.uk/discover-dante/doc/introducing-dante/page/12.

Monteverdi, Claudio. *Il ritorno d'Ulisse in patria*. Libretto by Giacomo Badoardo, Venice, 1640.

Mordine, Michael. "Odyssean Adventures in the *Cena Trimalchionis*." *Classical Antiquity*, vol. 32, no. 1, 2013, pp. 176–99.

Morris, Ian, and Barry B. Powell, editors. *A New Companion to Homer*. Brill, 1997.

Morrison, James V. *A Companion to Homer's* Odyssey. Greenwood Press, 2003.

Most, Glenn W. "Homer in Greek Culture from the Archaic to the Hellenistic Period." *The Homeric Epics and the Chinese* Book of Songs*: Foundational Texts Compared*, edited by Fritz-Heiner Mutschler, Cambridge Scholars Publishing, 2017, pp. 163–84.

Munro, D. B. *Homer's* Odyssey*, Books XIII–XXIV*. Clarendon Press, 1901.

Murnaghan, Sheila. *Disguise and Recognition in the* Odyssey. 1987. 2nd ed., Lexington Books, 2011.

———. Introduction. Lombardo, *Homer* [Hackett], pp. xiii–lxiii.

———. "Penelope's *Agnoia*: Knowledge, Power and Gender in the *Odyssey*." Doherty, *Homer's* Odyssey, pp. 231–46. Originally published in *Helios*, 1986.

Murnaghan, Sheila, and Deborah H. Roberts. "The Forecast Is Hurricane: Circe's Powers and Circe's Desires in Modern Women's Poetry." Cox and Theodorakopoulos, pp. 193–210.

———. "Penelope's Song: The Lyric Odysseys of Linda Pastan and Louise Glück." *Classical and Modern Literature*, vol. 22, 2002, pp. 1–33.

Murray, A. T., translator. *Homer: The* Odyssey. 1919. Edited by George Dimock, Harvard UP, 1998. Loeb Classical Library. 2 vols.

Murray, Jackie. "Race and Sexuality: Racecraft in the *Odyssey*." McCoskey, *Cultural History*, pp. 137–56.

Mykonos Vase with the fall of Troy. *Directorate of Archaeological Museums, Exhibitions and Educational Programs*, 2019–25, archaeologicalmuseums.gr/en/museum/5df34af3deca5e2d79e8c18e/archaeological-museum-of-mykonos.

Mylonas, George E. *Mycenae and the Mycenaean Age*. Princeton UP, 1966.

Myrsiades, Kostas, editor. *Approaches to Teaching Homer's* Iliad *and* Odyssey. Modern Language Association of America, 1987.

———, editor. *Reading Homer in the Twenty-First Century*. Special issue of *College Literature*. Vol. 34, no. 2, 2007.

Nagy, Gregory. *The Ancient Greek Hero in Twenty-Four Hours*. Harvard UP, 2013. *The Center for Hellenic Studies*, chs.harvard.edu/read/nagy-gregory-the-ancient-greek-hero-in-24-hours.

———. *The Best of the Achaeans*. Revised ed., Johns Hopkins UP, 1999.

———. *Comparative Studies in Greek and Indic Meter*. Harvard UP, 1974.

———. "A Cretan *Odyssey*, Part 1." *Classical Inquiries*, Center for Hellenic Studies, Harvard U, 17 Sept. 2015, classical-inquiries.chs.harvard.edu/a-cretan-odyssey-part-1/.

———. "A Cretan *Odyssey*, Part 2." *Classical Inquiries*, Center for Hellenic Studies, Harvard U 24 Sept. 2015, classical-inquiries.chs.harvard.edu/a-cretan-odyssey-part-2/.

———. "From Song to Text." Pache, pp. 80–95.

———. *Homer the Preclassic*. U of California P, 2010.

———, translator. "Proclus' Summary of the *Iliou Persis*, attributed to Arctinus of Miletus." *The Epic Cycle*, revised by Eugenia Lao, Center for Hellenic Studies, 2 Aug. 2016, chs.harvard.edu/primary-source/epic-cycle-sb/.

Narayana Rao, Velcheru. "A Ramayana of Their Own: Women's Oral Tradition in Telugu." *Many Ramayanas: The Diversity of a Narrative Tradition in South Asia*, edited by Paula Richman, U of California P, 1991, pp. 114–36.

Newey, Twila. "my heart weaving." *Sugar House Review*, 2021, www.sugarhousereview.com/sugarsuites1-newey.

Newmann, Fred. M., et al. *Authentic Intellectual Work and Standardized Tests: Conflict or Coexistence?* Consortium on Chicago School Research, 2001.

Newton, Rick. "Odysseus and Melanthius." *Greek, Roman, and Byzantine Studies*, vol. 38, no. 1, 1997, pp. 5–18.

Noble, Joseph V. "The Technique of Attic Vase-Painting." *American Journal of Archaeology*, vol. 64, no. 4, 1960, pp. 307–18.

O Brother, Where Art Thou? Directed by Joel Coen and Ethan Coen, Touchstone Pictures, 2000.

Olson, Stuart Douglas, editor. *Prolegomena*. De Gruyter, 2015, https://doi.org/10.1515/9781501501746. Vol. 1 of *Homer's* Iliad*: The Basel Commentary*.

O'Meally, Robert G. *Romare Bearden: A Black Odyssey*. DC Moore Gallery, 2008.

Owen, William B., and Edgar J. Goodspeed. *Homeric Vocabularies: Greek and English Vocabularies for the Study of Homer*. New ed., revised by Clyde Pharr, U of Oklahoma P, 1969.

Pache, Corinne Ondine, editor. *The Cambridge Guide to Homer*. Cambridge UP, 2020.

Page, Denys. *Folktales in Homer's* Odyssey. Harvard UP, 1973.

Palmer, George Herbert, translator. *The* Odyssey *of Homer*. 1894. *HathiTrust*, babel.hathitrust.org/cgi/pt?id=uc2.ark%3A%2F13960%2Ft88g8jw70&seq=5.

Paniagua, Christian. "Map of Hell." *The World of Dante*, edited by Deborah Parker, Institute for Advanced Technologies in the Humanities, U of Virginia, 2008, www.worldofdante.org/christianpaniagua_detail.html.

Pastan, Linda. *The Imperfect Paradise*. W. W. Norton, 1988.

———. "Rereading *The Odyssey* in Middle Age." Pastan, *Imperfect Paradise*, pp. 24–25.

———. "The Suitor." Pastan, *Imperfect Paradise*, p. 31.

Pausanias. *Description of Greece*. Translated by W. H. S. Jones and H. A. Ormerod, vol. 2, Harvard UP, 1926. Loeb Classical Library 188.

———. *Description of Greece*. Translated by W. H. S. Jones, vol. 3, Harvard UP, 1933. Loeb Classical Library 272.

Pedrick, Victoria. "Eurycleia and Eurynome as Penelope's Confidantes." *Epic and Epoch: Essays on the Interpretation and History of a Genre*, edited by Steven M. Oberhelman et al., Texas Tech UP, 1994, pp. 97–116.

Peradotto, John. *Man in the Middle Voice: Name and Narration in the* Odyssey. Princeton UP, 1990.

Pharr, Clyde. *Homeric Greek: A Book for Beginners*. Revised by John Wright, U of Oklahoma P, 1986.

Phelan, Peggy. *Unmarked: The Politics of Performance*. Routledge, 1993.

Pitt-Rivers, Julian. "Kith and Kin." *The Character of Kinship*, edited by Jack Goody, Cambridge UP, 1973, pp. 89–105.

Plato. *Republic*. Translated by C. D. C. Reeve, Hackett Publishing, 2004.

Pollitt, Katha. "Penelope Writes." *Antarctic Traveler*, by Pollitt, Knopf, 1983, pp. 14–15.

Pope, Alexander, translator. *The* Odyssey *of Homer*. 1725–26. Edited by Maynard Mack, Methuen, 1967.

Powell, Barry B. *Homer and the Origin of the Greek Alphabet*. Cambridge UP, 1991.

———, translator. *Homer: The* Odyssey. Oxford UP, 2014.

Probst, Robert E. "Reader Response Theory in the English Curriculum." *English Journal*, vol. 83, no. 3, 1994, pp. 37–44.

Pucci, Pietro. *Odysseus Polutropos: Intertextual Readings in the* Odyssey *and the* Iliad. Cornell UP, 1987.

Puhvel, Jaan. "'Meadow of the Otherworld' in Indo-European Tradition." *Zeitschrift für vergleichende Sprachforschung*, vol. 83, 1969, pp. 64–69.

Pulleyn, Simon, editor and translator. *Homer:* Odyssey *I*. Oxford UP, 2019.

Punter, Russell. *The* Odyssey. Illustrated by Fabio Fiorin, Usborne Publishing, 2021.

Purves, Alex. "Ajax and Other Objects: Homer's Vibrant Materialism." *Ramus*, vol. 44, 2015, pp. 75–94.

Putnam, Robert. *Bowling Alone: The Collapse and Revival of American Community*. Simon and Schuster, 2000.

Quintilian. *Institutio Oratoria*. Translated by H. E. Butler, Harvard UP, 1996.

Quito, Anne. "Drawing Is the Best Way to Learn, Even if You're No Leonardo da Vinci." *Quartz*, 15 Sept. 2018, qz.com/quartzy/1381916/drawing-is-the-best-way-to-learn-even-if-youre-no-leonardo-da-vinci/.

Raaflaub, Kurt. "A Historian's Headache: How to Read 'Homeric Society'?" *Archaic Greece: New Approaches and New Evidence*, edited by Nick Fisher and Hans van Wees, Duckworth / Classical Press of Wales, 1998, pp. 169–93.

Rabel, Robert J., editor. *Approaches to Homer: Ancient and Modern*. Classical Press of Wales, 2005.

Rada, J., and R. Rocchio. "Writing, Bodies, and Performance: Cultural Resistance behind Prison Walls." Lockard and Rankins-Robertson, *Prison Pedagogies*, pp. 171–89.

Rankine, Patrice D. *Ulysses in Black: Ralph Ellison, Classicism, and African American Literature*. U of Wisconsin P, 2006.

Rayor, Diane, translator. *The Homeric Hymns*. U of California P, 2014.

Rayor, Diane, and André Lardinois, translators. *Sappho: A New Translation of the Complete Works*. Cambridge UP, 2014.

Ready, Jonathan. "The Comparative Spectrum in Homer." *The American Journal of Philology*, vol. 129, no. 4, winter 2008, pp. 453–96.

Ready, Jonathan, and Christos Tsagalis, editors. *Homer in Performance: Rhapsodes, Narrators, and Characters*. U of Texas P, 2018.

Reardon, B. P., editor. *Collected Ancient Greek Novels*. U of California P, 1989.

Redfield, James M. "The Economic Man." Rubino and Shelmerdine, pp. 218–47.

———. *Nature and Culture in the* Iliad*: The Tragedy of Hector*. 1975. Expanded ed., Duke UP, 1994.

Red-figure calyx krater with death of Sarpedon. *Classical Art Research Centre*, U of Oxford, 2003–25, www.carc.ox.ac.uk/record/2F320D8E-61D8-4965-A2C5-C2E76A149354.

Richards, I. A. *The Philosophy of Rhetoric*. Oxford UP, 1936.

Rieu, E. V., translator. *Homer: The* Odyssey. Edited by D. C. H. Rieu, Penguin Classics, 2003.

Robertson, Suloni, illustrator. "Dante's *Inferno*." *Danteworlds*, edited by Guy Raffa, U of Texas, Austin, 2007, danteworlds.laits.utexas.edu/index2.html.

Robinson, F. P. *Effective Study*. Harper and Row, 1946.

Rogers, Brett M. "Cyber-Dogs, 'Gut Thinkings,' and the Limits of Recognition in Homer's *Odyssey*." *Artificial Intelligence in Greek and Roman Epic*, edited by Silvio Bär and Andriana Domouzi, Bloomsbury Academic, 2024, pp. 47–58.

———. "Hybrids and Homecomings in the *Odyssey* and *Alien Resurrection*." *Classical Traditions in Science Fiction*, edited by Rogers and B. E. Stevens, Oxford UP, 2015, pp. 217–42.

———. "The Postmodern Prometheus and Posthuman Reproductions in Science Fiction." *Frankenstein and Its Classics*, edited by J. Weiner et al., Bloomsbury Academic, 2018, pp. 107–22.

Rogers, Brett M., and Benjamin Eldon Stevens. "Classical Receptions in Science Fiction." *Classical Receptions Journal*, vol. 4, no. 1, 2012, pp. 127–47.

"Romare Bearden: *A Black Odyssey*: Archived Exhibition." *Smithsonian*, 2025, www.sites.si.edu/s/archived-exhibit?topicId=0TO36000000Tz69GAC.

Romm, James S. *The Edges of the Earth in Ancient Thought: Geography, Exploration, and Fiction*. Princeton UP, 1992.

Romney, Jonathan. "Double Vision." *The Guardian*, 19 May 2000, www.theguardian.com/film/2000/may/19/culture.features.

Rose, Peter. "Class Ambivalence in the *Odyssey*." *Historia*, vol. 24, no. 2, 1975, pp. 129–49.

———. *Sons of the Gods, Children of Earth: Ideology and Literary Form in Ancient Greece*. Cornell UP, 1995.

Rotundo, E. Anthony. *American Manhood: Transformations in Masculinity from the Revolution to the Modern Era*. Basic Books, 1993.

Rouse, W. H. D., translator. *The Story of Odysseus*. 1937. Mentor Classics, 1964.

Rubin, Gayle. "The Traffic in Women: Notes on the 'Political Economy' of Sex." *Toward an Anthropology of Women*, edited by Rayna Rapp, Monthly Review Press, 1975, pp. 157–210.

Rubino, Carl, and Cynthia Shelmerdine, editors. *Approaches to Homer*. 1983. U of Texas P, 2021.

Rutherford, R. B., editor. *Homer:* Odyssey *Books 19 and 20*. Cambridge UP, 1992.

Sahlins, Marshall. *What Kinship Is—and Is Not*. U of Chicago P, 2013.

Saïd, Suzanne. *Homer and the* Odyssey. Oxford UP, 2011.

Schein, Seth. "Female Representations and Interpreting the *Odyssey*." *The Distaff Side: Representing the Female in Homer's* Odyssey, edited by Beth Cohen, Oxford UP, 1995, pp. 17–28.

———, editor. *Reading the* Odyssey*: Selected Interpretive Essays*. Princeton UP, 1996.

Schliemann, Heinrich. *Ilios: The City and Country of the Trojans*. Harper Brothers, 1881.

———. *Troy and Its Remains*. Scribner, Welford, and Armstrong, 1875.

Schoder, Raymond V., and Vincent C. Horrigan. *A Reading Course in Homeric Greek: Book I*. Revised by Leslie Collins Edwards, 3rd ed., Focus, 2005.

Scodel, Ruth. *Listening to Homer*. U of Michigan P, 2009.

Segal, Charles. "Divine Justice in the *Odyssey*: Poseidon, Cyclops, and Helios." *American Journal of Philology*, vol. 113, no. 4, 1992, pp. 489–518.

Sélincourt, Aubrey de. *The World of Herodotus*. Little, Brown, 1962.

Shanahan, Timothy. "Letting the Text Take Center Stage." *American Educator*, vol. 37, no. 3, fall 2013, pp. 4–11, www.aft.org/periodical/american-educator/fall-2013/letting-text-take-center-stage.

Shay, Jonathan. *Achilles in Vietnam: Combat Trauma and the Undoing of Character*. Atheneum, 1994.

———. *Odysseus in America: Combat Trauma and the Trials of Homecoming*. Scribner, 2002.

Shelley, Mary. *Frankenstein; or, The Modern Prometheus: The 1818 Text*. Edited by Marilyn Butler, Oxford, 2009.

Sherratt, Susan. "Archaeological Contexts." J. Foley, *Companion*, pp. 119–41.

Shewring, Walter, translator. *The* Odyssey. Oxford UP, 1980.

Simms, Robert C., editor. *Brill's Companion to Prequels, Sequels, and Retellings of Classical Epic*. Brill, 2018.

Sinos, Dale S. *Achilles, Patroklos, and the Meaning of "Philos."* Institut für Sprachwissenschaft der Universität Innsbruck, 1980.

Slatkin, Laura. "Composition by Theme and the Mētis of the *Odyssey*." Schein, *Reading*, pp. 223–37.

———. "Homer's *Odyssey*." J. Foley, *Companion*, pp. 315–29.

Snodgrass, Anthony M. *Early Greek Armour and Weapons*. Edinburgh UP, 1964.

Snyder-Young, Dani. *Theatre of Good Intentions: Challenges and Hopes for Theatre and Social Change*. Palgrave Macmillan, 2013.

Sounder. Directed by Martin Ritt, Radnitz / Mattel Productions, 1972.

Spolin, Viola. *Improvisation for the Theater.* Northwestern UP, 1983.

Stanford, W. B., editor. *Homer:* Odyssey. 2nd ed., Bloomsbury, 1998. 2 vols.

———. *The Ulysses Theme: A Study in the Adaptability of a Traditional Hero.* 1954. 2nd ed., U of Michigan P, 1963.

Steadman, Geoffrey, editor. *Homer's* Odyssey *6–8: Greek Text with Facing Vocabulary and Commentary.* 2010, geoffreysteadman.com/homers-odyssey-6-8/. PDF download.

———. *Homer's* Odyssey *9–12: Greek Text with Facing Vocabulary and Commentary.* 2nd ed., 2016, geoffreysteadman.com/files-odyssey-9-12/. PDF download.

———. *Homer's* Odyssey *17–20: Greek Text with Facing Vocabulary and Commentary.* Beta version, 27 Jan. 2020, geoffreysteadman.com/odyssey-17-20-preview/. PDF download.

Steiner, Deborah, editor. *Homer:* Odyssey *Books 17–18.* Cambridge UP, 2010.

Steiner, George, editor. *Homer in English.* Penguin, 1996.

Stevens, Benjamin Eldon. "Dante and Homer." Pache, pp. 582–84.

Storace, Patricia. "Robert Fagles: The Art of Translation II." *The Paris Review*, vol. 41, summer 1999, pp. 143–64.

Sturt, Jemimah Makepiece. "Penelope's Musings." G. Steiner, p. 187.

Taylor, Charles H. *Essays on the* Odyssey*: Selected Modern Criticism.* Indiana UP, 1963.

Tebben, Joseph R. *Concordantia Homerica, Pars 1,* Odyssea*: A Computer Concordance to the van Thiel Edition of Homer's* Odyssey. Georg Olms Verlag, 1994.

Tennyson, Alfred. "The Lotos-Eaters." G. Steiner, pp. 133–38.

———. "Ulysses." G. Steiner, pp. 138–40.

———. "Ulysses." *Poetry Foundation*, 2022, www.poetryfoundation.org/poems/45392/ulysses.

Terracotta krater. *The Metropolitan Museum of Art*, 2000–24, www.metmuseum.org/art/collection/search/248904.

Thalmann, William G. "Female Slaves in the *Odyssey*." *Women and Slaves in Greco-Roman Culture: Differential Equations*, edited by Sandra R. Joshel and Sheila Murnaghan, Routledge, 1998, pp. 22–34.

———. *The Swineherd and the Bow: Representations of Class in the* Odyssey. Cornell UP, 1998.

Theocritus. "Cyclops." *Theocritus: Idylls and Epigrams,* translated by Daryl Hine, Athenaeum, 1982, pp. 42–44.

Thiel, Helmut van, editor. *Homeri Odyssea.* 1991. Cambridge UP, 2009.

Thomas, Roy, and Greg Tocchini. *Marvel Illustrated: The* Odyssey. Marvel Enterprises, 2008–09.

Traill, David A. "Insistent Questions." *Archaeology*, vol. 52, no. 4, 1999, pp. 55–56.

2001: A Space Odyssey. Directed by Stanley Kubrick, Metro-Goldwyn-Mayer, 1968.

Ulysses. Directed by Mario Camerini, Paramount Pictures, 1954.

Urquhart, Vicki, and Monette McIver. *Teaching Writing in the Content Areas.* Association for Supervision and Curriculum Development, 2005.

Van Nortwick, Thomas. “Penelope and Nausicaa.” *Transactions of the American Philological Association*, vol. 109, 1979, pp. 269–76.

Van Peteghem, Julie, et al. *Blackout Poetry from Hell: Ulysses. Padlet*, huntercollege68.padlet.org/julievp/blackout_dante. Accessed 8 May 2025.

Vega, Suzanne. “Calypso.” *Solitude Standing*. A and M Records, 1987.

Venkatraman, Padma. “Weeding Out Racism’s Invisible Roots: Rethinking Children’s Classics.” *School Library Journal*, 19 June 2020, slj.com/story/weeding-out-racisms-invisible-roots-rethinking-childrens-classics-libraries-diverse-books.

Vergil. *The* Aeneid. Translated by Sarah Ruden, Yale UP, 2021.

Vidal-Naquet, Pierre. “Land and Sacrifice in the *Odyssey*: A Study of Religious and Mythical Meanings.” Schein, *Reading*, pp. 33–54.

Vidan, Aida. *Embroidered with Gold, Strung with Pearls: The Traditional Ballads of Bosnian Women*. Center for Hellenic Studies, 2003.

Waal, Willemijn. “On the ‘Phoenician Letters’: The Case for an Early Transmission of the Greek Alphabet from an Archaeological, Epigraphic and Linguistic Perspective.” *Aegean Studies*, vol. 1, 2018, pp. 83–125, www.aegeussociety.org/wp-content/uploads/2018/12/Aegean-Studies-vol1-4-Waal.pdf. PDF download.

Wace, Alan J. B., and Frank H. Stubbings. *A Companion to Homer*. Macmillan, 1962.

Walcott, Derek. *The* Odyssey: *A Play*. Farrar, Straus and Giroux, 1993.

Wallinga, H. T. *Ships and Sea-Power before the Great Persian War: The Ancestry of the Ancient Trireme*. Brill, 1993.

Webster, T. B. L. “Homer and Attic Geometric Vases.” *The Annual of the British School at Athens*, vol. 50, 1955, pp. 38–50.

Weinbaum, Stanley G. “A Martian Odyssey.” 1934. *Project Gutenberg*, www.gutenberg.org/files/23731/23731-h/23731-h.htm.

Weiner, Jesse. “Classical Epic and the Poetics of Modern Fantasy.” *Classical Traditions in Modern Fantasy*, edited by B. Rogers and B. E. Stevens, Oxford UP, 2017, pp. 25–46.

West, Emily. “Circe, Calypso, Hidimbā: The *Odyssey* and Graeco-Aryan Proto-Epic.” *Journal of Indo-European Studies*, vol. 42, nos. 1–2, 2014, pp. 144–74.

West, Martin L., editor and translator. *Greek Epic Fragments: From the Seventh to the Fifth Centuries B.C.* Harvard UP, 2003. Loeb Classical Library 497.

———, editor and translator. *Homeric Hymns, Homeric Apocrypha, Lives of Homer*. Harvard UP, 2003. Loeb Classical Library 496.

———. *Indo-European Poetry and Myth*. Oxford UP, 2007.

———. *The Making of the* Odyssey. Oxford UP, 2014.

Whitley, James. “Homer and History.” Pache, pp. 257–66.

———. “Homer’s Entangled Objects: Narrative, Agency and Personhood in and out of Iron Age Texts.” *Cambridge Archaeological Journal*, vol. 23, 2013, pp. 395–416.

———. *Style and Society in Dark Age Greece*. Cambridge UP, 1991.

Whitman, Cedric. *Homer and the Heroic Tradition*. W. W. Norton, 1958.

Wicked. Directed by Jon M. Chu, Universal Pictures, 2024.

Wicked. Music and lyrics by Stephen Schwartz, 2003.

Wiggins, Grant, and Jay McTighe. *Understanding by Design.* 2nd ed., Association for Supervision and Curriculum Development, 2005.

Willett, John, editor and translator. *Brecht on Theatre: The Development of an Aesthetic.* Hill and Wang, 2001.

Willis, Ika. *Reception.* Routledge, 2018.

Wilson, Emily, translator. *The* Odyssey*: Homer.* W. W. Norton, 2018.

———, editor and translator. *The* Odyssey*: Homer.* Narrated by Claire Danes, audiobook ed., unabridged ed., Audible, 2018.

———, editor and translator. *The* Odyssey. Norton Critical Edition, W. W. Norton, 2020.

———. "Slaves and Sex in the *Odyssey.*" *Slavery and Sexuality in Classical Antiquity,* edited by Deborah Kamen and C. W. Marshall, U of Wisconsin P, 2021, pp. 15–39.

———. "Translating Homer as a Woman." Cox and Theodorakopoulos, pp. 279–98.

Winkler, John. *The Constraints of Desire: The Anthropology of Sex and Gender in Ancient Greece.* Routledge, 1990.

Winkler, Martin M. "Homer and Homerica on Screen." Pache, pp. 536–40.

The Wiz. Directed by Sidney Lumet, Universal Pictures, 1978.

The Wizard of Oz. Directed by Victor Fleming, Metro-Goldwyn-Mayer, 1939.

Wofford, Susanne. *The Choice of Achilles: The Ideology of Figure in the Epic.* Stanford UP, 1992.

Wohl, Victoria. "Standing by the Stathmos: The Creation of Sexual Ideology in the *Odyssey.*" *Arethusa,* vol. 26, 1993, pp. 19–50.

Wolfe, Jessica. "Homer in Renaissance Europe (1488–1649)." Pache, pp. 490–504.

Woolf, Virginia. "On Not Knowing Greek." *The Common Reader,* by Woolf, Harcourt, Brace and World, 1953, pp. 24–39.

Zeitlin, Froma. "Figuring Fidelity in Homer's *Odyssey.*" *The Distaff Side: Representing the Female in Homer's* Odyssey, edited by Beth Cohen, Oxford UP, 1995, pp. 117–54.

Zimmerman, Mary. *The Odyssey: A Play.* Northwestern UP, 2006.

Zinsser, William. *Writing to Learn.* Harper and Row, 1988.

Zwiers, Jeff, and Marie Crawford. *Academic Conversations.* Stenhouse Publishers, 2011.